MVS TSO
Part 1: Concepts and ISPF

Second Edition

Doug Lowe

Mike Murach & Associates, Inc.

2560 West Shaw Lane, Suite 101
Fresno, California 93711-2765

MVS TSO

Part 1: Concepts and ISPF

Second Edition

Doug Lowe

Development team

Author:	Doug Lowe
Writer/editor:	Anne Prince
Editor:	Sheila Lynch
Production director:	Steve Ehlers

Related books

MVS TSO, Part 2: Commands and Procedures by Doug Lowe
MVS JCL (Second Edition) by Doug Lowe
MVS Assembler Language by Kevin McQuillen and Anne Prince
OS Utilities by Doug Lowe

20 19 18 17 16 15 14 13 12 11 10 9 8 7 6

ISBN: 0-911625-56-9

Library of Congress Cataloging-in-Publication Data

Lowe, Doug.
   MVS TSO.

    Includes index.
    Contents: pt. 1. Concepts and ISPF - - pt. 2. Commands
and procedures.
    1. Time-sharing computer systems. 2. MVS (Computer
system) I. Title.
QA76.53.L69   1991   005.4'429   90-19907
ISBN 0-911625-56-9 (v. 1 : pbk. : alkaline)
ISBN 0-911625-57-7 (v. 2 : pbk. : alkaline)

Contents

Preface

If you're involved in any type of program development on an IBM mainframe computer running MVS, you need to know how to use TSO/ISPF, IBM's standard platform for application development. Unfortunately, TSO/ISPF isn't as easy to learn as it should be. It isn't particularly user-friendly. Its documentation is spread out over half a dozen or more IBM manuals which are, as you might guess, designed more for reference than for learning. And there aren't many effective training programs. So when it comes to mastering TSO/ISPF, you're pretty much on your own.

That's why you need this book. It will teach you how to use TSO/ISPF for the everyday tasks of program development: editing source programs; compiling, link-editing, and executing programs; displaying file contents; creating, copying, and deleting data sets; and much more. This book will help you master these essential ISPF tasks in no time.

Why this book is effective

This book is the first of a two-part revision of my 1984 book, *MVS TSO*. I believe it is effective for the same reasons the first edition remained successful for six years. It teaches you how to use the most essential features of ISPF almost immediately. It emphasizes the important aspects of ISPF rather than the trivial ones. It shows you how ISPF relates to TSO and MVS so you can make better use of your system's resources. And it teaches you how to treat the IBM manuals as the references they're supposed to be.

One of the most common failings of technical books is that they are poorly planned. All too often, they cover just about every aspect of a subject, without regard for what's important and what isn't. And many are organized in an illogical or haphazard way, with little concern for educational effectiveness. In contrast, I spent a great deal of time planning the content of this book before I wrote one word. I carefully chose what to include and, just as importantly, what to leave out. I won't waste your time with information that's interesting but not very useful.

Another common failing of technical books is that they are poorly illustrated. Most technical books simply don't have enough illustrations, and the illustrations they do include are often trivial or unrealistic. Because I believe the illustrations are at least as important as the text, I've placed a heavy emphasis on them in this book. So you'll find hundreds of illustrations that show you how to perform ISPF operations, teach you how to use ISPF commands, and explain important concepts. These illustrations not only help you learn new skills, but also serve as handy references later on.

How to use this book

I organized this book in the most logical sequence for a beginning TSO user. So if you're new to TSO, I suggest you start with chapter 1 and read each chapter in sequence. However, only chapters 1-4 depend on that sequence. So once you've finished those chapters, you can read any of the remaining chapters in any order you wish. And if you're already familiar with IBM mainframe computer systems, you can skip chapter 1 altogether.

A word of advice on using this book: TSO/ISPF is an interactive system, so it's best learned interactively. The most effective way to use this book, then, is alongside your terminal. That way, you can try out new TSO/ISPF features as you read about them. By comparing your experimentation with the examples in the book, you'll come to a deeper understanding of how TSO/ISPF works.

Who this book is for

This book is for anyone who uses TSO/ISPF. That includes both beginning and experienced programmers, application and systems programmers, operators, and college students enrolled in a programming course. The only prerequisite is a basic familiarity with computers.

MVS, TSO, and ISPF come in many different versions. There are three basic versions of the MVS operating system in use today: MVS/370, MVS/XA, and MVS/ESA. In addition, MVS must be used with a Job Entry Subsystem, either JES2 or JES3. There are also several releases of TSO in common use today. And although ISPF Version 3 is in widespread use, there are certainly many installations still using Version 2. The good news is that this book applies to all of these software versions. Whenever I introduce a feature that's unique to a particular version of MVS, TSO, or ISPF, I'll be sure to point it out. Otherwise, you can assume that everything presented in this book will work on any MVS system that runs ISPF.

About the second edition

As I've already mentioned, this book is the first of a two-part revision of my 1984 book, *MVS TSO*. TSO and ISPF have changed a lot since 1984. Since the first edition of this book was published, IBM has released several major versions of TSO and ISPF. They've added new commands and new utilities, released the VS COBOL II compiler, included two facilities for managing programming projects (LMF and SCLM), and introduced a TSO version of the REXX procedure language. And they've made minor improvements to just about every TSO and ISPF feature.

I couldn't possibly have kept the second edition to one volume without omitting many of these important features. That's why the second edition is in two parts. This book, *Part 1*, presents everything you need to know to use TSO/ISPF effectively for application programming. It covers all the new features of ISPF Versions 2 and 3, including LMF and SCLM. It shows you how to use the VS COBOL II interactive debugger. And it covers an optional program called SDSF that lets you manage background jobs more effectively than the standard ISPF OUTLIST utility.

Part 2 covers TSO commands and procedures. It shows you how to issue native TSO commands like ALLOCATE and LISTCAT, and it teaches you how to create CLIST and REXX procedures. In addition, it covers two ISPF features that require you to use CLIST or REXX procedures: edit macros and the dialog manager. Once you've mastered the basic ISPF features *Part 1* presents, you'll want to master the advanced techniques presented in *Part 2*.

Conclusion

I'm confident that this book will teach you how to use TSO/ISPF effectively. And I know you'll use it often as a desk reference after you've mastered the fundamentals. In fact, I guarantee it: If you ever regret purchasing this book, send it back and I'll refund your money. No questions asked.

As always, I'm interested in your questions, comments, criticisms, and suggestions. I'm especially interested in learning about any ISPF techniques you may have found useful that I didn't include in this book. So please feel free to use the postage-paid comment form at the back of this book. I look forward to hearing from you soon.

Doug Lowe
Fresno, California
September, 1990

Section 1

Introduction

Before you can start using TSO, you need to understand a few basic concepts. For example, you should understand the fundamental differences between mainframe computers, minicomputers, and microcomputers. You should understand the basic workings of the MVS operating system. And you should know how to operate a 3270 terminal. This section presents those basic concepts.

Chapter 1

Preliminary concepts and terminology

If you've never worked on an IBM mainframe computer system, or if you've had only limited experience with IBM mainframes, you need to learn a few basic concepts before you begin to study the details of TSO. This chapter presents those basic concepts. It's divided into three topics. Topic 1 is an introduction to mainframe computer systems. It explains the differences between mainframe computers and mini and microcomputers and introduces the basic features of mainframe computer operating systems. Topic 2 is a more specific introduction to MVS and TSO. And topic 3 presents the details of operating a 3270, the most commonly used terminal under MVS and TSO.

Some of the material in this chapter may be review for you, depending on your experience. As a result, I suggest you review the objectives and list of terms at the end of each topic to see whether you need to study the topic.

Topic 1 What every TSO user needs to know about IBM mainframe computers

This topic introduces you to the characteristics of data processing on IBM mainframe computers. Because many people have experience with computers that are quite different from IBM mainframe computers, this topic begins by exploring the similarities and differences between IBM mainframe computers and two other common types of computer systems: minicomputers and microcomputers. Then, it describes some of the basic features provided by mainframe computer operating systems. Finally, it introduces you to the three main families of IBM mainframe operating systems.

This topic is designed for readers who may have experience with computers, but not with mainframe computer systems. In other words, if you've used a personal computer or a minicomputer system, this topic will give you the background you need so you can start learning about TSO. If, on the other hand, your experience is with mainframe computers, IBM or not, this topic will be mostly review.

HOW MAINFRAME COMPUTERS COMPARE WITH MINICOMPUTERS AND MICROCOMPUTERS

You can divide most computer systems used for business purposes into three classes: *microcomputers*, *minicomputers*, and *mainframe computers*. Although these divisions are loosely based on the size of the computer systems, there are no hard and fast rules for deciding exactly where one category ends and the next begins. In other words, the categories overlap. As a result, the largest minicomputer systems are often larger than the smallest mainframe computers.

Several factors determine the "size" of a computer system. In particular, the size of a computer's hardware configuration, the nature of its applications, and the complexity of its system

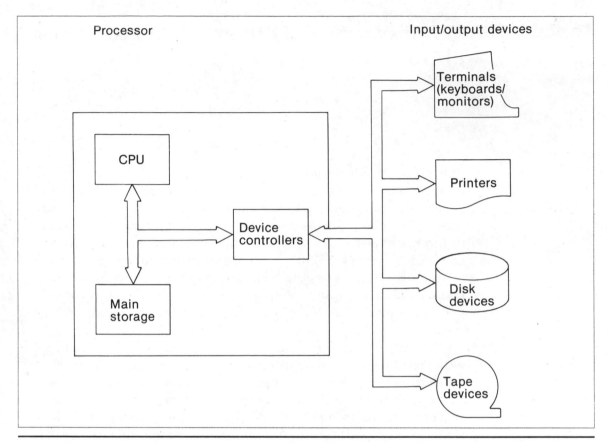

Figure 1-1   The basic components of a modern computer system

software help classify a system as a microcomputer, minicomputer, or mainframe.

Hardware configurations

Regardless of size, all computers consist of two basic types of components: *processors* and *input/output (I/O) devices*. Figure 1-1 illustrates these components. As you can see, the processor consists of three parts: the *central processing unit,* or *CPU*, executes instructions; *main storage* stores instructions and data processed by the CPU; and *device controllers* let the CPU and main storage connect to I/O devices. Input/output devices fall into two classes: those that provide input and output to the system, such as terminals and

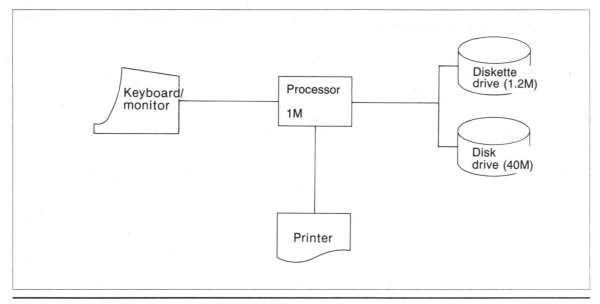

Figure 1-2   A typical microcomputer configuration

printers, and those that provide *secondary storage*, such as tape and
disk drives.

Although all computer systems consist of these basic components, the way those components are combined for a particular
computer system varies depending on the system's requirements.
Now, I'll describe the typical *configurations* of hardware equipment
for microcomputers, minicomputers, and mainframes.

Microcomputer configurations   Microcomputers are small,
single user systems that provide a simple processor and just a few
input/output devices. Figure 1-2 shows the configuration of a
typical microcomputer. This system consists of a processor with
1M of main storage (one M is about a million characters of data), a
keyboard, a display monitor, a printer, a diskette drive with a
capacity of 1.2M, and a 40M hard disk. A microcomputer system
like this usually costs $3,000-5,000.

Minicomputer configurations   Figure 1-3 shows a typical minicomputer configuration. Unlike microcomputers, most minicomputers provide more than one terminal so that several people can
use the system at one time. A system like this is sometimes called a
multi-user system. The minicomputer configuration in figure 1-3

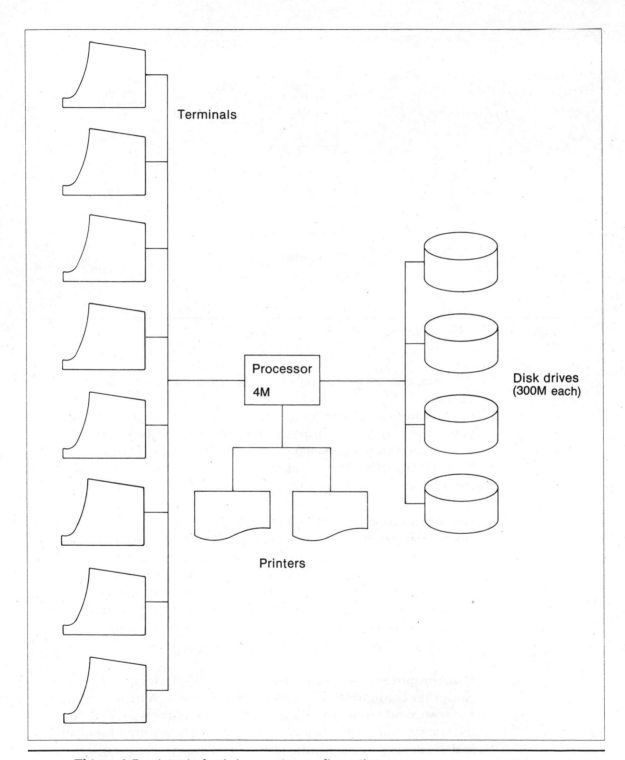

Figure 1-3   A typical minicomputer configuration

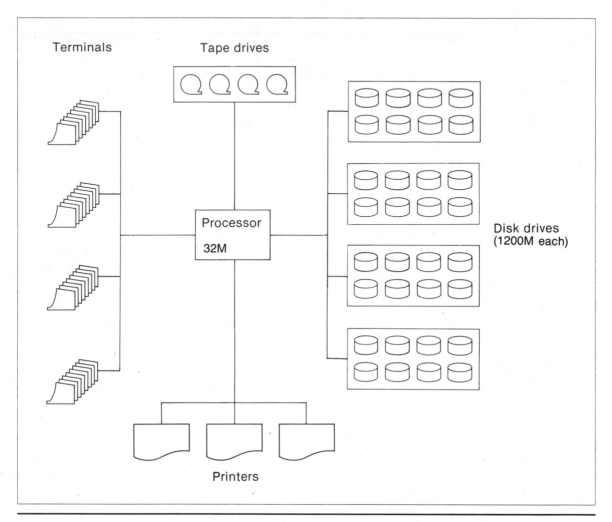

Figure 1-4   A typical mainframe computer configuration

has 4M of main storage, 8 terminals, two printers, and four disk drives totalling 1,200M. The cost of a configuration like this would probably be about $50,000.

Mainframe configurations   Figure 1-4 shows a typical configuration for a mainframe computer. Although it consists of the same basic types of components as the microcomputer and minicomputer, it has more I/O devices and larger storage capacities. For example, the configuration in figure 1-4 includes 32 disk drives, four tape drives, three printers, and a large number of terminals. The processor's main storage is 32M, and the total disk capacity is nearly 40 billion bytes. Such a system would cost well over a million dollars.

The System/360-370 family   Without doubt, the most popular family of mainframe computers ever is the System/360-370 family, introduced by IBM more than 20 years ago. The original System/360 was smaller than the smallest of today's microcomputers, offering only 8K of main storage. Today, the largest member of the family can be configured with more than 80,000 times as much main storage: 640M bytes.

As IBM enhanced the capabilities of the System/360 processors, it periodically assigned new names to them. In the 1970s, the most popular processor was the System/370. This was replaced in the 1980s by the 3080 and 3090 processors. Other popular processors include the 4300 series and the 9370. In 1990, a new line of processors called the System/390 was introduced. Because all these processors are compatible with the basic System/360-370 instruction sets and can run the same operating systems, they are all commonly referred to as System/360 or System/370 processors.

Applications

The nature of the applications performed by a computer is another aspect of its size. In general, larger computers are used for a broader range of applications than are smaller computers. That's because the larger computers support more users, with more diverse needs, than do smaller computers.

To illustrate, consider a typical bank. Loan officers, who use specialized techniques to make sound decisions about loans, often use microcomputers to make their calculations. Each branch may have a minicomputer to support a variety of needs for the individual branch. And the bank may have a centralized mainframe computer that supports all the bank's branches, providing for an even broader range of needs. In other words, the bank uses microcomputers for applications at the individual level, minicomputers at the departmental or branch level, and mainframe computers at the corporate level.

Sometimes, computers of various sizes have similar applications that vary only in the volume of data processed. For example, a corner retail store may use a microcomputer to manage its inventory, a larger retail store may use a minicomputer for inventory management, and a large chain of retail stores may use a central mainframe computer for inventory management. All three stores use their computers for essentially the same function; it's the volume of data processed that distinguishes them.

System software

Yet another distinction among computers is the scope of the *system software* required to manage the computer system's resources so that application programs can perform useful work. The cornerstone of system software is the *operating system*, a set of programs that directly controls the operation of the computer. Microcomputers have a relatively simple operating system, such as the MS-DOS operating system used on IBM Personal Computers. Minicomputer systems generally have more complex operating systems so that they can effectively manage a larger configuration of equipment. And mainframe computer systems have operating systems that are complex beyond imagination. The MVS operating system, which includes TSO, is among the most sophisticated and complex mainframe operating systems in use today.

One way to appreciate the increasing complexity of these operating systems is to consider the number of technical manuals that accompany an operating system. MS-DOS, the most commonly used microcomputer operating system, is thoroughly documented in a single manual. The operating system for a popular minicomputer system I've worked with is documented in about a dozen manuals. The subject of this book, the MVS operating system, has hundreds of manuals. In fact, IBM publishes a document called the *IBM System/370, 30xx, and 4300 Processors Bibliography*; it contains a 200-page section that lists over 10,000 publications related to the System/360-370 family.

Another factor that indicates the complexity of an operating system is the need for specialized programmers to maintain the operating system. Microcomputers almost never require programmers to maintain their operating systems; instead, the end user learns how to use the operating system without help. Since minicomputer systems are more complex, they sometimes require a programmer to keep the operating system working properly. Some minicomputer systems, however, don't require full-time programmers to maintain their operating systems. In contrast, mainframe installations cannot function without a staff of *systems programmers* working full-time to keep the system software in shape. The job of the systems programmer includes installing new system software, updating the software to reflect changes made to the hardware or software configuration, optimizing the software so it runs efficiently, and correcting errors in the operating system.

In many ways, it's the complexity of the operating system that most clearly distinguishes mainframe computers from smaller computers. So, the next section introduces you to several basic facilities provided by mainframe computer operating systems.

FIVE CHARACTERISTIC FEATURES OF MAINFRAME OPERATING SYSTEMS

To help you understand the nature of mainframe operating systems, I'll now describe five basic characteristics common to most of them. As you read about these characteristics, you'll note that some of them are found on microcomputer or minicomputer operating systems too, although not usually at the same level of sophistication as they're found on mainframes. The five characteristics are: virtual storage, multiprogramming, spooling, batch processing, and time-sharing.

Virtual storage

In most computer systems, the processor's main storage is among the most valuable of the system's resources. As a result, modern mainframe computer operating systems provide sophisticated services to make the best use of the available main storage. Among the most important of these services is virtual storage.

Simply put, *virtual storage* is a technique that lets a processor simulate an amount of main storage that is larger than the actual amount of *real storage*. For example, a processor that has 2M bytes of real storage might use virtual storage to simulate 16M bytes of main storage. To do this, the computer uses disk storage as an extension of real storage.

The key to understanding virtual storage is realizing that at any given moment, only the current program instruction and the data it accesses need to be in real storage. Other data and instructions can be placed temporarily on disk storage, and recalled into main storage when needed. In other words, virtual storage operating systems transfer data and instructions between real storage and disk storage as they are needed.

Although the details of how an operating system implements virtual storage varies from one system to the next, the basic concept is the same. Fortunately, virtual storage is largely transparent; from the user's point of view, virtual storage appears to be real storage.

Multiprogramming

Another feature common to all mainframe computers is *multiprogramming*. Multiprogramming means simply that the computer lets more than one program execute at the same time. Actually, that's misleading; at any given moment, only one program can have control of the CPU. Nevertheless, a multiprogramming system *appears* to execute more than one program at the same time.

The key to understanding multiprogramming is to realize that some processing operations—like reading data from an input device—take much longer than others. As a result, most programs that run on mainframe computers are idle a large percentage of the time, waiting for I/O operations to complete. If programs were run one at a time on a mainframe computer, the CPU would spend most of its time waiting. Multiprogramming simply reclaims the CPU during these idle periods and lets another program execute.

Multiprogramming, like virtual storage, is mostly transparent; each program appears to have exclusive use of the system. As a result, you don't have to worry about the details of how it works.

Spooling

A significant problem that must be overcome by multiprogramming systems is sharing access to input and output devices for the programs that execute together. For example, if two programs executing at the same time try to write output to a printer, the output from both programs is intermixed in the printout. One way to avoid this problem is to give one of the programs complete control of the printer. Unfortunately, that defeats the purpose of multiprogramming because the other program has to wait until the printer is available.

To provide shared access to printer devices, *spooling* is used. Spooling manages printer output for applications by intercepting printer output and directing it to a disk device instead. Then, when the program finishes, the operating system collects its spooled print output and directs it to the printer. In a multiprogramming environment, the operating system stores the spooled output separately on disk so it can print each program's output separately.

Another benefit of spooling is that programs can execute faster. That's because disk devices are much faster than printers. The operating system component that actually prints the spooled output is multiprogrammed along with the application programs, so the printer is kept as busy as possible. But the application programs themselves aren't slowed down by the relatively slow operation of the printer.

Batch processing

If you've used an IBM personal computer, you're probably familiar with batch files; a batch file contains a series of commands that are processed together as a batch. On a mainframe computer, *batch processing* is the normal way of using the computer system, and has been for decades.

When you use batch processing, your work is processed in units called *jobs*. A job may cause one or more programs to execute in sequence. For example, one job may invoke the programs necessary to update a file of employee records, print a report listing employee information, and produce payroll checks.

One of the problems that arises when batch processing is used is managing how work flows through the system. In a typical mainframe computer system, many users (perhaps hundreds) compete to use the system's resources. To manage this, the *Job Entry Subsystem*, or *JES*, processes each user's job in an orderly fashion. You'll learn more about JES in topic 2 of this chapter.

Time-sharing

Batch processing was the normal way to use mainframe computer systems in the early days of data processing. At that time, the primary input devices were card readers, which read decks of punched paper cards. As terminal devices became more and more common, users needed a more direct way to use the computer system. As a result, most modern mainframe computers provide time-sharing facilities.

In a *time-sharing* system, each user has access to the system through a terminal device. Instead of submitting jobs that are scheduled for later execution, the user enters commands that are processed immediately. As a result, time-sharing is sometimes called *interactive processing*, because it lets users interact directly with the computer. Sometimes, time-sharing processing is also called *foreground processing*, while batch job processing is called *background processing*.

Because of time-sharing, mainframe computer systems have two faces: batch job processing and time-sharing. In practice, you need to be familiar with both techniques of using your computer. As a programmer, you'll use your computer's time-sharing facilities most often to create, maintain, and store files of 80-character records, such as JCL statements and programs, so they can be processed as jobs in background mode. This book will teach you how to perform those functions using the time-sharing face of MVS, called TSO.

IBM MAINFRAME OPERATING SYSTEMS

Now that you're familiar with some basic features of mainframe operating systems, I'll introduce you to three major families of IBM mainframe operating systems: DOS, OS, and VM.

The DOS family of operating systems

DOS, which stands for *Disk Operating System*, was originally designed for small system configurations that had limited processing requirements. Although DOS was first introduced in the mid-1960s, it has evolved significantly from its original version. As a result, today's DOS has little resemblance to the original DOS.

DOS today is commonly called *DOS/VSE*, or just *VSE*; VSE stands for *Virtual Storage Extended*, which refers to the particular way it handles virtual storage. The most recent release of DOS/VSE supports a maximum of 40M bytes of virtual storage, and up to 12 jobs multiprogrammed together.

Although DOS/VSE has evolved into a respectable operating system, it's still most appropriate for smaller systems that don't have extensive processing requirements. For larger configurations, the OS family of operating systems is more appropriate.

The OS family of operating systems

OS, which stands for *Operating System*, was originally designed for installations that required the full range of processing possibilities. Originally, OS was intended to offer a smooth migration path from DOS. But the two operating systems have evolved along different paths, so that they now are fundamentally incompatible with one another. As a result, a conversion from DOS to OS is a significant undertaking.

In the late 1960s and early 1970s, there were two versions of OS in widespread use, called *OS/MFT* and *OS/MVT*. They differed in the way they handled multiprogramming. MFT stood for *Multiprogramming a Fixed number of Tasks*; it preallocated a fixed number of *partitions* where user jobs could execute. Under MFT, the size of each partition remained constant, as did the number of jobs that could be multiprogrammed. In contrast, MVT, which stood for *Multiprogramming a Variable number of Tasks*, allocated storage to each program as it entered the system. Under MVT, each program was allocated a *region* of storage as it executed, and the number of programs that could be multiprogrammed depended on the storage requirements of each program and the total amount of available storage.

Neither MFT or MVT provided virtual storage; when virtual storage was developed in the early 1970s, MFT and MVT were replaced by *OS/VS1* and *OS/VS2*. OS/VS1, or just *VS1*, provided the same fixed partition structure of MFT, only in a virtual storage environment. Similarly, OS/VS2, or just *VS2*, provided the variable region structure of MVT. Both VS1 and VS2 provide a maximum of

16M of virtual storage. There are still some shops that use VS1 and VS2 today.

The current form of OS is called *MVS*, which stands for *Multiple Virtual Storage*. (Originally, MVS was called OS/VS2 Release 2 MVS; what was originally called OS/VS2 Release 1 is now sometimes called *SVS*, for *Single Virtual Storage*.) In MVS, each multiprogrammed job is given its own virtual storage address space, which can be up to 16M or 2G (one G is about a billion characters of data), depending on which version of MVS you're using. The idea of multiple virtual address spaces is a bit confusing. Fortunately, like virtual storage and multiprogramming, it's entirely transparent. So don't worry about how it works.

Today, there are three common versions of MVS. Because IBM periodically repackages MVS and gives it a different name to reflect the new packaging, it's easy to become confused. So, throughout this book, I'll say just MVS when it doesn't really matter what version of MVS you're using. If I'm referring specifically to one of the versions that limits a user's address space to 16M, I'll call it *MVS/370*. This version is also sometimes called MVS Release 3.8. I'll use the term *MVS/XA* to refer to the newer MVS, which provides for user address spaces of up to 2G bytes. This version is sometimes called MVS/SP Version 2. I'll use the term *MVS/ESA* to refer to the most current version of MVS, which lets each user access as much as 16 *terrabytes* of virtual storage (a terrabyte is a trillion bytes). This version is sometimes called MVS/SP Version 3. Fortunately, most of the information in this book applies to any of the three MVS versions.

The VM operating system

A third IBM operating system, called *VM*, has a different approach to computer system management than DOS or OS. VM, which stands for *Virtual Machine*, uses a variety of techniques including virtual storage and multiprogramming to simulate more than one computer system (called a virtual machine) on a single real computer system. Within each simulated virtual machine, you must use a more conventional operating system like DOS or OS. VM provides a special operating system, called *CMS* (for *Conversational Monitor System*), that lets a single terminal user use a virtual machine interactively.

Although VM is used at some TSO installations, it's more commonly used along with DOS/VSE at smaller installations. In any event, whether or not your shop uses VM doesn't significantly affect the way you use TSO.

DISCUSSION

The purpose of this topic has been to orient you to the world of IBM mainframe data processing. As a result, you don't need to worry about many of the specifics this chapter presented; they'll be repeated in more detail in later chapters. Instead, I just want you to have a feel for mainframe computer systems, especially in contrast to other types of computer systems you may have encountered.

Terms

microcomputer
minicomputer
mainframe computer
processor
input/output device
I/O device
central processing unit
CPU
main storage
device controllers
secondary storage
configuration
multi-user system
system software
operating system
systems programmer
virtual storage
real storage
multiprogramming
spooling
batch processing

job
Job Entry Subsystem
JES
time-sharing
interactive processing
foreground processing
background processing
DOS
Disk Operating System
DOS/VSE
VSE
Virtual Storage Extended
OS
Operating System
OS/MFT
OS/MVT
partition
region
OS/VS1
OS/VS2
VS1

VS2
MVS
Multiple Virtual Storage
SVS
Single Virtual Storage
MVS/370
MVS/XA
MVS/ESA
terrabyte
VM
Virtual Machine
CMS
Conversational Monitor System

Objectives

1. Distinguish among three levels of computer systems: microcomputers, minicomputers, and mainframe computers.

2. Briefly describe five features of mainframe computer operating systems.

3. Identify the three major families of IBM operating systems.

Topic 2   An introduction to MVS and TSO

This topic introduces the basic characteristics of MVS and TSO. Although this book is about using TSO, you must understand the basics of its underlying operating system, MVS, before you can fully understand TSO. So I'll start by presenting the basic features of the MVS operating system. Then, I'll describe some of the basic features of TSO.

AN INTRODUCTION TO MVS

MVS, which stands for *Multiple Virtual Storage*, is the operating system that supports TSO. Although *TSO* stands for *Time Sharing Option*, it is not an option; it is an integral part of MVS. As a result, to use TSO effectively, you must understand the capabilities of MVS.

As I mentioned in topic 1, MVS is available in three versions: MVS/370, MVS/XA, and MVS/ESA. As a TSO user, the version of MVS your installation uses doesn't matter much. There are only a few instances where the MVS version affects how you use TSO.

Multiple Virtual Storage

In modern computer systems, main storage consists of millions of individual storage locations, each of which can store one *byte* of information. To refer to a particular storage location, you use an *address*, which indicates the storage location's offset from the beginning of memory. Thus, the first byte of memory is at address 0, the second byte is at address 1, and so on.

The complete range of addresses—and, as a result, storage locations—that can be accessed by the computer is called an *address space*. The maximum size of an address space is limited by the number of digits used to represent addresses. For example, suppose a computer keeps track of memory using six-digit decimal addresses. Such a computer could access up to 1,000,000 bytes of storage, with addresses ranging from 0 to 999,999.

Of course, real computers use binary numbers rather than decimal numbers to represent addresses. On System/370 processors, for example, addresses are represented by 24-bit binary numbers. As a result, an address space on a System/370 processor can be no larger than 16M, the largest number that can be represented in 24 bits. Newer models of the System/370 family can operate with 24-bit addresses in *370-mode*, or with 31-bit addresses in *XA-mode* (*XA* stands for *Extended Architecture*). With 31-bit addresses, an address space can be as large as 2G.

In simpler computer systems, the size of the address space limits the total amount of virtual storage the computer can simulate. System/370 computers, however, can keep track of several address spaces at once. Each address space is a complete range of addresses, from 0 to the maximum (16M or 2G). And the address spaces are independent of one another. As a result, to access a particular byte of main storage, you have to know not only the byte's storage address, but what address space the address applies to.

All versions of MVS use this multiple address space capability to implement multiprogramming. Thus, each batch job running under MVS executes in its own address space. Similarly, every TSO user who is using MVS is operating in his or her own address space. Figure 1-5 shows how this works. Here, you can see there are four address spaces; each address space supports a TSO user or a batch job. Each address space shares access to the CPU, and each is backed by a combination of real storage and disk storage.

As a TSO user, you have access to the full 16M or 2G storage limit. In actual practice, 6M or more of each address space may be occupied by the operating system. Although the storage required by the operating system overhead is unavailable to individual users, the remaining free storage is far more than is typically needed by a TSO user.

Jobs and Job Control Language

As you know, a *job* is the execution of one or more related programs in sequence. Each program executed by a job is called a *job step*. To illustrate, suppose you want to process a job that executes two programs: the first sorts a customer file into customer

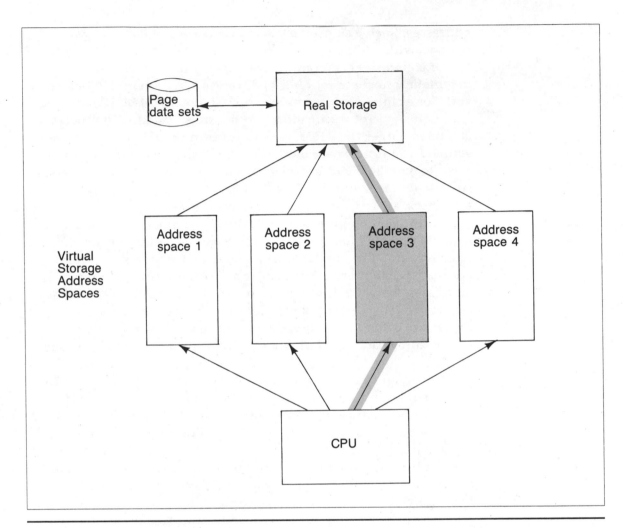

Figure 1-5   Multiple virtual storages

name sequence, and the second prints a report that lists customers by name. That's a two-step job, because it requires two programs. But no matter how many job steps your job contains, when you submit it to be processed by MVS, MVS treats it as a whole. In other words, every job begins with the execution of the first program and continues until the last program finishes executing, unless an error occurs.

Within a job, the *Job Control Language*, or *JCL*, provides the specifications necessary for MVS to process the job. Figure 1-6 shows a simple example of JCL for a job that prints the contents of a file

```
//MMA2COPY  JOB   USER=DLOWE,PASSWORD=XXXXXXXX
//          EXEC  PGM=IEBGENER
//SYSPRINT  DD    SYSOUT=A
//SYSUT1    DD    DSN=DLOWE.COPYLIB.COBOL(OPENITEM),DISP=SHR
//SYSUT2    DD    SYSOUT=A
//SYSIN     DD    DUMMY
```

Figure 1-6   JCL statements for a simple job

using a system utility called IEBGENER. Although you don't have to know JCL to use TSO, you won't last long in an MVS environment without it. In this book, I'll teach you only the JCL you need to know to use TSO. So if you want to learn more JCL than that, I suggest you read my book, *MVS JCL*.

The Job Entry Subsystem

To process a job on an MVS system, MVS uses an important component called the *Job Entry Subsystem*, or *JES*. Simply put, the Job Entry Subsystem is the MVS component that keeps track of jobs that enter the system, determines when they are executed, and sends each job's printed output to the correct printer.

To fully understand MVS Job Entry Subsystems, you must understand that the original versions of OS didn't provide a Job Entry Subsystem. On those systems, an operating system component called the *job scheduler* provided a relatively crude form of job entry and spooling. Because the OS job scheduler was inadequate for most installation's needs, other programs were widely used. These programs duplicated the functions of the job scheduler, but provided more efficient operation and comprehensive control than the job scheduler alone.

When MVS was announced, IBM integrated the functions performed by these other programs into the operating system by providing the Job Entry Subsystem. There are two versions of JES, called *JES2* and *JES3*. JES2 is designed for single-processor systems that don't have serious job scheduling problems. In contrast, JES3 is designed for large, multi-processor systems, where job

scheduling is highly complicated. Each MVS system uses either
JES2 or JES3; the two Job Entry Subsystems can't be used together
on the same system.

Figure 1-7 illustrates the basic job scheduling functions
provided by JES2 and JES3. When you submit a job for processing
under JES2 or JES3, the job's JCL statements and other input are
held in a *job queue* until JES2/JES3 determines that the job is ready
to be executed. Then, JES2/JES3 presents the job to MVS for execution. As the job executes, its printed output is collected in an *output
queue*. Then, when the job is finished, JES2/JES3 prints the spooled
output on an appropriate printer.

With either JES2 or JES3, you can assign each job a job class
and a priority to prioritize the jobs in the job queue. Then,
JES2/JES3 executes jobs with higher class and priority assignments, even if jobs with lower class and priority were waiting in
the queue longer. JES3 provides additional job scheduling functions that aren't available under JES2. For example, JES3 lets you
specify that a job must be executed every day at 10:00 am. Or you
can say that a job shouldn't start until another specific job finishes.

JES2 and JES3 also provide many options for the final disposition of spooled output data (called *SYSOUT data*), based on the one-
character *SYSOUT class* that's assigned to the data when it's created.
This SYSOUT class specifies what type of device to use for the
output. Normally, the SYSOUT class and JES2/JES3 cause SYSOUT
data to be printed automatically along with the rest of the job
output at a default printer. But you can also change the SYSOUT
class and use JES2 or JES3 commands to route SYSOUT data to a
specific local or remote printer or to delete or save the output
without printing it.

Data sets and data set names

Every DASD volume in an MVS installation contains a *Volume Table
of Contents*, or *VTOC*, that identifies each file residing on the
volume. Each VTOC entry gives the file's name, physical characteristics (block length, record length, organization, and so on), and its
location on the disk.

In MVS terminology, a file is called a *data set*; each data set has
a name that consists of one or more *qualifiers*. These qualifiers can
be a maximum of eight characters long, and are separated in the
data set name by periods. The maximum length of a data set name,

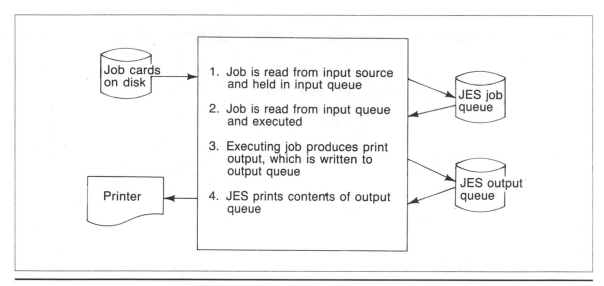

Figure 1-7   Spooling

including the periods, is 44 characters. This length allows for five eight-character qualifiers and four separating periods. Here are some examples of valid data set names:

```
MASTER
MASTER.DATA
TEST.MASTER.DATA
```

The first qualifier in a data set name is called the *high-level qualifier*. Your supervisor will let you know what high-level qualifier to use whenever you create a data set. Usually, the high-level qualifier indicates the catalog where the data set is stored. I'll discuss catalogs in a minute.

MVS lets you maintain many different types of files on DASD. Only two of them are important to TSO: sequential and partitioned. In a *sequential data set*, the records of the file can be retrieved only in the same order they were written. As a result, when a program reads the file, the records are always retrieved in the same order. To process a record in the middle of the file, you have to read all the preceding records. Under TSO, most of the sequential files you'll use will be spooled JES output: compiler listings, program output, and so on.

A *partitioned data set*, often called a *PDS* or *library*, consists of a *directory* and one or more *members*. A PDS directory is simply a list of the members in the library. Each member is functionally the same as a sequential data set. In fact, you can process an individual member of a partitioned data set as if it were a sequential data set. But the advantage of partitioned organization is that you can also process the entire library as a single file.

In a partitioned data set, each member has a one- to eight-character member name. To refer to a member, you specify the member name in parentheses following the data set name. For example,

```
TEST.COBOL(MKTG1200)
```

refers to the member MKTG1200 in the library TEST.COBOL.

Catalogs

MVS maintains a structure of *catalogs* to store the names and other information of commonly used files. To access a *cataloged data set*, you specify only the data set name. MVS locates the file by searching its catalogs. To access a file that isn't cataloged, you must supply the data set name and the vol-ser for the volume that contains the file. In all likelihood, however, all the files you'll access as a TSO user will be cataloged.

An MVS catalog structure consists of one *master catalog* and a number of *user catalogs*, as illustrated in figure 1-8. In general, the master catalog contains catalog entries for system files (files that begin with SYS1) and user catalogs. User catalogs contain catalog entries for users' data sets.

To determine what catalog a particular data set is in, MVS uses the data set name's high-level qualifier. For example, a data set named MMA.TEST.COBOL would be cataloged in the catalog indicated by the high-level qualifier, MMA. The high-level qualifier (in this case, MMA) doesn't necessarily have to be the name of the catalog. Instead, it can be a catalog *alias*. Each catalog can have many aliases; as a result, data sets with many different high-level qualifiers can be stored in the same catalog.

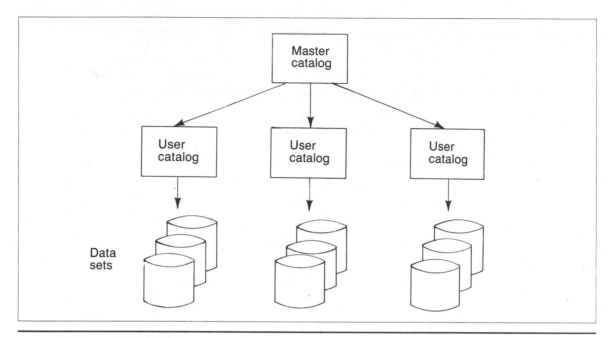

Figure 1-8   Catalogs and data sets

Data set allocation

When you request access to an existing data set, MVS uses information you provide in your JCL along with information in the data set
label and catalog to locate it. Similarly, when you create a new data
set, MVS uses the information you provide to locate and set aside
space for it. The process of locating an existing data set or space for
a new data set and preparing the system resources needed to use
the data set is called *allocation*. The allocation of direct-access space
is an important function of the MVS facilities that manage data.

One of the most important functions of JCL is to indicate the
data sets that need to be allocated for each job. To do that, you
include a *DD statement* for each data set the job needs. In figure 1-6,
you can see an example of a DD statement that allocates a data set.
Here, the DD statement labeled SYSUT1 allocates a member of a
partitioned data set named DLOWE.COPYLIB.COBOL(OPENITEM).

Security

In most MVS installations, *security* is a major concern. MVS provides for data set security by allowing you to set *passwords* for sensitive files. Then, only users who know the correct password can access the file.

Installations that need more security than standard MVS provides often use a special security system such as *RACF* (*Resource Access Control Facility*). RACF provides a multi-level password scheme that has different levels of access authority for different users. In addition, RACF provides for automatic cycling of passwords. For example, you can set up RACF so that you have to change your password every 10 days.

The Storage Management Subsystem

For MVS/ESA systems, IBM provides an optional data management environment called the *Storage Management Subsystem*, or *SMS*. Simply put, SMS automates many of the tasks of managing DASD space for large MVS installations. SMS is relatively new, but it should be available in more installations each year.

As a TSO user, SMS will affect you in two ways. First, every SMS data set must be cataloged, so you don't have to worry about uncataloged data sets. Second, SMS lets you assign classes to data sets to determine how they are handled. You can assign three types of classes to each data set: *data class*, which specifies basic data set characteristics like space requirements, record format, record length, and so on; *storage class*, which lets you specify the performance you require for the data set; and *management class*, which specifies how and when the data set is backed up or removed from DASD. Each installation determines its own classes and policies for using them, so if you're using SMS, you'll have to find out what data, storage, and management classes to use.

AN INTRODUCTION TO TSO

TSO stands for Time-Sharing Option. Originally, that's what TSO was: an optional feature of MVS that provided time-sharing capabilities. Quite simply, *time-sharing* allows users to share time and resources. The current versions of TSO still provide time-sharing capabilities, but TSO is no longer optional. Instead, it is an integral part of MVS and provides the primary interactive support for MVS.

MVS handles each TSO user in much the same way as it handles batch jobs. As a result, each TSO user has a unique address space for running programs. When a TSO user logs on to TSO, MVS initiates a terminal session using JCL that's unique to that user. This JCL includes DD statements that allocate the data sets that will be available to the user. And it specifies what *terminal monitor program* will be used to process the TSO user's terminal session. It can even specify a command or procedure that is executed automatically whenever that user logs on to TSO. The systems programmers who are responsible for maintaining TSO create this JCL, so you don't have to worry about it.

TSO commands

The most direct way to use TSO is by entering commands. You can do this whenever TSO indicates it is in *ready mode* by displaying this message on your terminal screen:

```
READY
```

TSO provides a total of 26 different commands that perform a variety of functions. Figure 1-9 lists some of the most common functions you can perform with these commands. For the most part, these functions fall into four basic categories: (1) managing data sets; (2) developing programs; (3) processing background jobs; and (4) changing your TSO environment.

There are many commands other than TSO commands you can enter at the READY prompt. For example, you can use AMS commands to define VSAM data sets. Or, you can use commands to invoke standard language compilers, such as VS COBOL II. All told, there are dozens of commands you can use under TSO.

Command procedures

A *command procedure* is a list of TSO commands that are executed together. Besides TSO commands, however, you can include procedure statements that provide many of the features of a high-level

Data set management functions

Dynamically allocate data sets
List data sets
Print data sets
Copy data sets
Delete data sets
Rename data sets
List catalog entries
List VTOC entries
Use VSAM AMS commands

Program development functions

Create and edit program source libraries
Compile a source program
Link-edit a compiled program
Test a link-edited program
View compiler and linkage-editor output
Route output to a printer

Batch job functions

Submit a job for background processing
Monitor the progress of a background job
View output from a background job
Route output to a local or remote site
Cancel submitted jobs

Other TSO functions

Help facility
Message broadcast
CLIST
REXX

Figure 1-9   Functions available under TSO

programming language: symbolic variables, conditional logic,
branching, and so on. As a result, you can easily create simple
applications using command procedures.

Today, TSO provides two command procedure facilities: *CLIST* and *REXX*. CLIST has been available under TSO for many years, while REXX, a procedure language originally used under VM, was only recently made available for TSO users. Both CLIST and REXX are covered in *Part 2: Commands and Procedures.*

TSO data sets

As you use TSO, you will need to create and modify data sets. For example, when you edit a program source file, you modify a member of a partitioned data set.

TSO uses standard MVS data set naming conventions, but adds some conventions of its own. Normally, TSO names any data set you create or modify in a TSO session according to these conventions. As you will see in a moment, however, these conventions are *not* absolute requirements.

In TSO, a data set name generally follows this format:

```
user-id.name.type
```

User-id is the TSO user identification number assigned to each user. *Name* is the name you create to identify the data set. And *type* is one of the values in figure 1-10 used to identify the type of data stored in the data set.

To illustrate this naming convention, suppose your user-id is TSO0001 and you want to create a COBOL source library named SOURCE. In this case, the TSO data set name is TSO0001.SOURCE.COBOL.

Normally, TSO supplies the user-id component of a data set name. For example, you can refer to TSO0001.SOURCE.COBOL simply as SOURCE.COBOL. TSO automatically adds your user-id to the name.

Incidentally, you can qualify the name component of a TSO data set name. For example, you can create a data set name like this:

```
TSO0001.SOURCE.TEST.COBOL
```

Here, the name component of the data set name is SOURCE.TEST. The only restriction on this kind of qualification is that the total length of the data set name, including the periods used to separate its components, can't be longer than 44 characters. That's because

Type	Meaning
ASM	Assembler language source code
CLIST	CLIST procedure
CNTL	JCL job stream used for batch job facility
COBOL	COBOL source code
DATA	Uppercase text data
EXEC	REXX procedure
FORT	FORTRAN source code
LOAD	Executable program module
OBJ	Object module
PLI	PL/I source code
TEXT	Upper and lowercase text data

Figure 1-10   Common data set types

the TSO data set name must conform to MVS naming requirements.

You specify partitioned data set members in the usual way: enclose the member name in parentheses following the data set name. For example, in the data set name

```
TSO0001.SOURCE.COBOL(MKTG1200)
```

the member name is MKTG1200. To access this data set, specify the data set name as SOURCE.COBOL(MKTG1200). (Remember, TSO automatically adds the user-id.)

Remember that these conventions are just that: conventions. They are not absolute requirements of MVS or TSO. In fact, TSO allows you to bypass these conventions by specifying a data set name in apostrophes, using any format you desire. As a result, you can refer to a data set named CUSTOMER.MASTER like this:

```
'CUSTOMER.MASTER'
```

When you use apostrophes like this, TSO doesn't add the user-id component to the data set name.

TSO session manager

TSO was first released in 1969. At that time, terminal devices such as the 2741, a hardcopy terminal that looked much like an IBM Selectric typewriter, were popular. The major characteristic of these terminals was that they processed input and output one line at a time. As a result, TSO was designed to interact with users one line at a time.

Two years later, IBM came out with the 3270 Information Display System, the system on which TSO is now most popular. Unlike earlier devices, the 3270 terminal can display a whole screen of data at a time. So when the 3270 was announced, IBM modified TSO slightly to allow for the new type of display. As a result, TSO causes 3270 terminals to display data one line at a time, starting at line 1 and moving down the screen until the display is filled. Then, the screen is erased and the next line starts again at the top.

The problem with this line-by-line display is that whenever you clear the screen, the data that was displayed is lost. So IBM introduced the *TSO session manager* to make it easy to recall data that has been cleared from the screen. The session manager records all line-oriented terminal activity in a special journal and provides simple commands to display journal entries on the terminal. Still, the TSO session manager doesn't change the inherent line-by-line nature of TSO.

ISPF

ISPF, which stands for *Interactive System Productivity Facility*, provides a menu-driven, full-screen interface to most of TSO's features. With ISPF, you invoke TSO's functions by selecting menu options and answering system prompts. Without ISPF, you invoke TSO functions using commands. Since most installations today use ISPF, this book focuses on using ISPF.

DISCUSSION

So far in this chapter, I've tried to give you a deeper level of understanding than most introductory courses on TSO do. That's because I think you'll be better able to take advantage of your system's resources if you understand how you're using them.

Unfortunately, the drawback of my approach is that I've given you more information than you absolutely need to begin using TSO. So if you're confused about the relationship between TSO and MVS, don't be frustrated. The relationship is complex, and you'll understand it better as you work with TSO.

In the next topic, I'll describe the 3270 Information Display System and show you how to access TSO. To be more specific, I'll introduce you to the 3270 terminal and show you how to use the keyboard. Then, I'll show you how to connect your terminal to TSO and log on.

Terms

MVS	high-level qualifier
Multiple Virtual Storage	sequential data set
TSO	partitioned data set
Time Sharing Option	PDS
byte	library
address	directory
address space	member
370-mode	catalog
XA-mode	cataloged data set
Extended Architecture	master catalog
job step	user catalog
Job Control Language	alias
JCL	allocation
Job Entry Subsystem	DD statement
JES	security
job scheduler	password
JES2	RACF
JES3	Resource Acquisition Control Facility
job queue	Storage Management Subsystem
output queue	SMS
SYSOUT data	data class
SYSOUT class	storage class
Volume Table of Contents	management class
VTOC	time-sharing
data set	terminal monitor program
qualifier	ready mode

command procedure
CLIST
REXX
user-id
name
type
TSO session manager
ISPF
Interactive System Productivity Facility
native TSO
line mode TSO

Objectives

1. Briefly describe how Multiple Virtual Storage is used to implement multiprogramming.

2. Briefly describe the function of the job control language and the job entry subsystem.

3. Briefly describe the following components of an MVS system:
   a. data sets
   b. catalogs
   c. data set allocation
   d. security

4. Describe the data set naming conventions under MVS and TSO.

5. Briefly describe the following components of TSO:
   a. command procedures
   b. the TSO session manager
   c. ISPF

Topic 3

How to use a 3270 Information Display System and access TSO

In this topic, I'll present the basic information you need to get started with TSO: how to use a 3270 terminal, and how to access TSO and log on and off.

If you've used 3270-type terminals before, feel free to skip the section on using a 3270 terminal. And if you've used TSO and already know how to log on, you can skip that section, too.

HOW TO USE THE 3270 INFORMATION DISPLAY SYSTEM

The 3270 family of terminal devices has been the standard for IBM mainframe computers since its introduction in 1971. Although other types of terminals can be used with MVS systems, 3270 devices are by far the most popular. So odds are you'll use a 3270 terminal to access TSO.

If you've never used a 3270 terminal, you need to know a little about it before you go on. This is especially true if you've used a PC but not a 3270, because there are many differences between the way PCs and 3270 terminals work. As a result, you'll probably find certain aspects of the 3270's operation confusing. But if you spend a few minutes now learning how the terminal works, you'll save yourself some frustration later on.

Components of a 3270 system

The *3270 Information Display System* is not a single terminal, but rather a system of terminals, printers, and controllers. Several display stations and printers can be connected to a single controller. The controller, in turn, is connected to the host

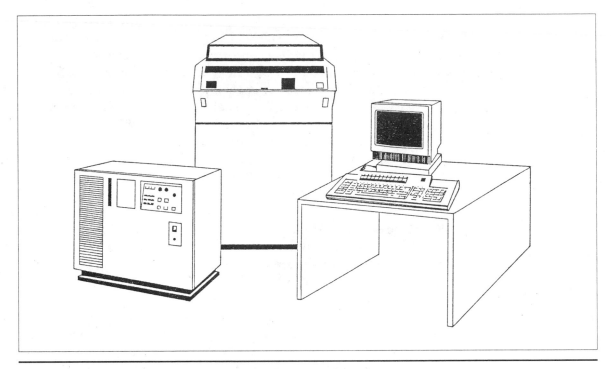

Figure 1-11   Components of a 3270 Information Display System

computer system, either by direct cable or over phone lines. Figure 1-11 illustrates these components.

3270 display stations   3270 terminals, officially called *display stations*, consist of a CRT monitor, a keyboard, and an electronics unit. For many years, the standard 3270 terminal was the 3278, which had a monitor capable of displaying 24 lines of 80 characters each. In the 1980s, IBM phased out this terminal and replaced it with smaller, lighter, and more reliable models, such as the 3178 and the 3191. These terminals have the same basic display characteristics (24 lines of 80 characters each), but have better-designed keyboard layouts.

These 3278-compatible terminals have monochrome displays. In other words, they display characters in a single color (usually green or white) against a dark background. In contrast, 3279-compatible display stations can display characters in seven different colors. Like the 3278, IBM phased out the original 3279 color terminal, replacing it with the 3189 and 3192 models, which have similar characteristics. Although a color terminal isn't a must for using TSO, it does make certain TSO functions easier to use.

Besides color, 3270 display stations can be configured with many different options. For example, you can configure a 3270 with a specialized keyboard for special applications or foreign languages. Other options include: a selector light pen that allows an operator to communicate with the host system without using the keyboard; extended highlighting that lets the terminal display underscored, blinking, or reversed characters; and graphics. None of these options affect the TSO functions presented in this book, so I won't mention them again.

3270 printers   In addition to display stations, printers can be attached to a 3270 controller. IBM offers a variety of 3270 printers, including dot-matrix printers that print up to 400 characters per minute, line printers that print up to 2,000 lines per minute, and laser printers that print 12 letter quality pages per minute.

As a TSO user, you can use TSO facilities to direct printed output to a 3270 printer. In addition, you can use a feature called *local print* that prints the contents of your terminal's screen on a 3270 printer. Since this operation doesn't involve transmission of data between the 3270 and the host computer, it's an efficient way to print.

3270 controllers   For many years, the standard 3270 controller was the 3274. Although many 3274 controllers are still in use, IBM has replaced the 3274 with the newer 3174 control unit. Depending on the model of 3274 or 3174, as many as 32 display stations and printers can be connected to the controller. From a practical standpoint, it doesn't matter what kind of controller your terminal is connected to.

3270-compatible devices and emulators   Because of the enormous popularity of the 3270 system, many manufacturers besides IBM offer compatible terminals, printers, and controllers. And most manufacturers of minicomputers and microcomputers offer *emulator programs* that allow their computers to behave as if they were 3270 devices. As a matter of fact, many of the examples in this book were tested using an emulator program running on an IBM Personal Computer. Because of cost advantages and additional benefits, it's becoming more and more common to see such products in use in 3270 networks.

How to use a 3270 display station

To use TSO effectively, you need to know how to use a 3270 display station effectively. If you've used a terminal device of any type in the past, this should present no special problems. Your main tasks are to learn how the 3270 display works and how to operate the 3270 keyboard.

Characteristics of the 3270 display screen   As I've already mentioned, most 3270 terminals display 24 rows of 80 characters. To control the way data is displayed, the 3270 treats its screen as a series of *fields*, each with various characteristics. For example, some screen fields let you key data into them, while others are protected from data entry.

Data-entry fields are called *unprotected fields* because they are *not* protected from operator entry. As a result, you can key data into an unprotected field. In contrast, display-only fields such as captions and data displayed by a program are called *protected fields* because they're protected from operator entry.

As a general convention, ISPF clearly identifies its unprotected fields with these characters:

===>

So whenever you see those characters, you know ISPF is letting you enter data.

Functions of the 3270 keys   The 3270 display station's keyboard is similar to a typewriter keyboard, with the addition of a few special keys. Although 3270 keyboards are available in many different configurations, the keyboard layout shown in figure 1-12 is typical. The keyboard contains five types of keys: (1) data-entry keys, (2) cursor-control keys, (3) editing keys, (4) attention keys, and (5) miscellaneous keys. Each keyboard in figure 1-12 highlights one of the five categories of keys.

The data-entry keys include the letters, numerals, and special characters (#, @, and so on) normally found on a typewriter keyboard. You use these keys for normal text and data entry. The Shift and Shift-lock keys work just as they do on a typewriter. On some keyboards, a special numeric keypad is included to speed entry of numeric data.

You use the cursor-control keys to change the location of the cursor on the terminal's screen. The *cursor* is a special character—

an underscore or a solid block—that shows the screen location of the next character entered at the keyboard. The cursor-control keys include four keys with arrows that move the cursor in the direction of the arrow: up, down, left, or right. Other cursor-control keys include the Tab key (it moves the cursor to the next unprotected field), the Back-tab key (it moves the cursor to the previous unprotected field), the Backspace key (it moves the cursor one position to the left and erases the character at that position), the New-line key (it moves the cursor to the first unprotected field on the next line), and the Home key (it moves the cursor to the first unprotected field on the screen). Incidentally, the Home key is the same as the Back-tab key. To make it function as a Home key, you have to press the Alt key first, then the Back-tab key.

The editing keys include the Insert key (â), used to insert data between characters already on the screen; the Delete key (â), used to delete a single character from the screen; the Erase-EOF (erase to end-of-field) key, used to delete an entire field; and the Erase-input (ErInp) key, used to erase all data entered on the screen.

The attention keys allow you to communicate with the system. For example, when you press the Enter key, TSO processes the data you've entered on the screen.

The *program function keys*, or *PF keys*, are attention keys you use to invoke a pre-defined TSO function. A 3270 display station can have up to 24 PF keys; most have 12. The PF keys are labelled PF1, PF2, and so on up to PF24.

If you study the PF keys in figure 1-12, you'll see that the PF1 through PF12 keys are located along the top row of the keyboard, on the same keys as the numerals. To use PF1-12, you must first depress the Alt key, then press the correct PF key. For example, to use PF8, you press Alt and 8.

In contrast, the PF13-24 keys in figure 1-12 are separated from the main keyboard. Because you don't have to use the Alt key, the PF13-24 keys are easier to use than the PF1-12 keys. But as I said, not all 3270 keyboards have all 24 PF keys. As a result, many TSO functions use both sets of PF keys. In other words, PF1 and PF13 have the same function, as do PF2 and PF14. This isn't true for all 3270 applications, but it generally is for TSO. To show that you can use both sets of keys, I usually refer to the keys in pairs in this book. Thus, PF1/13 means PF1 or PF13.

A 3270 keyboard also has two or three *program access keys* (or *PA keys)*, labelled PA1, PA2, and PA3. (Note that the keyboard in figure 1-12 doesn't have PA3.) The PA keys work like the PF keys

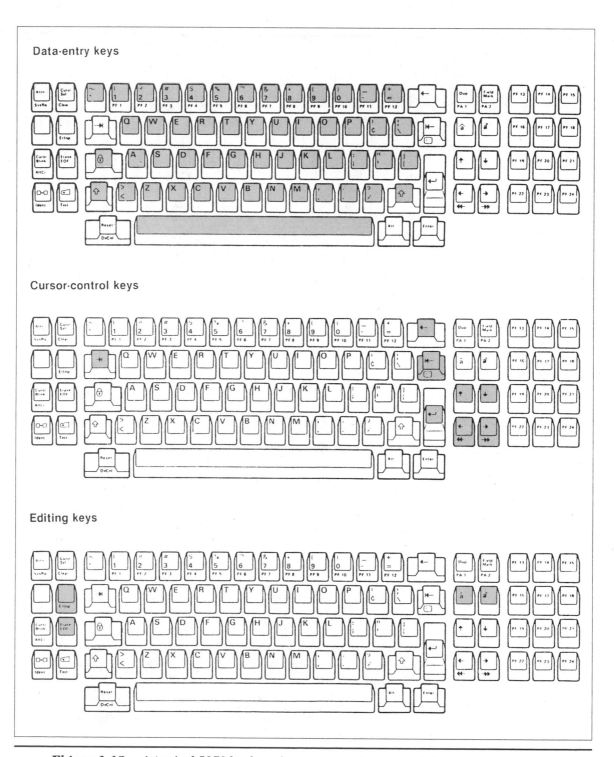

Figure 1-12   A typical 3270 keyboard arrangement (part 1 of 2)

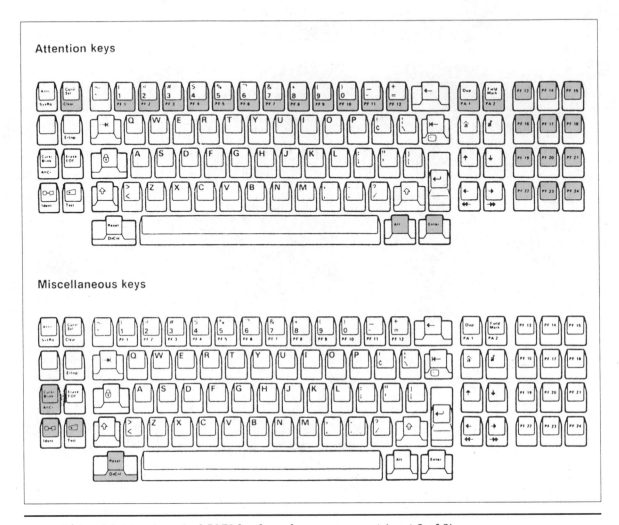

Figure 1-12   A typical 3270 keyboard arranagement (part 2 of 2)

except that no data is sent to the system when you use them. Instead, just an indication of which PA key was pressed is sent. PA1 is used as an *Interrupt key* for many TSO operations. In other words, when you press PA1, the TSO operation currently processing is immediately interrupted. PA2 allows you to redisplay the screen, ignoring any changes you may have made.

The *Clear key* works like a PA key, except it erases the screen and any data that was on the screen is lost. As a result, you shouldn't normally use the Clear key.

As you can see in figure 1-12, there are several other keys on a 3270 keyboard. But with the exception of the *Reset key*, you don't use them often. You use the Reset key whenever the terminal "locks up," that is, when you make an entry error and the terminal freezes the keyboard to prevent further data entry. In this case, the keyboard is released when you press the Reset key.

HOW TO ACCESS TSO

Accessing a TSO system involves two steps: connecting your terminal to TSO and entering a LOGON command. You use a related command, LOGOFF, to end a TSO session.

How to connect your terminal to TSO

Before you can log on and begin using TSO, you must connect your terminal to the TSO system. This is a two-step process. First, you must *physically* connect you terminal to the proper terminal network. Then, you must *logically* connect your terminal to TSO.

In all likelihood, your terminal is already physically connected to the computer system. If that's the case, all you have to do to get started is turn the terminal on. If your terminal is at a remote location, however, you may have to establish a connection between your terminal and the computer. The procedures for establishing a remote connection are varied, so you should ask your supervisor how to do it.

Most MVS installations support more than one on-line system. For example, a typical MVS system might support a CICS production system, a CICS development system, and TSO. (CICS is an IBM product that manages on-line transaction processing.) As a result, once you've made a physical connection to the computer network, you have to tell the network what application you want to be connected to. For example, figure 1-13 shows how I access TSO on my system. Here, I typed TSO to access TSO. Again, the procedure may vary slightly for your installation, so you'll have to find out what it is.

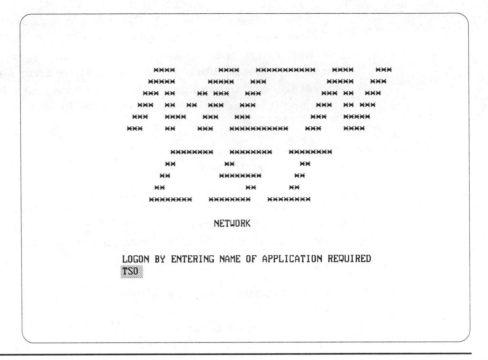

Figure 1-13   Accessing TSO

The LOGON command

Once you've connected your terminal to TSO, you can log on by
entering a LOGON command. The basic format of the LOGON
command is this:

```
LOGON user-id/password
```

For example, if your user-id is TSO0001 and your password is DAL,
you enter the LOGON command like this:

```
LOGON TSO0001/DAL
```

If you omit the parameters and enter just the word LOGON, TSO
prompts you for the missing information. Usually, though, it's
easier and faster to enter all the information in the LOGON
command.

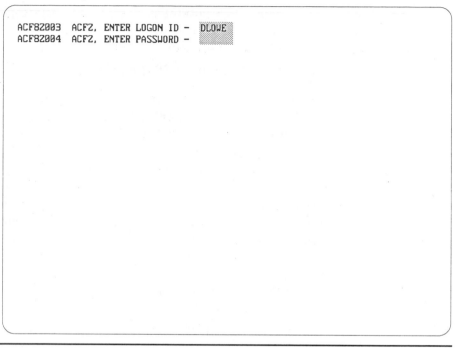

```
ACF82003  ACF2, ENTER LOGON ID -  DLOWE
ACF82004  ACF2, ENTER PASSWORD -
```

Figure 1-14   Logging on to TSO

You may also be required to specify an account number on your LOGON command. If so, you code it following the password like this:

```
LOGON TS00001/DAL ACCT(1234)
```

Here, the account number is 1234.

At some installations, the LOGON command is replaced by a logon screen, as shown in figure 1-14. Here, rather than enter a complete logon command, you just type your user-id and password in the appropriate fields. An appropriate LOGON command is then constructed for you.

In response to your LOGON command, TSO may display a number of messages. These messages, called *notices*, are created by systems programmers or operators and may contain information about new releases of software products, scheduled interruptions in the system's operation, and so on.

Usually, it's a good idea to scan these messages. But if you want, you can suppress the notices by specifying NONOTICE on your LOGON command, like this:

```
LOGON TSO0001/DAL NONOTICE
```

In this case, TSO doesn't display the notices.

When you issue a LOGON command, TSO submits a JCL procedure to JES2 or JES3. This procedure includes statements that describe the data sets to be used in your session and indicate whether the session manager or standard TSO is in effect. As a result, the procedure starts a foreground job to process your TSO session. But you don't have to worry about writing this procedure yourself. Normally, a systems programmer creates and maintains the logon JCL.

The LOGOFF command

The LOGOFF command has a simple format:

```
LOGOFF
```

When you enter a LOGOFF command, your TSO session is ended. In other words, your TSO foreground job is terminated. Before you can do more work, you must enter another LOGON command.

In many installations, TSO is set up so that it automatically logs you off if your terminal is idle for a certain period of time, for example, 15 minutes. That's because it generally costs more to sit idle for 15 minutes or more than it does to logoff and logon again later.

DISCUSSION

I included this topic just as a brief overview of how to use a 3270 terminal and how to access TSO. As you might guess, the best way to learn how to use a 3270 terminal is to use it for a while. It doesn't take long to master. And you'll get plenty of experience as you now go on to section 2.

Terms

3270 Information Display System
display station
local print
emulator program
field
unprotected field
protected field
cursor
program function key
PF key
program access key
PA key
Interrupt key
Clear key
Reset key
notice

Objectives

1. List the components of a typical 3270 system.

2. Find the data-entry, cursor-control, editing, PF, PA, and Reset keys on your keyboard, and explain how you use them.

3. Describe the procedure for logging on and off TSO.

Section 2

How to use ISPF

As a TSO user, you'll probably spend almost all of your terminal time using ISPF. ISPF provides a powerful and comprehensive program development environment that includes a text editor, utilities to manage data sets and libraries, and facilities to manage background job processing. The chapters in this section show you how to use these and other ISPF features.

If you've never used ISPF, you should read chapter 2 first. It presents the basics of using ISPF menus and panels and briefly describes each of the ISPF features presented in chapters 3-8. Because those chapters are independent of one another, however, you can read them in any sequence you wish once you've grasped the information presented in chapter 2.

Chapter 2

An introduction to ISPF

As I mentioned in chapter 1, ISPF provides a powerful environment for program development under TSO. Before you start learning how to use ISPF's individual features, such as its text editor or utility features, you need to learn the basics of using ISPF. For example, you need to learn how to work your way through ISPF's menus, how to enter commands, and so on. The two topics in this chapter present that information. Topic 1 presents the basics of using ISPF, and topic 2 shows you how to set up the ISPF working environment so it suits your needs.

Topic 1   The basics of using ISPF

ISPF, which stands for *Interactive System Productivity Facility*, is an optional IBM product that manages on-line applications under TSO. The part of ISPF that programmers use on a day-to-day basis is called *ISPF/PDF* (*PDF* stands for *Program Development Facility*). Throughout this book, whenever I mention ISPF, I am referring to ISPF/PDF. The other part of ISPF is called *dialog manager*; it lets you create your own applications that run under ISPF. I don't cover ISPF dialog manager in this book.

ISPF includes a variety of facilities that are useful for program development work: a powerful text editor, a set of utilities to create and manage data sets and libraries, and the ability to invoke language translators to compile and link-edit application programs. Although you can perform all these functions using native TSO commands, program development tasks are much easier to accomplish when you use ISPF's features.

In this topic, you'll learn the basics of using ISPF: how to access ISPF, what functions it provides from its main menu, how to select menu functions, and so on.

How to access ISPF

To gain access to ISPF, you must first connect your terminal to the host system (if necessary) and enter a valid TSO LOGON command, as I described in chapter 1. Once TSO displays its READY message, you can invoke ISPF by entering the command:

    ISPF

Then, ISPF displays its main menu, shown in figure 2-1.

In many installations, a TSO LOGON procedure is created to automatically invoke ISPF when you log on. In this case, the READY message never appears and you don't have to enter the ISPF command.

```
------------------------- ISPF/PDF PRIMARY OPTION MENU -------------------------
OPTION  ===>
                                                              USERID   - DLOWE
        0  ISPF PARMS  - Specify terminal and user parameters TIME     - 19:50
        1  BROWSE      - Display source data or output listings TERMINAL - 3278
        2  EDIT        - Create or change source data          PF KEYS  - 24
        3  UTILITIES   - Perform utility functions
        4  FOREGROUND  - Invoke language processors in foreground
        5  BATCH       - Submit job for language processing
        6  COMMAND     - Enter TSO command or CLIST
        7  DIALOG TEST - Perform dialog testing
        8  LM UTILITIES- Perform library administrator utility functions
        9  IBM PRODUCTS- Additional IBM program development products
       10  SCLM        - Software Configuration and Library Manager
        C  CHANGES     - Display summary of changes for this release
        S  SDSF        - Spool Display and Search Facility
        T  TUTORIAL    - Display information about ISPF/PDF
        X  EXIT        - Terminate ISPF using log and list defaults

    Enter END command to terminate ISPF.
```

Figure 2-1   ISPF's primary option menu

The primary option menu

Most of ISPF's functions are controlled by *menus* that present a list of processing options. As a result, to perform one of these functions, you simply specify the appropriate option.

The ISPF main menu shown in figure 2-1 is called the *primary option menu.* It offers you fourteen processing functions.

Option 0: ISPF PARMS   ISPF uses various default values throughout its many functions. For example, when you press PA1, you interrupt whatever function you're currently doing; that's the default value for PA1.

You use option 0 whenever you want to change the ISPF defaults. ISPF remembers the changes you make, so the next time you access ISPF, the changes are still in effect. I'll describe the most useful ISPF defaults in topic 2 of this chapter.

Option 1: BROWSE   This option lets you display the contents of a data set or an output listing, even when the records you want to look at are longer than the line on your screen. Normally, you'll use it to display compiler output. I describe browse in detail in chapter 3.

Option 2: EDIT   This option lets you create or change a data set or library member. It's probably the ISPF function you'll use most often. I describe it in chapter 4.

Option 3: UTILITIES   This option makes it easy for you to use some useful ISPF features—features otherwise available only through complicated TSO or JCL commands. For example, using the utility programs, you can easily create, rename, delete, move, or copy data sets. Or you can display partitioned data set directories, catalogs or VTOCs, or data set allocation information. I describe the utility functions in chapter 5.

Option 4: FOREGROUND   This option lets you execute the foreground processors for developing application programs. Because the foreground processors tie up your terminal as they execute, you can't use your terminal for other functions until they finish. I describe foreground processing in chapter 6.

Option 5: BATCH   This option lets you execute the batch processors for developing application programs. Although all these processors are available in foreground mode, batch jobs let you use your terminal for other functions while your job executes. However, overall response time for a batch job is often much slower than in foreground mode. That's because you have to wait for your job to be scheduled.

In chapter 7, I show you how to use the batch option. In addition, that chapter describes other ISPF facilities for background processing.

Option 6: COMMAND   This option lets you issue a TSO command or a CLIST or REXX procedure directly, bypassing ISPF's menu structure. If you want to learn how to use TSO commands or how to create CLIST or REXX procedures, I suggest you get a copy of *Part 2: Commands and Procedures*.

Option 7: DIALOG TEST   If you're responsible for developing applications using ISPF's dialog manager, you'll use option 7 a lot. It provides several features that make it easier to test and debug

ISPF *dialogs*. Since testing and debugging dialogs is beyond the scope of this book, I won't cover option 7.

Option 8: LM UTILITIES   This option lets you use the features of the *Library Management Facility*, or *LMF*. LMF controls who can access and move members of libraries that are under its control. Although it's the job of the system administrator to set up these controls, as a programmer, you may need to use some of the features of LMF to modify and move members. Even if you don't, it's worth knowing how LMF works if it's used in your shop. So I'll show you the basics of using LMF in chapter 8.

Option 9: IBM PRODUCTS   This option lets you use IBM program development products other than ISPF/PDF. I don't present any of these products in this book.

Option 10: SCLM   This option lets you use the features of the *Software Configuration and Library Manager*, or *SCLM*. SCLM provides services that let you control, maintain, and track the components of an application. Because it's a complicated program, I'll cover only its basics in chapter 8.

Option C: CHANGES   This option provides you with information on the changes that were made for your installation's release of ISPF. If you've just upgraded to a new release, the information this option presents can be useful.

Option T: TUTORIAL   This option displays instructions for using ISPF. I'll explain it briefly later in this chapter.

Option X: EXIT   This option terminates ISPF. I'll explain the details of using it in this chapter.

The format of ISPF displays

ISPF displays, or *panels*, come in two varieties: menus, which present options for your selection, and *entry panels*, which require you to enter data set names or other options. However, menus and entry panels all follow the same basic format. In particular, ISPF reserves the top two lines of all displays for system information, the third line to optionally display error messages, and the remainder of the screen (including line 3 if no message is displayed) to display data. In addition, ISPF uses the graphic:

```
===>
```

to indicate fields where you can enter data.

The first line of each display contains the display title. The title of the screen in figure 2-1 is this:

```
ISPF/PDF PRIMARY OPTION MENU
```

In addition, ISPF often uses the right-hand side of line 1 to display a short message. For example, during a browse operation, ISPF displays the current line and column numbers in this area. And it often displays short error messages in this area, too.

You use the second line to enter commands for processing by ISPF. For a menu screen, ISPF identifies the *command area* like this:

```
OPTION ===>
```

For other screens, ISPF identifies the command area like this:

```
COMMAND ===>
```

In either case, you can enter a variety of ISPF commands in the command area. If the cursor is positioned somewhere else on the screen, you can easily move it to the command area by pressing the home key. I'll have more to say about entering commands in this area in a minute.

Some ISPF displays don't let you enter a command. In this case, line 2 contains a message like this:

```
ENTER/VERIFY PARAMETERS BELOW:
```

Then, you enter data in the fields in the *data area*, below line 2.

The third screen line is normally blank, though in browse or edit mode, it does contain data. Whenever a short error message appears in line 1, you can obtain a longer version of it in line 3 by entering HELP in the command area or by pressing PF1/13.

How to use ISPF menus

ISPF's menus are easy to use. To select a menu option, enter the option's number or letter in the command area. For example, to select the edit option from the primary option menu, enter 2 like this:

```
OPTION ===> 2
```

When you press the Enter key, ISPF displays the first screen of the edit function.

Many of ISPF's primary options lead to additional menus. For example, if you select option 3 (utilities), the next screen ISPF displays is another menu, showing fourteen additional options. You can easily bypass the second menu screen by specifying both options at the primary menu. To do that, you separate the selections with a period. For example, if you enter the response

```
OPTION ===> 3.5
```

at the primary option menu, ISPF doesn't display the utilities menu. Instead, it automatically selects utility option 5.

You can also move directly from one option to another without displaying the primary option menu. For example, if you're editing a file, you can move directly to the utilities option. To do this, code an equals sign followed by the desired option number in the command area, like this:

```
COMMAND ===> =3
```

Then, when you press enter, ISPF goes directly to primary option 3.

How to enter commands in the command area

As I mentioned, you can enter a variety of commands in the command area of most ISPF panels. You can enter three kinds of commands in the command area: *ISPF commands*, *PDF primary commands*, and *TSO commands*. ISPF commands are commands that are built into ISPF and can be issued from any ISPF panel. PDF primary commands provide functions that are specific to certain ISPF options, such as the editor or the utilities. From a practical point of view, there is little difference between ISPF commands and PDF primary commands. So I'll refer to commands of both types simply as *primary commands*.

To issue a TSO command from the command area, you must precede the command with the word *TSO*, like this:

```
TSO LISTCAT
```

Here, the LISTCAT command is passed to TSO for processing. You can also invoke a CLIST or REXX procedure in this way.

If you want to enter the same command several times, you can use the Retrieve key, PF12/24. When you press this key, ISPF displays the last command you issued in the command area. Then, you can press the Enter key to issue the command again, you can modify the command before you reissue it, or you can press PF12/24 again to retrieve the previous command. You can continue to press PF12/24 to retrieve commands until all of the commands you've issued during the current ISPF session have been retrieved.

You can also enter several commands on the command line at once. To do that, just separate the commands with semicolons. To illustrate, suppose you want to make two text changes to a data set using the edit option. You could enter two CHANGE commands one at a time, or you could enter two CHANGE commands together, like this:

```
CHANGE 'MCA' 'CTA' ALL;CHANGE 'TWA' 'TCA' ALL
```

Then, ISPF executes the commands one at a time. If the first command fails for any reason, the second one isn't executed.

How to use the PF and PA keys

Besides entering commands in the command area, you can also control certain ISPF functions using the program access (PA) and program function (PF) keys. Figure 2-2 shows the default meanings of these keys.

As I said in chapter 1, many 3270 terminals require you to use the Alt key and one other key for PF1-12, while PF13-24 require only a single keystroke. As a result, all the function key assignments for ISPF are duplicated. So, you can use PF13 instead of PF1, PF14 instead of PF2, and so on. In this book, I indicate that by specifying function keys like this: PF4/16. That means you can use either PF4 or PF16.

Many of the PF and PA keys described in figure 2-2 are self-explanatory; others are discussed later in this book. Now, I want to explain how you use two of them: PF3/15 and PF4/16.

PF3/15, the End key, terminates an ISPF function. Whenever you have completed the processing for an ISPF function and want to return to the previous menu, use PF3/15.

Key	Title	Meaning
PA1	Attention	Interrupt the current operation.
PA2	Reshow	Redisplay the current screen.
PF1/13	Help	Enter the tutorial.
PF2/14	Split	Enter split-screen mode.
PF3/15	End	Terminate the current operation.
PF4/16	Return	Return to the primary option menu.
PF7/19	Up	Move the screen window up.
PF8/20	Down	Move the screen window down.
PF9/21	Swap	Activate the other logical screen in split-screen mode.
PF10/22	Left	Move the screen window left.
PF11/23	Right	Move the screen window right.
PF12/24	Retrieve	Redisplay the last ISPF command issued.

Figure 2-2   Commonly used attention and function keys

PF4/16, the Return key, is similar in function to PF3/15. The difference is that PF4/16 returns directly to the primary option menu, bypassing any intermediate panels.

Incidentally, you can change the meaning of any PF key by reassigning it using the ISPF Parms option. I'll show you how to do that in topic 2 of this chapter.

How to enter data set names

Most ISPF functions require you to enter one or more data set names. For example, figure 2-3 shows the entry panel for the edit option, which requires you to enter the name of the data set or library member you want to edit. ISPF data set names follow basically the same naming conventions as TSO data set names. Each data set name consists of three components: project-id, library-name, and type.

Each component of the data set name is eight or fewer alphanumeric characters, starting with a letter. The project-id identifies the project associated with the data set and usually defaults to the user-id from your LOGON command. The library-name can be any

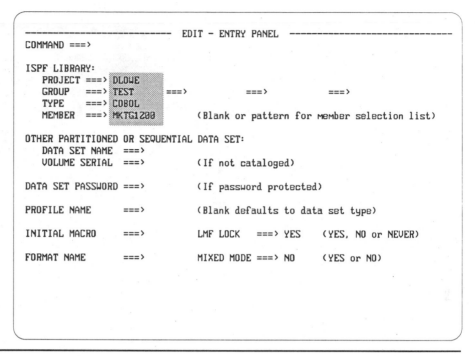

```
------------------------------ EDIT - ENTRY PANEL -----------------------------
COMMAND ===>

ISPF LIBRARY:
   PROJECT ===> DLOWE
   GROUP   ===> TEST        ===>          ===>          ===>
   TYPE    ===> COBOL
   MEMBER  ===> MKTG1200          (Blank or pattern for member selection list)

OTHER PARTITIONED OR SEQUENTIAL DATA SET:
   DATA SET NAME  ===>
   VOLUME SERIAL  ===>          (If not cataloged)

DATA SET PASSWORD ===>          (If password protected)

PROFILE NAME      ===>          (Blank defaults to data set type)

INITIAL MACRO     ===>          LMF LOCK   ===> YES   (YES, NO or NEVER)

FORMAT NAME       ===>          MIXED MODE ===> NO    (YES or NO)
```

Figure 2-3   Edit entry panel

name you want. The type indicates the nature of the data stored in the data set. Although you can code anything in the type field, you should stick to the valid TSO types I presented in figure 1-10.

The three components of a data set name are strung together to form the file's MVS data set name. As a result, the data set name for the file specified in figure 2-3 is DLOWE.TEST.COBOL.

If a data set has partitioned organization, you can specify the name of the member to be processed in the field labelled MEMBER. If you omit the member name from the entry panel, ISPF displays a list of all the members in the data set, as shown in figure 2-4. You then select the member to be processed by placing an S next to the member's name.

You can also display a member list by entering a pattern for the member name. A *pattern* consists of a partial member name plus the symbols * or % or both. An asterisk (*) represents a string of characters. For example, if I coded the pattern

    MKTG*

ISPF would display a member list of all the member names that begin with MKTG, regardless of how many additional characters

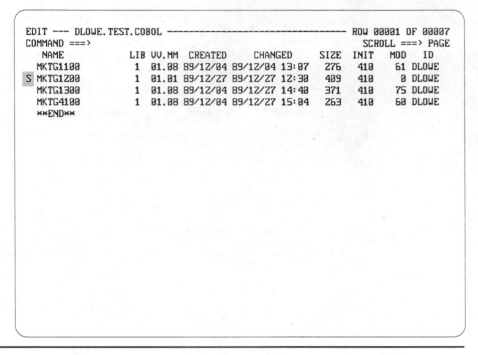

```
 EDIT --- DLOWE.TEST.COBOL ------------------------------- ROW 00001 OF 00007
 COMMAND ===>                                                  SCROLL ===> PAGE
    NAME        LIB VV.MM  CREATED    CHANGED     SIZE  INIT  MOD   ID
    MKTG1100     1  01.08 89/12/04 89/12/04 13:07  276  410   61 DLOWE
  S MKTG1200     1  01.01 89/12/27 89/12/27 12:30  409  410    0 DLOWE
    MKTG1300     1  01.08 89/12/04 89/12/27 14:40  371  410   75 DLOWE
    MKTG4100     1  01.08 89/12/04 89/12/27 15:04  263  410   60 DLOWE
    **END**
```

Figure 2-4   Edit member selection list

there are in the member name. A percent sign (%) represents a single character. So if I coded the pattern

    MKTG%%%

ISPF would display a member list of only those member names that begin with MKTG and consist of four additional characters.

To process a data set whose name doesn't follow the ISPF naming conventions, you must use the OTHER PARTITIONED OR SEQUENTIAL DATA SET field, shown in figure 2-3. If you enter a fully-qualified data set name here, you must enclose it in apostrophes, like this:

    DATA SET NAME ===> 'TESTLIB.COB'

In this example, the complete data set name is TESTLIB.COB. If you omit the apostrophes, ISPF adds your user-id to the beginning of the data set name.

If the data set isn't cataloged, you must enter a volume serial number. However, most ISPF data sets are cataloged. So you won't use the VOLUME SERIAL field often.

To process a data set that's protected by a standard MVS password, you must enter the correct password in the DATA SET PASSWORD field. However, if your installation uses RACF for password protection, you don't have to enter a password for the data set. That's because RACF uses your user-id to determine if you have access to a particular data set.

How to use split-screen mode

It can sometimes be advantageous to view two different ISPF panels at the same time. For example, while editing a data set, you might want to browse another data set that contains similar code. To do that, you can use *split-screen mode* to split the screen horizontally into two separate screens.

Figure 2-5 illustrates how split-screen mode works. In part 1 of the figure, I'm editing a COBOL program. To enter split-screen mode, I placed the cursor on the line where I wanted the split to occur. Then, I pressed PF2/14. When I did, ISPF split the screen horizontally into two *logical screens*, as in part 2 of the figure. Notice that the primary option menu is now available from the second logical screen. So I can perform any function I want from that screen.

ISPF treats each logical screen as an independent session. However, only one session can be active at a time. The session that's currently active is identified by the location of the cursor. When you first enter split-screen mode, ISPF positions the cursor in the second logical screen. So in part 2 of figure 2-5, the cursor is positioned in the command area of the primary option menu. To switch from one session to another, you use PF9/21.

To terminate split-screen mode, you simply end one of the sessions. For example, if I ended the edit session in the first logical screen in part 2 of figure 2-5, the primary option menu in the second logical screen would occupy the entire display.

Tutorial (Help)

The *ISPF tutorial* provides on-line instructions on how to use ISPF. You enter the tutorial in one of two ways. First, you can select option T from the primary option menu to display instructions on how to use the tutorial. Second, you can press the Help key

Place the cursor where you want to split the screen and press PF2/14

```
EDIT ---- DLOWE.TEST.COBOL(MKTG1200) - 01.02 ------------------ COLUMNS 007 072
COMMAND ===>                                                    SCROLL ===> PAGE
****** ******************************** TOP OF DATA *****************************
000100  IDENTIFICATION DIVISION.
000200 *
000300  PROGRAM-ID.     MKTG1200.
000400 *
000500  ENVIRONMENT DIVISION.
000600 *
000700  CONFIGURATION SECTION.
000800 *
000900  INPUT-OUTPUT SECTION.
001000 *
001100  FILE-CONTROL.
001200      SELECT CUSTMST  ASSIGN TO AS-CUSTMST.
001300      SELECT SALESMN  ASSIGN TO SALESMN
001400                      ORGANIZATION IS INDEXED
001500                      ACCESS IS RANDOM
001600                      RECORD KEY IS SM-SALESMAN-KEY.
001700      SELECT SALESRPT ASSIGN TO SALESRPT.
001800 *
001900  DATA DIVISION.
002000 *
002100  FILE SECTION.
```

Figure 2-5   Entering split-screen mode (part 1 of 2)

The screen is split into two logical screens

```
EDIT ---- DLOWE.TEST.COBOL(MKTG1200) - 01.02 ------------------ COLUMNS 007 072
COMMAND ===>                                                    SCROLL ===> PAGE
****** ******************************** TOP OF DATA *****************************
000100  IDENTIFICATION DIVISION.
000200 *
000300  PROGRAM-ID.     MKTG1200.
000400 *
000500  ENVIRONMENT DIVISION.
000600 *
000700  CONFIGURATION SECTION.
000800 *
000900  INPUT-OUTPUT SECTION.
001000 *
. . . . . . . . . . . . . . . . . . . . . . . . . . . . . . . .
------------------------ ISPF/PDF PRIMARY OPTION MENU -----------------------
OPTION  ===>
                                                      USERID   - DLOWE
     0  ISPF PARMS  - Specify terminal and user parameters  TIME     - 17:06
     1  BROWSE      - Display source data or output listings TERMINAL - 3278
     2  EDIT        - Create or change source data           PF KEYS  - 24
     3  UTILITIES   - Perform utility functions
     4  FOREGROUND  - Invoke language processors in foreground
     5  BATCH       - Submit job for language processing
     6  COMMAND     - Enter TSO command or CLIST
```

Figure 2-5   Entering split-screen mode (part 2 of 2)

(PF1/13) to immediately display the portion of the tutorial that describes the ISPF function you're currently performing.

In general, ISPF functions are simple and the entry panels are self-explanatory. However, it's easy to forget the formats of ISPF commands. So you'll probably find yourself using PF1/13 often when you begin to use ISPF.

List and log files

Some ISPF operations generate printed output. For example, when you compile a COBOL program, a compiler listing is generated. Printed output like this is collected in a special data set called a *list file*. When you terminate ISPF, you specify what happens to the contents of the listing data set. I'll explain how to terminate ISPF and how to specify the disposition of the listing data set in just a moment.

If you want to print the listing data set without terminating ISPF, you can use the LIST command. On the LIST command, you can code one of three options: PRINT, DELETE, or KEEP. If you enter LIST PRINT, the listing data set is printed and deleted. If you enter LIST DELETE, the listing data set is deleted without being printed. And if you enter LIST KEEP, the data set is deallocated. Then, when additional output is created, ISPF allocates a new listing data set.

If you code the LIST command without an option, ISPF displays the panel in figure 2-6. Here, you can enter process options that correspond to the PRINT, DELETE, and KEEP options: PD, D, and KN. If you specify PD, you also have to specify a SYSOUT class or a local printer ID.

In addition to compiler listings and other types of listings you request, ISPF maintains a record of ISPF operations in a special *log file*. As a programmer, the ISPF log is of little value. So you normally won't print it unless your installation has a policy that says you should. If you do need to print it, however, you can specify the appropriate option when you terminate ISPF, or you can issue the LOG command during an ISPF session. The LOG command has the same format as the LIST command.

```
--------------------      SPECIFY DISPOSITION OF LIST DATA SET  ----------------------
COMMAND ===>

   LIST DATA SET (DLOWE.SPF4.LIST) DISPOSITION:
        Process option   ===> PD
        SYSOUT class     ===> A
        Local printer ID ===>

   VALID PROCESS OPTIONS:
        PD - Print data set and delete
        D  - Delete data set without printing
        KN - Keep existing data set and continue with new data set

    Press ENTER key to process the list data set.
    Enter END command to exit without processing the list data set.

JOB STATEMENT INFORMATION:  (Required for system printer)
===> //DLOWEP  JOB (9999),'DOUG LOWE'
===> //*
===> //*
===> //*
```

Figure 2-6   The list data set disposition panel

How to terminate ISPF

The normal way to terminate ISPF is to select option X from the primary option menu (or by entering =X from most ISPF panels). This option simply returns to native TSO, using the default values for processing the log and list files.

If you haven't specified any default values or if you use the End key (PF3/15) to terminate ISPF, ISPF displays the termination panel, shown in figure 2-7. Here, you must specify process options for the log and list files. Three of the options are the same options that are available when you issue a LIST or LOG command: PD to print and delete the data set, D to delete the data set, and KN to keep the data set and allocate a new data set in the next session. The fourth option, K, keeps the data set and allocates the same data set in the next session.

For the list file, you'll usually specify PD to print the file. If you do, you have to specify either a SYSOUT class or a local printer-id. You can get the correct values for these fields from your super-

```
----------------          SPECIFY DISPOSITION OF LOG AND LIST DATA SETS '  -----------------
COMMAND ===>

LOG OPTIONS FOR THIS SESSION              LIST OPTIONS FOR THIS SESSION
----------------------------              ----------------------------
Process option    ===>  PD                Process option    ===> D
SYSOUT class      ===>  A                  SYSOUT class      ===>
Local printer ID ===>                      Local printer ID ===>

VALID PROCESS OPTIONS:
    PD - Print data set and delete
    D  - Delete data set without printing
    K  - Keep data set (allocate same data set in next session)
    KN - Keep data set and allocate new data set in next session

  Press ENTER key to complete ISPF termination.
  Enter END command to return to the primary option menu.

JOB STATEMENT INFORMATION:  (Required for system printer)
  ===> //DLOWEP  JOB (9999),'DOUG LOWE'
  ===> //*
  ===> //*
  ===> //*
```

Figure 2-7   The ISPF termination screen

visor. If you specify a SYSOUT class, ISPF submits a background
job to print and delete the data set. If you specify a printer-id, the
data set is routed to the printer you specify.

The user profile

For each ISPF user, ISPF maintains a *user profile*. The user profile
contains default values for many fields of the various entry panels.
Whenever you change one of these fields, ISPF stores the change in
your profile. Then, the next time you recall that panel, the changed
value is supplied by default. Because of the user profile, you have
to enter many ISPF fields only once. From then on, ISPF supplies
default values for the fields. (Incidentally, the PROFILE NAME
field in figure 2-3 applies only to the edit option; it has nothing to
do with the user profile.)

Discussion

Like most interactive programs, ISPF is easier to use than it is to describe. So if you're confused at this point, don't worry. ISPF is actually very easy to learn. After you've used ISPF for awhile, using its menus and filling in its entry panels will become second nature to you.

Terms

ISPF
Interactive System Productivity Facility
ISPF/PDF
ISPF/Program Development Facility
dialog manager
menu
primary option menu
dialog
Library Management Facility
LMF
Software Configuration and Library Manager
SCLM
panel
entry panel
command area
data area
pattern
split-screen mode
logical screen
ISPF tutorial
list file
log file
user profile

Objectives

1. Briefly describe the function of each of the ISPF primary options:
   a. ISPF parms
   b. browse
   c. edit
   d. utilities
   e. foreground
   f. batch
   g. command
   h. dialog test
   i. LM utilities
   j. IBM products
   k. SCLM
   l. changes
   m. tutorial
   n. exit

2. Describe the procedures for accessing and terminating ISPF.

3. Explain what split-screen mode is and how you use it.

4. Describe these ISPF features:
   a. user profile
   b. log file
   c. list file

5. Explain how to move back and forth between ISPF menus.

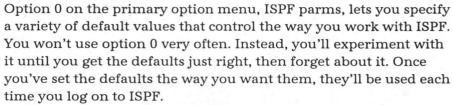

Topic 2

How to set up your ISPF defaults

Option 0 on the primary option menu, ISPF parms, lets you specify a variety of default values that control the way you work with ISPF. You won't use option 0 very often. Instead, you'll experiment with it until you get the defaults just right, then forget about it. Once you've set the defaults the way you want them, they'll be used each time you log on to ISPF.

Figure 2-8 shows the menu that's displayed when you select option 0 from the primary option menu. As you can see, it provides eight options that control various aspects of ISPF's operation. Of these eight, only the first five are important for most users, so I won't cover the last three. Keep in mind that you don't have to change *any* of these defaults if you don't want to; the standard default values are acceptable for most users.

Instead of discussing these options in the order they're listed in the menu, I'll describe them in a more logical sequence. First, I'll show you how to specify your terminal characteristics using option 0.1. Then, I'll show you how to set your PF key definitions using option 0.3. Next, I'll show you how to use option 0.4 to change the location of the command line. Finally, I'll show you how options 0.2 and 0.5 affect the way ISPF handles list and log data.

Option 0.1: Specifying terminal characteristics

The first ISPF parm option lets you specify the characteristics of the terminal you're using to access ISPF. In all likelihood, you won't have to change these settings. If you change terminal types, however, you may need to.

Figure 2-9 shows the panel ISPF displays when you select option 0.1. Here, you can enter data into five fields. In the first, you enter your terminal type. Most of the time, you'll enter 3278 here, even if your terminal is a 3278-compatible terminal such as a 3178 or a PC emulating a 3270. You enter one of the other values only if your terminal is not a 3278-compatible.

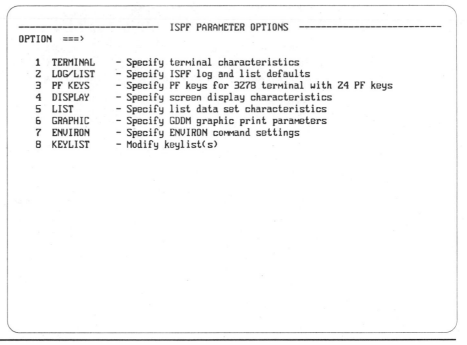

Figure 2-8   The ISPF options menu

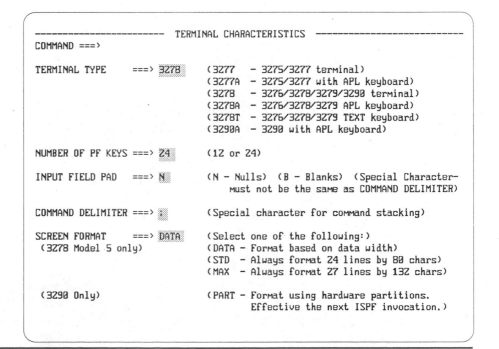

Figure 2-9   Setting terminal characteristics

The NUMBER OF PF KEYS field tells ISPF whether you have 12 or 24 PF keys. Newer 3270 terminals have 24, but some older models have only 12. ISPF usually sets this field to the correct value automatically, so you don't need to worry about it.

The INPUT FIELD PAD field tells ISPF what character to use as a "pad character" to fill out the unused positions of input fields. You should always leave this field at its default setting, N, so that ISPF uses nulls as pad characters. Any other value increases the amount of time required to transmit information from your terminal to the computer.

The COMMAND DELIMITER field lets you specify a non-standard character to separate commands entered in the command area. Normally, you use a semicolon for this purpose.

The last field, SCREEN FORMAT, applies to only two types of terminals: the 3278 model 5, which is capable of displaying 27 rows of 132 characters each; or the 3290, which can be divided into several partitions, each acting as an independent terminal. If you aren't using one of these terminals, the value of this field is ignored.

Option 0.3: Setting PF key definitions

Option 0.3 lets you change the commands associated with any of your terminal's PF keys. That way, you can set up ISPF so it works best for you. For example, if you often use a command to find the beginning of a COBOL program's Procedure Division, you can assign that command to a function key.

Figure 2-10 shows the entry panel option 0.3 uses to let you specify PF key definitions. Here, the definitions of PF13-24 are displayed. To display the definitions of PF1-12, just press the Enter key.

To change the definition of a PF key, type a new command over the old definition. You can use any ISPF command you want, including TSO. (You'll find a complete listing of available ISPF commands in the appendix.) If you code TSO for a PF key definition, ISPF lets you specify any TSO command or CLIST when you press that PF key.

Option 0.3 is most useful for terminals with 24 PF keys. On these terminals, I recommend you leave PF13-24 at their default settings. That way, everyone at your installation will have the same

```
----------------- PF KEY DEFINITIONS AND LABELS - PRIMARY KEYS -----------------
COMMAND ===>

NUMBER OF PF KEYS ===> 24                              TERMINAL TYPE ===> 3278

PF13 ===> HELP
PF14 ===> SPLIT
PF15 ===> END
PF16 ===> RETURN
PF17 ===> RFIND
PF18 ===> RCHANGE
PF19 ===> UP
PF20 ===> DOWN
PF21 ===> SWAP
PF22 ===> LEFT
PF23 ===> RIGHT
PF24 ===> RETRIEVE


PF13 LABEL ===>            PF14 LABEL ===>            PF15 LABEL ===>
PF16 LABEL ===>            PF17 LABEL ===>            PF18 LABEL ===>
PF19 LABEL ===>            PF20 LABEL ===>            PF21 LABEL ===>
PF22 LABEL ===>            PF23 LABEL ===>            PF24 LABEL ===>

Press ENTER key to display alternate keys.   Enter END command to exit.
```

Figure 2-10   Setting PF key definitions

set of standard PF key assignments. Then, you can use PF1-12 for special-purpose key assignments.

Once you've created special PF key assignments, you might want to display them at the bottom of the screen. To do that, enter this command in the command area:

    PFSHOW ON

Figure 2-11 shows the resulting PF key display. To remove the PF key display, enter the command PFSHOW OFF.

Option 0.4: Setting display characteristics

The entry panel for option 0.4, shown in figure 2-12, has four entry fields. The last three are meaningful only for ISPF applications developed according to IBM's CUA standard (*CUA* stands for *Common User Access*). Since ISPF/PDF isn't a CUA application, I won't cover these three fields in this book. So the only field you

```
------------------------ ISPF/PDF PRIMARY OPTION MENU ------------------------
OPTION  ===>
                                                              USERID   - DLOWE
       0  ISPF PARMS  - Specify terminal and user parameters  TIME     - 17:21
       1  BROWSE      - Display source data or output listings TERMINAL - 3278
       2  EDIT        - Create or change source data           PF KEYS  - 24
       3  UTILITIES   - Perform utility functions
       4  FOREGROUND  - Invoke language processors in foreground
       5  BATCH       - Submit job for language processing
       6  COMMAND     - Enter TSO command or CLIST
       7  DIALOG TEST - Perform dialog testing
       8  LM UTILITIES- Perform library administrator utility functions
       9  IBM PRODUCTS- Additional IBM program development products
      10  SCLM        - Software Configuration and Library Manager
       C  CHANGES     - Display summary of changes for this release
       S  SDSF        - Spool Display and Search Facility
       T  TUTORIAL    - Display information about ISPF/PDF
       X  EXIT        - Terminate ISPF using log and list defaults

Enter END command to terminate ISPF.



    F13=HELP     F14=SPLIT    F15=END      F16=RETURN   F17=RFIND    F18=RCHANGE
    F19=UP       F20=DOWN     F21=SWAP     F22=LEFT     F23=RIGHT    F24=RETRIEVE
```

Figure 2-11   Displaying PF key assignments

```
------------------------ DISPLAY CHARACTERISTICS ----------------------------
COMMAND ===>

COMMAND LINE PLACEMENT ===> ASIS      (ASIS   - Display as shown
                                                in panel definition.)

                                      (BOTTOM - Display as the last
                                                line on the screen or
                                                as the last line above
                                                the split line.)


ACTIVE WINDOW FRAME


            INTENSITY ===> HIGH     (HIGH or LOW)


                COLOR ===> YELLOW  (BLUE, RED, PINK, GREEN, TURQ,
                                    YELLOW or WHITE)

PANEL DISPLAY CUA MODE ===> YES     (YES or NO)
```

Figure 2-12   Setting display characteristics

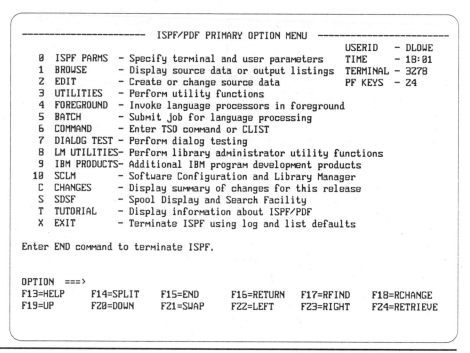

```
----------------------- ISPF/PDF PRIMARY OPTION MENU -----------------------
                                                    USERID   - DLOWE
    0  ISPF PARMS  - Specify terminal and user parameters    TIME     - 18:01
    1  BROWSE      - Display source data or output listings  TERMINAL - 3278
    2  EDIT        - Create or change source data            PF KEYS  - 24
    3  UTILITIES   - Perform utility functions
    4  FOREGROUND  - Invoke language processors in foreground
    5  BATCH       - Submit job for language processing
    6  COMMAND     - Enter TSO command or CLIST
    7  DIALOG TEST - Perform dialog testing
    8  LM UTILITIES- Perform library administrator utility functions
    9  IBM PRODUCTS- Additional IBM program development products
   10  SCLM        - Software Configuration and Library Manager
    C  CHANGES     - Display summary of changes for this release
    S  SDSF        - Spool Display and Search Facility
    T  TUTORIAL    - Display information about ISPF/PDF
    X  EXIT        - Terminate ISPF using log and list defaults

Enter END command to terminate ISPF.



OPTION  ===>
F13=HELP      F14=SPLIT     F15=END      F16=RETURN   F17=RFIND    F18=RCHANGE
F19=UP        F20=DOWN      F21=SWAP     F22=LEFT     F23=RIGHT    F24=RETRIEVE
```

Figure 2-13   An ISPF menu with the command line at the bottom

need to be concerned with here is the first, which lets you move the position of the command area from the top of the screen to the bottom.

Figure 2-13 shows the effect of specifying BOTTOM for this field. Here, you can see that the command line has been moved from the top of the screen to the bottom. If you've used an on-line system that has the command line at the bottom, such as VM/CMS, placing the command line at the bottom of the screen might make ISPF seem more familiar at first. I recommend you don't move it, though. Eventually, you'll get used to ISPF's standard command line placement.

Options 0.2 and 0.5: Controlling list and log data sets

As you recall, ISPF maintains a *list data set* and a *log data set* as you work. The list data set contains data you want printed; the log data

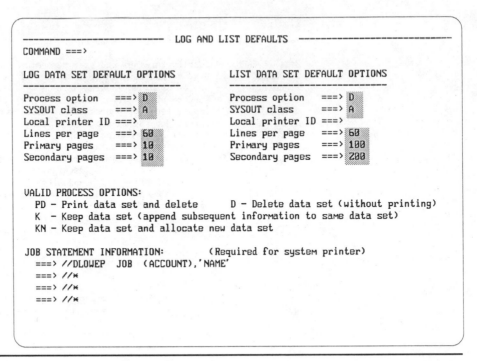

```
------------------------- LOG AND LIST DEFAULTS -------------------------
COMMAND ===>

LOG DATA SET DEFAULT OPTIONS            LIST DATA SET DEFAULT OPTIONS
---------------------------             ----------------------------
Process option    ===> D                Process option    ===> D
SYSOUT class       ===> A                SYSOUT class       ===> A
Local printer ID ===>                    Local printer ID ===>
Lines per page    ===> 60                Lines per page    ===> 60
Primary pages     ===> 10                Primary pages     ===> 100
Secondary pages   ===> 10                Secondary pages   ===> 200


VALID PROCESS OPTIONS:
  PD - Print data set and delete     D - Delete data set (without printing)
  K  - Keep data set (append subsequent information to same data set)
  KN - Keep data set and allocate new data set

JOB STATEMENT INFORMATION:           (Required for system printer)
  ===> //DLOWEP  JOB  (ACCOUNT),'NAME'
  ===> //*
  ===> //*
  ===> //*
```

Figure 2-14   Setting log and list data set defaults

set contains a record of your ISPF activity. Two ISPF parm options control the way ISPF processes these data sets: 0.2 and 0.5.

When you terminate ISPF using the X option, ISPF processes the list and log data sets according to the defaults. Option 0.2 lets you set those defaults. As you can see in figure 2-14, the entry panel for option 0.2 is similar to the panel displayed when you exit ISPF using PF3. Here, you can specify a processing option, SYSOUT class, printer ID, lines per page, and an estimate of the number of pages that will be required.

Option 0.5, shown in figure 2-15, lets you control the basic characteristics of the list data set: the record format, record length, and line length. Usually, the default settings for these fields are appropriate. However, if you want to print data that's wider than 120 characters, you'll have to specify a larger record and line length.

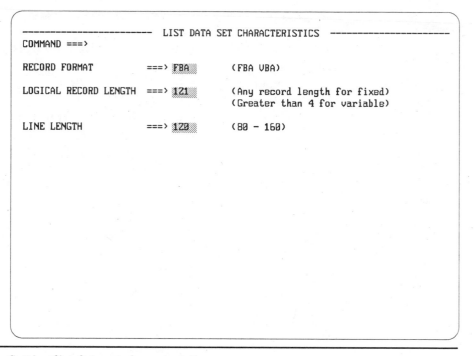

Figure 2-15   Setting list data set characteristics

Discussion

As I said at the start of this topic, you won't use option 0 often. So don't worry about memorizing any of its settings. Instead, experiment a little at first to get ISPF set up the way you want it. Then, use option 0 only when a change is warranted. For example, you might use it when you change terminal types or when you change a PF key assignment.

Terms

CUA
Common User Access
list data set
log data set

Objective

Perform the following functions using the appropriate ISPF options:

    a.   specify the terminal characteristics

    b.   set your PF key definitions

    c.   move the command line to the bottom of the screen

    d.   control the list and log data sets

Chapter 3

How to browse a data set

In this chapter, you'll learn how to use ISPF's browse option to examine the contents of a data set or member. There are two topics in this chapter. Topic 1 shows you the basics of using browse. When you've completed it, you can move on to chapter 4 if you wish...and you should if you're new to ISPF. Topic 2 presents advanced features of browse. You won't need these features initially, but they'll prove useful as you gain experience with ISPF.

Topic 1   Basic browse operations

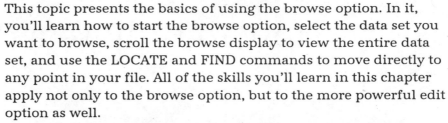

This topic presents the basics of using the browse option. In it, you'll learn how to start the browse option, select the data set you want to browse, scroll the browse display to view the entire data set, and use the LOCATE and FIND commands to move directly to any point in your file. All of the skills you'll learn in this chapter apply not only to the browse option, but to the more powerful edit option as well.

You'll use browse most often to examine files containing records larger than 80 bytes. In particular, you'll use browse to display SYSOUT data sets, which contain 133-byte records. The first byte in each record of this type is a printer-control character and the remaining 132 bytes contain alphanumeric data. When browse displays this type of data set, it displays only the 132 bytes of data, omitting the printer-control character at the beginning of each record.

How to begin a browse session

To begin a browse session, select option 1 from the primary option menu. Then, ISPF displays the browse entry panel, shown in figure 3-1. Here, you enter the name of the data set you want to browse. The shaded part of this example shows I'm going to browse a data set named DLOWE.MKTG1200.LIST. This data set is a compiler listing from a COBOL compilation.

Note that although the browse entry panel indicates that the PROJECT, GROUP, TYPE, and MEMBER fields identify an "ISPF library," you can access either a standard sequential data set or a partitioned data set using these fields. If the data set is partitioned, you can specify a member name in the MEMBER field. For a sequential data set, though, you must leave the MEMBER field blank.

If the data set is partitioned, you should know about two additional techniques: concatenating libraries and using a member list.

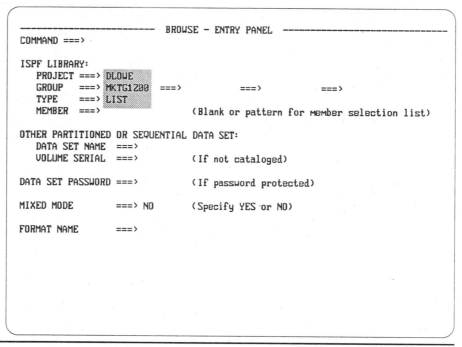

```
-------------------------- BROWSE - ENTRY PANEL  --------------------------------
COMMAND ===>

ISPF LIBRARY:
    PROJECT ===> DLOWE
    GROUP   ===> MKTG1200  ===>          ===>          ===>
    TYPE    ===> LIST
    MEMBER  ===>                     (Blank or pattern for member selection list)

OTHER PARTITIONED OR SEQUENTIAL DATA SET:
    DATA SET NAME  ===>
    VOLUME SERIAL  ===>               (If not cataloged)

DATA SET PASSWORD ===>                (If password protected)

MIXED MODE        ===> NO            (Specify YES or NO)

FORMAT NAME       ===>
```

Figure 3-1   Browse entry panel

How to concatenate libraries   You may have noticed in figure
3-1 that the GROUP field lets you specify up to four distinct
libraries as input to browse. Each of these libraries must have the
same project and type, but the group name can vary.

   If you specify more than one library, browse *concatenates* the
libraries when it searches for the member you specify. In other
words, to locate the member you specify, browse searches the
libraries in the order you list them. For example, suppose you code
the data set name entries like this:

```
PROJECT ===> DLOWE
LIBRARY ===> TEST     ===> MASTER
TYPE    ===> COBOL
MEMBER  ===> MKTG1200
```

Browse searches DLOWE.TEST.COBOL first to locate the member
named MKTG1200. If the member isn't found, browse searches
DLOWE.MASTER.COBOL next.

```
BROWSE - DLOWE.TEST.COBOL --------------------------------- ROW 00001 OF 00004
COMMAND ===>                                                SCROLL ===> PAGE
  NAME            VV.MM  CREATED    CHANGED      SIZE  INIT  MOD   ID
  MKTG1100        01.08 89/12/04 89/12/27 13:07   276  410   61 DLOWE
S MKTG1200        01.00 89/12/27 89/12/27 17:56   410  410    0 DLOWE
  MKTG1300        01.08 89/12/04 89/12/27 14:40   371  410   75 DLOWE
  MKTG4100        01.08 89/12/04 89/12/27 15:04   263  410   60 DLOWE
  **END**
```

Figure 3-2   Browse member list panel

How to display a member list   If the data set you specify in the
browse entry panel is partitioned, and you specify only a pattern of
the member name, or you don't specify a member name at all,
browse displays a *member list*, as shown in figure 3-2. This display
lists all the members from each library specified on the entry
panel. If the libraries contain more members than can be shown
on a single screen, you can use PF7/19 and PF8/20 to scroll
forward and backward through the list.

    To select the member you want to browse, type an S (for
"select") next to the member name and press the Enter key. In
figure 3-2, the member named MKTG1200 is selected.

The browse data display

After you specify the data set you want to display, browse displays
the first 22 lines of the source data, as shown in figure 3-3. In this
case, the first 22 lines of the VS COBOL II compiler listing indicate
what compiler options are in effect. As you can see, the right-hand

```
  BROWSE -- DLOWE.MKTG1200.LIST --------------------- LINE 00000000 COL 001 080
  COMMAND ===>                                             SCROLL ===> HALF
********************************** TOP OF DATA ***************************************
1PP 5668-958 REL. 2.0, 09/08/86, IBM VS COBOL II.                          DATE
0
        IGYOS4013-I   AN OPTIONS PARAMETER LIST WAS FOUND AS INPUT TO THE COMPI

1PP 5668-958 REL. 2.0, 09/08/86, IBM VS COBOL II.                          DATE
0*OPTIONS IN EFFECT*
        NOADV
          APOST
          BUFSIZE(4096)
        NOCOMPILE(E)
          DATA(31)
        NODECK
        NODUMP
        NODYNAM
        NOFASTSRT
        NOFDUMP
          FLAG(I)
          LIB
          LINECOUNT(60)
        NOLIST
          MAP
```

Figure 3-3 Browse data display

side of line 1 shows the current line number and the columns currently displayed. Here, the current line is line 0, and columns 1 through 80 are shown.

Sometimes, you'll want to identify individual columns between the left and right margins. To do that, enter the COLUMNS command in the command area. Then, browse displays a line at the top of the data area like the one in figure 3-4. As you can see, this line makes it easy to figure out the column locations of the data. To remove this line from the display, enter the RESET command.

Going back to figure 3-3, notice the TOP OF DATA indication on line 3. *Top of data* is ISPF's term for the first line of the source file. Likewise, *bottom of data* means the last line of the source file.

How to scroll through a data set

Browse displays up to 22 lines of 80-character data at a time in an area called the *screen window*. If the file contains more than 22

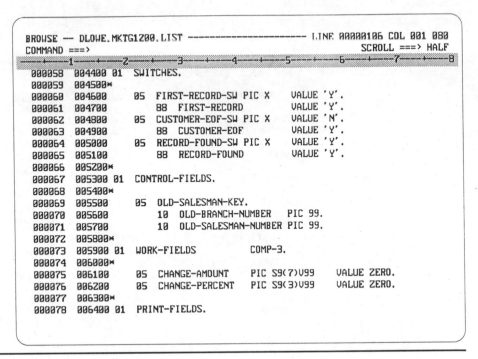

Figure 3-4   Displaying a COLS line

records or the records are more than 80 bytes long, you must *scroll*
the screen window to view all the data. Scrolling functions let you
specify both the direction and the amount of the move.

To specify the scroll direction, you use PF keys. Figure 3-5
shows the default PF key assignments for scrolling. As you can see,
PF7/19 moves the screen window up, PF8/20 moves it down,
PF10/22 moves it left, and PF11/23 moves it right. As a result, the
data *appears* to move on the screen. For example, when you move
the screen window down by using PF8/20, the data on the screen
appears to move up. Similarly, when you move the screen window
right using PF11/23, the screen data appears to move left.

You specify the amount of the scroll by entering a value in the
SCROLL field at the right-hand side of line 2 in the browse display
panel. Figure 3-6 shows the valid scroll amount values. Normally,
this value defaults to HALF. That means the screen window is
moved a half page in the direction indicated by the PF key you use.
(A *page* is 22 lines or 80 columns, depending on the direction of the

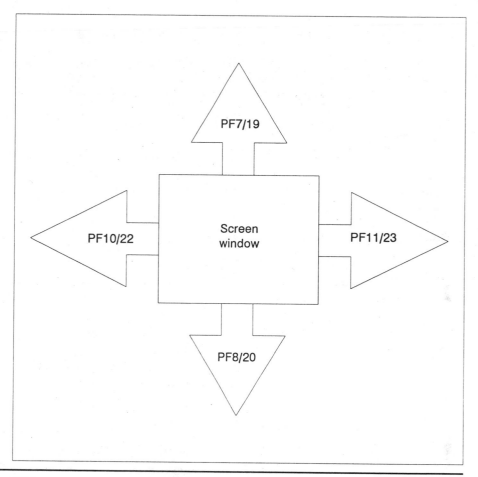

Figure 3-5   PF keys used for scrolling under ISPF

scroll.) For example, if you scroll down (PF8/20) HALF, the screen window is moved down 11 lines. If you scroll right (PF11/23) HALF, the window is moved 40 columns to the right.

To change the scroll amount, simply position the cursor in the SCROLL field (using the Tab key) and type in a new scroll amount. For example, to scroll a full page, enter the SCROLL field like this:

```
SCROLL ===> PAGE
```

Then, use a scrolling PF key to move the screen window 22 lines up or down or 80 columns left or right.

Value	Meaning
HALF	Move the screen window half a page (11 lines or 40 columns).
PAGE	Move the screen window one page (22 lines or 80 columns).
n	Move the screen window *n* lines or columns.
MAX	Move the screen window to top, bottom, left, or right margin.
CSR	Move the screen window so data at the current cursor position ends up at the top, bottom, left, or right of the screen.
DATA	Move the screen window one line or column less than a full page.

Figure 3-6   Scroll amounts

You can move the screen window a specific number of lines or columns by entering a number from 1 to 9999 in the SCROLL field. For example, if you enter

```
SCROLL ===> 50
```

the scrolling keys move the screen window 50 lines or columns.

You can easily move the screen window to the top or bottom of the data or to the left or right margin by entering MAX in the SCROLL field. Then, if you use PF7/19, the screen window is moved to the top of the data (line 0), while PF8/20 moves the window to the bottom of the data. Similarly, PF10/22 returns the screen window to the left margin (column 1), while PF11/23 moves the window to the right margin.

If you enter CSR in the SCROLL field, the amount of the scroll depends on the location of the cursor. If you press PF7/19, the screen window is moved so the current cursor line appears at the top of the screen. If you use PF8/20, the window is moved so the current cursor line appears at the bottom of the screen. PF10/22 moves the window so the current cursor column appears at the left margin of the screen. And PF11/23 moves the window so the current cursor column appears at the right screen margin.

The last value you can specify in the SCROLL field is DATA. This option moves the screen window one line or one column less than a full page. So if you use PF7/19, the line that is at the top of the screen before a scroll is at the bottom of the screen after the scroll. If you use PF8/20, the line that is at the bottom of the screen before a scroll is at the top of the screen after the scroll. If you use PF10/22, the column that is at the left of the screen before a scroll is at the right of the screen after the scroll. And if you use PF11/23, the column that is at the right of the screen before a scroll is at the left of the screen after the scroll.

Whenever you change the SCROLL field, the new value you enter remains as the default for subsequent scroll operations. As a result, if you want to scroll through a listing a page at a time, you need to change the scroll amount to PAGE only once.

If you want to change the scroll amount for a single scroll operation without replacing the default in the SCROLL field, you can enter the scroll amount in the command area instead. The scroll amount in the command area temporarily overrides the scroll amount in the SCROLL area. For example, if you enter

```
ENTER COMMAND ===> HALF              SCROLL ===> PAGE
```

the scroll moves the window a half page, but PAGE remains as the default scroll amount. So the next time you use one of the scrolling keys, the window will move a full page.

Figure 3-7 shows the effect of a half-page scroll for the browse session started in figures 3-1 and 3-3. Here, I simply typed HALF in the SCROLL field and pressed PF8/20. Now, the current line number is 11. If I pressed PF7/19 at this point, browse would return to the display in figure 3-3.

Figure 3-8 shows the effect of a half-page scroll right using PF11/23. Part 1 shows the display before the scroll; part 2 shows the display after the scroll. Here, you can see that the display has been shifted 40 characters.

Using the scrolling keys is a satisfactory way to view a listing only when the listing is small. Normally, however, a source listing like this contains hundreds or thousands of print lines. Obviously, scrolling a page at a time isn't acceptable for a large file. So, browse provides two commands, LOCATE and FIND, that let you move rapidly through a listing.

Part 1:

Before the scroll

```
 BROWSE -- DLOWE.MKTG1200.LIST ----------------------- LINE 00000000 COL 001 080
 COMMAND ===>                                           SCROLL ===> HALF
********************************* TOP OF DATA *********************************
1PP 5668-958 REL. 2.0, 09/08/86, IBM VS COBOL II.                          DATE
0
        IGYOS4013-I   AN OPTIONS PARAMETER LIST WAS FOUND AS INPUT TO THE COMPI

1PP 5668-958 REL. 2.0, 09/08/86, IBM VS COBOL II.                          DATE
0*OPTIONS IN EFFECT*
        NOADV
          APOST
          BUFSIZE(4096)
        NOCOMPILE(E)
          DATA(31)
        NODECK
        NODUMP
        NODYNAM
        NOFASTSRT
        NOFDUMP
          FLAG(I)
          LIB
          LINECOUNT(60)
        NOLIST
          MAP
```

Part 2:

After the scroll

```
 BROWSE -- DLOWE.MKTG1200.LIST ----------------------- LINE 00000011 COL 001 080
 COMMAND ===>                                           SCROLL ===> HALF
          DATA(31)
        NODECK
        NODUMP
        NODYNAM
        NOFASTSRT
        NOFDUMP
          FLAG(I)
          LIB
          LINECOUNT(60)
        NOLIST
          MAP
        NONUMBER
          OBJECT
          OFFSET
        NOOPTIMIZE
          OUTDD(SYSOUT   )
        NOPFDSGN
        NORENT
          RESIDENT
        NOSEQUENCE
          SIZE(4194304)
          SOURCE
```

Figure 3-7   Effect of a half-page scroll down

Part 1:

Before the scroll

```
  BROWSE -- DLOWE.MKTG1200.LIST --------------------- LINE 00000506 COL 001 080
  COMMAND ===>                                          SCROLL ===> HALF
  ----+----1----+----2----+----3----+----4----+----5----+----6----+----7----+----8
  PP 5668-958 REL. 2.0, 09/08/86, IBM VS COBOL II.                MKTG1200  DATE
  AN "M" PRECEDING A DATA-NAME REFERENCE INDICATES THAT THE DATA-NAME IS MODIFIED

     DEFINED   CROSS-REFERENCE OF DATA NAMES   REFERENCES

         205   BL-CHANGE-AMOUNT . . . . . . .  M421
         207   BL-CHANGE-PERCENT. . . . . . .  208 M426
         208   BL-CHANGE-PERCENT-R. . . . . .  M428
         203   BL-SALES-LAST-YTD. . . . . . .  M418
         201   BL-SALES-THIS-YTD. . . . . . .  M417
          90   BRANCH-TOTAL-LAST-YTD. . . . .  M391 418 419 422 423 M432 443
         197   BRANCH-TOTAL-LINE. . . . . . .  429
          89   BRANCH-TOTAL-THIS-YTD. . . . .  M390 417 419 M432
          75   CHANGE-AMOUNT. . . . . . . . .  M329 331 333 M399 401 403 M419 421 42
          76   CHANGE-PERCENT . . . . . . . .  M333 336 M403 406 M423 426 M443 446
         163   CL-BRANCH-NO . . . . . . . . .  M287 M300 M311 M322
         177   CL-CHANGE-AMOUNT . . . . . . .  M331
         179   CL-CHANGE-PERCENT. . . . . . .  180 M336
         180   CL-CHANGE-PERCENT-R. . . . . .  M338
         171   CL-CUSTOMER-NAME . . . . . . .  M326
         169   CL-CUSTOMER-NO . . . . . . . .  M325
```

Part 2:

After the scroll

```
  BROWSE -- DLOWE.MKTG1200.LIST --------------------- LINE 00000506 COL 041 120
  COMMAND ===>                                          SCROLL ===> HALF
  ----+----5----+----6----+----7----+----8----+----9----+----0----+----1----+----2
  OBOL II.                 MKTG1200  DATE 12/14/89  TIME 17.16.18    PAGE    11
  NDICATES THAT THE DATA-NAME IS MODIFIED BY THIS REFERENCE.

     REFERENCES

  .  M421
  .  208 M426
  .  M428
  .  M418
  .  M417
  .  M391 418 419 422 423 M432 443
  .  429
  .  M390 417 419 M432
  .  M329 331 333 M399 401 403 M419 421 423 M439 441 443
  .  M333 336 M403 406 M423 426 M443 446
  .  M287 M300 M311 M322
  .  M331
  .  180 M336
  .  M338
  .  M326
  .  M325
```

Figure 3-8   Effect of a half-page scroll right

The LOCATE command

```
LOCATE  {line-number}
        {label      }
```

Explanation

line-number	A line number relative to the first line of the file (line 0).
label	A previously defined label that refers to a line of the file.

Figure 3-9   The LOCATE command

The LOCATE command

The LOCATE command lets you move the display to a known point in the source file. Figure 3-9 shows the format of the LOCATE command. Here, you can specify either a line number or a label. I'll get to the label in just a moment. As for the line number, it's simply the relative line number you want to display. (The first line in the file is relative line zero.) For example, if you enter the command

```
LOCATE 1000
```

in the command line and press the Enter key, the display moves directly to line 1000. You can easily determine the line number of a line currently displayed by reading the LINE indication at the top of the screen.

You can assign a label to any line in the source file by scrolling the file so the line appears at the top of the screen window. Then, you enter a period followed by a one- to eight-character label in the command area. For example, figure 3-10 shows you how to assign the label PROC to line 18000 of the source listing. Then at any time during the browse session, you can return directly to this page by entering the command:

```
LOCATE PROC
```

The period that precedes the label is required when you define the label, but not when you refer to it in a LOCATE command unless

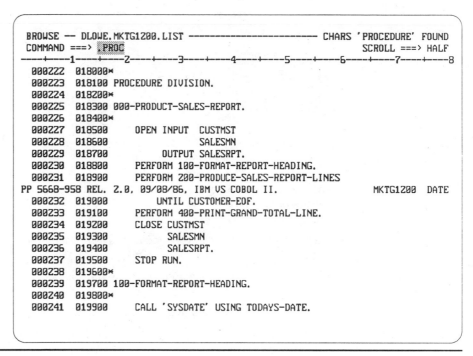

```
 BROWSE -- DLOWE.MKTG1200.LIST ----------------------- CHARS 'PROCEDURE' FOUND
 COMMAND ===> .PROC                                          SCROLL ===> HALF
 ----+----1----+----2----+----3----+----4----+----5----+----6----+----7----+----8
   000222  018000*
   000223  018100 PROCEDURE DIVISION.
   000224  018200*
   000225  018300 000-PRODUCT-SALES-REPORT.
   000226  018400*
   000227  018500     OPEN INPUT  CUSTMST
   000228  018600                 SALESMN
   000229  018700          OUTPUT SALESRPT.
   000230  018800     PERFORM 100-FORMAT-REPORT-HEADING.
   000231  018900     PERFORM 200-PRODUCE-SALES-REPORT-LINES
 PP 5668-958 REL. 2.0, 09/08/86, IBM VS COBOL II.                MKTG1200   DATE
   000232  019000         UNTIL CUSTOMER-EOF.
   000233  019100     PERFORM 400-PRINT-GRAND-TOTAL-LINE.
   000234  019200     CLOSE CUSTMST
   000235  019300           SALESMN
   000236  019400           SALESRPT.
   000237  019500     STOP RUN.
   000238  019600*
   000239  019700 100-FORMAT-REPORT-HEADING.
   000240  019800*
   000241  019900     CALL 'SYSDATE' USING TODAYS-DATE.
```

Figure 3-10   Assigning a label

your label begins with a numeral. Then, you must include the period in the LOCATE command to distinguish it from a line number.

Using labels is an efficient way to locate commonly displayed sections of a listing. For example, I sometimes place a label at the beginning of the Working-Storage Section, the Procedure Division, and one or more paragraphs in my COBOL programs. That way, I don't have to remember the line numbers for those lines.

The FIND command

If you don't know the number of the line you need to display, you can use the FIND command to locate a line that contains a specified string of characters. Figure 3-11 gives the basic format of the FIND command, but there are additional options that I'll cover in topic 2.

In its simplest form, you enter the FIND command like this:

```
FIND PROCEDURE
```

The FIND command

```
                        ( NEXT  )
                        | PREV  |
FIND  string    [ { FIRST } ]
                        | LAST  |
                        ( ALL   )
```

Explanation

string	The text string to be found. Must be in apostrophes or quotes if it contains spaces or commas.
NEXT	Start search at current line and locate the next occurrence of the string. This is the default.
PREV	Start search at current line and locate the previous occurrence of the string (search backwards).
FIRST	Start search at top of data and locate the first occurrence of the string.
LAST	Start search at bottom of data and locate the last occurrence of the string (search backwards).
ALL	Same as FIRST, but also indicate a count of the occurrences of the string in the file.

Figure 3-11   The FIND command

This FIND command locates the next occurrence of the text PROCE-DURE. In the case of a COBOL program, that's probably the start of the Procedure Division. If the search string contains blanks or commas, enclose it in apostrophes, like this:

```
FIND 'PROCEDURE DIVISION'
```

If the search string contains apostrophes, enclose it in quotes, like this:

```
FIND "VALUE 'PROCEDURE'"
```

Here, the FIND command searches for the text, VALUE 'PROCEDURE'. Likewise, if the search string contains quotes, enclose it in apostrophes, like this:

```
FIND 'VALUE "PROCEDURE"'
```

Here, the FIND command searches for VALUE "PROCEDURE".

The amount of text you specify in a search string is a matter of efficiency, so you should understand the efficiency tradeoffs involved. On one hand, the more characters you specify in the search string, the longer the search takes. On the other hand, the fewer characters you specify, the greater the chance that the FIND command will locate the wrong text.

To illustrate, suppose you are at the start of a COBOL compiler listing and you want to find the beginning of the Procedure Division. You could enter the command

```
FIND 'PROCEDURE DIVISION.'
```

but that's probably too many characters in the search string. Or you could enter the command

```
FIND P
```

but that's probably not enough characters, since there are probably many occurrences of the letter P before the Procedure Division header.

In general, you should specify only as many characters in the search string as are necessary to distinguish it from other text in the file. But don't be overly concerned about specifying too many characters. Although search time increases slightly for each character in the search string, the unnecessary terminal I/O that results when a FIND locates the wrong text is by far the greater inefficiency.

How to change the search direction   Normally, a FIND command search begins at the current line and continues to the end of the source file. So if the text you're looking for is located *before* the current line, FIND won't locate it. However, you can change the direction of the search by specifying a search direction on the FIND command.

If you specify PREV for the search direction, the search begins at the current line and continues *backwards* until the text is found or the top of the data is reached. If you specify FIRST, the search starts at the top of the data and continues until the text is found or the bottom of the data is reached. If you specify LAST, the search starts at the bottom of the data and works backwards.

If you specify ALL as the search direction, the search works like FIRST except that it doesn't stop when it finds the search string. Instead, it continues, locating all occurrences of the string. When the FIND operation completes, it displays the first occurrence, along with a count indicating how many occurrences of the string it found. Since FIND ALL locates all occurrences of a string in the file, it takes a little longer than FIND FIRST. As a result, you shouldn't use FIND ALL unless you really need to know how many occurrences of a string there are in the file.

How to recall a FIND command   If you need to enter the same FIND command more than once in a single browse session, you may find PF5/17 useful. PF5/17 repeats the most recent FIND command you issued. So once you've entered a FIND command, you can recall it easily using PF5/17.

Alternatively, if you know that you'll be repeating a FIND command before you enter it on the command line, precede the command with an ampersand (&). Then, the command remains on the command line after it's executed. To execute the command again, press the Enter key.

How to terminate browse

To terminate a browse operation, you can press the End key, PF3/15. If you entered a member name on the browse entry panel, this returns you to that panel. Then, you can enter another data set to browse, or press PF3/15 again to return to the primary option menu. If you selected the member you're browsing from a member list, pressing the End key returns you to the member list display. Then, you can select another member to browse, or you can press PF3/15 again to return to the browse entry panel. Alternatively, you can return directly to the primary option menu from the browse data display by pressing the Return key, PF4/16.

Discussion

At the start of this topic, I said you'd use browse most often for SYSOUT data sets like compiler listings, storage dumps, and so on. However, browse is useful for other types of data sets as well. In fact, you can use browse for any sequential or partitioned file, regardless of the file's record length. For example, you can browse sequential data sets created by a program you're testing. In the next topic, I'll show you some advanced features that not only help you browse SYSOUT data sets, but are useful for examining other types of sequential data sets as well.

Terms

concatenate
top of data
bottom of data
screen window
scroll
page

Objectives

1. Explain how to concatenate libraries on the browse entry panel.

2. Browse a data set using scrolling, LOCATE, and FIND to move the screen window to various parts of the listing.

Topic 2   Advanced browse operations

In topic 1 of this chapter, I showed you the basics of using browse. In this topic, you'll learn advanced features of browse, including advanced options of the FIND command, how to browse recursively, how to display hexadecimal data, and how to display carriage-control and non-displayable characters. If you're a first-time ISPF user, you should skip this topic for now and come back to it when you need to use the advanced browse capabilities it presents.

ADVANCED OPTIONS OF THE FIND COMMAND

Figure 3-12 presents the expanded format of the FIND command. In addition to the search direction (NEXT, PREV, etc.), the FIND command lets you specify a *match condition* (CHARS, PREFIX, etc.), column limitations, and advanced options in the search string.

Match conditions

Normally when you specify a string in a FIND command, any combination of characters that match the string satisfies the FIND. For example, if you code this FIND command,

```
FIND ABC
```

any of these strings will match:

```
ABC
ABCDEF
DEFABC
123ABCDEF
```

The FIND command

```
                  (NEXT )        (CHARS )
                  |PREV |        |PREFIX|
FIND string   [{ FIRST }]    [{ SUFFIX }]    [col-1 [col-2]]
                  |LAST |        |WORD  |
                  (ALL  )        (      )
```

Explanation

string	The text string to be found. Must be in apostrophes or quotes if it contains spaces or commas. May also be text, picture, hex string, or *, as explained in figure 3-14.
NEXT	Start search at current line and locate the next occurrence of the string. This is the default.
PREV	Start search at current line and locate the previous occurrence of the string (search backwards).
FIRST	Start search at top of data and locate the first occurrence of the string.
LAST	Start search at bottom of data and locate the last occurrence of the string (search backwards).
ALL	Same as FIRST, but also indicate a count of the occurrences of the string in the file.
CHARS	Any occurrence of the string satisfies the search. This is the default.
PREFIX	The string must be at the beginning of a word to satisfy the search.
SUFFIX	The string must be at the end of a word to satisfy the search.
WORD	The string must be surrounded by spaces or special characters to satisfy the search.
col-1	Starting column number. If col-2 is not specified, the string must begin in this column to satisfy the search.
col-2	Ending column number. If specified, the entire string must be found between col-1 and col-2 to satisfy the search.

Figure 3-12   Complete format of the FIND command

Search options	Examples					
CHARS 'HE'	**HE**	**HE**ED	S**HE**D	S**HE**	$**HE**ED	-**HE**$
PREFIX 'HE'	HE	**HE**ED	SHED	SHE	$**HE**ED	-HE$
SUFFIX 'HE'	HE	HEED	SHED	S**HE**	$HEED	-HE$
WORD 'HE'	**HE**	HEED	SHED	SHE	$HEED	-**HE**$

Figure 3-13   Examples of match conditions

That's because each of these strings contains the characters ABC. You'd also get the same results if you coded the match condition CHARS in the command, since it's the default.

By specifying a match condition other than CHARS, you can indicate that a string matches only if it appears at the beginning of a word (PREFIX), the end of a word (SUFFIX), or as a word itself (WORD). As far as browse is concerned, a *word* is a string of alphanumeric characters with a blank or special character at each end. As a result, ABC is a word in each of these strings:

```
ABC
ABC 123
DEF ABC 123
'ABC'
ABC$
```

In these examples, the special characters are not considered part of the word.

Figure 3-13 shows how match conditions affect a search. Here, the shading shows which strings match the search string. Note that a string that makes up a word by itself does *not* satisfy a search for a PREFIX or SUFFIX.

Column limitations

You can easily limit a search to a single column or range of columns by specifying column numbers in the FIND command. If you specify a single column number, the string must start in that column to satisfy the search. For example, this command:

```
FIND X 72
```

String	Meaning
text	String containing no blanks or commas
'text'	String enclosed in apostrophes; may include blanks or commas
T'text'	Same as 'text', except upper and lowercase letters are treated the same
X'hex-digits'	Hexadecimal string
P'picture'	Picture string
*	Use string from previous FIND

Figure 3-14 String types

looks for an X in column 72. Similarly,

```
FIND 120-READ 12
```

looks for 120-READ beginning in column 12.

If you specify two column numbers, the string must be located between the columns you specify to qualify. For example,

```
FIND 120-READ 16 72
```

searches for 120-READ between columns 16 and 72.

String formats

The string you specify in a FIND command can have one of several formats, as shown in figure 3-14. You already know about the first two. Now, I'll explain the others.

Text strings   The T format means that it doesn't matter whether the characters in the string are upper or lowercase. So, if you code

```
FIND T'PERFORM'
```

any of these strings satisfy the search:

```
PERFORM
perform
Perform
pERforM
```

Without the T option, only the first string (PERFORM) would
satisfy the search.

Hexadecimal strings   During a normal browse operation, any
non-displayable characters, such as packed-decimal numbers, are
displayed as periods. Using the H string option, however, you can
search for the hexadecimal values of such characters. Later in this
topic, I'll show you how to display the hexadecimal values.

To illustrate, suppose you are browsing an inventory file and
you want to locate a record with a unit price of $15.95. Knowing
that the unit-price field begins in column 58, and that the
PICTURE of the packed-decimal (COMP-3) unit-price field is
S9(5)V99, you could code a FIND command like this:

```
FIND X'0001595F' 58
```

Then, a hexadecimal value of 0001595F (decimal value positive
15.95) starting in column 58 satisfies the search.

Picture strings   Picture strings allow you to specify that the character in a specific position of the search string must be a particular
type of character, rather than a particular character. For example,
you can specify that the first character of a string must be alphanumeric, the second numeric, and the third alphabetic. You do this
by coding special characters to represent character types.

Figure 3-15 shows the special characters you can include in a
picture string and what they mean. In each case, a single occurrence of one of these characters corresponds to a single occurrence
of any character of the correct type. As a result, if you specify ¬ in
the first position of a picture string, the text must contain a non-
blank character in its first position to satisfy the search.

Figure 3-16 shows a few examples of picture strings and how
they are satisfied. If you'll take a few moments to study this figure,
you should have no problem understanding how picture strings
work.

Use previous string   You can code an asterisk as a search string,
like this:

```
FIND *
```

Then, browse uses the string you specified in the previous FIND
command as its search argument. This feature makes it easy to

Character	Meaning
=	Any character
¬	Any non-blank character
.	Any undisplayable character
#	Any numeric character
-	Any non-numeric character (including a blank)
@	Any alphabetic character
<	Any lowercase alphabetic character
>	Any uppercase alphabetic character
$	Any special character

Figure 3-15   Valid picture characters

Picture string	Examples			
P'==='	ABC-123	PERFORM 120-READ	A BC DE
P'@@@'	ABC-123	PERFORM 120-READ	A BC DE
P'###'	ABC-123	PERFORM 120-READ	A BC DE
P'$'	ABC-123	PERFORM 120-READ	A BC DE
P'===$###'	ABC-123	PERFORM 120-READ	A BC DE

Figure 3-16   Examples of picture strings

locate every occurrence of a string in a file, since you need to specify the string only once.

On the other hand, you can achieve the same effect by pressing PF5/17. That way, you recall the previous FIND command without entering anything in the command area. Or, you can precede the initial FIND command with an ampersand (&) and it will remain in the command area after it's executed.

Complex FIND commands

Although you don't usually need to, you can combine search direction, match condition, column limitation, and advanced string formats to create complex FIND commands. To illustrate, consider this command:

```
FIND P'##@$' PREV WORD 8
```

Here, the FIND command looks backwards for a word consisting of two numeric characters followed by a single alphabetic character followed by a single special character, starting in column 8. Like I said, though, you probably won't need FIND commands that are this complex very often.

How to browse recursively

Sometimes during a browse session, you may need to look at the contents of another member or data set. For example, if you're looking at a compiler listing, you may want to compare it to a previous compiler listing for the same program. If you don't have a hard copy of the previous compiler listing, you can use the BROWSE command to look at it without ending your current browse session. This is called *recursive browsing*.

The format of the BROWSE command is

```
BROWSE [member-name]
```

Note that this format doesn't allow you to specify the name of a partitioned data set. So if you specify a member name, the member must be in the same data set as the member you're currently browsing. For example, if you're browsing a member named MKT1200B in the data set DLOWE.TEST.LIST and you want to browse the member named MKT1200A in the same data set, you'd enter this command:

```
BROWSE MKT1200A
```

If you want to browse a data set other than the one you're currently browsing, enter the BROWSE command without a member name. Then, the browse entry panel I presented in figure 3-1 is displayed. From this panel, you can enter the name of any data set you want to browse.

When you're finished with a recursive browse session, you end it by pressing the End key, PF3/15 just as you would to end any other browse session. Then, you're returned to the browse session you were executing before you began the recursive browse session.

Instead of using the BROWSE command to start a recursive browse session, you might want to use the split screen feature I presented in chapter 2. Then, you can start a browse session in the second screen to display another file. The advantage of using the split screen feature is that both browse sessions are visible on the screen at the same time. The disadvantage is that each browse session has fewer screen lines to work with.

HOW TO DISPLAY HEXADECIMAL CODES: THE HEX COMMAND

If you're browsing a file that contains non-displayable characters, such as packed-decimal fields, you can display each character as a two-digit hexadecimal code by entering this command:

```
HEX ON
```

Figure 3-17 shows a hexadecimal browse display. Here, each row of 80 characters takes three lines: one for the normal character display and two for the hexadecimal display.

To determine a character's hexadecimal value, you simply take the digit that appears in the first row directly below that character followed by the the digit that appears in the second row directly below it. As a result, the hexadecimal value of the numeral 0 in column 11 of the first displayed line is F0.

HOW TO DISPLAY CARRIAGE-CONTROL AND NON-DISPLAYABLE CHARACTERS

At the beginning of the first topic of this chapter, I mentioned that browse normally omits the first byte of each record in a print file from its display. That's because the byte contains a control character that controls printer spacing. If you want browse to display this character, enter this command:

```
DISPLAY CC
```

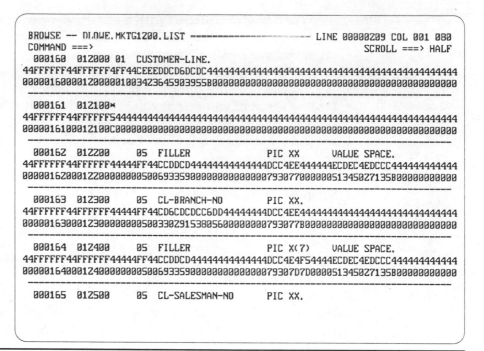

```
BROWSE -- DLOWE.MKTG1200.LIST --------------------- LINE 00000209 COL 001 080
COMMAND ===>                                              SCROLL ===> HALF
  000160  012000 01  CUSTOMER-LINE.
44FFFFFF44FFFFFF4FF44CEEEDDCD6DCDC444444444444444444444444444444444444444444444
000001600001200000100342364590395SB00000000000000000000000000000000000000000000
--------------------------------------------------------------------------------
  000161  012100*
44FFFFFF44FFFFFFS44444444444444444444444444444444444444444444444444444444444444
0000016100012100C00000000000000000000000000000000000000000000000000000000000000
--------------------------------------------------------------------------------
  000162  012200    05  FILLER             PIC XX       VALUE SPACE.
44FFFFFF44FFFFFF44444FF44CCDDCD44444444444444DCC4EE444444ECDEC4EDCCC444444444444
000001620001220000000005006933590000000000000007930770000005134502713SB000000000
--------------------------------------------------------------------------------
  000163  012300    05  CL-BRANCH-NO        PIC XX.
44FFFFFF44FFFFFF44444FF44CD6CDCDCC6DD44444444DCC4EE444444444444444444444444444444
0000016300012300000000500330291538056000000007930778000000000000000000000000000
--------------------------------------------------------------------------------
  000164  012400    05  FILLER             PIC X(7)     VALUE SPACE.
44FFFFFF44FFFFFF44444FF44CCDDCD44444444444444DCC4E4F54444ECDEC4EDCCC444444444444
00000164000124000000000500693359000000000000007930707D000005134502713SB000000000
--------------------------------------------------------------------------------
  000165  012500    05  CL-SALESMAN-NO      PIC XX.
```

Figure 3-17   A hexadecimal display

Then, browse displays the control characters, as figure 3-18 illustrates.

Figure 3-19 shows the printer-control characters you're likely to encounter. In figure 3-18, the first line contains a form feed and the second line is double-spaced. Similarly, the ninth line contains a form feed and the tenth line is double-spaced. All other lines in the display are single-spaced.

You can suppress the printer control characters again by entering this command:

```
DISPLAY NOCC
```

Then, the display is shifted to the left one character and the first byte of each record is omitted.

The DISPLAY command has one other use: it lets you change the character used to represent non-displayable characters. Initially, the period is used to represent data that can't be displayed. This can be confusing, though, if actual periods occur in

```
 BROWSE -- DLOWE.MKTG1200.LIST ---------------------- LINE 00000000 COL 001 080
 COMMAND ===>                                                   SCROLL ===> DATA
**************************** TOP OF DATA *****************************************
1PP 5668-958 REL. 2.0, 09/08/86, IBM VS COBOL II.                          DATE
0
        IGYOS4013-I   AN OPTIONS PARAMETER LIST WAS FOUND AS INPUT TO THE COMPI


        IGYOS4020-W   NORES    OPTION DISCARDED DUE TO OPTION CONFLICT RESOLUTI
                      TAKES PRECEDENCE.

1PP 5668-958 REL. 2.0, 09/08/86, IBM VS COBOL II.                          DATE
0*OPTIONS IN EFFECT*
      NOADV
        APOST
        BUFSIZE(4096)
      NOCOMPILE(E)
        DATA(31)
      NODECK
      NODUMP
      NODYNAM
      NOFASTSRT
      NOFDUMP
        FLAG(I)
```

Figure 3-18   A display that contains carriage-control characters

Character	Meaning
blank	Space one line before printing.
0	Space two lines before printing.
-	Space three lines before printing.
1	Skip to the top of the next page before printing.

Figure 3-19   Common printer-control characters

the records. To change the character used to represent non-displayable data, enter a DISPLAY command like this:

    DISPLAY

This command causes browse to display non-displayable characters as blanks. In some cases, the browse display is easier to view after you make this change.

DISCUSSION

Quite frankly, I doubt you'll use the browse features presented in this topic very often. However, there are cases where one or more of these features can be a real time-saver. So even though you may not use them often enough to become proficient at them, it's good to know they're available when you need them.

Terms

match condition
word
recursive browse

Objective

Use advanced FIND options, recursive browsing, the HEX command, and the DISPLAY command to efficiently browse data sets.

Chapter 4

How to edit a data set

One of the most important tasks of program development is creating and maintaining source programs. To do this under ISPF, you use the source file editor, option 2 on the primary option menu. This chapter explains how to use the editor.

There are three topics in this chapter. Topic 1 explains the basics of using the editor: how to specify a source file or member, how to use basic editing commands, and how to save edited data. Topic 2 describes the edit profile and how to change it. (The edit profile controls a variety of editing features, including tabbing, line numbering, and so on.) And topic 3 explains some of the more advanced editing features, such as the CHANGE command.

Topic 1   Basic edit operations

This topic presents the basics of using the ISPF text editor. Here, you'll learn how to start the editor, select the data set or member you want to edit, make basic changes to the text, and save your changes and exit from the editor. Although you'll use the editor most often to edit a member of a partitioned data set, you can also use the editor to edit a standard sequential data set, as long as the data set's records are not longer than 255 bytes. Throughout this chapter, I'll use the term *source member* to refer to the data you're editing, whether it's a PDS member or a sequential data set.

Before I get into the details of using the ISPF editor, I want to be sure you understand what's going on during an edit session. Once you specify the source member you want to edit, ISPF reads the entire member into virtual storage. As you use the editor, any changes you make are applied to the virtual storage copy of the source member. In other words, the source member still exists in its unedited state on disk. The updated member isn't written back to disk until you terminate edit or save the member explicitly. At that time, if you say you want to save the edited member, the editor copies the virtual storage version of the member back to disk.

How to start the editor

To start the ISPF editor, you select option 2 from the primary option menu. Then, ISPF displays the edit entry panel, shown in figure 4-1. The edit entry panel is similar to the browse entry panel. On it, you enter the name of the source member you want to edit. The shaded part of this example shows I'm going to edit a member named MKTG1200 in a library named DLOWE.TEST.COBOL.

If the data set is partitioned, you should know about two additional techniques: concatenating libraries and using a member list. These techniques work the same as they do for browse, so if you've already read about them in chapter 3, you can skip over them here.

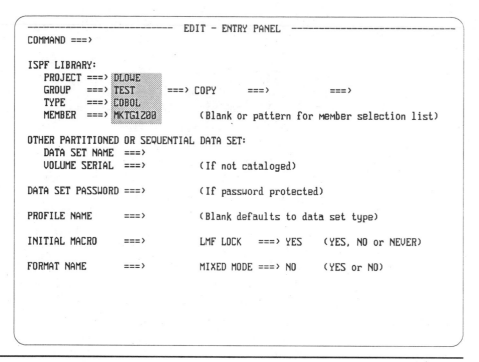

```
------------------------------ EDIT - ENTRY PANEL ------------------------------
COMMAND ===>

ISPF LIBRARY:
    PROJECT ===> DLOWE
    GROUP   ===> TEST      ===> COPY      ===>           ===>
    TYPE    ===> COBOL
    MEMBER  ===> MKTG1200          (Blank or pattern for member selection list)

OTHER PARTITIONED OR SEQUENTIAL DATA SET:
    DATA SET NAME  ===>
    VOLUME SERIAL  ===>           (If not cataloged)

DATA SET PASSWORD ===>           (If password protected)

PROFILE NAME      ===>           (Blank defaults to data set type)

INITIAL MACRO     ===>           LMF LOCK   ===> YES     (YES, NO or NEVER)

FORMAT NAME       ===>           MIXED MODE ===> NO      (YES or NO)
```

Figure 4-1   Edit entry panel

How to concatenate libraries   As you can see in figure 4-1, edit lets you specify up to four distinct libraries as input. Each of these libraries must have the same project and type, but the group name can vary.

If you specify more than one library, edit *concatenates* the libraries when it searches for the member you specify. In other words, to locate the member you specify, edit searches the libraries in the order you list them. For example, suppose you code the LIBRARY entries like this:

```
PROJECT ===> DLOWE
LIBRARY ===> TEST        ===> MASTER
TYPE    ===> COBOL
MEMBER  ===> MKTG1200
```

In this example, edit searches DLOWE.TEST.COBOL first to locate the MKTG1200 member. If it can't find the member there, it searches DLOWE.MASTER.COBOL.

If you use concatenated libraries, however, you should realize that the concatenation applies only when you retrieve the member. When you save a member at the end of your edit session, the updated member is always stored in the first library you specify on the entry panel. So, in the preceding example, MKTG1200 is saved in DLOWE.TEST.COBOL, even if it was retrieved from DLOWE.MASTER.COBOL.

Concatenated libraries are useful because they let you create a hierarchy of libraries. For example, you can create a single master library for a project and multiple test libraries: one for each programmer on the project. Then, you can store completed programs in the master library and use the test libraries for programs still under development. You'll learn more about how to work with a hierarchy like this in chapter 8.

How to display a member list   If the data set you specify in the edit entry panel is partitioned, and you specify only a pattern for the member name, or you don't specify a member name at all, edit displays a *member list*, as shown in figure 4-2. This display lists all the members from each library specified on the entry panel. If the libraries contain more members than can be shown on a single screen, you can use PF7/19 and PF8/20 to scroll forward and backward through the list.

To select the member you want to edit, type an S (for "select") next to the member name and press the Enter key. In figure 4-2, I selected the member named MKTG1200.

The edit data display

Figure 4-3 shows the edit data display for an existing source member. The edit display for a newly created source member is somewhat different. You'll learn about the differences later in this topic. As you can see in figure 4-3, the edit display for an existing source member consists of three distinct areas.

The top two screen lines make up the *heading area*. In this area, the editor displays informative messages and lets you enter commands.

The first six columns of lines 3-24 are the *line command area*. In this area, the editor displays a line number for each line of the source member. Besides displaying line numbers, the line command area serves another function. In it, you can enter line

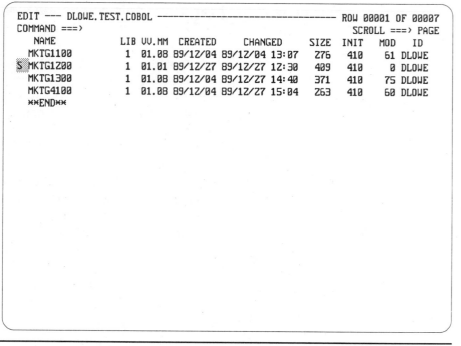

Figure 4-2   Edit member list panel

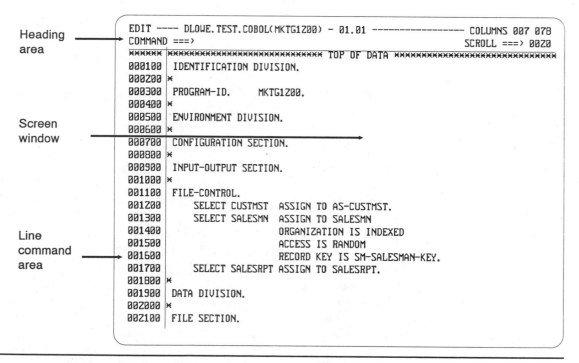

Figure 4-3   Edit data display

commands that perform certain editing functions, such as deleting or inserting lines. You'll learn how to use the most common line commands later in this topic.

The remaining columns of lines 3-24 are the *screen window*. Here, data from the source member is displayed. You can change the data in this area by simply typing over it. In addition, you can use your terminal's editing keys, like the Insert, Delete, and Erase-EOF keys, for more complicated editing. As soon as you press the Enter key, edit stores any changes you've made in the virtual storage copy of the source member.

Since the screen window here is only 72 characters long, only 72 characters of each source record can be displayed. The COLUMNS message in line 1 of figure 4-3 indicates that columns 7 through 78 are currently displayed. You can use the scrolling functions just as you do for browse to move the screen window right or left if you want to display the entire source record. PF10/22 moves the window left, and PF11/23 moves it right. Usually, though, you don't need to see or change data outside the columns that are normally displayed in the screen window.

Of course, you can also use scrolling functions to move the screen window up or down, just as in browse. PF7/19 moves the screen window up, and PF8/20 moves it down. And you can use the LOCATE and FIND commands to scroll the window as well. I'll present the format of these commands in topic 3 of this chapter.

Line numbers   During an editing session, the editor assigns *line numbers*, or *sequence numbers*, to each line of your source member, keeping the numbers in sequence as you add and delete lines. As I mentioned a minute ago, these line numbers appear on the edit display to the left of the screen window. In most cases, edit also stores the line numbers in the source records themselves. Depending on the type of data set, a source member has either COBOL format numbering, standard (STD) format numbering, both COBOL and standard format numbering, or no numbering at all.

COBOL source files have COBOL format numbers. That means the line numbers are six digits long and are stored in the first six positions of each record. As a result, if you scrolled to column 1 in figure 4-3, you'd see that the first six columns of each record contain a sequence number that matches the line number in the line command area.

Standard format numbers are eight digits long, but edit displays only the last six digits. For fixed-length records, they're stored in the last eight positions of each record. For variable-length records, they're stored in the first eight positions. Standard fixed-length numbering is used for all non-COBOL source files, including assembler, PL/I, CLIST, REXX, and CNTL (JCL) files.

Unnumbered data sets, quite naturally, have no line numbers at all. When you edit an unnumbered data set, the editor still creates sequence numbers and displays them in the line command area, but it discards them when you end the edit session. Unnumbered data sets typically contain test data.

In a minute, when I show you how to edit a source member, you'll see how the editor keeps the line numbers in sequence as you change a source member. Then, in topic 2, you'll learn how to specify (1) what numbering format a file should have, (2) what numbers the editor should assign to new lines, and (3) when you want the editor to renumber a member.

How to edit a source member

In edit, you use two types of commands, primary commands and line commands. You enter *primary commands* in the command input area, and they generally apply to the entire source member. In contrast, you enter *line commands* in the line command area, and they affect individual lines. When you enter a line command, you have to type over the line numbers that normally appear in that area.

In general, you use line commands more often than primary commands. As a result, this topic covers the most commonly used line commands and only one primary command. Then, topics 2 and 3 describe the less commonly used line commands, as well as the most commonly used primary commands.

Figure 4-4 summarizes the line commands covered in this topic. As you can see, line commands let you insert, delete, repeat, copy, or move single lines or blocks of lines.

How to insert lines   You use the I line command to insert blank lines into a source member. You can code an I by itself to insert one line, or you can code an I followed by a number to insert a block of lines.

Inserting lines

I	Insert a single line following this line.
In	Insert n lines following this line.

Deleting lines

D	Delete this line.
Dn	Delete n lines starting with this line.
DD	Delete the block of lines beginning with the first DD command and ending with the second DD command.

Repeating lines

R	Repeat this line.
Rn	Repeat this line n times.
RR	Repeat a block of lines.
RRn	Repeat a block of lines n times.

Copying and moving lines

C	Copy this line.
Cn	Copy n lines starting with this line.
CC	Copy a block of lines.
M	Move this line.
Mn	Move n lines starting with this line.
MM	Move a block of lines.
A	Copy or move lines after this line.
An	Repeat the copy or move n times after this line.
B	Copy or move lines before this line.
Bn	Repeat the copy or move n times before this line.

Figure 4-4   Basic line commands

Figure 4-5 shows how the INSERT command works. As you can see, part 1 contains two INSERT commands. The first inserts a single line following line 300; the second inserts four lines following line 800. In other words, the insertion comes immedi-

Part 1:

The I line commands
specify the location
and number of lines to
be inserted

```
EDIT ---- DLOWE.TEST.COBOL(MKTG1Z00) - 01.01 --------------- COLUMNS 007 078
COMMAND ===>                                                 SCROLL ===> PAGE
****** ****************************** TOP OF DATA ******************************
000100  IDENTIFICATION DIVISION.
000200 *
I       PROGRAM-ID.       MKTG1Z00.
000400 *
000500  ENVIRONMENT DIVISION.
000600 *
000700  CONFIGURATION SECTION.
I4     *
000900  INPUT-OUTPUT SECTION.
001000 *
001100  FILE-CONTROL.
001200      SELECT CUSTMST   ASSIGN TO AS-CUSTMST.
001300      SELECT SALESMN   ASSIGN TO SALESMN
001400                       ORGANIZATION IS INDEXED
001500                       ACCESS IS RANDOM
001600                       RECORD KEY IS SM-SALESMAN-KEY.
001700      SELECT SALESRPT ASSIGN TO SALESRPT.
001800 *
001900  DATA DIVISION.
002000 *
002100  FILE SECTION.
```

Part 2:

When you press the
Enter key, edit inserts
blanks lines

```
EDIT ---- DLOWE.TEST.COBOL(MKTG1Z00) - 01.01 --------------- COLUMNS 007 078
COMMAND ===>                                                 SCROLL ===> PAGE
****** ****************************** TOP OF DATA ******************************
000100  IDENTIFICATION DIVISION.
000200 *
000300  PROGRAM-ID.       MKTG1Z00.
'''''''
000400 *
000500  ENVIRONMENT DIVISION.
000600 *
000700  CONFIGURATION SECTION.
000800 *
'''''''
'''''''
'''''''
'''''''
000900  INPUT-OUTPUT SECTION.
001000 *
001100  FILE-CONTROL.
001200      SELECT CUSTMST   ASSIGN TO AS-CUSTMST.
001300      SELECT SALESMN   ASSIGN TO SALESMN
001400                       ORGANIZATION IS INDEXED
001500                       ACCESS IS RANDOM
001600                       RECORD KEY IS SM-SALESMAN-KEY.
```

Figure 4-5   Inserting lines

Part 3:

You can enter data
into any or all of the
blank lines

```
EDIT ---- DLOWE.TEST.COBOL(MKTG1200) - 01.01 -------------- COLUMNS 007 078
COMMAND ===>                                                  SCROLL ===> PAGE
****** ************************** TOP OF DATA ********************************
000100  IDENTIFICATION DIVISION.
000200  *
000300  PROGRAM-ID.      MKTG1200.
''''''  AUTHOR.          DOUG LOWE.
000400  *
000500  ENVIRONMENT DIVISION.
000600  *
000700  CONFIGURATION SECTION.
000800  *
''''''      SOURCE-COMPUTER.     IBM-370.
''''''      OBJECT-COMPUTER.     IBM-370.
''''''  *
''''''
000900  INPUT-OUTPUT SECTION.
001000  *
001100  FILE-CONTROL.
001200      SELECT CUSTMST  ASSIGN TO AS-CUSTMST.
001300      SELECT SALESMN  ASSIGN TO SALESMN
001400                      ORGANIZATION IS INDEXED
001500                      ACCESS IS RANDOM
001600                      RECORD KEY IS SM-SALESMAN-KEY.
```

Part 4:

When you press the
Enter key, edit
numbers the new lines
and deletes the ones
you didn't use

```
EDIT ---- DLOWE.TEST.COBOL(MKTG1200) - 01.01 -------------- COLUMNS 007 078
COMMAND ===>                                                  SCROLL ===> PAGE
****** ************************** TOP OF DATA ********************************
000100  IDENTIFICATION DIVISION.
000200  *
000300  PROGRAM-ID.      MKTG1200.
000310  AUTHOR.          DOUG LOWE.
000400  *
000500  ENVIRONMENT DIVISION.
000600  *
000700  CONFIGURATION SECTION.
000800  *
000810  SOURCE-COMPUTER.     IBM-370.
000820  OBJECT-COMPUTER.     IBM-370.
000830  *
000900  INPUT-OUTPUT SECTION.
001000  *
001100  FILE-CONTROL.
001200      SELECT CUSTMST  ASSIGN TO AS-CUSTMST.
001300      SELECT SALESMN  ASSIGN TO SALESMN
001400                      ORGANIZATION IS INDEXED
001500                      ACCESS IS RANDOM
001600                      RECORD KEY IS SM-SALESMAN-KEY.
001700      SELECT SALESRPT ASSIGN TO SALESRPT.
```

Figure 4-5   Inserting lines (continued)

ately after the line where the INSERT command appears. Even though the sequence numbers are erased on the lines containing line commands, you can easily figure out what they are because the lines in the source member are numbered in increments of 100.

Part 2 of figure 4-5 shows the effect of the two INSERT commands. As you can see, one blank line is inserted following line 300 and four blank lines are inserted following line 800.

Notice that the inserted lines in part 2 of figure 4-5 have apostrophes in the line command area instead of line numbers. That's because the insertion isn't permanent until you enter data on the inserted line. When you press the Enter key, the editor deletes any inserted lines that don't contain data.

To illustrate, part 3 of figure 4-5 shows the data entered into the inserted lines. Note that there isn't any data in the fourth line that was inserted after line 800. Part 4 of figure 4-5 shows the screen after the Enter key was pressed. As you can see, edit automatically generates line numbers for the inserted lines that contain data and deletes the fourth line following line 800, the line that doesn't contain data.

How to delete lines   You use the D line command to delete lines from your source member. You can code the DELETE command in one of three ways: (1) code a D to delete a single line; (2) code a D followed by a number to delete more than one line; and (3) code DD on two lines to delete those lines and every line between them.

Figure 4-6 shows how the D command works. Part 1 contains two D commands. The first deletes line 310. The second, a D3 command, deletes three lines starting with line 810. Part 2 of figure 4-6 shows the display after the deletions. As you can see, lines 310, 810, 820, and 830 were deleted.

Figure 4-7 shows how to delete a block of lines using the DD command. The commands in this figure delete the same lines as the commands in figure 4-6. Again, a D command deletes line 310. This time, though, a pair of DD commands, rather than a D3 command, deletes lines 810, 820, and 830. The effect is the same as in figure 4-6.

The lines indicated by a pair of DD commands do *not* have to be on the same display panel. To delete a block of lines that spans multiple panels, locate the first line you want to delete and enter a DD command at that line. Then, scroll to the panel containing the last line you want to delete and enter a DD command at that line. Or, if you prefer, mark the last line you want to delete and then

Part 1:

The D line commands tell which lines to delete

```
EDIT ---- DLOWE.TEST.COBOL(MKTG1Z00) - 01.01 ----------------- COLUMNS 007 078
COMMAND ===>                                                   SCROLL ===> PAGE
****** *************************** TOP OF DATA *********************************
000100  IDENTIFICATION DIVISION.
000200 *
000300  PROGRAM-ID.      MKTG1Z00.
D       AUTHOR.          DOUG LOWE.
000400 *
000500  ENVIRONMENT DIVISION.
000600 *
000700  CONFIGURATION SECTION.
000800 *
D3      SOURCE-COMPUTER.    IBM-370.
000820  OBJECT-COMPUTER.    IBM-370.
000830 *
000900  INPUT-OUTPUT SECTION.
001000 *
001100  FILE-CONTROL.
001200      SELECT CUSTMST  ASSIGN TO AS-CUSTMST.
001300      SELECT SALESMN  ASSIGN TO SALESMN
001400                      ORGANIZATION IS INDEXED
001500                      ACCESS IS RANDOM
001600                      RECORD KEY IS SM-SALESMAN-KEY.
001700      SELECT SALESRPT ASSIGN TO SALESRPT.
```

Part 2:

When you press the Enter key, edit deletes the lines

```
EDIT ---- DLOWE.TEST.COBOL(MKTG1Z00) - 01.01 ----------------- COLUMNS 007 078
COMMAND ===>                                                   SCROLL ===> PAGE
****** *************************** TOP OF DATA *********************************
000100  IDENTIFICATION DIVISION.
000200 *
000300  PROGRAM-ID.      MKTG1Z00.
000400 *
000500  ENVIRONMENT DIVISION.
000600 *
000700  CONFIGURATION SECTION.
000800 *
000900  INPUT-OUTPUT SECTION.
001000 *
001100  FILE-CONTROL.
001200      SELECT CUSTMST  ASSIGN TO AS-CUSTMST.
001300      SELECT SALESMN  ASSIGN TO SALESMN
001400                      ORGANIZATION IS INDEXED
001500                      ACCESS IS RANDOM
001600                      RECORD KEY IS SM-SALESMAN-KEY.
001700      SELECT SALESRPT ASSIGN TO SALESRPT.
001800 *
001900  DATA DIVISION.
002000 *
002100  FILE SECTION.
```

Figure 4-6   Deleting lines

```
EDIT ---- DLOWE.TEST.COBOL(MKTG1200) - 01.01 ------------------ COLUMNS 007 078
COMMAND ===>                                                        SCROLL ===> PAGE
****** ***************************** TOP OF DATA *****************************
000100  IDENTIFICATION DIVISION.
000200 *
000300  PROGRAM-ID.     MKTG1200.
D       AUTHOR.         DOUG LOWE.
000400 *
000500  ENVIRONMENT DIVISION.
000600 *
000700  CONFIGURATION SECTION.
000800 *
DD      SOURCE-COMPUTER.   IBM-370.
000820  OBJECT-COMPUTER.   IBM-370.
DD     *
000900  INPUT-OUTPUT SECTION.
001000 *
001100  FILE-CONTROL.
001200     SELECT CUSTMST  ASSIGN TO AS-CUSTMST.
001300     SELECT SALESMN  ASSIGN TO SALESMN
001400                     ORGANIZATION IS INDEXED
001500                     ACCESS IS RANDOM
001600                     RECORD KEY IS SM-SALESMAN-KEY.
001700     SELECT SALESRPT ASSIGN TO SALESRPT.
```

Figure 4-7   Deleting a block of lines

scroll backwards and mark the first line. Either way, when you enter the second DD command, the indicated lines are deleted.

How to repeat lines   The R command lets you repeat a single line or a group of lines one or more times. ISPF inserts the repeated lines immediately following the source line. Figure 4-8 shows an example of repeating a single line six times. In part 1, line 11100 contains an R6 command. Part 2 shows the effect of the REPEAT command: line 11100 is duplicated in lines 11110 through 11160.

Figure 4-9 shows how to repeat a block of lines. In part 1, the first RR command marks the start of the block. The second RR command indicates the end of the block and the number of times to repeat the block (in this case, three). Part 2 shows the effect of these RR commands: the block of lines is duplicated three times.

Like the DD command, you can use the RR command to repeat a block of lines that spans multiple panels. To do that, enter the first RR command to mark the start of the block, then scroll to the

Part 1:

The R line command
tells what line to
repeat and how many
times to repeat it

```
EDIT ---- DLOWE.TEST.COBOL(MKTG1200) - 01.01 ----------------- COLUMNS 007 078
COMMAND ===>                                                    SCROLL ===> PAGE
009800 *
009900  01  HEADING-LINE-4.
010000 *
010100      05  FILLER       PIC X(20)    VALUE 'BRANCH   SALESMAN  SA'.
010200      05  FILLER       PIC X(20)    VALUE 'LESMAN               '.
010300      05  FILLER       PIC X(20)    VALUE '      CUSTOMER  CUSTO'.
010400      05  FILLER       PIC X(20)    VALUE 'MER                  '.
010500      05  FILLER       PIC X(20)    VALUE '            SALES    '.
010600      05  FILLER       PIC X(20)    VALUE '    SALES            '.
010700      05  FILLER       PIC X(12)    VALUE 'ANGE  CHANGE'.
010800 *
010900  01  HEADING-LINE-5.
011000 *
R6          05  FILLER       PIC X(20)    VALUE '
011200 *
011300  01  CUSTOMER-LINE.
011400 *
011500      05  FILLER           PIC XX      VALUE SPACE.
011600      05  CL-BRANCH-NO      PIC XX.
011700      05  FILLER           PIC X(7)    VALUE SPACE.
011800      05  CL-SALESMAN-NO    PIC XX.
011900      05  FILLER           PIC X(5)    VALUE SPACE.
```

Part 2:

When you press the
Enter key, edit repeats
the line 6 times

```
EDIT ---- DLOWE.TEST.COBOL(MKTG1200) - 01.01 ----------------- COLUMNS 007 078
COMMAND ===>                                                    SCROLL ===> PAGE
009800 *
009900  01  HEADING-LINE-4.
010000 *
010100      05  FILLER       PIC X(20)    VALUE 'BRANCH   SALESMAN  SA'.
010200      05  FILLER       PIC X(20)    VALUE 'LESMAN               '.
010300      05  FILLER       PIC X(20)    VALUE '      CUSTOMER  CUSTO'.
010400      05  FILLER       PIC X(20)    VALUE 'MER                  '.
010500      05  FILLER       PIC X(20)    VALUE '            SALES    '.
010600      05  FILLER       PIC X(20)    VALUE '    SALES            '.
010700      05  FILLER       PIC X(12)    VALUE 'ANGE  CHANGE'.
010800 *
010900  01  HEADING-LINE-5.
011000 *
011100      05  FILLER       PIC X(20)    VALUE '                    '.
011110      05  FILLER       PIC X(20)    VALUE '                    '.
011120      05  FILLER       PIC X(20)    VALUE '                    '.
011130      05  FILLER       PIC X(20)    VALUE '                    '.
011140      05  FILLER       PIC X(20)    VALUE '                    '.
011150      05  FILLER       PIC X(20)    VALUE '                    '.
011160      05  FILLER       PIC X(20)    VALUE '                    '.
011200 *
011300  01  CUSTOMER-LINE.
```

Figure 4-8   Repeating lines

Part 1:

The RR line commands mark the first and last lines to be repeated

```
EDIT ---- DLOWE.TEST.COBOL(MKTG1200) - 01.01 --------------- COLUMNS 007 078
COMMAND ===>                                                 SCROLL ===> PAGE
032400 *
032500   250-PRINT-HEADING-LINES.
032600 *
032700       ADD 1              TO PAGE-COUNT.
032800       MOVE PAGE-COUNT     TO HDG1-PAGE-NUMBER.
032900       MOVE HEADING-LINE-1 TO PRINT-AREA.
033000       PERFORM 260-WRITE-PAGE-TOP-LINE.
RR           MOVE HEADING-LINE-2 TO PRINT-AREA.
033200       MOVE 1             TO SPACE-CONTROL.
RR3          PERFORM 270-WRITE-REPORT-LINE.
033400 *
033500   260-WRITE-PAGE-TOP-LINE.
033600 *
033700       WRITE PRINT-AREA
033800          AFTER ADVANCING PAGE.
033900       MOVE 1 TO LINE-COUNT.
034000 *
034100   270-WRITE-REPORT-LINE.
034200 *
034300       WRITE PRINT-AREA
034400          AFTER ADVANCING SPACE-CONTROL LINES.
034500       ADD SPACE-CONTROL TO LINE-COUNT.
```

Part 2:

When you press the Enter key, edit repeats the block of lines 3 times

```
EDIT ---- DLOWE.TEST.COBOL(MKTG1200) - 01.01 --------------- COLUMNS 007 078
COMMAND ===>                                                 SCROLL ===> PAGE
032400 *
032500   250-PRINT-HEADING-LINES.
032600 *
032700       ADD 1              TO PAGE-COUNT.
032800       MOVE PAGE-COUNT     TO HDG1-PAGE-NUMBER.
032900       MOVE HEADING-LINE-1 TO PRINT-AREA.
033000       PERFORM 260-WRITE-PAGE-TOP-LINE.
033100       MOVE HEADING-LINE-2 TO PRINT-AREA.
033200       MOVE 1             TO SPACE-CONTROL.
033300       PERFORM 270-WRITE-REPORT-LINE.
033310       MOVE HEADING-LINE-2 TO PRINT-AREA.
033320       MOVE 1             TO SPACE-CONTROL.
033330       PERFORM 270-WRITE-REPORT-LINE.
033340       MOVE HEADING-LINE-2 TO PRINT-AREA.
033350       MOVE 1             TO SPACE-CONTROL.
033360       PERFORM 270-WRITE-REPORT-LINE.
033370       MOVE HEADING-LINE-2 TO PRINT-AREA.
033380       MOVE 1             TO SPACE-CONTROL.
033390       PERFORM 270-WRITE-REPORT-LINE.
033400 *
033500   260-WRITE-PAGE-TOP-LINE.
033600 *
```

Figure 4-9   Repeating a block of lines

panel containing the end of the block and enter the second RR command.

How to copy lines   A copy operation is similar to a repeat operation except that besides specifying the line or group of lines to be copied, you indicate where the lines are copied to (called the *destination*). To mark the lines to copy, you use the C, Cn, or CC commands. To mark the copy destination, you use an A or a B command. If you specify A, the source lines are placed after the destination line. If you specify B, the source lines are placed before the destination line.

To illustrate, consider figure 4-10. Here, the group of lines from line 2300 to line 2500 is copied after line 2700. Part 1 of figure 4-10 shows the line commands entered for this copy operation; part 2 shows the completion of the copy.

As with the other line commands, you don't have to enter all the commands necessary for a copy operation on a single panel. In fact, you can mark a block of lines by placing the first CC command on one panel, the second CC command on another panel, and the A or B command on yet another panel.

You can combine a copy and repeat operation into a single operation by specifying a number on the A or B command. For example, had A3 been specified in part 1 of figure 4-10, part 2 would show that the copied lines were repeated three times following line 2700.

How to move lines   A move operation is similar to a copy operation with one exception: the source lines are deleted from their original location when they're moved. The commands you enter for a move are the same as for a copy, except you specify M, Mn, or MM rather than C, Cn, or CC.

Figure 4-11 shows a typical move operation. Part 1 shows the line commands used for the move, while part 2 shows the effect of the move. As you can see, the source lines that were moved no longer appear in their original location. This example also shows the effect of using B rather than A to mark the destination.

The RESET command   Many edit commands display informational messages at various screen locations or at various points in your source text. And many commands generate error messages that are displayed in the heading area of the screen. Once you've read these messages, you can remove them by entering a RESET

Part 1:

The CC line commands tell what block of lines to copy; the A line command marks the destination

```
EDIT ---- DLOWE.TEST.COBOL(MKTG1Z00) - 01.01 ------------------ COLUMNS 007 078
COMMAND ===>                                                    SCROLL ===> PAGE
002100  FILE SECTION.
002200 *
CC      FD  CUSTMST
002400      RECORD CONTAINS 42 CHARACTERS.
CC     *
002600  COPY CUSTMAST.
A      *
002800  WORKING-STORAGE SECTION.
002900 *
003000  01  SWITCHES.
003100 *
003200      05  FIRST-RECORD-SW PIC X     VALUE 'Y'.
003300          88  FIRST-RECORD          VALUE 'Y'.
003400      05  CUSTOMER-EOF-SW PIC X     VALUE 'N'.
003500          88  CUSTOMER-EOF          VALUE 'Y'.
003600      05  RECORD-FOUND-SW PIC X     VALUE 'Y'.
003700          88  RECORD-FOUND          VALUE 'Y'.
003800 *
003900  01  CONTROL-FIELDS.
004000 *
004100      05  OLD-SALESMAN-KEY.
004200          10  OLD-BRANCH-NUMBER   PIC 99.
```

Part 2:

When you press the Enter key, edit copies the lines

```
EDIT ---- DLOWE.TEST.COBOL(MKTG1Z00) - 01.01 ------------------ COLUMNS 007 078
COMMAND ===>                                                    SCROLL ===> PAGE
002100  FILE SECTION.
002200 *
002300  FD  CUSTMST
002400      RECORD CONTAINS 42 CHARACTERS.
002500 *
002600  COPY CUSTMAST.
002700 *
002710  FD  CUSTMST
002720      RECORD CONTAINS 42 CHARACTERS.
002730 *
002800  WORKING-STORAGE SECTION.
002900 *
003000  01  SWITCHES.
003100 *
003200      05  FIRST-RECORD-SW PIC X     VALUE 'Y'.
003300          88  FIRST-RECORD          VALUE 'Y'.
003400      05  CUSTOMER-EOF-SW PIC X     VALUE 'N'.
003500          88  CUSTOMER-EOF          VALUE 'Y'.
003600      05  RECORD-FOUND-SW PIC X     VALUE 'Y'.
003700          88  RECORD-FOUND          VALUE 'Y'.
003800 *
003900  01  CONTROL-FIELDS.
```

Figure 4-10 Copying lines

Part 1:

The MM line commands tell what block of lines to move; the B line command marks the destination

```
EDIT ---- DLOWE.TEST.COBOL(MKTG1200) - 01.01 ---------------- COLUMNS 007 078
COMMAND ===>                                                  SCROLL ===> PAGE
002100  FILE SECTION.
002200 *
B       FD  SALESRPT
002400      LABEL RECORDS ARE STANDARD
002500      RECORD CONTAINS 132 CHARACTERS.
002600 *
002700  01  PRINT-AREA.
002800 *
002900      05  PRINT-LINE  PIC X(132).
003000 *
MM      FD  CUSTMST
003200      RECORD CONTAINS 42 CHARACTERS.
003300 *
003400  COPY CUSTMAST.
003500 *
003600  FD  SALESMN
003700      RECORD CONTAINS 29 CHARACTERS.
003800 *
003900  COPY SALESMAN.
MM     *
004100  WORKING-STORAGE SECTION.
004200 *
```

Part 2:

When you press the Enter key, edit moves the lines

```
EDIT ---- DLOWE.TEST.COBOL(MKTG1200) - 01.01 ---------------- COLUMNS 007 078
COMMAND ===>                                                  SCROLL ===> PAGE
002100  FILE SECTION.
002200 *
002210  FD  CUSTMST
002220      RECORD CONTAINS 42 CHARACTERS.
002230 *
002240  COPY CUSTMAST.
002250 *
002260  FD  SALESMN
002270      RECORD CONTAINS 29 CHARACTERS.
002280 *
002290  COPY SALESMAN.
002291 *
002300  FD  SALESRPT
002400      LABEL RECORDS ARE STANDARD
002500      RECORD CONTAINS 132 CHARACTERS.
002600 *
002700  01  PRINT-AREA.
002800 *
002900      05  PRINT-LINE  PIC X(132).
003000 *
004100  WORKING-STORAGE SECTION.
004200 *
```

Figure 4-11 Moving lines

primary command. Although RESET removes messages that appear within your source text, it doesn't affect the text itself. I'll point out specific times to use RESET throughout the rest of this chapter.

How to create a new member

So far, all of the examples in this topic have dealt with existing source members. Most of that information applies to new members as well, but you should be aware of a few extra points.

To create a new source member, specify a member name that doesn't exist in the library on the edit entry panel in figure 4-1. The library, though, must exist. (You'll learn how to use the data set utility to create a library in chapter 5.)

Once you've filled in the edit entry panel, ISPF creates an empty workspace in virtual storage. When you end the edit session, ISPF writes the new member onto disk in the library you specified.

Figure 4-12 shows the edit display for a new COBOL member. Here, there are no line numbers or source data. You simply type in the data you want from column 7 on, using the New-line key to move from one line to the next. When you fill up the screen, you can press the Enter key. Then, edit adds the lines to the virtual storage copy of the source member and replaces the apostrophes in columns 1-6 with appropriate line numbers.

Unfortunately, if you press the Enter key after filling up a screen, you don't get a new blank screen. So, if you want to enter additional lines, you have to use the INSERT command. Then, you can go back and enter data on the blank lines you insert.

I've found the fastest way to create a new member is *not* to press the Enter key at the end of the first screen. Instead, set the SCROLL amount to 20, and in the last line of the screen, enter an I20 command. Then, use PF8/20 to scroll forward 20 lines. The result is a screen much like the one you began with in figure 4-12. The only difference is that the first line doesn't say TOP OF DATA; instead, it's the last line you entered. You can then key data into this screen just like you did for the original screen. You can continue using this technique until you've completed your new source member.

```
EDIT ---- DLOWE.TEST.COBOL(MKTG3100) - 01.00 ------------------ COLUMNS 007 078
COMMAND ===>                                                   SCROLL ===> PAGE
****** ***************************** TOP OF DATA ******************************
,,,,,,
,,,,,,
,,,,,,
,,,,,,
,,,,,,
,,,,,,
,,,,,,
,,,,,,
,,,,,,
,,,,,,
,,,,,,
,,,,,,
,,,,,,
,,,,,,
,,,,,,
,,,,,,
,,,,,,
,,,,,,
,,,,,,
****** ************************* BOTTOM OF DATA ******************************
```

Figure 4-12   Creating a new member

How to terminate edit

The usual way to end an edit session is to press the End key,
PF3/15. When you do this, ISPF saves your changed member in the
primary library (the first library specified in a chain of concatenated libraries) and returns to the entry panel. Then, you can enter
another member to edit or press PF3/15 again to return to the
primary option menu. If you aren't going to edit another member,
you can use PF4/16 instead. This key also saves the changed
member, but it returns directly to the primary option menu.

If you want to terminate the edit session *without* saving your
changes, you can enter CANCEL in the command input area and
press the enter key. CANCEL returns to the entry panel without
copying the edited member back to the disk.

A related command, SAVE, saves the member without terminating edit. When you enter SAVE in the command area, the
virtual storage version of the member is copied to disk and the edit

session continues. In other words, the member you just saved is still on the screen and you can continue making changes to it.

Terms

source member
concatenate
member list
heading area
line command area
screen window
line number
sequence number
primary command
line command
destination

Objective

Edit a data set using the insert, delete, repeat, copy, and move line commands.

Topic 2 How to control the edit profile

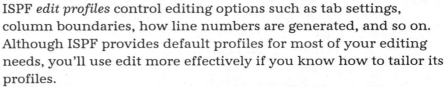

ISPF *edit profiles* control editing options such as tab settings, column boundaries, how line numbers are generated, and so on. Although ISPF provides default profiles for most of your editing needs, you'll use edit more effectively if you know how to tailor its profiles.

This topic is divided into two parts. In the first part, you'll learn what the edit profile is, how to display it, how to switch to a different profile, and how to lock a profile so it can't be changed. In the second part, you'll learn how to change the individual settings of a profile.

THE EDIT PROFILE

For each user, ISPF maintains a number of separate edit profiles. The default edit profiles correspond to data set types and are named accordingly. For example, COBOL is the default profile for data sets whose type is COBOL. If you want, you can create additional edit profiles with names you make up. So if you have more than one profile requirement for COBOL files, you can create profiles named COB1, COB2, and COB3.

Normally, you don't specify a profile when you edit a data set or member. The profile automatically defaults to the data set's type. So if you edit a COBOL file, you automatically receive the COBOL profile. However, you can specify an alternate edit profile on the edit entry panel, as shown in figure 4-13. Here, an edit profile named COB1 is specified. Even though the data set type is COBOL, the COB1 profile is selected for this editing session.

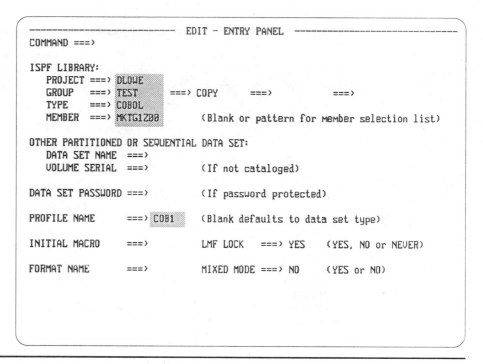

Figure 4-13   Specifying an alternate profile

How to display the edit profile

During an editing session, you can display the edit profile by entering this primary command:

    PROFILE

The profile display looks like the shaded portion of figure 4-14.

The first four lines indicate the profile name (COBOL), the source member's record format and length (FIXED and 80), and the settings of various *edit modes*. Except for the PROFILE and IMACRO modes, each is either on or off. Thus, in figure 4-14, CAPS mode is on, while HEX mode is off.

Following the four mode lines are lines showing the current settings for TABS, BOUNDS, and MASK. As you'll see later in this topic, TABS controls the location of tab stops, BOUNDS controls the left and right margins, and MASK controls the format of the line that's inserted with an INSERT command. The TABS and MASK lines are displayed only if they contain data, in other words, only if

```
EDIT ---- DLOWE.TEST.COBOL(MKTG1200) - 01.01 ---------------- COLUMNS 007 078
COMMAND ===>                                                  SCROLL ===> PAGE
****** ************************************ TOP OF DATA ***********************************
=PROF> ....COBOL (FIXED - 80)....RECOVERY OFF....NUMBER ON COB..............
=PROF> ....CAPS ON....HEX OFF....NULLS ON STD....TABS ON 0.................
=PROF> ....AUTOSAVE ON....AUTONUM OFF....AUTOLIST OFF....STATS ON..........
=PROF> ....PROFILE UNLOCK....IMACRO NONE....PACK OFF....NOTE ON...........
=TABS>      *                              *               *
=BNDS> <                                                                    >
=MASK>      05  FILLER        PIC X(20)    VALUE '                   '.
=COLS> ---1----+----2----+----3----+----4----+----5----+----6----+----7---+
000100  IDENTIFICATION DIVISION.
000200 *
000300  PROGRAM-ID.      MKTG1200.
000400 *
000500  ENVIRONMENT DIVISION.
000600 *
000700  CONFIGURATION SECTION.
000800 *
000900  INPUT-OUTPUT SECTION.
001000 *
001100  FILE-CONTROL.
001200      SELECT CUSTMST  ASSIGN TO AS-CUSTMST.
001300      SELECT SALESMN  ASSIGN TO SALESMN
```

Figure 4-14   An edit profile display

you've set tabs or entered a non-blank mask line. The BNDS line is displayed only if you've changed the boundaries from the default setting.

The last line is a COLS line, similar to the one in browse, that identifies column positions. If you want to display a COLS line anywhere in your source text during an edit session, enter COLS in the line command area of any line and edit automatically inserts a COLS line at that point. To remove a COLS line from the display, delete it using a D line command or enter a RESET command, as described in topic 1.

You control the settings for each of the profile options using commands that I describe later in this topic. When you terminate edit, any profile changes you've made are saved as part of the profile, unless the profile is locked. I'll show you how to lock a profile in a moment.

How to switch to a different profile or create a new profile

When you use the PROFILE command, you can specify a profile name that causes edit to switch to a different profile. For example, if you enter this command:

```
PROFILE COB3
```

edit retrieves the profile named COB3. If there is no COB3 profile, edit creates one using the current profile settings. Thus, to create a new profile, you simply change the profile settings individually using the commands I'll describe next, then issue a PROFILE command specifying the new profile name.

How to lock an edit profile

Normally, any changes you make to the edit profile are saved when you end an edit session. However, once you get a profile set up the way you want it, you can lock it so that any changes made to the profile during an edit session affect only that session. In other words, any changes you make to a locked profile are not saved in the profile permanently.

To lock a profile, enter this command:

```
PROFILE LOCK
```

Then, the current profile settings are saved in the edit profile. So the next time you use that profile, it has the same settings as it did when you locked it, even if you changed the settings in a previous edit session. The only exception is that the CAPS, NUMBER, PACK, and STATS modes are set each time you begin an edit session based on the data you're editing. I'll have more to say about these modes later in this topic.

HOW TO CHANGE PROFILE SETTINGS

You use a variety of commands to change profile settings. Here, you'll first learn the profile settings for four important editing functions: tabbing, boundary control, masking, and line numbering. Then, you'll learn the remaining edit mode settings.

How to use tabs

When you edit a source member, you often need to move the cursor to a particular column to align text. For example, you may want to place all the PIC clauses of a COBOL program in column 36. Normally, you use a cursor key or the space bar to move the cursor to a particular column. If you use edit's tabbing feature, however, you can move the cursor to a particular column location, called a *tab stop*, using a single keystroke.

Edit provides two types of tabs: hardware and logical. When you use *hardware tabs*, you use the 3270's Tab key to move the cursor immediately to the next tab stop. When you use *logical tabs*, you enter a special *tab character*, usually the # key or the @ key, whenever you want to align text at a tab stop. Then, when you press the Enter key, edit replaces the tab characters with the correct number of spaces to align the tabbed text properly.

To illustrate logical tabbing, suppose you have tab stops set at columns 36 and 48. Now, consider figure 4-15. Part 1 of this figure, contains text for a record description using the @ key as a tab character. Part 2 of figure 4-15 shows how the text is aligned as a result of logical tabbing.

Notice in the last line of the SALESMAN-TOTAL-LINE in part 2 of the figure that the PIC clause isn't aligned at a tab stop. That's because the data that's aligned at column 36 extends past column 48, and there aren't any tab stops defined past column 48. Any time the editor doesn't find a tab stop, as in this case, it inserts a single space in place of the tab character. You can see that's what happened in figure 4-15.

To implement a hardware tab stop, edit uses a special control character called an *attribute byte*. Attribute bytes control various characteristics of the fields on a 3270 screen, such as whether or not an operator can enter data into the field. Each attribute byte takes up one position on the screen, but it displays as a blank so you can't see it. The only reason you need to be aware of the presence of attribute bytes when you use hardware tabbing is this: You can't modify the character immediately to the left of a hardware tab stop because that position contains an attribute byte. In other words, if you define a hardware tab in column 32, you can't change the data in column 31.

When you edit a COBOL source program, you'll probably use hardware tabs most in the Data Division. That's because you want to align PIC clauses and other information in columns, and there's

Part 1:

The @ symbol is the tab character

```
EDIT ---- DLOWE.TEST.COBOL(MKTG1Z00) - 01.01 -------------- COLUMNS 007 078
COMMAND ===>                                                SCROLL ===> PAGE
014100 *
014Z00  01  SALESMAN-TOTAL-LINE.
014300 *
014400      05  FILLER@PIC X(63)@VALUE SPACE.
014500      05  FILLER@PIC X(19)@VALUE 'SALESMAN TOTALS:'.
014600      05  SL-SALES-THIS-YTD@PIC Z,ZZZ,ZZ9.99-.
014700      05  FILLER@PIC XX@VALUE SPACE.
014800      05  SL-SALES-LAST-YTD@PIC Z,ZZZ,ZZ9.99-.
014900      05  FILLER@PIC XX@VALUE SPACE.
015000      05  SL-CHANGE-AMOUNT@PIC Z,ZZZ,ZZ9.99-.
015100      05  FILLER@PIC X@VALUE SPACE.
015Z00      05  SL-CHANGE-PERCENT@PIC ZZZ9-.
015300      05  SL-CHANGE-PERCENT-R@REDEFINES SL-CHANGE-PERCENT@PIC X(5).
015400 *
015500  01  BRANCH-TOTAL-LINE.
015600 *
015700      05  FILLER         PIC X(65)   VALUE SPACE.
015800      05  FILLER         PIC X(17)   VALUE 'BRANCH TOTALS:'.
015900      05  BL-SALES-THIS-YTD PIC Z,ZZZ,ZZ9.99-.
016000      05  FILLER         PIC XX      VALUE SPACE.
016100      05  BL-SALES-LAST-YTD PIC Z,ZZZ,ZZ9.99-.
016Z00      05  FILLER         PIC XX      VALUE SPACE.
```

Part 2:

When you press the Enter key, edit moves the text to the proper tab stops

```
EDIT ---- DLOWE.TEST.COBOL(MKTG1Z00) - 01.01 -------------- COLUMNS 007 078
COMMAND ===>                                                SCROLL ===> PAGE
014100 *
014Z00  01  SALESMAN-TOTAL-LINE.
014300 *
014400      05  FILLER          PIC X(63)   VALUE SPACE.
014500      05  FILLER          PIC X(19)   VALUE 'SALESMAN TOTALS:'.
014600      05  SL-SALES-THIS-YTD PIC Z,ZZZ,ZZ9.99-.
014700      05  FILLER          PIC XX      VALUE SPACE.
014800      05  SL-SALES-LAST-YTD PIC Z,ZZZ,ZZ9.99-.
014900      05  FILLER          PIC XX      VALUE SPACE.
015000      05  SL-CHANGE-AMOUNT  PIC Z,ZZZ,ZZ9.99-.
015100      05  FILLER          PIC X       VALUE SPACE.
015Z00      05  SL-CHANGE-PERCENT PIC ZZZ9-.
015300      05  SL-CHANGE-PERCENT-R REDEFINES SL-CHANGE-PERCENT PIC X(5).
015400 *
015500  01  BRANCH-TOTAL-LINE.
015600 *
015700      05  FILLER          PIC X(65)   VALUE SPACE.
015800      05  FILLER          PIC X(17)   VALUE 'BRANCH TOTALS:'.
015900      05  BL-SALES-THIS-YTD PIC Z,ZZZ,ZZ9.99-.
016000      05  FILLER          PIC XX      VALUE SPACE.
016100      05  BL-SALES-LAST-YTD PIC Z,ZZZ,ZZ9.99-.
016Z00      05  FILLER          PIC XX      VALUE SPACE.
```

Figure 4-15 Logical tabbing

```
EDIT ---- DLOWE.TEST.COBOL(MKTG1200) - 01.01 ----------------- COLUMNS 007 078
COMMAND ===>                                                   SCROLL ===> PAGE
=COLS> ---1----+----2----+----3----+----4----+----5----+----6----+----7----+---
014100 *
014200  01  SALESMAN-TOTAL-LINE.
=TABS>      *                              *             *
014300 *
014400      05  FILLER            PIC X(63)   VALUE SPACE.
014500      05  FILLER            PIC X(19)   VALUE 'SALESMAN TOTALS:'.
014600      05  SL-SALES-THIS-YTD PIC Z,ZZZ,ZZ9.99-.
014700      05  FILLER            PIC XX      VALUE SPACE.
014800      05  SL-SALES-LAST-YTD PIC Z,ZZZ,ZZ9.99-.
014900      05  FILLER            PIC XX      VALUE SPACE.
015000      05  SL-CHANGE-AMOUNT  PIC Z,ZZZ,ZZ9.99-.
015100      05  FILLER            PIC X       VALUE SPACE.
015200      05  SL-CHANGE-PERCENT PIC ZZZ9-.
015300      05  SL-CHANGE-PERCENT-R REDEFINES SL-CHANGE-PERCENT
015400                            PIC X(5).
015500 *
015600  01  BRANCH-TOTAL-LINE.
015700 *
015800      05  FILLER            PIC X(65)   VALUE SPACE.
015900      05  FILLER            PIC X(17)   VALUE 'BRANCH TOTALS:'.
016000      05  BL-SALES-THIS-YTD PIC Z,ZZZ,ZZ9.99-.
```

Figure 4-16   Defining tab stops

usually no need to enter data in the positions occupied by attribute
bytes. In the Procedure Division and other sections of your
program where you need to enter data in a more free-form fashion,
you'll probably use logical tabbing.

You use two commands to control tabbing. The TABS line
command defines the location of each tab stop. The TABS primary
command activates hardware or logical tabs. Note that although
these two commands have the same name, they have distinct functions. The TABS line command lets you specify the position of each
tab stop, while the TABS primary command lets you activate TABS
mode and control how tabbing works.

How to define tab stops   When you enter TABS in the line
command area and press the Enter key, ISPF responds with a tab
line as shown in figure 4-16 (the tab line is shaded). The tab line
defines the location of each tab stop. Initially, it's blank. To define
a tab stop, you enter an asterisk (*) immediately to the left of the
desired tab position. For example, the asterisks in columns 11, 35,
and 47 of the tab line in figure 4-16 define tab stops in columns 12,

---

The TABS command

TABS $\mathtt{[} \left\{ \begin{matrix} \underline{\mathtt{ON}} \\ \mathtt{OFF} \end{matrix} \right\} \mathtt{]}$ [tab-character] $\mathtt{[} \left\{ \begin{matrix} \underline{\mathtt{STD}} \\ \mathtt{ALL} \end{matrix} \right\} \mathtt{]}$

Explanation

ON/OFF   Says whether to activate or deactivate TABS mode. On is the default.

tab-character   Specifies a character used for logical tabbing. If omitted, hardware tabbing is assumed.

STD/ALL   Says whether to insert attribute bytes for each tab stop. If you code ALL, attribute bytes are inserted even if that causes non-blank data to be overlaid. If you code STD, only non-blank data is replaced by attribute bytes. STD is the default.

Figure 4-17   The TABS primary command

36, and 48. You place the asterisk to the left of the tab stop because the asterisk defines the location of the attribute byte for hardware tabbing, not the tab stop itself. This is true even if you use logical tabs rather than hardware tabs.

How to activate TABS mode   Once you've defined a tab line, you use a TABS primary command to activate tabbing. Figure 4-17 shows the format of the TABS primary command. As you can see, it has three options. ON/OFF indicates whether you're activating or deactivating TABS mode. If you specify ON, tabbing is activated. If you specify OFF, tabbing is turned off and any attribute characters inserted for hardware tabbing are removed. If you don't specify ON or OFF, ON is assumed.

The next option, tab-character, says what character is used for logical tabbing. For example, if you want the pound sign to be the logical tab character, you enter this command:

```
TABS ON #
```

Then, you use the pound sign to move from one tab stop to another.

If you omit the tab-character, hardware tabbing is assumed. Then, attribute bytes are inserted before each tab stop, and you use the Tab key rather than logical tab characters to move from one tab stop to the next.

The ALL and STD options pertain to hardware tabbing only. They determine whether existing data is overlaid with attribute bytes. If you say STD or let it default, attribute bytes are not inserted if they overlay non-blank data. If you say ALL, attribute bytes are inserted for every tab stop, even if non-blank data is overlaid. In either case, the attribute bytes appear on the screen only; they're never transferred to the source member.

For hardware tabbing, you can remove attribute bytes from a single line by (1) pressing the Erase-EOF key to blank out the line command area, or (2) placing the cursor directly under an attribute byte. In either case, the attribute bytes in the line are removed when you press the Enter key. They're inserted again the next time you press the Enter key.

Why would you want to temporarily remove attribute bytes from a single line? One case is when you're entering code for the Working-Storage Section of a COBOL source program. Here, you might use hardware tabbing to tab to position 48 for the VALUE clauses. Sometimes, though, you need to create a long VALUE clause that starts before column 48 and continues to the end of the line. To enter that VALUE clause, you first need to remove the attribute characters for that line.

How to change column boundaries

Left and right margins or *boundaries* determine the range of columns for editing data. Normally, the boundaries are set based on the type field of the file or library name.

For a COBOL file, the left margin is column 7 and the right margin is column 72. Although you can change the data in columns 1-6 and 73-80, the edit commands you learn about in topic 3 will affect only the data in columns 7-72.

For an ASM file (assembler source code), the boundaries are set at columns 1 and 71. For other file types, the left margin is column 1 and the right margin is the last position of the record.

To change boundary settings, you can use either the BOUNDS line command or the BOUNDS primary command. If you enter BOUNDS in the line command area, edit responds by displaying a bounds line, as illustrated in figure 4-18. When this line is displayed, enter a less-than sign (<) to mark the new left boundary

```
EDIT ---- DLOWE.TEST.COBOL(MKTG1200) - 01.01 ---------------- COLUMNS 007 078
COMMAND ===>                                                    SCROLL ===> PAGE
014100 *
014200  01  SALESMAN-TOTAL-LINE.
=BNDS>                       <                                                 >
014300 *
014400      05  FILLER              PIC X(63)   VALUE SPACE.
014500      05  FILLER              PIC X(19)   VALUE 'SALESMAN TOTALS:'.
014600      05  SL-SALES-THIS-YTD   PIC Z,ZZZ,ZZ9.99-.
014700      05  FILLER              PIC XX      VALUE SPACE.
014800      05  SL-SALES-LAST-YTD   PIC Z,ZZZ,ZZ9.99-.
014900      05  FILLER              PIC XX      VALUE SPACE.
015000      05  SL-CHANGE-AMOUNT    PIC Z,ZZZ,ZZ9.99-.
015100      05  FILLER              PIC X       VALUE SPACE.
015200      05  SL-CHANGE-PERCENT   PIC ZZZ9-.
015300      05  SL-CHANGE-PERCENT-R REDEFINES SL-CHANGE-PERCENT
015400                              PIC X(5).
015500 *
015600  01  BRANCH-TOTAL-LINE.
015700 *
015800      05  FILLER              PIC X(65)   VALUE SPACE.
015900      05  FILLER              PIC X(17)   VALUE 'BRANCH TOTALS:'.
016000      05  BL-SALES-THIS-YTD   PIC Z,ZZZ,ZZ9.99-.
016100      05  FILLER              PIC XX      VALUE SPACE.
```

Figure 4-18   Changing the edit boundaries

and a greater-than sign (>) to mark the new right boundary. The positions that contain the < or > characters are considered to be within the boundaries.

To restore the boundaries to the default values, enter a BOUNDS line command and erase the bounds line using the Erase-EOF key. To remove the boundary line from the display, delete the line using the D line command or enter the RESET command. The RESET command does *not* affect the boundary settings.

You can also change the boundaries using the BOUNDS primary command. To do that, enter a command like this:

    BOUNDS 30 56

In this example, the left boundary is set to 30 and the right boundary is set to 56. This command does not cause the bounds line to be displayed. To change the boundaries back to their defaults, enter the BOUNDS primary command without specifying the boundaries.

How to use edit masks

An *edit mask* is a pre-defined line that's used as the initial contents of each line you insert using an I line command. You use an edit mask to create repetitive lines. Initially, the edit mask is blank. As a result, any lines you insert with an I command are blank. To change the mask, enter MASK in the line command area. Edit responds by displaying a mask line, as shown in part 1 of figure 4-19. Then, enter your edit mask. In this example, I entered a dummy field description as the mask.

Part 1 of figure 4-19 also contains an I line command that inserts 7 lines. Part 2 shows the result of this insertion. As you can see, the mask line is copied into each inserted line. The mask line remains in effect until you change it again, using another MASK command. You can remove the mask line display with a D line command or a RESET primary command. But the mask line is still active even though it's not displayed. The only way to deactivate the mask line is to change it to blanks using another MASK command.

Often, a better way to achieve the effect of an edit mask is to insert one blank line, enter data on it, and repeat the line using an R command. The advantage of this technique is that you don't have to reset the mask line once you're through.

How to control line numbers

To control how edit maintains *line numbers*, also called *sequence numbers*, you use the five commands shown in figure 4-20. The NUMBER command determines the format of the line numbers and whether they're displayed in the data window. The NONUMBER command turns number mode off; it has the same effect as entering NUMBER OFF. The AUTONUM command says whether or not line numbers are automatically resequenced when you terminate edit. The RENUM command says to resequence the line numbers. And the UNNUM command removes line numbers.

The NUMBER and NONUMBER commands   You use the NUMBER and NONUMBER commands to control the setting of NUMBER mode. If you say NUMBER ON COBOL, NUMBER ON STD, or NUMBER ON STD COBOL, edit checks that the member has valid COBOL, standard, or both COBOL and standard line

Part 1:

The MASK line command defines the line to be inserted with an I command

```
EDIT ---- DLOWE.TEST.COBOL(MKTG1200) - 01.01 ---------------- COLUMNS 007 078
COMMAND ===>                                                 SCROLL ===> PAGE
=MASK>       05  FILLER      PIC X(20)   VALUE '                    '.
009900  01   HEADING-LINE-4.
010000  *
010100       05  FILLER      PIC X(20)   VALUE 'BRANCH   SALESMAN  SA'.
010200       05  FILLER      PIC X(20)   VALUE 'LESMAN              '.
010300       05  FILLER      PIC X(20)   VALUE '      CUSTOMER  CUSTO'.
010400       05  FILLER      PIC X(20)   VALUE 'MER                 '.
010500       05  FILLER      PIC X(20)   VALUE '          SALES     '.
010600       05  FILLER      PIC X(20)   VALUE '    SALES           '.
010700       05  FILLER      PIC X(12)   VALUE 'ANGE  CHANGE'.
010800  *
010900  01   HEADING-LINE-5.
I7       *
011100  *
011200  01   CUSTOMER-LINE.
011300  *
011400       05  FILLER          PIC XX       VALUE SPACE.
011500       05  CL-BRANCH-NO     PIC XX.
011600       05  FILLER          PIC X(7)     VALUE SPACE.
011700       05  CL-SALESMAN-NO   PIC XX.
011800       05  FILLER          PIC X(5)     VALUE SPACE.
011900       05  CL-SALESMAN-NAME PIC X(25).
```

Part 2:

When you press the Enter key, edit inserts the mask line 7 times

```
EDIT ---- DLOWE.TEST.COBOL(MKTG1200) - 01.01 ---------------- COLUMNS 007 078
COMMAND ===>                                                 SCROLL ===> PAGE
=MASK>       05  FILLER      PIC X(20)   VALUE '                    '.
009900  01   HEADING-LINE-4.
010000  *
010100       05  FILLER      PIC X(20)   VALUE 'BRANCH   SALESMAN  SA'.
010200       05  FILLER      PIC X(20)   VALUE 'LESMAN              '.
010300       05  FILLER      PIC X(20)   VALUE '      CUSTOMER  CUSTO'.
010400       05  FILLER      PIC X(20)   VALUE 'MER                 '.
010500       05  FILLER      PIC X(20)   VALUE '          SALES     '.
010600       05  FILLER      PIC X(20)   VALUE '    SALES           '.
010700       05  FILLER      PIC X(12)   VALUE 'ANGE  CHANGE'.
010800  *
010900  01   HEADING-LINE-5.
011000  *
''''''       05  FILLER      PIC X(20)   VALUE '                    '.
''''''       05  FILLER      PIC X(20)   VALUE '                    '.
''''''       05  FILLER      PIC X(20)   VALUE '                    '.
''''''       05  FILLER      PIC X(20)   VALUE '                    '.
''''''       05  FILLER      PIC X(20)   VALUE '                    '.
''''''       05  FILLER      PIC X(20)   VALUE '                    '.
''''''       05  FILLER      PIC X(20)   VALUE '                    '.
011100  *
011200  01   CUSTOMER-LINE.
```

Figure 4-19   Using an edit mask

Command	Meaning
NUMBER $\left[\begin{Bmatrix} ON \\ OFF \end{Bmatrix}\right]$ $\left[\begin{Bmatrix} STD \\ COBOL \\ STD\ COBOL \end{Bmatrix}\right]$ [DISPLAY]	Defines how line numbers are stored in the member.
NONUMBER	Turns number mode off.
AUTONUM $\left[\begin{Bmatrix} ON \\ OFF \end{Bmatrix}\right]$	Says whether or not line numbers should be resequenced whenever the member is saved.
RENUM $\left[\begin{Bmatrix} ON \\ OFF \end{Bmatrix}\right]$ $\left[\begin{Bmatrix} STD \\ COBOL \\ STD\ COBOL \end{Bmatrix}\right]$ [DISPLAY]	Resequences the line numbers unless OFF is specified. OFF turns number mode off. You can specify standard or COBOL numbers if you want.
UNNUM	Replaces line numbers with blanks and turns off NUMBER mode.

Figure 4-20   Primary commands used to control line numbering

numbers. If it doesn't, edit resequences the numbers so they're valid. Once NUMBER mode is on, edit automatically maintains line numbers, generating new line numbers for inserted lines and resequencing existing line numbers whenever necessary. As a result, you don't have to renumber the source member to insert, move, copy, or repeat lines. If you say NUMBER OFF, edit ignores any line numbers it finds in the file. Instead, it creates its own sequence numbers for temporary use.

If you code any of the NUMBER ON commands, you can also code the DISPLAY option. This option says to display the generated sequence numbers in the data window. If you specify DISPLAY, edit scrolls the display window left or right to display the sequence numbers. Note that even if the sequence numbers are displayed in the edit window, they can't be modified.

When you start an edit session, edit scans the source file to determine what types of line numbers are present and sets the NUMBER mode accordingly. This is true even if you locked the profile. However, if the profile is locked and the editor changes the NUMBER mode, the change is *not* saved in the profile permanently.

Because NUMBER mode is set automatically, you usually won't use the NUMBER command. The one time you're likely to use the NUMBER command is when you're creating an unnumbered test file. In that case, you'll probably need to issue a NUMBER OFF command. You can also turn NUMBER mode off by entering the NONUMBER command.

The AUTONUM command   The AUTONUM command controls AUTONUM mode, which says whether or not a member should be renumbered automatically each time it's saved. Normally, AUTONUM is off. If you like your members numbered in regular increments, use AUTONUM mode.

The RENUM command   You use the RENUM command to resequence line numbers. RENUM starts with 100 for the first line number and then numbers by 100s. You can force COBOL or standard numbers or both by specifying COBOL, STD, or STD COBOL on the RENUM command. You can also turn NUMBER mode on or off using RENUM. ON is the default. If you specify OFF, the STD, COBOL, and STD COBOL options have no effect. Since edit automatically resequences line numbers whenever necessary, you won't use the RENUM command often.

The UNNUM command   You use the UNNUM command to remove line numbers from a member. UNNUM replaces any existing line numbers with blanks and turns off NUMBER mode. To restore sequence numbers, use the RENUM or NUMBER command.

Other edit modes

I've already described three edit modes: TABS, NUMBER, and AUTONUM. Figure 4-21 lists all the edit modes. For each of them (other than TABS, NUMBER, and IMACRO), the command you use

Mode	Function
TABS	Controls logical and hardware tabbing.
NUMBER	Controls how line numbers are maintained.
AUTONUM	Controls automatic resequencing.
STATS	Controls automatic maintenance of library statistics.
NULLS	Controls how trailing blanks are handled on the 3270 screen.
AUTOLIST	Controls automatic printing.
RECOVERY	Controls the automatic journal kept for recovery purposes.
HEX	Controls hexadecimal display.
CAPS	Controls automatic conversion of lowercase data to uppercase.
PACK	Controls how data is stored.
AUTOSAVE	Controls automatic saving of modifications.
NOTES	Controls displaying of notes.
IMACRO	Controls the edit macro that is run at the beginning of an edit session.

Figure 4-21   Edit modes

to turn them on or off is the mode name followed by the word ON or OFF. So, to activate AUTOLIST mode, you code this command:

```
AUTOLIST ON
```

Now, I'll describe each of the remaining edit modes in detail.

STATS mode   If STATS mode is on, ISPF automatically maintains statistics for each member in the library. These statistics are displayed on member selection lists and may be created, reset, or deleted using option 3.5, the reset utility. I'll present the reset utility in chapter 5.

Figure 4-22 shows a typical member selection list. Here, you can see the library statistics. The VV.MM field contains a version and modification level number. Version is initially set to 1 and can be changed using the reset utility or by entering a VERSION primary command. Each time you edit a member, ISPF automatically adds 1 to the modification level number. As a result, a newly

```
┌──────────────────────────────────────────────────────────────────────┐
│ EDIT --- DLOWE.TEST.COBOL --------------------------------- ROW 00001 OF 00004 │
│ COMMAND ===>                                                SCROLL ===> PAGE │
│    NAME            VV.MM  CREATED    CHANGED       SIZE  INIT   MOD   ID     │
│    MKTG1100        01.08 89/12/04 89/12/27 13:07   276   410    61 DLOWE     │
│    MKTG1200        01.00 89/12/27 89/12/27 17:56   410   410     0 DLOWE     │
│    MKTG1300        01.08 89/12/04 89/12/27 14:40   371   410    75 DLOWE     │
│    MKTG4100        01.08 89/12/04 89/12/27 15:04   263   410    60 DLOWE     │
│    **END**                                                                   │
│                                                                              │
│                                                                              │
│                                                                              │
│                                                                              │
│                                                                              │
│                                                                              │
│                                                                              │
│                                                                              │
└──────────────────────────────────────────────────────────────────────┘
```

Figure 4-22   An edit member selection list

created member has a VV.MM of 1.00, while a member that's been edited four times since its creation has a VV.MM of 1.04. You can also change the modification level number by entering a LEVEL primary command. The highest value both the version and modification level number can have is 99. If you modify a member more than 99 times, the modification level number stays at 99.

The CREATED and CHANGED fields show the date the member was created and the date and time it was last edited. The SIZE, INIT, and MOD fields show the current number of lines in the member, the number of lines initially in this version, and the number of lines that have been modified since the version was created. Finally, the ID field shows the user-id of the person who edited the member most recently.

For members with standard line numbers, STATS mode affects how the line numbers are maintained. If STATS mode is on, only six digits of each eight digit line number are used as a sequence number. The last two digits are reserved for the *modification flag*. These digits indicate how many times each line has been modified. If the modification flag is 00, the line hasn't been changed since the member was created. If the modification flag is 02, the line has been modified twice. When STATS mode is off, all eight digits of the line number are used for sequencing. STATS mode doesn't affect line numbering for COBOL members.

NULLS mode   NULLS mode controls how trailing blanks are sent to the screen. If NULLS mode is off, all blanks are sent to the screen. If NULLS mode is on (the default), trailing blanks—the ones that follow the last non-blank character on each line—are sent to the screen as null characters (hex zeros) rather than as blanks.

When NULLS mode is on, response time is better and it's easier to use the Insert key. Response time is improved because null characters are not actually sent to the terminal. For remote terminals, the difference in response time can be significant. But for local terminals, you probably won't notice a difference. As for the Insert key, if NULLS mode is off, each line is filled with blanks. Since all blanks are considered to be data, you can't use the Insert key to insert characters unless you first erase trailing blanks using the Erase-EOF key. When NULLS mode is on, you don't have to use the Erase-EOF key before you can use the Insert key because source lines aren't padded with blanks.

The disadvantage of NULLS mode is that you have to use the space bar to move the cursor across the screen when you're entering new text. If you use a cursor key instead, the entire line is compressed when you press the Enter key. For example, suppose you enter a line like this, using the right arrow key instead of the space bar to space between 05, FILLER, PIC, and X:

```
05  FILLER          PIC X.
```

When you press the Enter key, the nulls you skipped over with the cursor key are removed, and the line looks like this:

```
05FILLERPICX.
```

Whether you specify NULLS ON or OFF depends largely on your personal editing style. If you frequently use the cursor keys rather than the space bar to move the cursor across the screen, you should specify NULLS OFF. On the other hand, if you find yourself constantly using the Erase-EOF key to delete trailing blanks so you can use the Insert key, change NULLS to ON. I think it's best to develop the habit of using the Space bar rather than a cursor key. That way, you can set NULLS mode ON and use the Insert key easily. But again, it's a matter of personal choice.

AUTOLIST mode   When you terminate edit, a source listing is automatically generated if you made any changes to the source member and if AUTOLIST mode is on. The source listing is written to the list data set, which isn't printed until you terminate ISPF.

For programs in development, you don't want AUTOLIST mode on. Otherwise, each time you edit your program, a source listing is generated. On the other hand, AUTOLIST mode is a good idea for programs in production. That way, each time maintenance is done to the program, it's automatically documented.

RECOVERY mode   If you're worried about system crashes, you can use RECOVERY mode to keep a record of all changes you make during an edit session in a special disk file called the *recovery data set*. The recovery data set is closed only when edit terminates normally. If the system crashes, the recovery data set is left open. When the system comes up and you edit the member again, edit displays a panel that lets you apply the changes stored in the recovery data set. Of course, the price you pay for this extra protection is increased response time.

If RECOVERY mode is on, you can also use the UNDO command. The UNDO command lets you reverse the changes you make to a source member during an edit session. To use this feature, enter UNDO in the command area. When you do, the last modification you made is reversed. You can enter the UNDO command as many times as you want, until all modifications you made during the current edit session are reversed.

Note that RECOVERY mode works only for existing source members; it has no effect on a new member until the member is saved. As a result, if you use RECOVERY mode, it's a good idea to explicitly save new members early in the edit session by entering a SAVE command. That way, RECOVERY becomes active for the member.

HEX mode   When HEX mode is on, data is displayed in hexadecimal format. The format, shown in figure 4-23, is the same as the browse hexadecimal display. While in HEX mode, you can change the contents of any byte by changing the character or the two-byte hex code. Thus, you can use HEX mode to create or modify packed-decimal test data. Or, you can create program literals (such as COBOL VALUE clauses) that contain non-displayable data.

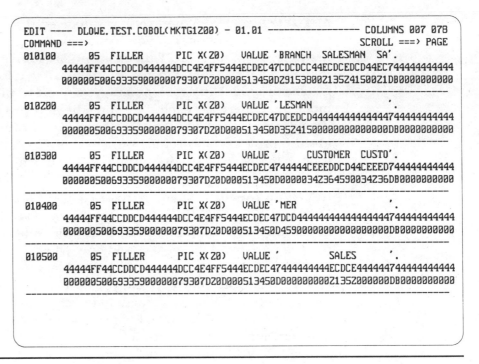

Figure 4-23   Edit hexadecimal display

CAPS mode   When CAPS mode is on, any lowercase letters you enter are automatically converted to uppercase letters. When CAPS mode is off, no automatic conversion from lower to uppercase occurs. Normally, CAPS mode is on when you're editing COBOL and other types of source files. The only times you would normally deactivate CAPS mode is when you're entering text data like program documentation or when you're creating program literals that require lowercase letters.

Whether or not CAPS mode is on, you can convert specific lines of data from uppercase to lowercase or from lowercase to uppercase using the LC and UC line commands. LC converts all the characters on the line where it's specified to lowercase letters. UC converts all the characters on a line to uppercase letters. To convert a block of lines, enter the number of lines following the LC or UC command or enter LCLC or UCUC on the first and last lines you want to convert. The setting of CAPS mode is not affected by these commands.

PACK mode   PACK mode determines whether data is stored in compressed format. If PACK mode is on, the editor automatically compresses the data when you save it. The advantage of using compressed format is that it saves space. A disadvantage is that compressed data requires additional processing when it's read or written. Unless space management is a high priority in your shop, you'll want to turn PACK mode off.

AUTOSAVE mode   I mentioned in the last topic that when you end an edit session using the End key (PF3/15), which executes the END command, the modifications you've made are saved automatically only if AUTOSAVE mode is on. Since you'll almost always want to save the modifications you've made, you'll want to set AUTOSAVE mode on. To do that, enter the command

AUTOSAVE ON

or just

AUTOSAVE

since ON is the default.

If for some reason you want to turn AUTOSAVE mode off, enter the command

AUTOSAVE OFF PROMPT

or just

AUTOSAVE OFF

If you enter one of these commands then try to end an edit session after changing the source member, the editor notifies you that the member was changed. At that point, you can either enter a SAVE command to save the changes before ending the session, you can enter a CANCEL command to end the session without saving the changes, or you can enter an AUTOSAVE ON command so that when you end the edit session, the changes are saved automatically.

You can also enter the command

AUTOSAVE OFF NOPROMPT

to turn AUTOSAVE mode off. But if you do, edit doesn't let you know if any changes were made when you end the edit session. Instead, it just ends the edit session without saving the changes. Since you can easily lose work this way without knowing it, I recommend you never use NOPROMPT. So if you need to turn AUTOSAVE mode off, use AUTOSAVE OFF PROMPT.

NOTES mode   NOTES mode determines whether notes are displayed when you insert an edit model into the member you're editing. Since I don't cover edit models in this book, I won't say any more about NOTES mode.

IMACRO mode   The IMACRO command specifies the name of an *initial macro* that's saved in the edit profile. For example, if you enter a command like this:

```
IMACRO COBMAC
```

the macro named COBMAC is saved in the current edit profile. Then, the macro is executed every time you edit a member that uses that profile. If you specify an initial macro then decide you don't want it saved in the edit profile, enter this command:

```
IMACRO NONE
```

Then, no initial macro is associated with the edit profile. The use of edit macros is beyond the scope of this book, however. If you want to learn how to create an edit macro, get a copy of *Part 2: Commands and Procedures.*

DISCUSSION

With the exception of TABS mode, most of the features I presented in this topic are useful only for special applications. As a result, you don't have to study every detail in this topic. Using hardware and logical tabs, however, can save you a lot of time. So I suggest you start using the TABS commands right away.

Terms

edit profile	tab character
edit mode	attribute byte
tab stop	boundary
hardware tab	edit mask
logical tab	line number

sequence number
modification flag
recovery data set
initial macro

Objectives

1. Explain the function of the edit profile.

2. Explain the difference between logical tabbing and hardware tabbing.

3. Use the commands described in this text to modify profile settings for:

    a. locking a profile
    b. tabs
    c. boundaries
    d. masks
    e. line numbers
    f. statistics
    g. null characters
    h. automatic printing
    i. recovery
    j. hexadecimal display
    k. upper and lowercase characters
    l. packed decimal data
    m. automatic saving
    n. initial macros

Topic 3 Advanced edit operations

In the first topic of this chapter, I presented the basics of using edit. This topic builds on that base. Here, I present edit commands that let you do more sophisticated editing.

The FIND and CHANGE commands

Two editing commands, FIND and CHANGE, have nearly identical formats. Both of these commands are shown in figure 4-24. The operation of the FIND command under edit is the same as under browse, with the exception of the X/NX and range options. I'll explain the range option in a minute. I'll explain the X/NX option when I show you how to exclude lines later in this topic.

You use the CHANGE command to find a character string and replace it with another string. The only difference between the format of this command and the FIND command is that you specify two strings for a CHANGE command, while a FIND command requires only one string. Since you already know how to use FIND, the rest of this section describes CHANGE.

The basic operation of the CHANGE command proceeds in two phases. First, edit locates an occurrence of string-1 just as if it executed a FIND command. Second, edit changes the located text to string-2. For example, this command:

```
CHANGE ABC DEF
```

locates the string *ABC* and changes it to *DEF*.

Normally, you don't have to use quotes or apostrophes to enclose strings in a CHANGE command. However, if a string contains spaces, commas, quotes, or apostrophes, or if the string is the same as a keyword (like ALL), you must enclose it in quotes or apostrophes. If the string contains an apostrophe, enclose it in quotes, like this:

```
"VALUE 'TOTAL' "
```

The FIND/CHANGE command

$$\left\{\begin{matrix} \text{FIND} \\ \text{CHANGE} \end{matrix}\right\} \quad \text{string-1} \;\; [\text{string-2}] \;\; [\text{range}] \;\; [\left\{\begin{matrix} \underline{\text{NEXT}} \\ \text{PREV} \\ \text{FIRST} \\ \text{LAST} \\ \text{ALL} \end{matrix}\right\}] \;\; [\left\{\begin{matrix} \text{CHARS} \\ \text{PREFIX} \\ \text{SUFFIX} \\ \text{WORD} \end{matrix}\right\}]$$

$$[\left\{\begin{matrix} \text{X} \\ \text{NX} \end{matrix}\right\}] \quad [\text{col-1} \; [\text{col-2}]]$$

Explanation

FIND	Look for string-1 in the text.
CHANGE	Look for string-1 in the text and, if found, replace it with string-2.
string-1	The text string to be found. Must be in apostrophes or quotes if it contains spaces or commas. May be a hex string in the form X'hex-digits', a text string in the form T'text-string', or a picture string in the form P'picture-string'.
string-2	The replacement value for string-1. Must be in apostrophes or quotes if it contains spaces or commas. May be a hex value in the form H'hex-digits'. Valid only for CHANGE.
range	A range of lines identified by two labels. The default range is the first and last lines of the file.
NEXT	Start search at current line and locate the next occurrence of string-1. This is the default.
PREV	Start search at current line and locate the previous occurrence of string-1 (search backwards).
FIRST	Start search at top of data and locate the first occurrence of string-1.
LAST	Start search at bottom of data and locate the last occurrence of string-1 (search backwards).
ALL	Same as FIRST, but also indicate a count of the occurrences of string-1 in the file.

Figure 4-24   The FIND/CHANGE command (part 1 of 2)

Explanation, continued

CHARS	Any occurrence of string-1 satisfies the search. This is the default.
PREFIX	String-1 must be at the beginning of a word to satisfy the search.
SUFFIX	String-1 must be at the end of a word to satisfy the search.
WORD	String-1 must be surrounded by spaces or special characters to satisfy the search.
X NX	Controls the search of excluded lines. X says to search only excluded lines; NX says to search only lines that are not excluded. If neither X nor NX is coded, all lines, excluded or not, are searched.
col-1	Starting column number. If col-2 is *not* specified, string-1 must begin in this column to satisfy the search. Default value is the current left boundary.
col-2	Ending column number. If specified, string-1 must be found between col-1 and col-2 to satisfy the search. Default value is the current right boundary.

Figure 4-24   The FIND/CHANGE command (part 2 of 2)

Here, the string is VALUE 'TOTAL'. Likewise, if the string contains quotes, enclose it in apostrophes, like this:

```
'VALUE  "TOTAL "'
```

Here, the string is VALUE "TOTAL". If you don't use quotes or apostrophes, the end of the string is marked by a space or comma.

How to specify a search range   By default, the range of a search operation is the entire source member. However, you can limit the search to a specific range of lines by including the range option on the CHANGE command. To specify a range, enter the labels you've assigned to the first and last line you want to search. For example, the command

```
CHANGE ABC DEF .BEGIN .END
```

searches all the lines between and including the lines you assigned the .BEGIN and .END labels.

How to change the search direction   You can change the search direction of a CHANGE command by specifying PREV, FIRST,

LAST, or ALL. PREV means to search backwards; FIRST means start at the top of the data and search forwards; and LAST means start at the bottom of the data and search backwards. If you specify ALL on a CHANGE command, all occurrences of string-1 in the entire source member are changed to string-2. To illustrate, consider figure 4-25. Here, all occurrences of GTL- are changed to GL-. Part 1 of figure 4-25 shows the edit display before the CHANGE command executes, while part 2 shows the effect of the CHANGE command. As you can see, five lines have been changed. Each is marked by ==CHG> in the line command area. That makes it easy to verify that your CHANGE command worked as you intended.

As this example shows, the CHANGE command doesn't require that string-1 and string-2 be the same length. If they aren't, edit automatically adjusts the source line so that the change is made correctly. Figure 4-26 shows some more examples of changes involving strings of different lengths. If you'll study this figure for a moment, you'll see that edit shifts the text left or right to make up for any difference in string length. However, this shifting occurs only within the word or words directly affected by the change. Edit doesn't shift data that isn't directly affected by the change unless necessary. As a result, column alignments are often, but not always, maintained.

How to specify a match condition, column limitations, or a string type   You can specify a match condition for string-1 by specifying that string-1 must be a separate word (WORD), the start of a word (PREFIX), or the end of a word (SUFFIX). You can also specify column limitations to say what columns are searched for string-1. The default values for the column limitations are the current column boundaries. You can code either string as a hex value, and you can also code string-1 as a text or picture string. Chapter 3 describes each of these options in detail, so I won't describe them again here.

How to exclude lines

There are two ways you can exclude lines from a display. First, you can use a set of line commands. Second, you can use the EXCLUDE primary command. Note that when you use either of these methods to exclude lines, the lines aren't removed from the source member. They just aren't displayed.

Part 1:

The CHANGE
command specifies
the text change

```
EDIT ---- DLOWE.TEST.COBOL(MKTG1200) - 01.01 --------------- COLUMNS 007 078
COMMAND ===> CHANGE GTL- GL- ALL                           SCROLL ===> PAGE
016300        05  FILLER              PIC XX      VALUE SPACE.
016400        05  BL-CHANGE-AMOUNT    PIC Z,ZZZ,ZZ9.99-.
016500        05  FILLER              PIC X       VALUE SPACE.
016600        05  BL-CHANGE-PERCENT   PIC ZZZ9-.
016700        05  BL-CHANGE-PERCENT-R REDEFINES BL-CHANGE-PERCENT
016800                                PIC X(5).
016900 *
017000 01  GRAND-TOTAL-LINE.
017100 *
017200        05  FILLER              PIC X(66)   VALUE SPACE.
017300        05  FILLER              PIC X(14)   VALUE 'GRAND TOTALS:'.
017400        05  GTL-SALES-THIS-YTD  PIC ZZZ,ZZZ,ZZ9.99-.
017500        05  GTL-SALES-LAST-YTD  PIC ZZZ,ZZZ,ZZ9.99-.
017600        05  GTL-CHANGE-AMOUNT   PIC ZZZ,ZZZ,ZZ9.99-.
017700        05  FILLER              PIC X       VALUE SPACE.
017800        05  GTL-CHANGE-PERCENT  PIC ZZZ9-.
017900        05  GTL-CHANGE-PERCENT-R REDEFINES GTL-CHANGE-PERCENT
018000                                PIC X(5).
018100 *
018200    PROCEDURE DIVISION.
018300 *
018400    000-PRODUCE-SALES-REPORT.
```

Part 2:

When you press the
Enter key, edit
changes the text

```
EDIT ---- DLOWE.TEST.COBOL(MKTG1200) - 01.01 ------------ CHARS 'GTL-' CHANGED
COMMAND ===>                                               SCROLL ===> PAGE
016300        05  FILLER              PIC XX      VALUE SPACE.
016400        05  BL-CHANGE-AMOUNT    PIC Z,ZZZ,ZZ9.99-.
016500        05  FILLER              PIC X       VALUE SPACE.
016600        05  BL-CHANGE-PERCENT   PIC ZZZ9-.
016700        05  BL-CHANGE-PERCENT-R REDEFINES BL-CHANGE-PERCENT
016800                                PIC X(5).
016900 *
017000 01  GRAND-TOTAL-LINE.
017100 *
017200        05  FILLER              PIC X(66)   VALUE SPACE.
017300        05  FILLER              PIC X(14)   VALUE 'GRAND TOTALS:'.
==CHG>        05  GL-SALES-THIS-YTD   PIC ZZZ,ZZZ,ZZ9.99-.
==CHG>        05  GL-SALES-LAST-YTD   PIC ZZZ,ZZZ,ZZ9.99-.
==CHG>        05  GL-CHANGE-AMOUNT    PIC ZZZ,ZZZ,ZZ9.99-.
017700        05  FILLER              PIC X       VALUE SPACE.
==CHG>        05  GL-CHANGE-PERCENT   PIC ZZZ9-.
==CHG>        05  GL-CHANGE-PERCENT-R REDEFINES GL-CHANGE-PERCENT
018000                                PIC X(5).
018100 *
018200    PROCEDURE DIVISION.
018300 *
018400    000-PRODUCE-SALES-REPORT.
```

Figure 4-25 Using the CHANGE command

String-1	String-2	Text change
BF-ITEM-NO	BF-ITEM-DESCR	Before: 05 BF-ITEM-NO PIC X(20). After: 05 BF-ITEM-DESCR PIC X(20). Before: MOVE BF-ITEM-NO TO WS-ITEM. After: MOVE BF-ITEM-DESCR TO WS-ITEM.
BF-ITEM-DESCR	BF-ITEM-NO	Before: 05 BF-ITEM-DESCR PIC X(20). After: 05 BF-ITEM-NO PIC X(20). Before: MOVE BF-ITEM-DESCR TO WS-ITEM. After: MOVE BF-ITEM-NO TO WS-ITEM.

Figure 4-26   Changes involving strings of different lengths

Excluded lines are sometimes useful when you have many similar lines of source text, such as a long series of MOVE statements or individual field descriptions within a record description. By excluding these lines, you can display and edit the text that surrounds these lines without unnecessary scrolling.

Line commands for excluding and redisplaying lines   You use the group of line commands shown in figure 4-27 to exclude a line or a group of lines from the display. To illustrate, consider figure 4-28. In part 1 of this figure, I coded two XX commands to exclude the individual fields of a record description. Part 2 shows the display after edit excluded the lines. As you can see, edit replaces the entire group of lines with a single line that indicates how many lines it excluded from the display.

You can process the line that displays in place of excluded lines with most of the line commands you already know. For example, if you delete it with a D command, edit deletes all the excluded lines. If you copy, move, or repeat it with a C, M, or R command, edit copies, moves, or repeats all the excluded lines.

To redisplay all or a portion of the excluded text, you use an F, L, or S command. The F command redisplays a line or lines starting at the beginning of the excluded lines, while L starts at the

Command	Meaning
X	Exclude this line.
Xn	Exclude n lines.
XX	Exclude this line and all lines between the two XX commands.
F	Show the first line of the excluded text.
Fn	Show the first n lines.
L	Show the last line of the excluded text.
Ln	Show the last n lines.
S	Show one line of the excluded text.
Sn	Show n lines.

Figure 4-27   Line commands for excluding and redisplaying source lines

end of the excluded lines. For example, if you exclude lines 2010, 2020, and 2030, then enter F2, edit redisplays lines 2010 and 2020. On the other hand, if you enter L2, edit redisplays lines 2020 and 2030.

The S command selects lines to redisplay by checking the indentation level of the text. S always redisplays those lines with the leftmost indentation. Figure 4-29 shows how the S command works. In part 1, I excluded 16 lines of Procedure Division code from the display. Part 2 shows the S command I entered to redisplay part of the excluded lines. Part 3 shows the redisplayed text.

The S command checks for indentation by scanning the source text from left to right until it finds a non-blank character. In a COBOL program, that means comment lines are usually the first to be redisplayed because the S command finds an asterisk in column 7 first. That's good if the comment lines contain text. But if the comments are blank, it doesn't help much to redisplay them. So when you use the S command, remember that blank comment lines rather than important program lines may be selected for redisplay.

Part 1:

The XX line commands mark the first and last lines to be excluded

```
EDIT ---- DLOWE.TEST.COBOL(MKTG1200) - 01.01 ------------------ COLUMNS 007 078
COMMAND ===>                                                 SCROLL ===> PAGE
009800 *
009900  01  HEADING-LINE-4.
XX            *
010100      05  FILLER      PIC X(20)    VALUE 'BRANCH   SALESMAN   SA'.
010200      05  FILLER      PIC X(20)    VALUE 'LESMAN                '.
010300      05  FILLER      PIC X(20)    VALUE '     CUSTOMER   CUSTO'.
010400      05  FILLER      PIC X(20)    VALUE 'MER                   '.
010500      05  FILLER      PIC X(20)    VALUE '        SALES        '.
010600      05  FILLER      PIC X(20)    VALUE '   SALES             '.
XX            05  FILLER      PIC X(12)    VALUE 'ANGE   CHANGE'.
010800 *
010900  01  HEADING-LINE-5.
011000 *
011100      05  FILLER      PIC X(20)    VALUE '  NO         NO      NA'.
011200      05  FILLER      PIC X(20)    VALUE 'ME                    '.
011300      05  FILLER      PIC X(20)    VALUE '      NO      NAME    '.
011400      05  FILLER      PIC X(20)    VALUE '                      '.
011500      05  FILLER      PIC X(20)    VALUE '     THIS YTD        '.
011600      05  FILLER      PIC X(20)    VALUE ' LAST YTD         AM'.
011700      05  FILLER      PIC X(12)    VALUE 'OUNT     %'.
011800 *
011900  01  CUSTOMER-LINE.
```

Part 2:

When you press the Enter key, edit displays a message instead of the lines

```
EDIT ---- DLOWE.TEST.COBOL(MKTG1200) - 01.01 ------------------ COLUMNS 007 078
COMMAND ===>                                                 SCROLL ===> PAGE
009800 *
009900  01  HEADING-LINE-4.
- - - - - - - - - - - - - - - - - - - - - - 8 LINE(S) NOT DISPLAYED
010800 *
010900  01  HEADING-LINE-5.
011000 *
011100      05  FILLER      PIC X(20)    VALUE '  NO         NO      NA'.
011200      05  FILLER      PIC X(20)    VALUE 'ME                    '.
011300      05  FILLER      PIC X(20)    VALUE '      NO      NAME    '.
011400      05  FILLER      PIC X(20)    VALUE '                      '.
011500      05  FILLER      PIC X(20)    VALUE '     THIS YTD        '.
011600      05  FILLER      PIC X(20)    VALUE ' LAST YTD         AM'.
011700      05  FILLER      PIC X(12)    VALUE 'OUNT     %'.
011800 *
011900  01  CUSTOMER-LINE.
012000 *
012100      05  FILLER           PIC XX       VALUE SPACE.
012200      05  CL-BRANCH-NO     PIC XX.
012300      05  FILLER           PIC X(7)     VALUE SPACE.
012400      05  CL-SALESMAN-NO   PIC XX.
012500      05  FILLER           PIC X(5)     VALUE SPACE.
012600      05  CL-SALESMAN-NAME PIC X(25).
```

Figure 4-28   Excluding lines

Part 1:

The XX line commands mark the lines to be excluded

```
EDIT ---- DLOWE.TEST.COBOL(MKTG1200) - 01.01 ----------------- COLUMNS 007 078
COMMAND ===>                                                  SCROLL ===> PAGE
021400              MOVE CM-SALESMAN-KEY TO OLD-SALESMAN-KEY
021500              MOVE 'N'              TO FIRST-RECORD-SW
021600          ELSE
XX                  IF CM-SALESMAN-KEY NOT GREATER OLD-SALESMAN-KEY
021800              PERFORM 220-PRINT-CUSTOMER-LINE
021900              PERFORM 280-ACCUMULATE-SALES-TOTALS
022000              ELSE
022100                  IF CM-BRANCH-NUMBER GREATER OLD-BRANCH-NUMBER
022200                      PERFORM 290-PRINT-SALESMAN-TOTAL-LINE
022300                      PERFORM 300-PRINT-BRANCH-TOTAL-LINE
022400                      PERFORM 220-PRINT-CUSTOMER-LINE
022500                      PERFORM 280-ACCUMULATE-SALES-TOTALS
022600                      MOVE CM-SALESMAN-KEY TO OLD-SALESMAN-KEY
022700                  ELSE
022800                      PERFORM 290-PRINT-SALESMAN-TOTAL-LINE
022900                      PERFORM 220-PRINT-CUSTOMER-LINE
023000                      PERFORM 280-ACCUMULATE-SALES-TOTALS
023100                      MOVE CM-SALESMAN-NUMBER
XX                              TO OLD-SALESMAN-NUMBER
023300          ELSE      PERFORM 290-PRINT-SALESMAN-TOTAL-LINE
023400          PERFORM 290-PRINT-SALESMAN-TOTAL-LINE
023500          PERFORM 300-PRINT-BRANCH-TOTAL-LINE.
```

Part 2:

The S line command tells how many lines to redisplay

```
EDIT ---- DLOWE.TEST.COBOL(MKTG1200) - 01.01 ----------------- COLUMNS 007 078
COMMAND ===>                                                  SCROLL ===> PAGE
021400              MOVE CM-SALESMAN-KEY TO OLD-SALESMAN-KEY
021500              MOVE 'N'              TO FIRST-RECORD-SW
021600          ELSE
S6    - - - - - - - - - - - - - - - - 16 LINE(S) NOT DISPLAYED
023300          ELSE
023400              PERFORM 290-PRINT-SALESMAN-TOTAL-LINE
023500              PERFORM 300-PRINT-BRANCH-TOTAL-LINE.
023600 *
023700  210-READ-CUSTOMER-RECORD.
023800 *
023900      READ CUSTMST
024000          AT END
024100              MOVE 'Y' TO CUSTOMER-EOF-SW.
024200 *
024300  220-PRINT-CUSTOMER-LINE.
024400 *
024500      IF FIRST-RECORD
024600          MOVE CM-BRANCH-NUMBER   TO CL-BRANCH-NO
024700          MOVE CM-SALESMAN-NUMBER TO CL-SALESMAN-NO
024800          MOVE CM-SALESMAN-KEY    TO SM-SALESMAN-KEY
024900          MOVE 'Y'                TO RECORD-FOUND-SW
025000          PERFORM 230-READ-SALESMAN-RECORD
```

Figure 4-29 Redisplaying excluded lines

Part 3:

When you press the
Enter key, edit
redisplays the six
lines with the leftmost
indentation

```
EDIT ---- DLOWE.TEST.COBOL(MKTG1Z00) - 01.01 ------------------ COLUMNS 007 078
COMMAND ===>                                                    SCROLL ===> PAGE
021400              MOVE CM-SALESMAN-KEY TO OLD-SALESMAN-KEY
021500              MOVE 'N'             TO FIRST-RECORD-SW
021600          ELSE
021700              IF CM-SALESMAN-KEY NOT GREATER OLD-SALESMAN-KEY
021800                  PERFORM 220-PRINT-CUSTOMER-LINE
021900                  PERFORM 280-ACCUMULATE-SALES-TOTALS
022000              ELSE
022100                  IF CM-BRANCH-NUMBER GREATER OLD-BRANCH-NUMBER
- - - - - - - - - - - - - - - - - - - - - - 5 LINE(S) NOT DISPLAYED
022700                  ELSE
- - - - - - - - - - - - - - - - - - - - - - 5 LINE(S) NOT DISPLAYED
023300          ELSE
023400              PERFORM 290-PRINT-SALESMAN-TOTAL-LINE
023500              PERFORM 300-PRINT-BRANCH-TOTAL-LINE.
023600 *
023700  210-READ-CUSTOMER-RECORD.
023800 *
023900      READ CUSTMST
024000          AT END
024100              MOVE 'Y' TO CUSTOMER-EOF-SW.
024200 *
024300  220-PRINT-CUSTOMER-LINE.
```

Figure 4-29   Redisplaying excluded lines (continued)

You can also use a RESET command to redisplay excluded
lines. Simply enter RESET EXCLUDED and edit redisplays all the
excluded lines.

The EXCLUDE primary command   You use the EXCLUDE
primary command to locate lines that contain a specific character
string and exclude them from the display. As you can see in figure
4-30, the EXCLUDE command is almost identical to the FIND
command. The only difference is that the X/NX option isn't available with EXCLUDE.

When you enter an EXCLUDE command, edit searches for lines
that contain the string you specify. When it finds a line, it excludes
it from the display. So the command

```
EXCLUDE ABC ALL
```

excludes all the lines that contain the characters *ABC*.

How to use FIND and CHANGE with excluded lines   When I
presented the FIND and CHANGE commands earlier in this topic, I

The EXCLUDE command

$$\text{EXCLUDE string-1 [range] } \left[\left\{ \begin{array}{l} \text{NEXT} \\ \text{PREV} \\ \text{FIRST} \\ \text{LAST} \\ \text{ALL} \end{array} \right\} \right] \left[\left\{ \begin{array}{l} \text{CHARS} \\ \text{PREFIX} \\ \text{SUFFIX} \\ \text{WORD} \end{array} \right\} \right] \text{ [col-1 [col-2]]}$$

Explanation

string-1	The text string to be found. Must be in apostrophes or quotes if it contains spaces or commas. May be a hex string in the form X'hex-digits', a text string in the form T'text-string', or a picture string in the form P'picture-string'.
range	A range of lines identified by two labels. The default range is the first and last lines of the file.
NEXT	Start search at current line and locate the next occurrence of string-1. This is the default.
PREV	Start search at current line and locate the previous occurrence of string-1 (search backwards).
FIRST	Start search at top of data and locate the first occurrence of string-1.
LAST	Start search at bottom of data and locate the last occurrence of string-1 (search backwards).
ALL	Same as FIRST, but also indicate a count of the occurrences of string-1 in the file.
CHARS	Any occurrence of string-1 satisfies the search. This is the default.
PREFIX	String-1 must be at the beginning of a word to satisfy the search.
SUFFIX	String-1 must be at the end of a word to satisfy the search.
WORD	String-1 must be surrounded by spaces or special characters to satisfy the search.
col-1	Starting column number. If col-2 is *not* specified, string-1 must begin in this column to satisfy the search. Default value is the current left boundary.
col-2	Ending column number. If specified, string-1 must be found between col-1 and col-2 to satisfy the search. Default value is the current right boundary.

Figure 4-30   The EXCLUDE command

Part 1:

The EXCLUDE ALL command specifies that all lines are to be excluded

```
EDIT ---- DLOWE.TEST.COBOL(MKTG1Z00) - 01.01 ----------------- COLUMNS 007 078
COMMAND ===> EXCLUDE ALL                                        SCROLL ===> PAGE
010800 *
010900  01   HEADING-LINE-5.
011000 *
011100       05  FILLER      PIC X(Z0)   VALUE '  NO        NO      NA'.
011200       05  FILLER      PIC X(Z0)   VALUE 'ME                    '.
011300       05  FILLER      PIC X(Z0)   VALUE '        NO      NAME  '.
011400       05  FILLER      PIC X(Z0)   VALUE '                     '.
011500       05  FILLER      PIC X(Z0)   VALUE '      THIS YTD       '.
011600       05  FILLER      PIC X(Z0)   VALUE ' LAST YTD        AM'.
011700       05  FILLER      PIC X(1Z)   VALUE 'OUNT    %'.
011800 *
011900  01   CUSTOMER-LINE.
012000 *
012100       05  FILLER          PIC XX      VALUE SPACE.
012200       05  CL-BRANCH-NO     PIC XX.
012300       05  FILLER          PIC X(7)    VALUE SPACE.
012400       05  CL-SALESMAN-NO   PIC XX.
012500       05  FILLER          PIC X(5)    VALUE SPACE.
012600       05  CL-SALESMAN-NAME PIC X(Z5).
012700       05  FILLER          PIC X(4)    VALUE SPACE.
012800       05  CL-CUSTOMER-NO   PIC ZZZZ9.
012900       05  FILLER          PIC XXX     VALUE SPACE.
```

Figure 4-31   Using the EXCLUDE command

mentioned that you use the X/NX option with excluded lines. If you specify X on a FIND or CHANGE command, only excluded lines are searched. If you say NX, only the lines that are *not* excluded are searched. If you don't say X or NX, all the source member's lines, excluded or not, are searched by the FIND or CHANGE command.

FIND and CHANGE are also useful if you want to exclude all the lines in a member that *don't* contain a particular character string. To do that, enter the EXCLUDE ALL command. When you do, edit excludes every line in the member from the display. Next, enter a FIND or CHANGE command. Then, all the lines that contain the character string you specify are redisplayed.

To illustrate, consider figure 4-31. In part 1, I entered the EXCLUDE ALL command and edit excluded all the lines from the display, as you can see in part 2 of the figure. Then, I entered this FIND command:

```
FIND 01 ALL
```

Part 2:

When you press the
Enter key, edit
excludes all the lines;
the FIND command
specifies the lines you
want to redisplay

```
EDIT ---- DLOWE.TEST.COBOL(MKTG1200) - 01.01 ------------------ COLUMNS 007 078
COMMAND ===> FIND 01 ALL                                    SCROLL ===> PAGE
****** **********************************  TOP OF DATA  ******************************
- - - - - - - - - - - - - - - - - - - -  410 LINE(S) NOT DISPLAYED
****** **********************************  BOTTOM OF DATA  ***************************
```

Part 3:

When you press the
Enter key, edit
displays all the lines
containing 01

```
EDIT ---- DLOWE.TEST.COBOL(MKTG1200) - 01.01 ------------------- 16 CHARS '01'
COMMAND ===>                                                SCROLL ===> PAGE
****** **********************************  TOP OF DATA  ******************************
- - - - - - - - - - - - - - - - - - - - - - 36 LINE(S) NOT DISPLAYED
003700  01  PRINT-AREA.
- - - - - - - - - - - - - - - - - - - - - -  5 LINE(S) NOT DISPLAYED
004300  01  SWITCHES.
- - - - - - - - - - - - - - - - - - - - - -  8 LINE(S) NOT DISPLAYED
005200  01  CONTROL-FIELDS.
- - - - - - - - - - - - - - - - - - - - - -  5 LINE(S) NOT DISPLAYED
005800  01  WORK-FIELDS        COMP-3.
- - - - - - - - - - - - - - - - - - - - - -  4 LINE(S) NOT DISPLAYED
006300  01  PRINT-FIELDS.
- - - - - - - - - - - - - - - - - - - - - -  6 LINE(S) NOT DISPLAYED
007000  01  TOTAL-FIELDS       COMP-3.
- - - - - - - - - - - - - - - - - - - - - -  8 LINE(S) NOT DISPLAYED
007900  01  DATE-FIELDS.
- - - - - - - - - - - - - - - - - - - - - -  3 LINE(S) NOT DISPLAYED
008300  01  NEXT-REPORT-LINE   PIC X(132).
- - - - - - - - - - - - - - - - - - - - - -  1 LINE(S) NOT DISPLAYED
008500  01  COMPANY-NAME.
- - - - - - - - - - - - - - - - - - - - - -  5 LINE(S) NOT DISPLAYED
009100  01  REPORT-TITLE.
- - - - - - - - - - - - - - - - - - - - - -  7 LINE(S) NOT DISPLAYED
```

Figure 4-31   Using the EXCLUDE command (continued)

The DELETE command

```
DELETE  [ALL] [range] [{ X  }]
                       { NX }
```

Explanation

ALL   Delete all lines that are within the specified range or are excluded or not
                excluded. You cannot specify ALL by itself.

range   A range of lines identified by two labels. The default range is the first and last
                lines of the file.

X   Delete only excluded lines.

NX   Delete only non-excluded lines.

Note: You must specify ALL or range, and you cannot specify ALL by itself.

Figure 4-32   The DELETE command

In part 3, you can see that edit redisplayed all the lines that contain
the characters 01. In other words, all the lines that don't contain
the characters 01 are excluded from the display.

How to delete excluded lines   In topic 1 of this chapter, you
learned how to delete lines using the DELETE line command. You
can also delete lines using the DELETE primary command. The
format of this command is presented in figure 4-32.

   With the DELETE primary command, you can delete all
excluded or non-excluded lines. For example, suppose you want to
delete all lines that contain the string PRODUCT-TOTAL. To do
that, you could enter this sequence of commands:

```
EXCLUDE ALL
FIND PRODUCT-TOTAL ALL
DELETE ALL NX
```

Here, the EXCLUDE and FIND commands exclude the entire file,
then display the lines to be deleted. Then, the DELETE command
deletes all the displayed lines.

You can also code a range on the DELETE primary command. However, because it's easier to delete a range of lines using the DELETE line command, you probably won't use the range option often. If you want to code a range option, you code it just like you do on a FIND or CHANGE command.

How to locate a line by its type

In chapter 3, you learned how to use the LOCATE command with browse to position the display at a known point in the file. In edit, you can also use LOCATE to position the display at a particular type of line. Figure 4-33 presents the format of the LOCATE command for locating a line by its type. As you can see, you can specify a search direction and a range of lines just like you can for the FIND, CHANGE, and EXCLUDE commands. The other option you specify determines the type of line you want to search for.

The type options you can specify are CHANGE, LABEL, EXCLUDED, ERROR, COMMAND, and SPECIAL. CHANGE searches for a line that contains the characters ==CHG> in the line command area. LABEL searches for a line with a label. EXCLUDED searches for an excluded line. ERROR searches for a line that contains the characters ==ERR> in the line command area. The editor adds these characters to a line when an error occurs during the processing of an edit command. COMMAND searches for a line that has a pending line command. For example, the C line command is pending until you specify the destination for the copy. SPECIAL searches for special lines that aren't part of the source member, such as the lines that are displayed as a result of issuing the PROFILE command.

To illustrate how this form of the LOCATE command works, consider figure 4-34. In part 1 of this figure, I entered this command:

    LOCATE CHANGE

Then, in part 2 of the figure, the first line that contains the characters ==CHG> is at the top of the display. This is the form of the LOCATE command you'll probably use most often.

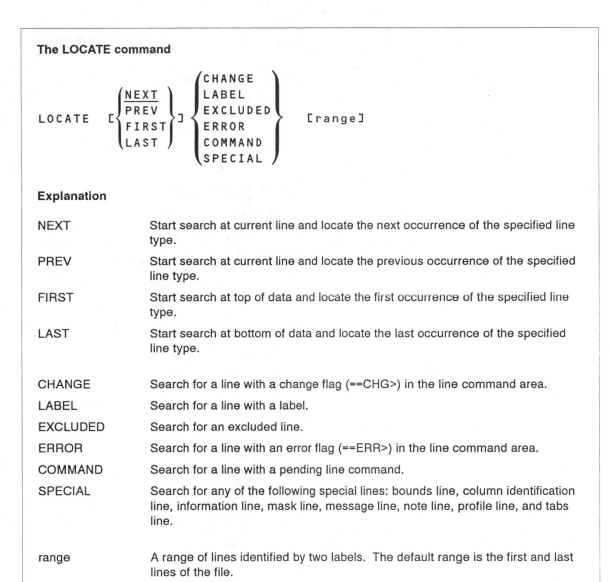

The LOCATE command

LOCATE   [{ NEXT / PREV / FIRST / LAST }] { CHANGE / LABEL / EXCLUDED / ERROR / COMMAND / SPECIAL }   [range]

Explanation

NEXT	Start search at current line and locate the next occurrence of the specified line type.
PREV	Start search at current line and locate the previous occurrence of the specified line type.
FIRST	Start search at top of data and locate the first occurrence of the specified line type.
LAST	Start search at bottom of data and locate the last occurrence of the specified line type.
CHANGE	Search for a line with a change flag (==CHG>) in the line command area.
LABEL	Search for a line with a label.
EXCLUDED	Search for an excluded line.
ERROR	Search for a line with an error flag (==ERR>) in the line command area.
COMMAND	Search for a line with a pending line command.
SPECIAL	Search for any of the following special lines: bounds line, column identification line, information line, mask line, message line, note line, profile line, and tabs line.
range	A range of lines identified by two labels. The default range is the first and last lines of the file.

Figure 4-33   The LOCATE command for locating a line by its type

Part 1:

The LOCATE
command specifies
the type of line to be
located

```
EDIT ---- DLOWE.TEST.COBOL(MKTG1200) - 01.01 ----------------- COLUMNS 007 078
COMMAND ===> LOCATE CHANGE                                     SCROLL ===> PAGE
016300        05  FILLER              PIC XX       VALUE SPACE.
016400        05  BL-CHANGE-AMOUNT    PIC Z,ZZZ,ZZ9.99-.
016500        05  FILLER              PIC X        VALUE SPACE.
016600        05  BL-CHANGE-PERCENT   PIC ZZZ9-.
016700        05  BL-CHANGE-PERCENT-R REDEFINES BL-CHANGE-PERCENT
016800                                PIC X(5).
016900 *
017000  01  GRAND-TOTAL-LINE.
017100 *
017200        05  FILLER              PIC X(66)    VALUE SPACE.
017300        05  FILLER              PIC X(14)    VALUE 'GRAND TOTALS:'.
==CHG>        05  GL-SALES-THIS-YTD   PIC ZZZ,ZZZ,ZZ9.99-.
==CHG>        05  GL-SALES-LAST-YTD   PIC ZZZ,ZZZ,ZZ9.99-.
==CHG>        05  GL-CHANGE-AMOUNT    PIC ZZZ,ZZZ,ZZ9.99-.
017700        05  FILLER              PIC X        VALUE SPACE.
==CHG>        05  GL-CHANGE-PERCENT   PIC ZZZ9-.
==CHG>        05  GL-CHANGE-PERCENT-R REDEFINES GL-CHANGE-PERCENT
018000                                PIC X(5).
018100 *
018200  PROCEDURE DIVISION.
018300 *
018400  000-PRODUCE-SALES-REPORT.
```

Part 2:

When you press the
Enter key, edit scrolls
to the specified type of
line

```
EDIT ---- DLOWE.TEST.COBOL(MKTG1200) - 01.01 ----------------- COLUMNS 007 078
COMMAND ===>                                                  SCROLL ===> PAGE
==CHG>        05  GL-SALES-THIS-YTD   PIC ZZZ,ZZZ,ZZ9.99-.
==CHG>        05  GL-SALES-LAST-YTD   PIC ZZZ,ZZZ,ZZ9.99-.
==CHG>        05  GL-CHANGE-AMOUNT    PIC ZZZ,ZZZ,ZZ9.99-.
017700        05  FILLER              PIC X        VALUE SPACE.
==CHG>        05  GL-CHANGE-PERCENT   PIC ZZZ9-.
==CHG>        05  GL-CHANGE-PERCENT-R REDEFINES GL-CHANGE-PERCENT
018000                                PIC X(5).
018100 *
018200  PROCEDURE DIVISION.
018300 *
018400  000-PRODUCE-SALES-REPORT.
018500 *
018600        OPEN INPUT  CUSTMST
018700                    SALESMN
018800             OUTPUT SALESRPT.
018900        PERFORM 100-FORMAT-REPORT-HEADING.
019000        PERFORM 200-PRODUCE-SALES-REPORT-LINES
019100             UNTIL CUSTOMER-EOF.
019200        PERFORM 400-PRINT-GRAND-TOTAL-LINE.
019300        CLOSE CUSTMST
019400              SALESMN
019500              SALESRPT.
```

Figure 4-34   The LOCATE command as it's used to locate a changed line

Data shift command	Column shift command	Meaning
<	(	Shift this line left 2 positions.
<n	(n	Shift this line left n positions.
<<	((	Shift a block of lines left 2 positions.
<<n	((n	Shift a block of lines left n positions.
>	)	Shift this line right 2 positions.
>n	)n	Shift this line right n positions.
>>	))	Shift a block of lines right 2 positions.
>>n	))n	Shift a block of lines right n positions.

Figure 4-35 Line commands for shifting data

How to shift source text

You use the group of commands shown in figure 4-35 to shift the contents of a line or group of lines one or more positions to the left or right. A common use for the shift commands is to change the indentation level of a group of source statements. In many cases, it's easier to use the 3270 Delete and Insert keys to shift data left or right. But when many lines of data are involved, the shift commands can be a real time-saver.

Edit provides two types of shift operations: column and data. When you shift data with a column shift, the data is simply moved a specified number of columns to the left or right. Then, data that is shifted beyond the right or left margin is lost, and spaces are inserted where needed.

A data shift is more complex, because ISPF tries not to lose meaningful data. So when you shift data with a data shift, non-blank characters are never deleted, words are not combined, and spaces within apostrophes are not deleted. Often, the effect of a column and data shift is the same. However, in cases where data might be lost, a data shift displays an error message instead of dropping the data. As a result, I recommend you use data shifting rather than column shifting.

You indicate whether you want a column or a data shift by using a greater-than or less-than sign or a left or right parenthesis.

If you use a greater-than (>) or less-than (<) sign, a data shift is performed. Parentheses cause a column shift.

To shift data on a single line, you use a single shift character. To shift data on multiple lines, you use a pair of shift commands, each consisting of two shift characters, just like other group line commands such as DD, CC, and so on. If you specify a number on the shift command, the data is shifted left or right the number of columns you specify. Otherwise, the data is shifted two columns.

To illustrate shifting, consider figure 4-36. Here, a group of lines is shifted four characters to the right. In part 1, you can see the original data and the shift commands. In part 2, you can see the effect of the shift. Note that when you're shifting a block of code, you specify the number of columns on only one of the shift commands; it doesn't matter which one.

Another thing to note is that a shift command works only within the column boundaries, as shown in figure 4-37. In part 1, you can see the original text, the BNDS line, and the shift command. Part 2 shows the effect of the shift. Notice that data outside the boundaries isn't shifted.

External data sets

Edit provides several options that involve data sets or members other than the one you're editing. You can copy or move lines from another data set or member into the source member you're editing. Or, you can copy or move lines from the member you're editing to create or replace another data set or member. To perform these operations, you use one of the primary commands summarized in figure 4-38 along with the MOVE/COPY line commands you learned in topic 1.

How to copy or move data from an external data set   To move or copy data from a data set or member into the source member you're editing, you use a COPY or MOVE primary command. For example, if you enter this command:

```
COPY CUSTMST
```

Part 1:

The >> line commands
mark the first and last
lines to be shifted right

```
EDIT ---- DLOWE.TEST.COBOL(MKTG1200) - 01.01 ---------------- COLUMNS 007 078
COMMAND ===>                                                  SCROLL ===> PAGE
031400 *
031500  250-PRINT-HEADING-LINES.
031600 *
>>              ADD 1              TO PAGE-COUNT.
031800         MOVE PAGE-COUNT     TO HDG1-PAGE-NUMBER.
031900         MOVE HEADING-LINE-1 TO PRINT-AREA.
032000         PERFORM 260-WRITE-PAGE-TOP-LINE.
032100         MOVE HEADING-LINE-2 TO PRINT-AREA.
032200         MOVE 1              TO SPACE-CONTROL.
032300         PERFORM 270-WRITE-REPORT-LINE.
032400         MOVE HEADING-LINE-3 TO PRINT-AREA.
032500         PERFORM 270-WRITE-REPORT-LINE.
032600         MOVE HEADING-LINE-4 TO PRINT-AREA.
032700         MOVE 2              TO SPACE-CONTROL.
032800         PERFORM 270-WRITE-REPORT-LINE.
032900         MOVE HEADING-LINE-5 TO PRINT-AREA.
033000         MOVE 1              TO SPACE-CONTROL.
033100         PERFORM 270-WRITE-REPORT-LINE.
>>4            MOVE 2              TO SPACE-CONTROL.
033300 *
033400  260-WRITE-PAGE-TOP-LINE.
033500 *
```

Part 2:

When you press the
Enter key, edit shifts
the lines 4 positions to
the right

```
EDIT ---- DLOWE.TEST.COBOL(MKTG1200) - 01.01 ---------------- COLUMNS 007 078
COMMAND ===>                                                  SCROLL ===> PAGE
031400 *
031500  250-PRINT-HEADING-LINES.
031600 *
031700             ADD 1              TO PAGE-COUNT.
031800             MOVE PAGE-COUNT TO HDG1-PAGE-NUMBER.
031900             MOVE HEADING-LINE-1 TO PRINT-AREA.
032000             PERFORM 260-WRITE-PAGE-TOP-LINE.
032100             MOVE HEADING-LINE-2 TO PRINT-AREA.
032200             MOVE 1              TO SPACE-CONTROL.
032300             PERFORM 270-WRITE-REPORT-LINE.
032400             MOVE HEADING-LINE-3 TO PRINT-AREA.
032500             PERFORM 270-WRITE-REPORT-LINE.
032600             MOVE HEADING-LINE-4 TO PRINT-AREA.
032700             MOVE 2              TO SPACE-CONTROL.
032800             PERFORM 270-WRITE-REPORT-LINE.
032900             MOVE HEADING-LINE-5 TO PRINT-AREA.
033000             MOVE 1              TO SPACE-CONTROL.
033100             PERFORM 270-WRITE-REPORT-LINE.
033200             MOVE 2              TO SPACE-CONTROL.
033300 *
033400  260-WRITE-PAGE-TOP-LINE.
033500 *
```

Figure 4-36   Shifting a block of lines

Part 1:

The BNDS line shows
the new column
boundaries; the))
commands mark the
lines to be shifted

```
EDIT ---- DLOWE.TEST.COBOL(MKTG1Z00) - 01.01 ----------------- COLUMNS 007 078
COMMAND ===>                                                   SCROLL ===> PAGE
012000 *
=BNDS>                                   <                                    >
))             05   FILLER               PIC XX        VALUE SPACE.
012200         05   CL-BRANCH-NO          PIC XX.
012300·        05   FILLER               PIC X(7)      VALUE SPACE.
012400         05   CL-SALESMAN-NO        PIC XX.
012500         05   FILLER               PIC X(5)      VALUE SPACE.
012600         05   CL-SALESMAN-NAME      PIC X(25).
012700         05   FILLER               PIC X(4)      VALUE SPACE.
012800         05   CL-CUSTOMER-NO        PIC ZZZZ9.
012900         05   FILLER               PIC XXX       VALUE SPACE.
013000         05   CL-CUSTOMER-NAME      PIC X(25).
013100         05   FILLER               PIC X(5)      VALUE SPACE.
013200         05   CL-SALES-THIS-YTD     PIC ZZ,ZZ9.99-.
013300         05   FILLER               PIC X(5)      VALUE SPACE.
013400         05   CL-SALES-LAST-YTD     PIC ZZ,ZZ9.99-.
013500         05   FILLER               PIC X(5)      VALUE SPACE.
013600         05   CL-CHANGE-AMOUNT      PIC ZZ,ZZ9.99-.
013700         05   FILLER               PIC X         VALUE SPACE.
013800         05   CL-CHANGE-PERCENT     PIC ZZZ9-.
013900         05   CL-CHANGE-PERCENT-R   REDEFINES CL-CHANGE-PERCENT
))4                                       PIC X(5).
```

Part 2:

When you press the
Enter key, edit shifts
only the data within
the boundaries

```
EDIT ---- DLOWE.TEST.COBOL(MKTG1Z00) - 01.01 ----------------- COLUMNS 007 078
COMMAND ===>                                                   SCROLL ===> PAGE
=BNDS>                                   <                                    >
012100         05   FILLER               PIC XX        VALUE SPACE.
012200         05   CL-BRANCH-NO          PIC XX.
012300         05   FILLER               PIC X(7)      VALUE SPACE.
012400         05   CL-SALESMAN-NO        PIC XX.
012500         05   FILLER               PIC X(5)      VALUE SPACE.
012600         05   CL-SALESMAN-NAME      PIC X(25).
012700         05   FILLER               PIC X(4)      VALUE SPACE.
012800         05   CL-CUSTOMER-NO        PIC ZZZZ9.
012900         05   FILLER               PIC XXX       VALUE SPACE.
013000         05   CL-CUSTOMER-NAME      PIC X(25).
013100         05   FILLER               PIC X(5)      VALUE SPACE.
013200         05   CL-SALES-THIS-YTD     PIC ZZ,ZZ9.99-.
013300         05   FILLER               PIC X(5)      VALUE SPACE.
013400         05   CL-SALES-LAST-YTD     PIC ZZ,ZZ9.99-.
013500         05   FILLER               PIC X(5)      VALUE SPACE.
013600         05   CL-CHANGE-AMOUNT      PIC ZZ,ZZ9.99-.
013700         05   FILLER               PIC X         VALUE SPACE.
013800         05   CL-CHANGE-PERCENT     PIC ZZZ9-.
013900         05   CL-CHANGE-PERCENT-R   REDEFINES CL-CHANGE-PERCENT
014000                                    PIC X(5).
014100 *
```

Figure 4-37   Effect of a shift within boundaries

Command	Meaning
COPY [member] [{AFTER BEFORE} label]	Copy the named member to the position marked by an A or B line command or the specified label.
MOVE [member] [{AFTER BEFORE} label]	Copy the named member to the position marked by an A or B line command or the specified label, then delete the member from its original location.
CREATE [member] [range]	Create a new member with the range of lines marked by C or M commands or the specified labels.
REPLACE [member] [range]	Create a new member or replace an existing member with the range of lines marked by C or M commands or the specified labels.

Note: If the member name is omitted from any of these commands, a panel is displayed for entering the data set and member information.

Figure 4-38   Commands used for merging and segmenting data

ISPF searches the library you specified on the edit entry panel to locate the member named CUSTMST. Then, it copies that member into the member you're editing. If you enter this command:

```
MOVE CUSTMST
```

the effect is the same except that CUSTMST is deleted from the library after it's included in the member you're editing.

To indicate where the copied or moved data should be placed, you use an A or B line command. These commands have the same meaning as when they're used for a line copy or move operation. Thus, A means place the data after the line containing the A command; B means place the data before the line. Normally, you enter the A or B command on the same panel as you enter the COPY or MOVE primary command. However, you can enter them on different panels if you wish.

You can also indicate where the data is placed by coding the BEFORE or AFTER option on a MOVE or COPY command. If you

code BEFORE, the data is placed immediately before the line that
contains the label you specify. If you code AFTER, the data is
placed after the line that contains the label. You probably won't
use these options often since it's easier to just enter the A or B line
command.

Figure 4-39 shows an example of a copy operation. In part 1,
you can see the A line command and the COPY primary command.
Part 2 shows the result of the copy operation: the text from
CUSTMAST follows the line that contained the A line command.

Normally, ISPF searches for the member specified on the COPY
or MOVE command in the same library that contains the member
you're editing. However, these members may not be in the same
library. For example, the source member MKTG1200 might be in a
library named DLOWE.TEST.COBOL, while CUSTMAST might be
in DLOWE.COPY.COBOL.

ISPF provides two ways to specify a different library for the
copy/move member. The first is to list a series of concatenated
libraries on the edit entry panel. Thus, you can enter these values
on the entry panel:

```
PROJECT ===>    DLOWE
LIBRARY ===>    TEST        ===>   COPY        ===>
TYPE    ===>    COBOL
```

Then, DLOWE.TEST.COBOL and DLOWE.COPY.COBOL are
searched in order.

Alternatively, you can omit the member name from the COPY
or MOVE command. Then, edit responds with a panel like the one
in figure 4-40. On it, you supply the data set and member name for
the member to be copied or moved. If you're not sure what library
contains the member, you can list a series of libraries for concatenation.

If you don't want to copy all of a member, you can specify a
range of line numbers on edit's COPY or MOVE panel. For
example, if you enter these values:

```
FIRST LINE    ===> 1000
LAST LINE     ===> 4000
NUMBER TYPE   ===> COBOL
```

only lines 1000 to 4000 are copied or moved. If the library type is
COBOL, you should specify COBOL for the NUMBER TYPE. Otherwise, specify STANDARD or RELATIVE. STANDARD means the
source member has non-COBOL numbering. RELATIVE means the

Part 1:

The COPY command specifies the member to be copied; the A command marks its destination

```
EDIT ---- DLOWE.TEST.COBOL(MKTG1200) - 01.02 ---------------- COLUMNS 007 078
COMMAND ===> COPY CUSTMAST                                     SCROLL ===> PAGE
002100  FILE SECTION.
002200 *
002300  FD  CUSTMST
002400      RECORD CONTAINS 42 CHARACTERS.
A      *
002600 *
002700  FD  SALESMN
002800      RECORD CONTAINS 29 CHARACTERS.
002900 *
003000  COPY SALESMAN.
003100 *
003200  FD  SALESRPT
003300      LABEL RECORDS ARE STANDARD
003400      RECORD CONTAINS 132 CHARACTERS.
003500 *
003600  01  PRINT-AREA.
003700 *
003800      05  PRINT-LINE  PIC X(132).
003900 *
004000  WORKING-STORAGE SECTION.
004100 *
004200  01  SWITCHES.
```

Part 2:

When you press the Enter key, edit copies the member CUSTMAST into the member MKTG1200

```
EDIT ---- DLOWE.TEST.COBOL(MKTG1200) - 01.02 ----------- MEMBER CUSTMAST COPIED
COMMAND ===>                                              SCROLL ===> PAGE
002100  FILE SECTION.
002200 *
002300  FD  CUSTMST
002400      RECORD CONTAINS 42 CHARACTERS.
002500 *
002510  01  CUSTOMER-MASTER-RECORD.                                      000100
002520 *                                                                 000200
002530      05  CM-CUSTOMER-KEY.                                         000300
002540          10  CM-SALESMAN-KEY.                                     000400
002550              15  CM-BRANCH-NUMBER    PIC XX.                      000500
002560              15  CM-SALESMAN-NUMBER  PIC XX.                      000600
002570          10  CM-CUSTOMER-NUMBER      PIC X(5).                    000700
002580      05  CM-CUSTOMER-NAME            PIC X(25).                   000800
002590      05  CM-SALES-THIS-YTD           PIC S9(5)V99 COMP-3.         000900
002591      05  CM-SALES-LAST-YTD           PIC S9(5)V99 COMP-3.         001000
002600 *
002700  FD  SALESMN
002800      RECORD CONTAINS 29 CHARACTERS.
002900 *
003000  COPY SALESMAN.
003100 *
003200  FD  SALESRPT
```

Figure 4-39 Copying external data

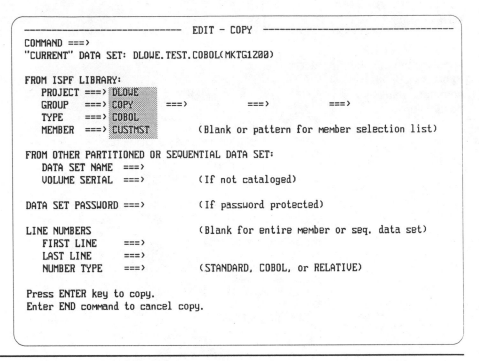

```
------------------------------- EDIT - COPY --------------------------------
COMMAND ===>
"CURRENT" DATA SET: DLOWE.TEST.COBOL(MKTG1Z00)

FROM ISPF LIBRARY:
   PROJECT ===> DLOWE
   GROUP   ===> COPY       ===>          ===>          ===>
   TYPE    ===> COBOL
   MEMBER  ===> CUSTMST            (Blank or pattern for member selection list)

FROM OTHER PARTITIONED OR SEQUENTIAL DATA SET:
   DATA SET NAME  ===>
   VOLUME SERIAL  ===>           (If not cataloged)

DATA SET PASSWORD ===>           (If password protected)

LINE NUMBERS                     (Blank for entire member or seq. data set)
   FIRST LINE    ===>
   LAST LINE     ===>
   NUMBER TYPE   ===>            (STANDARD, COBOL, or RELATIVE)

Press ENTER key to copy.
Enter END command to cancel copy.
```

Figure 4-40   The COPY entry panel

FIRST LINE and LAST LINE are relative to the beginning of the member and have nothing to do with line numbers in the member.

How to create or replace an external data set   The CREATE and REPLACE commands let you move or copy data from the member you're editing to another member. When you use CREATE, data is copied or moved from the member you're editing to a new member. If a member with the same name already exists, an error results. When you use REPLACE, an existing member is replaced. If a member with the same name doesn't exist, a new member is created. To avoid replacing data accidentally, you should use CREATE unless you're sure you want to replace an existing member.

To specify what lines you want to copy or move, you can use the COPY or MOVE line commands, usually in block form (CC or MM). If you use MM, the lines you specify are deleted from the member you're editing after they're moved to the new member. If you use CC, they're not deleted.

You can also determine what lines are copied or moved by coding the range option on a CREATE or REPLACE command. The range option consists of two labels. The first label identifies the first line you want to copy or move and the last label identifies the last line you want to copy or move.

Figure 4-41 shows an example of a create operation. In part 1, I coded two CC line commands and a CREATE command. Part 2 of figure 4-41 shows the contents of the new member the CREATE command created.

If you specify a member name on a REPLACE command, edit searches for the member in the libraries you specified on the edit entry panel. If the member isn't found in one of those libraries, the new member is always created in the first library you specified. A new member is also created in the first library when you specify a member name on a CREATE command. To create a member in a different library, omit the member name from the CREATE or REPLACE command. Edit responds with a panel like the one in figure 4-42. On this panel, you specify any library or sequential data set. You can also specify whether the member will be stored in packed decimal format.

How to edit recursively

Just as you can invoke a browse session from within another browse session, you can invoke an edit session from within another edit session. This is particularly useful if you're debugging a program and subprogram at the same time. Then, you can make a change to the subprogram without leaving the edit session for the main program. This is called *recursive editing*.

To invoke an edit session from within edit, use the EDIT command. Its format is

```
EDIT [member]
```

If you specify a member name, the editor retrieves the member with that name from the data set you're currently editing. If you omit the member name, the edit entry panel is displayed. On this panel, you can enter the name of any source member you want to edit.

To exit from a recursive edit session, you press the End key or enter the CANCEL command just like you would for any edit session. Then, you're returned to the edit session you were executing before you entered the EDIT command.

Part 1:

The CREATE
command specifies
the new member
name; the CC
commands mark the
lines to be copied into
the new member

```
EDIT ---- DLOWE.TEST.COBOL(MKTG1200) - 01.02 ------------------ COLUMNS 007 078
COMMAND ===> CREATE REPORTFD                                    SCROLL ===> PAGE
002700 FD  SALESMN
002800     RECORD CONTAINS 29 CHARACTERS.
002900 *
003000 COPY SALESMAN.
003100 *
CC        FD  SALESRPT
003300     LABEL RECORDS ARE STANDARD
003400     RECORD CONTAINS 132 CHARACTERS.
003500 *
003600 01  PRINT-AREA.
003700 *
CC         05  PRINT-LINE  PIC X(132).
003900 *
004000 WORKING-STORAGE SECTION.
004100 *
004200 01  SWITCHES.
004300 *
004400     05  FIRST-RECORD-SW PIC X    VALUE 'Y'.
004500         88  FIRST-RECORD         VALUE 'Y'.
004600     05  CUSTOMER-EOF-SW PIC X    VALUE 'N'.
004700         88  CUSTOMER-EOF         VALUE 'Y'.
004800     05  RECORD-FOUND-SW PIC X    VALUE 'Y'.
```

Part 2:

The new member
REPORTFD

```
EDIT ---- DLOWE.TEST.COBOL(REPORTFD) - 01.00 ------------------ COLUMNS 007 078
COMMAND ===>                                                    SCROLL ===> PAGE
****** ***************************** TOP OF DATA ***********************************
003200 FD  SALESRPT
003300     LABEL RECORDS ARE STANDARD
003400     RECORD CONTAINS 132 CHARACTERS.
003500 *
003600 01  PRINT-AREA.
003700 *
003800     05  PRINT-LINE  PIC X(132).
****** ***************************** BOTTOM OF DATA ********************************
```

Figure 4-41   Creating a member

```
------------------------------- EDIT - CREATE -------------------------------
COMMAND ===>
"CURRENT" DATA SET: DLOWE.TEST.COBOL(MKTG12ØØ)

TO ISPF LIBRARY:
    PROJECT ===> DLOWE
    GROUP   ===> COPY
    TYPE    ===> COBOL
    MEMBER  ===> REPORTFD

TO OTHER PARTITIONED DATA SET MEMBER:
    DATA SET NAME  ===>
    VOLUME SERIAL  ===>              (If not cataloged)

DATA SET PASSWORD ===>              (If password protected)

SPECIFY PACK OPTION FOR "CREATE" DATA SET ===> NO  (YES or NO)

Press ENTER key to create.
Enter END command to cancel create.
```

Figure 4-42   The CREATE entry panel

Instead of using the EDIT command to start a recursive edit session, you might want to use the split screen feature presented in chapter 2. Then, you can start an edit session in the second screen to edit another file. The advantage of the split screen feature is that both edit sessions are visible on your screen at the same time. The disadvantage is that each edit session has fewer lines to work with.

Whether you use the split screen feature or recursive editing, ISPF does not allow you to edit the same member in two simultaneous editing sessions. If you need to work on two portions of a member at the same time, the best way to do it is to exclude the lines between the two sections of the source member. That way, you can easily scroll between the two sections.

Discussion

Although you probably won't use most of the features I presented in this topic every day, I think you'll find them quite useful on occasion. In particular, the merge and segment functions can save you a lot of time when you reuse portions of an existing library member. And the FIND and CHANGE commands provide an easy way of finding and changing lines of data.

Term

recursive edit

Objective

Edit a data set, using the commands described in this topic to do the following:

1. exclude lines using either the EXCLUDE primary command or the exclude line commands

2. change a text string to a different string of characters

3. locate a line by its type

4. delete lines using the DELETE primary command

5. shift data

6. add data from an existing member to the member you're editing

7. create a new member or replace an existing one with data from the member you're editing

8. edit recursively

Chapter 5

How to perform utility functions

When you select option 3 from the primary option menu, ISPF displays the utility selection menu shown in figure 5-1. This chapter shows you how to perform the utility functions you'll use most often from this menu. It's divided into three topics. Topic 1 shows you how to manage your data sets using the data set list utility. Because this utility is so versatile, you'll use it to perform many of your everyday functions. Topic 2 presents some additional utilities for managing your libraries and data sets. These utilities include the library utility, the data set utility, the move/copy utility, the reset utility, and the hardcopy utility. Finally, topic 3 presents the compare and search utilities.

Another utility you may use frequently is the outlist utility. However, outlist isn't presented in this chapter. Instead, since you use it when you submit background jobs, it's covered in chapter 7 along with other ISPF features used for background processing.

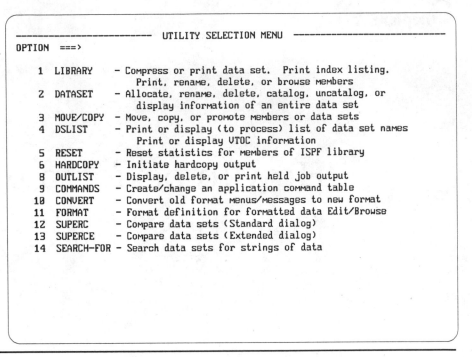

```
---------------------------- UTILITY SELECTION MENU ----------------------------
OPTION ===>

     1  LIBRARY    - Compress or print data set.  Print index listing.
                         Print, rename, delete, or browse members
     2  DATASET    - Allocate, rename, delete, catalog, uncatalog, or
                         display information of an entire data set
     3  MOVE/COPY  - Move, copy, or promote members or data sets
     4  DSLIST     - Print or display (to process) list of data set names
                         Print or display VTOC information
     5  RESET      - Reset statistics for members of ISPF library
     6  HARDCOPY   - Initiate hardcopy output
     8  OUTLIST    - Display, delete, or print held job output
     9  COMMANDS   - Create/change an application command table
    10  CONVERT    - Convert old format menus/messages to new format
    11  FORMAT     - Format definition for formatted data Edit/Browse
    12  SUPERC     - Compare data sets (Standard dialog)
    13  SUPERCE    - Compare data sets (Extended dialog)
    14  SEARCH-FOR - Search data sets for strings of data
```

Figure 5-1   The utility selection menu

Topic 1

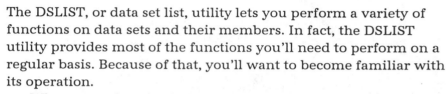

Option 3.4: The DSLIST utility

The DSLIST, or data set list, utility lets you perform a variety of functions on data sets and their members. In fact, the DSLIST utility provides most of the functions you'll need to perform on a regular basis. Because of that, you'll want to become familiar with its operation.

When you select the data set list utility, option 4 on the utility menu, ISPF displays the entry panel presented in figure 5-2. On this panel, you enter an option code to specify the function you want to perform. There are three valid option codes:

P   Print data set list
V   Display VTOC information
PV Print VTOC information

If you leave the OPTION field blank, ISPF displays a data set list based on the information you enter in the DSNAME LEVEL and VOLUME fields. This is the option you'll use most often.

In this topic, you'll first learn not only how to display a data set list, but how to manage your data sets and members from this list. Then, you'll learn some of the primary commands available with the DSLIST utility. Last, you'll learn how to use the P, V, and PV options to print a data set list and to display or print VTOC information.

How to display a data set list

If you want to display a data set list, you leave the OPTION field on the entry panel blank. To specify what data sets you want to list, enter the appropriate values in the DSNAME LEVEL and VOLUME fields. In the DSNAME LEVEL field, you enter the level qualifiers for the data sets you want to list. For example, to display all data sets with the high-level qualifier DLOWE, you enter DLOWE in the DSNAME LEVEL field. You can enter any number of levels to identify the data sets you want to display.

```
------------------------------ DATA SET LIST UTILITY ------------------------------
OPTION  ===>

   blank - Display data set list *           P  - Print data set list
   V     - Display VTOC information only     PV - Print VTOC information only

Enter one or both of the parameters below:
   DSNAME LEVEL  ===> DLOWE
   VOLUME        ===>


   INITIAL DISPLAY VIEW      ===> VOLUME    (VOLUME,SPACE,ATTRIB,TOTAL)
   CONFIRM DELETE REQUEST    ===> YES       (YES or NO)

* The following line commands will be available when the list is displayed:

   B - Browse data set      C - Catalog data set      F - Free unused space
   E - Edit data set        U - Uncatalog data set    = - Repeat last command
   D - Delete data set      P - Print data set
   R - Rename data set      X - Print index listing
   I - Data set information M - Display member list
   S - Information (short)  Z - Compress data set      TSO cmd, CLIST or REXX exec
```

Figure 5-2   The data set list utility entry panel

If you enter a qualifier in the DSNAME LEVEL field and leave the VOLUME field blank, ISPF displays all cataloged data sets that meet the qualification. However, if you also specify a volume serial number in the VOLUME field, ISPF displays only the data sets on the specified volume that meet the qualification. Because ISPF uses the volume table of contents to create this list, a data set doesn't have to be cataloged to be included in the list.

You can also specify a volume in the VOLUME field without specifying a qualifier in the DSNAME LEVEL field. If you do, ISPF displays all the data sets on the volume.

The entry you make in the INITIAL DISPLAY VIEW field determines the information ISPF displays for each data set in the list. The valid options are VOLUME, SPACE, ATTRIB, and TOTAL. If you're displaying a data set list so you can perform a particular function on one or more data sets, it doesn't matter what option you specify. However, if you need specific information on a data set, you need to know what option provides the information you need.

```
DSLIST - DATA SETS BEGINNING WITH DLOWE ---------------------------- ROW 1 OF 36
COMMAND ===>                                                  SCROLL ===> PAGE

COMMAND      NAME                                    MESSAGE           VOLUME
-------------------------------------------------------------------------------
             DLOWE.CMPCOLM.PROF                                        TS0002
             DLOWE.CMPCOLM.STMTS                                       TS0002
             DLOWE.COBOL.PROF                                          TS0002
             DLOWE.COBOL.STMTS                                         TS0002
             DLOWE.COPY.COBOL                                          TS0004
             DLOWE.COPY1.COBOL                                         TS0004
             DLOWE.CUSTMAST.DATA                                       TS0004
             DLOWE.C5F47.TEXT                                          TS0003
             DLOWE.C5F51.TEXT                                          TS0003
             DLOWE.C5F52.TEXT                                          TS0003
             DLOWE.C5F59.LIST                                          TS0003
             DLOWE.C5F61.TEXT                                          TS0003
             DLOWE.ISPPROF                                             TS0001
             DLOWE.MKTG1200.LINKLIST                                   TS0004
             DLOWE.MKTG1200.LIST                                       TS0003
             DLOWE.MKTG1300.LIST                                       TS0004
             DLOWE.PROC.PROF                                           TS0002
             DLOWE.PROC.STMTS                                          TS0002
             DLOWE.SALESMAN.DATA                                       TS0004
```

Figure 5-3   A data set list with a VOLUME display

Figures 5-3 through 5-6 present the output for each of the display options. In each case, I specified DLOWE in the DSNAME LEVEL field and left the VOLUME field blank. As you can see, the VOLUME option displays the volume where each of the data sets in the list reside. The SPACE option displays information on track allocation and usage. The ATTRIB option displays the characteristics of the data sets. And the TOTAL option displays all the above information, along with the creation and expiration dates and the date each data set was last referred to. The TOTAL option is a little harder to work with than the other options, however, because it displays two lines of information for each data set.

Notice the COMMAND column in each of the data set lists in figures 5-3 through 5-6. As you'll see in a minute, you can enter a variety of line commands in this area. In addition, you can enter TSO commands and CLIST and REXX procedures here. You'll learn how to do that later in this topic.

```
DSLIST - DATA SETS BEGINNING WITH DLOWE -------------------------- ROW 1 OF 36
COMMAND ===>                                                  SCROLL ===> PAGE

COMMAND       NAME                              TRACKS %USED XT  DEVICE
-------------------------------------------------------------------------------
              DLOWE.CMPCOLM.PROF                     1   100  1  3380
              DLOWE.CMPCOLM.STMTS                    1   100  1  3380
              DLOWE.COBOL.PROF                       1   100  1  3380
              DLOWE.COBOL.STMTS                      1   100  1  3380
              DLOWE.COPY.COBOL                      15     6  1  3380
              DLOWE.COPY1.COBOL                     15     6  1  3380
              DLOWE.CUSTMAST.DATA                    1   100  1  3380
              DLOWE.C5F47.TEXT                       1   100  1  3380
              DLOWE.C5F51.TEXT                       1   100  1  3380
              DLOWE.C5F52.TEXT                       1   100  1  3380
              DLOWE.C5F59.LIST                       1   100  1  3380
              DLOWE.C5F61.TEXT                       1   100  1  3380
              DLOWE.ISPPROF                          2    50  1  3380
              DLOWE.MKTG1200.LINKLIST                1   100  1  3380
              DLOWE.MKTG1200.LIST                    4   100  1  3380
              DLOWE.MKTG1300.LIST                    3   100  1  3380
              DLOWE.PROC.PROF                        1   100  1  3380
              DLOWE.PROC.STMTS                       1   100  1  3380
              DLOWE.SALESMAN.DATA                    1   100  1  3380
```

Figure 5-4   A data set list with a SPACE display

```
DSLIST - DATA SETS BEGINNING WITH DLOWE -------------------------- ROW 1 OF 36
COMMAND ===>                                                  SCROLL ===> PAGE

COMMAND       NAME                             DSORG  RECFM  LRECL  BLKSZ
-------------------------------------------------------------------------------
              DLOWE.CMPCOLM.PROF                PS     FB       80   1600
              DLOWE.CMPCOLM.STMTS               PS     FB       80   1600
              DLOWE.COBOL.PROF                  PS     FB       80   1600
              DLOWE.COBOL.STMTS                 PS     FB       80   1600
              DLOWE.COPY.COBOL                  PO     FB       80   3120
              DLOWE.COPY1.COBOL                 PO     FB       80   3120
              DLOWE.CUSTMAST.DATA               PS     FB       42    420
              DLOWE.C5F47.TEXT                  PS     FBA     133   3325
              DLOWE.C5F51.TEXT                  PS     FBA     133   3325
              DLOWE.C5F52.TEXT                  PS     FBA     133   3325
              DLOWE.C5F59.LIST                  PS     FBA     133   3325
              DLOWE.C5F61.TEXT                  PS     FBA     133   3325
              DLOWE.ISPPROF                     PO     FB       80   3120
              DLOWE.MKTG1200.LINKLIST           PS     FA      121    121
              DLOWE.MKTG1200.LIST               PS     FBA     133   3059
              DLOWE.MKTG1300.LIST               PS     FBA     133   3059
              DLOWE.PROC.PROF                   PS     FB       80   1600
              DLOWE.PROC.STMTS                  PS     FB       80   1600
              DLOWE.SALESMAN.DATA               PS     FB       29    290
```

Figure 5-5   A data set list with an ATTRIB display

```
DSLIST - DATA SETS BEGINNING WITH DLOWE ------------------------- ROW 1 OF 36
COMMAND ===>                                                    SCROLL ===> PAGE

COMMAND       NAME                                        MESSAGE        VOLUME
  TRACKS %   XT DEVICE  DSORG RECFM LRECL BLKSZ CREATED    EXPIRES      REFERRED
------------------------------------------------------------------------------
             DLOWE.CMPCOLM.PROF                                          TS0002
   1 100     1 3380     PS    FB      80   1600 1990/01/11 ***NONE*** 1990/01/11
------------------------------------------------------------------------------
             DLOWE.CMPCOLM.STMTS                                         TS0002
   1 100     1 3380     PS    FB      80   1600 1990/01/11 ***NONE*** 1990/01/11
------------------------------------------------------------------------------
             DLOWE.COBOL.PROF                                            TS0002
   1 100     1 3380     PS    FB      80   1600 1990/01/11 ***NONE*** 1990/01/11
------------------------------------------------------------------------------
             DLOWE.COBOL.STMTS                                           TS0002
   1 100     1 3380     PS    FB      80   1600 1990/01/11 ***NONE*** 1990/01/11
------------------------------------------------------------------------------
             DLOWE.COPY.COBOL                                            TS0004
  15   6     1 3380     PO    FB      80   3120 1989/12/27 ***NONE*** 1990/01/22
------------------------------------------------------------------------------
             DLOWE.COPY1.COBOL                                           TS0004
  15   6     1 3380     PO    FB      80   3120 1989/12/04 ***NONE*** 1989/12/27
------------------------------------------------------------------------------
```

Figure 5-6   A data set list with a TOTAL display

When you display a data set list, you can use the standard scrolling commands to scroll up and down in the list. However, the LEFT and RIGHT commands operate differently. Instead of scrolling the data left and right, they scroll through the four different views. For example, if the VOLUME view is currently displayed and you scroll right, ISPF displays the SPACE view. If you scroll right again, ISPF displays the ATTRIB view. If you scroll right again, ISPF displays the TOTAL view. And if you scroll right one more time, ISPF displays the VOLUME view once again. If you scroll left, ISPF displays the views in reverse order. This feature is useful if you don't know what view you want or if you need to see more than one view.

The last entry field on the panel in figure 5-2 is CONFIRM DELETE REQUEST. ISPF uses this field when you delete a data set from the data set list display. In a moment, you'll learn how to use this field.

Code	Function
B	Browse a data set
C	Catalog a data set
D	Delete a data set
E	Edit a data set
F	Free the unused space in a data set
I	Display information for a data set
M	Display a member list
P	Print a data set
R	Rename a data set
S	Display a shortened version of the information for a data set
U	Uncatalog a data set
X	Print a data set index listing
Z	Compress a data set
=	Repeat the last command

Figure 5-7   The codes for the functions you can perform as you display a data set list

How to manage your files from a data set or member list

You can perform a variety of functions from a data set list panel. These functions and their codes are listed in figure 5-7. To perform any of these functions, you just enter the appropriate letter or symbol to the left of the data set in the list. Since ISPF doesn't display these function codes on the data set list display, be sure you know the codes for the functions you want to perform before you display the data set list. Now, you'll learn how to perform each of these functions.

How to display a member list   If a data set that's displayed in a list is a partitioned data set, you can list the members in the data set by entering the M line command. For example, I entered M next to the data set DLOWE.TEST.COBOL in the first part of figure 5-8. Part 2 of the figure shows the member list ISPF displayed. On this panel, you can enter the browse, edit, print, rename, and

Part 1:

To display a member list for a partitioned data set, enter an M next to the data set name

```
DSLIST - DATA SETS BEGINNING WITH DLOWE ------------------------- ROW 20 OF 36
COMMAND ===>                                                   SCROLL ===> PAGE

COMMAND      NAME                                    MESSAGE          VOLUME
--------------------------------------------------------------------------------
             DLOWE.SCFILE.LIST                                        TS0003
             DLOWE.SEARCH.STMTS                                       TS0002
             DLOWE.SPF1.TEXT                                          TS0004
             DLOWE.SRCHFOR.LIST                                       TS0003
             DLOWE.SRCHFOR.STMTS                                      TS0004
             DLOWE.SUBPROG.LOAD                                       TS0003
             DLOWE.SUPERC.LIST                                        TS0003
             DLOWE.SUPERC.STMTS                                       TS0003
             DLOWE.SUPERC.TEXT                                        TS0004
             DLOWE.SYSDATE.LINKLIST                                   TS0004
             DLOWE.SYSTIME.LINKLIST                                   TS0004
     M       DLOWE.TEST.COBOL                                         TS0002
             DLOWE.TEST.LOAD                                          TS0003
             DLOWE.TEST.OBJ                                           TS0003
             DLOWE.TESTMKTG.COBOL                                     TS0002
             DLOWE.TEST1.COBOL                                        TS0002
             DLOWE.TSO.TEXT                                           TS0003
************************** END OF DATA SET LIST **************************
```

Part 2:

The member list is displayed

```
DSLIST -- DLOWE.TEST.COBOL --------------------------------- ROW 00001 OF 00004
COMMAND ===>                                               SCROLL ===> PAGE
          NAME     RENAME      VV.MM    CHANGED      SIZE INIT  MOD   ID
          MKTG1100             01.08 89/12/27 13:07   276  410   61 DLOWE
          MKTG1200             01.01 90/01/22 17:30   410  410    0 DLOWE
          MKTG1300             01.08 89/12/27 14:40   371  410   75 DLOWE
          MKTG4100             01.08 89/12/27 15:04   263  410   60 DLOWE
          **END**
```

Figure 5-8   Displaying a member list from a data set list delete line commands. You can also enter TSO commands and CLIST and REXX procedures on individual lines.

Another way to display a member list is by entering the B or E line command from a data set list to browse or edit a partitioned data set. However, when you enter one of these commands, the member list ISPF displays doesn't contain the extended line command area, so you can't enter TSO commands or CLIST or REXX procedures on it. The only line command you can enter is S to select the member you want to browse or edit.

How to browse or edit a data set or member   I already told you how you can browse or edit a member by entering the B or E line command on a data set list entry for a partitioned data set, then selecting the member you want to browse or edit. I also told you how you can browse or edit a data set by using the M line command to display a member list, then entering the B or E line command on the member you want to browse or edit. But there's another way you can browse or edit a member without displaying a member list. To do that, you have to specify the name of the member on the data set list panel. Figure 5-9 illustrates how this works.

In part 1 of figure 5-9, I entered the E line command on the line that contains the partitioned data set DLOWE.TEST.COBOL. Then, I entered the name of the member I wanted to edit, MKTG1200, in parentheses following the name of the data set. When I pressed the Enter key, ISPF displayed the edit display panel, as you can see in part 2 of the figure.

Notice that the edit entry panel was bypassed in this example. This is true whether you enter the E line command with a member name from a data set list panel or you enter the E line command from a member list panel. Because ISPF doesn't display the edit entry panel, you can't specify an edit profile or an initial macro.

You can also enter the name of the member you want to edit without moving the cursor all the way to the end of the data set name. To do that, enter the B or E line command, followed by at least one space, followed by a slash (/) and the member name enclosed in parentheses. For example, I could obtain the same results as in figure 5-9 by entering this command in the line command area:

```
E /(MKTG1200)
```

Part 1:

Enter the E line command next to the data set you want to edit and enter the member name in parentheses to the right of the data set name

```
DSLIST - DATA SETS BEGINNING WITH DLOWE -------------------------- ROW 20 OF 39
COMMAND ===>                                                    SCROLL ===> PAGE

COMMAND        NAME                                  MESSAGE          VOLUME
-----------------------------------------------------------------------------
               DLOWE.SALESMAN.DATA                                    TS0002
               DLOWE.SCFILE.LIST                                      TS0003
               DLOWE.SEARCH.STMTS                                     TS0002
               DLOWE.SPF007.OUTLIST                                   TEST07
               DLOWE.SPF3.OUTLIST                                     TS0003
               DLOWE.SRCHFOR.LIST                                     TS0003
               DLOWE.SRCHFOR.STMTS                                    TS0004
               DLOWE.SUBPROG.LOAD                                     TS0001
               DLOWE.SUPERC.LIST                                      TS0003
               DLOWE.SUPERC.STMTS                                     TS0003
               DLOWE.SUPERC.TEXT                                      TS0004
               DLOWE.SYSDATE.LINKLIST                                 TS0004
               DLOWE.SYSTIME.LINKLIST                                 TS0001
               DLOWE.TEST.CNTL                                        TS0002
        E      DLOWE.TEST.COBOL(MKTG1200)                             TS0002
               DLOWE.TEST.LOAD                                        TS0002
               DLOWE.TEST.OBJ                                         TS0003
               DLOWE.TESTMKTG.COBOL                                   TS0002
               DLOWE.TEST1.COBOL                                      TS0002
```

Part 2:

ISPF displays the edit display panel

```
EDIT ---- DLOWE.TEST.COBOL(MKTG1200) - 01.13 ------------------ COLUMNS 007 078
COMMAND ===>                                                    SCROLL ===> 0020
****** *************************** TOP OF DATA ***************************
000100  IDENTIFICATION DIVISION.
000200 *
000300  PROGRAM-ID.      MKTG1200.
000400 *
000500  ENVIRONMENT DIVISION.
000600 *
000700  CONFIGURATION SECTION.
000800 *
000900  INPUT-OUTPUT SECTION.
001000 *
001100  FILE-CONTROL.
001200      SELECT CUSTMST  ASSIGN TO AS-CUSTMST.
001300      SELECT SALESMN  ASSIGN TO SALESMN
001400                      ORGANIZATION IS INDEXED
001500                      ACCESS IS RANDOM
001600                      RECORD KEY IS SM-SALESMAN-KEY.
001700      SELECT SALESRPT ASSIGN TO SALESRPT.
001800 *
001900  DATA DIVISION.
002000 *
002100  FILE SECTION.
```

Figure 5-9   Editing a member from the data set list panel

Part 1:

Enter the D line command next to the data set you want to delete

```
DSLIST - DATA SETS BEGINNING WITH DLOWE ------------------- 1 MEMBER PROCESSED
COMMAND ===>                                                SCROLL ===> PAGE

COMMAND      NAME                          TRACKS %USED XT  DEVICE
-----------------------------------------------------------------------------
             DLOWE.SALESMAN.DATA               1  100  1   3380
             DLOWE.SCFILE.LIST                 1  100  1   3380
             DLOWE.SEARCH.STMTS                1    0  1   3380
             DLOWE.SPFLOGZ.LIST                8   12  1   3380
             DLOWE.SPF007.OUTLIST              1  100  1   3380
             DLOWE.SPF3.OUTLIST                1  100  1   3380
             DLOWE.SRCHFOR.LIST                1  100  1   3380
             DLOWE.SRCHFOR.STMTS               1  100  1   3380
             DLOWE.SUBPROG.LOAD                2   50  1   3380
             DLOWE.SUPERC.LIST                 1  100  1   3380
             DLOWE.SUPERC.STMTS                1    0  1   3380
             DLOWE.SUPERC.TEXT                 1  100  1   3380
             DLOWE.SYSDATE.LINKLIST            1  100  1   3380
             DLOWE.SYSTIME.LINKLIST            1  100  1   3380
             DLOWE.TEST.CNTL                  30    3  1   3380
             DLOWE.TEST.COBOL                 30   10  1   3380
             DLOWE.TEST.LOAD                   9   88  3   3380
             DLOWE.TEST.OBJ                   39  100 12   3380
  D          DLOWE.TESTMKTG.COBOL            15   40  1   3380
```

Figure 5-10   Deleting a data set

Here, the slash represents the data set name that appears on the line where you enter the command, in this case, DLOWE.TEST.COBOL. When you enter a command like this, don't worry if part of the member name you type overlaps part of the data set name. ISPF automatically remembers the name of the data set and substitutes it for the slash.

How to delete a data set or member   From the DSLIST utility, you can delete either an entire data set or selected members of a partitioned data set. Figure 5-10 shows you how to delete an entire data set. In part 1, I entered the D line command for the data set named DLOWE.TESTMKTG.COBOL. When I pressed the Enter key, the confirm delete panel in part 2 of the figure appeared. ISPF displays this panel only if you specify YES in the CONFIRM DELETE REQUEST field on the DSLIST entry panel.

If I press the Enter key at this point, ISPF scratches the data set and removes it from the catalog, unless the file hasn't expired. If it hasn't expired, ISPF displays the confirm purge panel presented in

Part 2:

Confirm or cancel the
delete request

```
-------------------------------- CONFIRM DELETE --------------------------------
COMMAND ===>

DATA SET NAME: DLOWE.TESTMKTG.COBOL
VOLUME:        TSO002
CREATION DATE: 1989/12/27


INSTRUCTIONS:

    Press ENTER key to confirm delete request.
       (The data set will be deleted and uncataloged.)

    Enter END command to cancel delete request.
```

Part 3:

Confirm or cancel the
purge request

```
------------------------------- CONFIRM PURGE ----------------------------------
COMMAND ===>

 The data set being deleted has an expiration date which has not expired.

DATA SET NAME:     DLOWE.TESTMKTG.COBOL
VOLUME:            TSO002
CREATION DATE:     1989/12/27
EXPIRATION DATE:   1990/12/31

PURGE DATA SET ===> YES     (YES or NO)

INSTRUCTIONS:

    Enter YES to confirm the purge request.
       (A request will be issued for the data set
          to be deleted and uncataloged)

    Enter NO or END command to cancel the purge request.
```

Figure 5-10   Deleting a data set (continued)

part 3 of figure 5-10. ISPF displays this panel whether or not you specified YES in the CONFIRM DELETE REQUEST field. If you want to continue with the delete operation, enter YES in the PURGE DATA SET field. Otherwise, enter NO. You can also cancel the delete function from either of the confirm panels by pressing the End key, PF3/15.

To delete selected members of a partitioned data set, first, enter the M line command for the data set to display a member list. Note that you can't enter the name of a member on the data set list panel for a delete function like you can for a browse or edit function. Then, when the member list is displayed, enter the D line command for the member you want to delete. In part 1 of figure 5-11, I entered a D next to a member named MKTG4100. When you press the Enter key, ISPF deletes the member and displays a message on the member list that indicates the member was deleted. You can see this message in part 2 of figure 5-11.

How to rename a data set or member   To rename a data set, enter the R line command as illustrated in part 1 of figure 5-12. Here, I entered an R next to the data set named DLOWE.TEST1.COBOL. When you press the Enter key, ISPF displays the panel in part 2 of the figure. On this panel, you enter the new name for the data set. In this case, I entered DLOWE.TESTMKTG.COBOL. Then, when you press the Enter key, ISPF renames the data set.

To rename specific members of a partitioned data set, first display a member list for the data set. Then, enter the R line command for the member you want to rename as well as the new name for the member. In part 1 of figure 5-13, I'm renaming the member MKTG4100 to MKTG1400. When you press the Enter key, ISPF renames the member and displays a message indicating that the member has been renamed. You can see this message in part 2 of figure 5-13. Unfortunately, this message indicates only that the member was renamed; it does not indicate what the new name is. To update the list to include the new name, you have to return to the data set list panel and display the member list again.

How to print a data set or member   To print a data set, enter the P line command next to it on the data set list panel. When you press the Enter key, ISPF records the contents of the data set in the list data set. Then, when you log off, you can direct the list data set to a local printer or submit a job to print it on a system printer. Or,

Part 1:

Enter the D line
command next to the
member you want to
delete

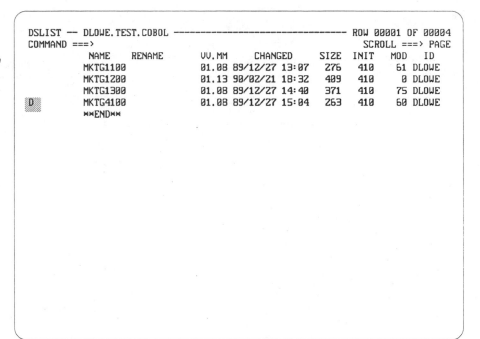

```
DSLIST -- DLOWE.TEST.COBOL ------------------------ ROW 00001 OF 00004
COMMAND ===>                                             SCROLL ===> PAGE
          NAME    RENAME       UV.MM    CHANGED     SIZE  INIT  MOD   ID
          MKTG1100             01.08 89/12/27 13:07   276   410   61  DLOWE
          MKTG1200             01.13 90/02/21 18:32   409   410    0  DLOWE
          MKTG1300             01.08 89/12/27 14:40   371   410   75  DLOWE
    D     MKTG4100             01.08 89/12/27 15:04   263   410   60  DLOWE
          **END**
```

Part 2:

ISPF deletes the
member

```
DSLIST -- DLOWE.TEST.COBOL ------------------------ ROW 00001 OF 00004
COMMAND ===>                                             SCROLL ===> PAGE
          NAME    RENAME       UV.MM    CHANGED     SIZE  INIT  MOD   ID
          MKTG1100             01.08 89/12/27 13:07   276   410   61  DLOWE
          MKTG1200             01.13 90/02/21 18:32   409   410    0  DLOWE
          MKTG1300             01.08 89/12/27 14:40   371   410   75  DLOWE
          MKTG4100 *DELETED
          **END**
```

Figure 5-11   Deleting a member of a partitioned data set

Part 1:

Enter the R line
command next to the
data set you want to
rename

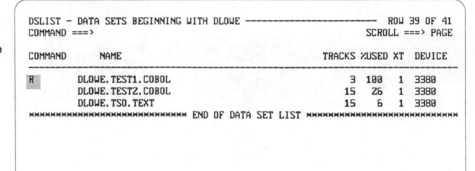

```
DSLIST - DATA SETS BEGINNING WITH DLOWE ------------------------ ROW 39 OF 41
COMMAND ===>                                                 SCROLL ===> PAGE

COMMAND      NAME                                     TRACKS %USED XT DEVICE
--------------------------------------------------------------------------------
   R         DLOWE.TEST1.COBOL                             3  100   1 3380
             DLOWE.TESTZ.COBOL                            15   26   1 3380
             DLOWE.TSO.TEXT                               15    6   1 3380
*******************************  END OF DATA SET LIST  **************************
```

Part 2:

Specify the new data
set name

```
------------------------------- RENAME DATA SET -------------------------------
COMMAND ===>

DATA SET NAME:  DLOWE.TEST1.COBOL
VOLUME:         TS0002

ENTER NEW NAME BELOW:     (The data set will be recataloged.)

ISPF LIBRARY:
    PROJECT ===> DLOWE
    GROUP   ===> TESTMKTG
    TYPE    ===> COBOL

OTHER PARTITIONED OR SEQUENTIAL DATA SET:
    DATA SET NAME  ===>
```

Figure 5-12   Renaming a data set

Part 1:

Enter the R line
command next to thew
member name in the
RENAME column

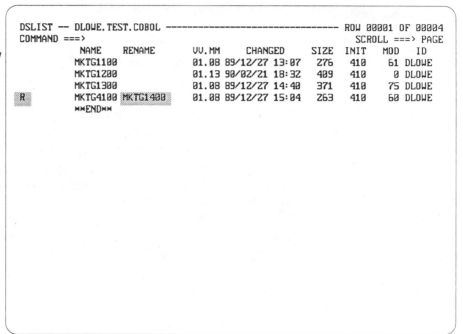

Part 2:

ISPF renames the
member

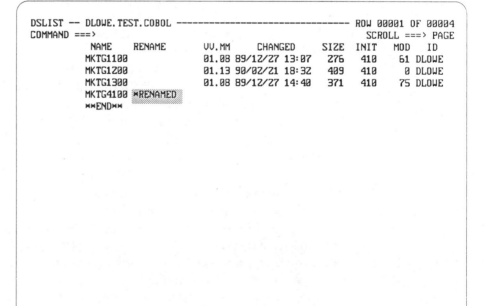

Figure 5-13   Renaming a member of a partitioned data set

you can use the LIST command presented in chapter 2 to print the list data set without logging off.

If the data set is partitioned, the contents of each member is printed, preceded by an index listing. Normally, you'll want to print only specific members of a partitioned data set, so you'll use the function only for sequential data sets. However, note that you cannot use this function to print data sets that contain printer control characters. To do that, you have to use the hardcopy utility, which is presented in the next topic.

To print a specific member of a partitioned data set, first display the member list for the data set. Then, enter the P line command for the member you want to print. When you press the Enter key, ISPF prints the member to the list data set.

How to display data set information   If you enter the I line command on a data set list, ISPF displays a complete list of information on the data set's library, including the location of the data set, its characteristics, and its space allocation and current utilization. If you enter the S line command, ISPF displays a shortened version of this information.

Figures 5-14 and 5-15 show the information that's displayed when you specify these options. Notice that the only information not included in the shortened listing is the maximum number of directory blocks that can be allocated to the library, the number of directory blocks that are currently used, and the number of members in the library. Because these two displays are almost identical, you'll probably never need to use the shortened version.

If your installation uses SMS, the information that's displayed is a bit different. Figure 5-16 shows the display for a managed data set when you specify the I line command. As you can see, ISPF displays the management, storage, and data classes in addition to the other information.

How to catalog or uncatalog a data set   You can change a data set's catalog status by entering the C or U line command on the data set list panel. If you enter C, ISPF adds the data to the catalog. If you enter U, ISPF removes the data set from the catalog. Note that the uncatalog function doesn't delete the data set; it just removes its entry from the catalog. The main difference between cataloged and uncataloged data sets is that when you refer to a data set that isn't cataloged, you must specify the serial number for the volume that contains the file.

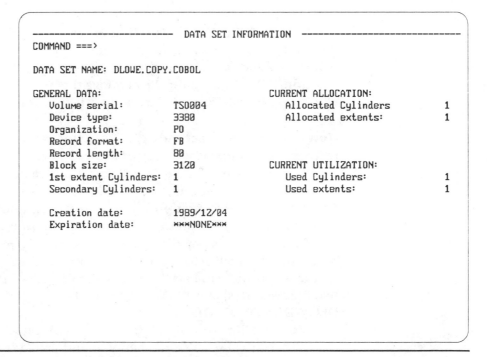

```
------------------------- DATA SET INFORMATION -------------------------------
COMMAND ===>

DATA SET NAME: DLOWE.COPY.COBOL

GENERAL DATA:                               CURRENT ALLOCATION:
    Volume serial:        TS0004                Allocated cylinders      1
    Device type:          3380                  Allocated extents:       1
    Organization:         PO                    Maximum dir. blocks:     1
    Record format:        FB
    Record length:        80
    Block size:           3120              CURRENT UTILIZATION:
    1st extent cylinders: 1                     Used cylinders:          1
    Secondary cylinders:  1                     Used extents:            1
                                                Used dir. blocks:        1
    Creation date:        1989/12/04            Number of members:       3
    Expiration date:      ***NONE***
```

Figure 5-14   A library information display

```
------------------------- DATA SET INFORMATION -------------------------------
COMMAND ===>

DATA SET NAME: DLOWE.COPY.COBOL

GENERAL DATA:                               CURRENT ALLOCATION:
    Volume serial:        TS0004                Allocated Cylinders      1
    Device type:          3380                  Allocated extents:       1
    Organization:         PO
    Record format:        FB
    Record length:        80
    Block size:           3120              CURRENT UTILIZATION:
    1st extent Cylinders: 1                     Used Cylinders:          1
    Secondary Cylinders:  1                     Used extents:            1

    Creation date:        1989/12/04
    Expiration date:      ***NONE***
```

Figure 5-15   A shortened library information display

```
-------------------------- DATA SET INFORMATION --------------------------
COMMAND ===>

DATA SET NAME: DLOWE.MKTG.COBOL

GENERAL DATA:                            CURRENT ALLOCATION:
   Management Class:     M1                 Allocated cylinders      5
   Storage class:        S1                 Allocated extents:       1
      Volume serial:     TS0001             Maximum dir. blocks:     2
      Device type:       3380
   Data class:           D1
      Organization:      PO              CURRENT UTILIZATION:
      Record format:     FB                 Used cylinders:          1
      Record length:     80                 Used extents:            1
      Block size:        3120               Used dir. blocks:        1
      1st extent cylinders: 5               Number of members:       3
      Secondary cylinders:  1

      Creation date:     1989/12/04
      Expiration date:   ***NONE***
```

Figure 5-16   A library information display for an SMS-managed data set

Most ISPF functions, including browse and edit, assume that your data sets are cataloged. And when you allocate a new data set using the allocate function of the data set utility, presented in the next topic, ISPF automatically catalogs the new data set. So you won't use the catalog and uncatalog functions often.

How to print a data set index   The X line command lets you print a data set index, a listing of useful information about the data set. For a sequential data set, this index includes general information about the data set, such as its volume, record format, and allocation. This information is the same information that's displayed when you enter the I line command for a data set.

If the data set is partitioned, the general information is followed by statistics for each of its members. The statistics that are included are the same statistics that are displayed in a member list. Figure 5-17 shows the index listing for the partitioned data set DLOWE.TEST.COBOL.

Like the P line command, the X line command sends output to the ISPF list data set. Then, when you end your ISPF session, you

```
PROJECT: DLOWE                                                          DATE: 90/01/19
GROUP:   TEST                                                           TIME: 16:17
TYPE:    COBOL                                                          PAGE: 001

GENERAL DATA:               GENERAL DATA:                    CURRENT ALLOCATION:
  VOLUME SERIAL: TSO002        RECORD FORMAT:      FB           1 CYLINDER
  DEVICE TYPE:   3380          RECORD LENGTH:      80           1 EXTENT
  ORGANIZATION:  PO            BLOCK SIZE:         3,120        1 DIRECTORY BLOCK
  CREATION DATE: 89/12/27      1ST EXTENT SIZE:    1
  EXPIRATION DATE: **NONE**    SECONDARY QUAN:     1          CURRENT UTILIZATION:
                                                                1 CYLINDER
                                                                1 EXTENT
                                                                1 DIRECTORY BLOCK
                                                                4 MEMBERS

MEMBER    TTR    VERS.MOD  CREATION   DATE AND TIME          CURRENT    INITIAL    MODIFIED   USER
NAME      (HEX)  LEVEL     DATE       LAST MODIFIED          NO. LINES  NO. LINES  NO. LINES  ID
MKTG1100  000310 01.08     89/12/04   89/12/27  13:07        276        410        61         DLOWE
MKTG1200  000705 01.00     89/12/27   89/12/27  17:56        410        410        0          DLOWE
MKTG1300  000507 01.08     89/12/04   89/12/27  14:40        371        410        75         DLOWE
MKTG4100  00060C 01.08     89/12/04   89/12/27  15:04        263        410        60         DLOWE
MAXIMUMS:        01.08                89/12/27  17:56        410        410        75
TOTALS:                                                      1,320      1,640      196
END OF MEMBER LIST
```

Figure 5-17 A library index listing

can print the list data set on a local printer or submit a job to print it on a system printer. Or, you can use the LIST command to print it without ending the session.

How to compress a data set   As you may know, a partitioned data set consists of an *index* (or *directory*) followed by one or more members. Whenever you edit and save a member, ISPF adds the new version of the member to the end of the data set and updates the index to point to the member's new location. The space occupied by the old version of the member becomes unusable. As a result, a PDS can soon become filled with unusable space. To reclaim this unusable space, you must *compress* the library. It's important that you compress your libraries often. If you don't, they'll quickly use up all the space allocated to them.

To compress a partitioned data set, enter the Z line command on the data set list panel. When you press the Enter key, ISPF invokes a standard utility program named IEBCOPY. IEBCOPY moves all the members to the beginning of the data set, right after the index, and releases the space that was unusable so you can use it again.

How to free a data set's unused space   Sometimes when you allocate a data set, you don't know how much space it will need. If you allocate too much space to a data set, you can free the unused space by entering the F line command from the data set list. For example, in part 1 of figure 5-18, you can see that the data set named DLOWE.TEST1.COBOL has 20 tracks allocated to it, but only three (15%) are being used. When I enter F in the line command area for that data set, the seventeen unused tracks are freed, as you can see in part 2 of the figure.

When you free unused space, you should realize that the example in figure 5-18 works only if you allocated the data set in tracks. If you allocated the data set in cylinders, only the unused cylinders are freed. For example, suppose you allocated five cylinders to a data set that resides on a 3380 device. Since a 3380 has 15 tracks per cylinder, a total of 75 tracks are allocated. If 35 of those tracks are currently unused and you enter a free line command, only 30 tracks, or two cylinders, are freed. In other words, you can't free a portion of a cylinder if you allocated the data set in cylinders.

If you use the free line command to free the unused space in a data set, you should know that you can still add or change records

Part 1:

To free unused space
in a data set, enter an
F name next to the
data set name

```
DSLIST - DATA SETS BEGINNING WITH DLOWE ------------------------ ROW 20 OF 36
COMMAND ===>                                                 SCROLL ===> PAGE

COMMAND      NAME                              TRACKS %USED XT  DEVICE
------------------------------------------------------------------------------
             DLOWE.SCFILE.LIST                    1   100   1   3380
             DLOWE.SEARCH.STMTS                   1     0   1   3380
             DLOWE.SPF1.TEXT                      1   100   1   3380
             DLOWE.SRCHFOR.LIST                   1   100   1   3380
             DLOWE.SRCHFOR.STMTS                  1   100   1   3380
             DLOWE.SUBPROG.LOAD                   2    50   1   3380
             DLOWE.SUPERC.LIST                    1   100   1   3380
             DLOWE.SUPERC.STMTS                   1     0   1   3380
             DLOWE.SUPERC.TEXT                    1   100   1   3380
             DLOWE.SYSDATE.LINKLIST               1   100   1   3380
             DLOWE.SYSTIME.LINKLIST               1   100   1   3380
             DLOWE.TEST.COBOL                    15    60   1   3380
             DLOWE.TEST.LOAD                      5    60   1   3380
             DLOWE.TEST.OBJ                      30    70   1   3380
             DLOWE.TESTMKTG.COBOL               15    33   1   3380
   F         DLOWE.TEST1.COBOL                   20    15   1   3380
             DLOWE.TSO.TEXT                      15     6   1   3380
*************************** END OF DATA SET LIST ***************************
```

Part 2:

The unused space is
freed

```
DSLIST - DATA SETS BEGINNING WITH DLOWE ------------------------ ROW 20 OF 36
COMMAND ===>                                                 SCROLL ===> PAGE

COMMAND      NAME                              TRACKS %USED XT  DEVICE
------------------------------------------------------------------------------
             DLOWE.SCFILE.LIST                    1   100   1   3380
             DLOWE.SEARCH.STMTS                   1     0   1   3380
             DLOWE.SPF1.TEXT                      1   100   1   3380
             DLOWE.SRCHFOR.LIST                   1   100   1   3380
             DLOWE.SRCHFOR.STMTS                  1   100   1   3380
             DLOWE.SUBPROG.LOAD                   2    50   1   3380
             DLOWE.SUPERC.LIST                    1   100   1   3380
             DLOWE.SUPERC.STMTS                   1     0   1   3380
             DLOWE.SUPERC.TEXT                    1   100   1   3380
             DLOWE.SYSDATE.LINKLIST               1   100   1   3380
             DLOWE.SYSTIME.LINKLIST               1   100   1   3380
             DLOWE.TEST.COBOL                    15    60   1   3380
             DLOWE.TEST.LOAD                      5    60   1   3380
             DLOWE.TEST.OBJ                      30    70   1   3380
             DLOWE.TESTMKTG.COBOL               15    33   1   3380
             DLOWE.TEST1.COBOL                    3   100   1   3380
             DLOWE.TSO.TEXT                      15     6   1   3380
*************************** END OF DATA SET LIST ***************************
```

Figure 5-18   Freeing unused space in a data set

or members in the data set. To do that, however, MVS must allocate an additional extent to the data set. So, you should use the F line command only for files that won't need the extra space in the near future.

How to repeat a line command   If you want to issue the same command for more than one data set in a data set list, there are two ways you can do it. First, you can enter the command for each data set you want to process. For example, if you want to delete two data sets, you could enter the D line command on the two lines containing those data sets. This is the method you'll probably use if you're entering one of the one-character line commands.

The other method of repeating a command is most useful when you want to repeat a CLIST, REXX, or TSO line command. For example, suppose you want to execute a CLIST named MKTG1000 for two data sets. To do that, enter the CLIST name on the line containing the first data set you want to process, then enter the repeat command, =, on the line containing the second data set. Then, ISPF executes the CLIST for both data sets.

You can also enter the repeat command after processing a line command. Then, ISPF executes the last command you issued for the data set on the line where you enter the repeat command. For example, if you executed the MKTG1000 CLIST for one data set, then entered the repeat line command for another data set, ISPF would execute the CLIST again for the second data set. Unfortunately, the repeat command is only valid on a data set list. It is not valid on a member list.

How to perform multiple commands   You already know that you can enter the same line command on multiple lines of a data set or member list panel. You can also enter any number of different commands on a data set list or member list panel. For example, figure 5-19 shows how you can print, rename, and delete data set members at the same time. In part 1 of the figure, I entered the P line command to print the member named MKTG1200, the R line command to rename the member named MKTG1400 to MKTG4100, and the D line command to delete the member named MKTG5100. Then, when I pressed the Enter key, ISPF performed all three operations, as you can see in the second part of the figure.

When you enter multiple commands on a data set list or member list panel, the commands are processed from top to

Part 1:

Enter the line
commands you want
to execute

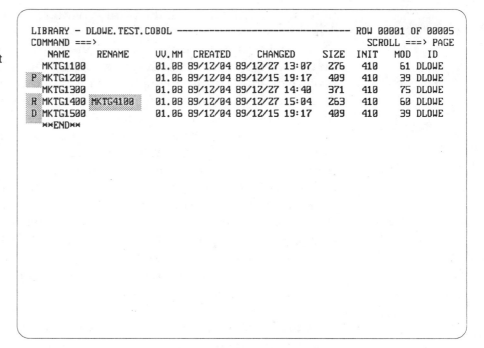

Part 2:

ISPF executes the
commands

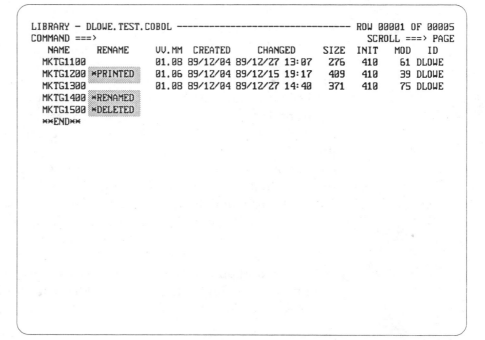

Figure 5-19   Printing, renaming, and deleting members

bottom. So, in figure 5-19, the print function is performed first, followed by the rename function, followed by the delete function.

In most cases, you can process all the line commands you enter on a panel by pressing the Enter key once. However, if you request browse or edit facilities using the B or E line commands, ISPF doesn't process any commands entered after these commands until you press the Enter key again. For example, suppose you enter a rename, edit, and delete command on a member list panel as in part 1 of figure 5-20. When you press the Enter key, ISPF processes the rename command, then, when it executes the edit command, it displays the edit display panel shown in part 2 of figure 5-20. When you finish editing the file and press the End key, PF3/15, ISPF returns you to the member list panel shown in part 3 of figure 5-20. As you can see, the panel indicates that ISPF executed both the rename and edit functions. However, ISPF didn't execute the delete function. To execute that function, you must press the Enter key again.

How to execute a TSO command or CLIST or REXX procedure from a data set or member list You can also enter a TSO command or a CLIST or REXX procedure in the line command area of a data set list or member list panel. Although I won't present TSO commands or CLIST or REXX procedures in this book, you need to understand how to enter them in a data set or member list. So I'll explain how to enter a TSO command or CLIST or REXX procedure now. If you want to learn more about TSO commands and CLIST and REXX procedures, I recommend *Part 2: Commands and Procedures.*

For now, the only thing you need to know about TSO commands and CLIST and REXX procedures in general is that you can code operands on them. For example, to submit a job for background processing, you can issue a TSO SUBMIT command. On the command, you code one operand: the name of the data set or member that contains the job you want to submit. If you enter the SUBMIT command as a line command on a data set list or member list panel, it automatically uses the fully-qualified name of the data set or member on that line as its operand.

To illustrate, consider figure 5-21. Here, I entered the SUBMIT line command on the line in a member list panel that contains the member named MKTG1200. As you can see at the top of the panel,

Part 1:

Enter the line
commands you want
to execute

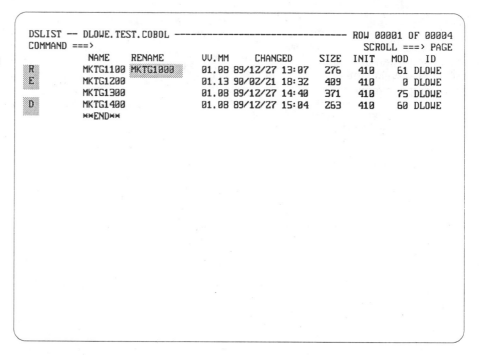

Part 2:

When ISPF reaches
the E line command, it
displays the edit
display panel

Figure 5-20 Entering multiple line commands that include an edit command

Part 3:

ISPF returns to the
member list panel
without executing the
remaining commands

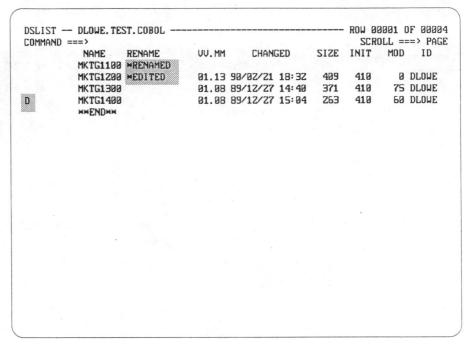

```
DSLIST -- DLOWE.TEST.COBOL ------------------------------- ROW 00001 OF 00004
COMMAND ===>                                                  SCROLL ===> PAGE
         NAME    RENAME      UU.MM    CHANGED      SIZE  INIT  MOD   ID
         MKTG1100 *RENAMED
         MKTG1200 *EDITED    01.13 90/02/21 18:32  409   410    0 DLOWE
         MKTG1300            01.08 89/12/27 14:40  371   410   75 DLOWE
    D    MKTG1400            01.08 89/12/27 15:04  263   410   60 DLOWE
         **END**
```

Figure 5-20   Entering multiple line commands that include an edit command
(continued)

the member is stored in a data set named DLOWE.TEST.CNTL.
When I press the Enter key, this command is issued:

```
SUBMIT 'DLOWE.TEST.CNTL(MKTG1200)'
```

This command submits the job contained in the member
MKTG1200 for background processing.

You can also execute a TSO command or CLIST or REXX procedure for a specific member from a data set list. This works the
same as it does for a browse or edit function. So, after you enter
the name of the TSO command or CLIST or REXX procedure , enter
the member name in parentheses following the name of the data
set. Or, follow the TSO command or CLIST or REXX procedure
with a space and a slash, followed immediately by the member
name enclosed in parentheses. For example, if I enter the
command

```
SUBMIT /(MKTG1200)
```

```
DSLIST -- DLOWE.TEST.CNTL ------------------------------- ROW 00001 OF 00010
COMMAND ===>                                                  SCROLL ===> PAGE
         NAME     RENAME      VV.MM    CHANGED      SIZE  INIT   MOD   ID
         AMSDEFIN             01.05 90/02/08 17:17   27    32    12 DLOWE
         COBUCG              01.02 90/02/20 18:59   10    11     4 DLOWE
         COBUCLG             01.03 90/02/21 18:20   11    11     1 DLOWE
         COB2UCG             01.00 90/02/21 18:54   11    11     0 DLOWE
         DEFESDS             01.00 90/02/08 17:27   15    15     0 DLOWE
         DEFKSDS             01.00 90/02/08 17:18   18    18     0 DLOWE
         LDCSTMST            01.02 90/02/08 19:06    9     9     2 DLOWE
         LDSLSMAN            01.02 90/02/08 18:10    9     9     2 DLOWE
 SUBMIT  MKTG1200            01.15 90/02/08 19:43   11    11    11 DLOWE
         SUBPROG             01.00 90/02/07 14:06    5     5     0 DLOWE
         **END**
```

Figure 5-21 Submitting a member for background processing using the TSO SUBMIT command

on a line containing the data set named DLOWE.TEST.CNTL, the resulting command looks like this:

```
SUBMIT 'DLOWE.TEST.CNTL(MKTG1200)'
```

As you can see, ISPF replaces the slash symbol with the fully–qualified data set name.

You can also execute TSO commands and CLIST and REXX procedures that require more than one operand from a data set list using a slash. To do that, enter the TSO command or CLIST or REXX procedure, followed by a space and a slash, followed by a member name enclosed in parentheses, if appropriate. Then, type a space and the second operand or variable. For example, if I enter the command

```
%COB2UCLG /(MKTG1200) DLOWE.COPY.COBOL
```

on a line containing the data set named DLOWE.TEST.COBOL, the resulting command looks like this:

```
%COB2UCLG 'DLOWE.TEST.COBOL(MKTG1200)' DLOWE.COPY.COBOL
```

The first few times you use the slash symbol in a TSO command or CLIST or REXX procedure, you might want to check that the command that's submitted is what you expect. To do that, issue the SHOWCMD ON primary command before you enter the TSO line command or CLIST or REXX procedure. Then, every time you enter a line command, ISPF displays a panel that shows what the actual command looks like before it's submitted to TSO. For example, figure 5-22 shows the panel ISPF displayed when I entered SHOWCMD ON followed by the SUBMIT line command I just presented. Notice that if the command isn't what you intended, you can change it from this panel. To process the command, press the Enter key. To exit from the panel without processing the command, press the End key, PF3/15. To discontinue displaying the expanded commands, issue the SHOWCMD OFF command.

Data set list utility primary commands

The data set list utility includes six primary commands you can use to manipulate the data sets in a data set list: CONFIRM, FIND, LOCATE, SAVE, SHOWCMD, and SORT. You can use three of these commands, LOCATE, SAVE, and SORT, plus one other command, SELECT, in a member list. In fact, you can use these four commands in any member list, not just member lists displayed from the DSLIST utility. However, you'll probably use them most often within DSLIST.

Here, I'll show you how to use only the SELECT, FIND, LOCATE, SORT, and SAVE commands. I've already shown you how to use the SHOWCMD command, and since the CONFIRM command accomplishes the same thing as specifying YES or NO in the CONFIRM DELETE REQUEST field on the entry panel, I won't cover it here.

How to automatically select members in a member list   If you want to issue the same line command for several members in a member list, you can often do it most efficiently using the SELECT primary command. Its format is

```
SELECT pattern [line-command]
```

When you issue a SELECT command, ISPF executes the line command you specify for every member in the member list that

```
------------------------- DATA SET LIST UTILITY -----------------------------
COMMAND ===>

Data Set Name: DLOWE.TEST.CNTL

Command before expansion:
     SUBMIT /(MKTG1200)

Command after expansion:
===> SUBMIT 'DLOWE.TEST.CNTL(MKTG1200)'



The expanded command field shown above can be modified.


Press ENTER key to process the command.
Enter END command to return without processing the command.
```

Figure 5-22 The SHOWCMD panel

matches the pattern you specify. Note that all the members in the member list that match the pattern are processed, whether or not they are currently displayed on the screen.

To illustrate how the SELECT command works, suppose you want to delete all the members in a list that begin with TEST. To do that, you could display the member list, then manually enter a D next to each member you want to delete. Or, you could enter this SELECT command:

    SELECT TEST* D

Then, ISPF deletes all the members that begin with TEST automatically, without requiring you to enter a separate D line command for each one.

If you use an asterisk by itself in a SELECT command, ISPF selects all the members in the member list for processing, Thus, if you want to delete all the members in a member list, enter this command:

    SELECT * D

Of course, a SELECT command like this can be dangerous. So be sure to review the member list carefully to avoid deleting members inadvertently.

If you omit the line command on a SELECT command, ISPF issues an S line command for each selected member. This is appropriate for ISPF options such as browse or edit that use the S line command to select members from a member list. Under DSLIST, however, the S line command displays brief information about the data set. So you'll usually include a line command on SELECT commands you use under DSLIST.

How to find character strings in a data set name   You can use the FIND command within the data set utility to locate character strings in a data set list. The format and operation of the FIND command are the same as they are for the browse feature. You can look back to figure 3-11 for a description of this command if you need to.

You'll probably use the FIND command most often with data set lists that take up several screens. Then, instead of scrolling through the list looking for particular entries, you can use the FIND command to locate the entries for you. For example, in the data set list in the first part of figure 5-23, I entered the command

```
FIND SUPERC ALL
```

In the second part of the figure, you can see that the first data set name that contains the characters SUPERC is at the top of the display.

How to sort a data set or member list   If a data set or member list is several pages long, it's sometimes easier to find the entry you need if the entries are sorted in a particular sequence. For example, it's easier to find a data set on a particular volume if the entries are sorted by volume serial number. To sort a data set list in this sequence or in a variety of other sequences, you use the SORT command.

The format of the SORT command is

```
SORT [field-1 [field-2]]
```

Here, field-1 is the *major sort field* and field-2 is the *minor sort field*. If you specify both fields, ISPF sorts the list by the major sort field first, then by the minor sort field. Figure 5-24 presents the fields

Part 1:

Enter the FIND
command

```
DSLIST - DATA SETS BEGINNING WITH DLOWE ------------------------------ ROW 1 OF 38
COMMAND ===> FIND SUPERC ALL                                        SCROLL ===> PAGE

COMMAND       NAME                                    MESSAGE              VOLUME
------------------------------------------------------------------------------------
              DLOWE.CMPCOLM.PROF                                            TS0002
              DLOWE.CMPCOLM.STMTS                                          TS0002
              DLOWE.COBOL.PROF                                              TS0002
              DLOWE.COBOL.STMTS                                            TS0002
              DLOWE.COPY.COBOL                                              TS0004
              DLOWE.COPY1.COBOL                                            TS0004
              DLOWE.CUSTMAST.DATA                                          TS0004
              DLOWE.C5F47.TEXT                                              TS0003
              DLOWE.C5F51.TEXT                                              TS0003
              DLOWE.C5F52.TEXT                                              TS0003
              DLOWE.C5F59.LIST                                              TS0003
              DLOWE.C5F61.TEXT                                              TS0003
              DLOWE.ISPPROF                                                TS0001
              DLOWE.MKTG1200.LINKLIST                                      TS0004
              DLOWE.MKTG1200.LIST                                          TS0003
              DLOWE.MKTG1300.LIST                                          TS0004
              DLOWE.PROC.PROF                                              TS0002
              DLOWE.PROC.STMTS                                              TS0002
              DLOWE.SALESMAN.DATA                                          TS0004
```

Part 2:

The cursor is posi-
tioned at the first data
set that contains the
specified characters

```
DSLIST - DATA SETS BEGINNING WITH DLOWE ------------------- 3 - CHARS 'SUPERC'
COMMAND ===>                                                    SCROLL ===> PAGE

COMMAND       NAME                                    MESSAGE              VOLUME
------------------------------------------------------------------------------------
              DLOWE.SUPERC.LIST                                            TS0003
              DLOWE.SUPERC.STMTS                                          TS0003
              DLOWE.SUPERC.TEXT                                            TS0004
              DLOWE.SYSDATE.LINKLIST                                      TS0004
              DLOWE.SYSTIME.LINKLIST                                      TS0004
              DLOWE.TEST.COBOL                                            TS0002
              DLOWE.TEST.LOAD                                              TS0003
              DLOWE.TEST.OBJ                                                TS0003
              DLOWE.TESTMKTG.COBOL                                        TS0002
              DLOWE.TEST1.COBOL                                            TS0002
              DLOWE.TSO.TEXT                                              TS0003
*************************** END OF DATA SET LIST ***************************
```

Figure 5-23   Using the FIND command with a data set list

Sort fields you can use in a data set list

Field name	Field description	Sort sequence
BLKSZ	Block size	Descending
CREATED	Creation date	Descending
DEVICE	Device type	Ascending
DSORG	Data set organization	Ascending
EXPIRES	Expiration date	Ascending
LRECL	Logical record length	Descending
MESSAGE	Command completion message	Ascending
NAME	Data set name	Ascending
RECFM	Record format	Ascending
REFERRED	Date last accessed	Descending
TRACKS	Data set size	Descending
VOLUME	Volume serial number	Ascending
XT	Extents used	Descending
%USED	Percent used space	Descending

Sort fields you can use in a member list

Field name	Field description	Sort sequence
CHANGED	Date and time of last change	Descending
CREATED	Creation date	Descending
ID	Last user to access member	Ascending
INIT	Initial number of records	Descending
LIB	Library in concatenation sequence	Ascending
NAME	Member name	Ascending
MM	Modification level	Ascending
MOD	Number or modified records	Descending
SIZE	Current number of records	Descending
VV	Version number	Ascending

Figure 5-24   Sort fields you can use in a data set or member list

you can use for the sort operation in data set and member lists. If you don't specify any fields on the SORT command, ISPF sorts the list by data set or member name. This is the sequence the data sets appear in when a list is first displayed.

Part 1:

Enter the SORT
command

```
DSLIST - DATA SETS BEGINNING WITH DLOWE ---------------------------- ROW 1 OF 38
COMMAND ===> SORT VOLUME                                    SCROLL ===> PAGE

COMMAND      NAME                           TRACKS %USED XT  DEVICE
---------------------------------------------------------------------------
             DLOWE.CMPCOLM.PROF                  1   100  1   3380
             DLOWE.CMPCOLM.STMTS                 1   100  1   3380
             DLOWE.COBOL.PROF                    1   100  1   3380
             DLOWE.COBOL.STMTS                   1   100  1   3380
             DLOWE.COPY.COBOL                   15     6  1   3380
             DLOWE.COPY1.COBOL                  15     6  1   3380
             DLOWE.CUSTMAST.DATA                 1   100  1   3380
             DLOWE.C5F47.TEXT                    1   100  1   3380
             DLOWE.C5F51.TEXT                    1   100  1   3380
             DLOWE.C5F52.TEXT                    1   100  1   3380
             DLOWE.C5F59.LIST                    1   100  1   3380
             DLOWE.C5F61.TEXT                    1   100  1   3380
             DLOWE.ISPPROF                       2    50  1   3380
             DLOWE.MKTG1200.LINKLIST             1   100  1   3380
             DLOWE.MKTG1200.LIST                 4   100  1   3380
             DLOWE.MKTG1300.LIST                 3   100  1   3380
             DLOWE.PROC.PROF                     1   100  1   3380
             DLOWE.PROC.STMTS                    1   100  1   3380
             DLOWE.SALESMAN.DATA                 1   100  1   3380
```

Part 2:

The data set list is
sorted by the fields
you specify

```
DSLIST - DATA SETS BEGINNING WITH DLOWE ---------------------------- ROW 1 OF 38
COMMAND ===>                                                SCROLL ===> PAGE

COMMAND      NAME                          MESSAGE            VOLUME
---------------------------------------------------------------------------
             DLOWE.ISPPROF                                    TS0001
             DLOWE.SPF2.LIST                                  TS0002
             DLOWE.TEST.COBOL                                 TS0002
             DLOWE.TESTMKTG.COBOL                             TS0002
             DLOWE.TEST1.COBOL                                TS0002
             DLOWE.CMPCOLM.PROF                               TS0002
             DLOWE.CMPCOLM.STMTS                              TS0002
             DLOWE.COBOL.PROF                                 TS0002
             DLOWE.COBOL.STMTS                                TS0002
             DLOWE.PROC.PROF                                  TS0002
             DLOWE.PROC.STMTS                                 TS0002
             DLOWE.SEARCH.STMTS                               TS0002
             DLOWE.TEST.OBJ                                   TS0003
             DLOWE.TSO.TEXT                                   TS0003
             DLOWE.SPFLOG1.LIST                               TS0003
             DLOWE.TEST.LOAD                                  TS0003
             DLOWE.MKTG1200.LIST                              TS0003
             DLOWE.SUBPROG.LOAD                               TS0003
             DLOWE.C5F47.TEXT                                 TS0003
```

Figure 5-25   Sorting a data set list

To illustrate, I entered this command for the data set list in part 1 of figure 5-25:

```
SORT VOLUME
```

This command sorts the list by volume. The result of this command is illustrated in the second part of figure 5-25. Notice that the display view changed so that the major sort field, in this case, VOLUME, is now displayed.

How to locate a data set or member   Once a data set or member list has been sorted, you can use the LOCATE command to scroll to a particular location in the list. To do this, you just enter the LOCATE command followed by the value you want to scroll to. This value must be contained in the major sort field, the field the list was sorted by.

Since ISPF sorts a data set list by data set name by default, you can enter a LOCATE command that specifies a data set name without having to sort the list. But if you want to locate a data set using any other field, you have to sort the list by that field first. The same is true for a member list, which ISPF sorts by member name by default.

Figure 5-26 illustrates the LOCATE command. In part 1 of the figure, I entered this command after sorting the list by volume serial number:

```
LOCATE TSO003
```

As you can see in part 2 of the figure, the list was scrolled so that the first data set that resides on volume TSO003 is at the top of the display.

When you use LOCATE, you should be aware that if the value you specify isn't located, the list is still scrolled. It's positioned at the first entry that follows the entry that would have contained the specified value. For example, in figure 5-26, if there weren't any data sets listed on volume TSO003, the list would have been positioned at the first entry on TSO004.

How to save a data set or member list   You can save a data set or member list to a sequential data set using the SAVE command. For example, to save the list to a data set named VOLSORT, code the SAVE command like this:

```
SAVE VOLSORT
```

Part 1:

Enter the LOCATE command

```
DSLIST - DATA SETS BEGINNING WITH DLOWE ---------------------- ROW 1 OF 38
COMMAND ===> LOCATE TSD003                                     SCROLL ===> PAGE

COMMAND      NAME                                      MESSAGE        VOLUME
-------------------------------------------------------------------------------
             DLOWE.ISPPROF                                            TS0001
             DLOWE.SPF2.LIST                                          TS0002
             DLOWE.TEST.COBOL                                         TS0002
             DLOWE.TESTMKTG.COBOL                                     TS0002
             DLOWE.TEST1.COBOL                                        TS0002
             DLOWE.CMPCOLM.PROF                                       TS0002
             DLOWE.CMPCOLM.STMTS                                      TS0002
             DLOWE.COBOL.PROF                                         TS0002
             DLOWE.COBOL.STMTS                                        TS0002
             DLOWE.PROC.PROF                                          TS0002
             DLOWE.PROC.STMTS                                         TS0002
             DLOWE.SEARCH.STMTS                                       TS0002
             DLOWE.TEST.OBJ                                           TS0003
             DLOWE.TSO.TEXT                                           TS0003
             DLOWE.SPFLOG1.LIST                                       TS0003
             DLOWE.TEST.LOAD                                          TS0003
             DLOWE.MKTG1200.LIST                                      TS0003
             DLOWE.SUBPROG.LOAD                                       TS0003
             DLOWE.C5F47.TEXT                                         TS0003
```

Part 2:

The list is scrolled so the first data set with the specified sort field is at the top

```
DSLIST - DATA SETS BEGINNING WITH DLOWE ---------------------- ROW 13 OF 38
COMMAND ===>                                                   SCROLL ===> PAGE

COMMAND      NAME                                      MESSAGE        VOLUME
-------------------------------------------------------------------------------
             DLOWE.TEST.OBJ                                           TS0003
             DLOWE.TSO.TEXT                                           TS0003
             DLOWE.SPFLOG1.LIST                                       TS0003
             DLOWE.TEST.LOAD                                          TS0003
             DLOWE.MKTG1200.LIST                                      TS0003
             DLOWE.SUBPROG.LOAD                                       TS0003
             DLOWE.C5F47.TEXT                                         TS0003
             DLOWE.C5F51.TEXT                                         TS0003
             DLOWE.C5F52.TEXT                                         TS0003
             DLOWE.C5F59.LIST                                         TS0003
             DLOWE.C5F61.TEXT                                         TS0003
             DLOWE.SCFILE.LIST                                        TS0003
             DLOWE.SRCHFOR.LIST                                       TS0003
             DLOWE.SUPERC.LIST                                        TS0003
             DLOWE.SUPERC.STMTS                                       TS0003
             DLOWE.COPY.COBOL                                         TS0004
             DLOWE.COPY1.COBOL                                        TS0004
             DLOWE.MKTG1300.LIST                                      TS0004
             DLOWE.CUSTMAST.DATA                                      TS0004
```

Figure 5-26   Using the LOCATE command with a data set list

ISPF adds the qualifier DATASETS to the end of the data set name. So in this case, the complete name of the data set is DLOWE.VOL-SORT.DATASETS.

Usually, you'll save a data set or member list so you can print it in a specific order. When you print a data set list by specifying the print option on the DSLIST entry panel, or a member list by specifying the print index line command from a data set list display, the list is first sorted by data set or member name. So if you want to print a data set or member list in another order, you must sort it, save the list to a sequential data set, and then print that data set.

You can also save a data set or member list in the ISPF list data set by entering the SAVE command without any operands. Then, you can print the data set when you end your ISPF session, or you can print it without ending the session using the LIST command.

Other DSLIST functions

Up to now, I've discussed only what you can do when you leave the option field on the DSLIST entry panel blank. But, as I mentioned at the beginning of this topic, there are three other options you can choose. I'll show you how to use those options now.

How to print a data set list   To print a data set list, you enter P in the OPTION field on the DSLIST entry panel. Along with this option, you enter the DSNAME LEVEL and VOLUME parameters just like you do when display a data set list. In part 1 of figure 5-27, I requested ISPF to print all the data sets with the qualifier DLOWE on volume TSO002. Part 2 of the figure shows the output, which ISPF stores in the ISPF list data set.

The data set listing in part 2 of figure 5-27 contains most of the information that's included in a data set list display when you specify the TOTAL option. The only fields missing are the device type and the expiration and last referral dates. Note that the format of this report doesn't depend on the value in the INITIAL DISPLAY VIEW field. This field affects only a displayed data set list.

How to display or print VTOC information   The *VTOC*, which stands for *Volume Table of Contents*, is a directory of all data sets stored on a volume. With early versions of ISPF, you used the list VTOC utility to display and print VTOC information. However, this

```
-------------------------------- DATA SET LIST UTILITY --------------------------------
OPTION  ===> P

    blank - Display data set list *          P  - Print data set list
    V    - Display VTOC information only     PV - Print VTOC information only

  Enter one or both of the parameters below:
    DSNAME LEVEL  ===> DLOWE
    VOLUME        ===> TSO00Z


    INITIAL DISPLAY VIEW     ===> SPACE    (VOLUME,SPACE,ATTRIB,TOTAL)
    CONFIRM DELETE REQUEST   ===> YES      (YES or NO)

  * The following line commands will be available when the list is displayed:

    B - Browse data set      C - Catalog data set      F - Free unused space
    E - Edit data set        U - Uncatalog data set     = - Repeat last command
    D - Delete data set      P - Print data set
    R - Rename data set      X - Print index listing
    I - Data set information M - Display member list
    S - Information (short)  Z - Compress data set        TSO cmd, CLIST or REXX exec
```

Figure 5-27   Printing a data set list (part 1 of 2)

utility is no longer available. Fortunately, its functions have been
incorporated into the data set list utility.

  To display VTOC information, you enter V in the OPTION field
on the entry panel of the data set list utility. To print VTOC information, enter PV. Then, in the VOLUME field, specify the name of
the volume you want VTOC information displayed or printed for.
In part 1 of figure 5-28, for example, I entered V to display VTOC
information for the volume TSO001. Part 2 of the figure shows the
resulting display. The printed output contains the same information, so I won't show it here.

  Except for the unit type and the number of free extents, the
information on this display is grouped into three categories. The
first group contains information on the volume in general: the
number of tracks, the percent of the tracks that are used, and the
number of tracks per cylinder. The second group contains information on the VTOC: the number of tracks in the VTOC, the percent
of the tracks that are used, and the number of unused data set
control blocks. (*Data set control blocks*, or *DSCBs*, store the label
information for the data sets on a volume.) The last group

```
LISTING OF DATA SETS BEGINNING WITH DLOWE                                          DATE: 90/01/25
                                                                                   TIME: 16:54
VOLUME - TS0002    UNIT - 3380                                                      PAGE:     1

VOLUME DATA:              VTOC DATA:
  TRACKS:      13,275       TRACKS:        44      FREE SPACE:       TRACKS    CYLINDERS
  %USED:           96       %USED:         52        SIZE:             469          0
  TRKS/CYLS:       15       FREE DSCBS:    15        LARGEST:           16          0

                                           FREE EXTENTS:     171

  DATA SET NAME            VOLUME  ORG  RECFM  LRECL  BLKSZ  TRKS  %USED  XT  CREATED
--------------------------------------------------------------------------------------------
DLOWE.CMPCOLM.PROF         TS0002   PS   FB      80   1600     1    100   1  1990/01/11
DLOWE.CMPCOLM.STMTS        TS0002   PS   FB      80   1600     1    100   1  1990/01/11
DLOWE.COBOL.PROF           TS0002   PS   FB      80   1600     1    100   1  1990/01/11
DLOWE.COBOL.STMTS          TS0002   PS   FB      80   1600     1    100   1  1990/01/11

DLOWE.PROC.PROF            TS0002   PS   FB      80   1600     1    100   1  1990/01/05
DLOWE.PROC.STMTS           TS0002   PS   FB      80   1600     1    100   1  1990/01/05
DLOWE.SEARCH.STMTS         TS0002   PS   FB      80   1600     1      0   1  1990/01/11
DLOWE.SPF2.TEXT            TS0002   PS   FBA    121   3146    18      5   1  1990/01/25

DLOWE.TEST.COBOL           TS0002   PO   FB      80   3120    15     60   1  1989/12/27
DLOWE.TESTMKTG.COBOL       TS0002   PO   FB      80   3120    15     33   1  1989/12/27
DLOWE.TEST1.COBOL          TS0002   PO   FB      80   3120     3    100   1  1989/12/27
```

Figure 5-27 Printing a data set list (part 2 of 2)

Part 1:

Specify the display
VTOC option and the
volume

```
-------------------------- DATA SET LIST UTILITY --------------------------
OPTION  ===> U

  blank - Display data set list *         P - Print data set list
  V     - Display VTOC information only   PV - Print VTOC information only

Enter one or both of the parameters below:
  DSNAME LEVEL  ===>
  VOLUME        ===> TS0001


  INITIAL DISPLAY VIEW     ===> SPACE    (VOLUME,SPACE,ATTRIB,TOTAL)
  CONFIRM DELETE REQUEST   ===> YES      (YES or NO)

* The following line commands will be available when the list is displayed:

B - Browse data set      C - Catalog data set     F - Free unused space
E - Edit data set        U - Uncatalog data set   = - Repeat last command
D - Delete data set      P - Print data set
R - Rename data set      X - Print index listing
I - Data set information M - Display member list
S - Information (short)   Z - Compress data set       TSO cmd, CLIST or REXX exec
```

Part 2:

The VTOC information
for the volume is
displayed

```
VTOC SUMMARY INFORMATION FOR VOLUME TS0001 ---------------------------------
COMMAND ===>

UNIT:  3380

VOLUME DATA:             VTOC DATA            FREE SPACE:    TRACKS    CYLS
  TRACKS:     13,275       TRACKS:      23      SIZE:        3,457     192
  %USED:          73       %USED:       90      LARGEST:     2,102     140
  TRKS/CYLS:      15       FREE DSCBS: 131
                                               FREE EXTENTS:   140
```

Figure 5-28   Displaying VTOC information

contains information on the free space on the volume: the number of tracks and cylinders that are free and the largest contiguous free space in tracks and cylinders.

Discussion

As you can see, the DSLIST utility provides many of the functions you'll need to perform on a regular basis. For example, if you're a COBOL programmer, you can invoke the edit function from DSLIST to create your source members and the jobs to process them. Then, you can issue a TSO SUBMIT command from DSLIST to submit the jobs for processing. And, you can invoke the browse function from DSLIST to look at the output from a job if you route the output to a disk file. This is much more efficient than jumping back and forth between ISPF's edit, background, and browse options.

There are, however, some functions you can't invoke from DSLIST. For example, you can't allocate data sets from DSLIST. To do that, you have to use the data set utility. You'll learn about this utility along with some other utilities for managing libraries and data sets in the next topic.

Terms

index
directory
compress
major sort field
minor sort field
VTOC
Volume Table of Contents
Data Set Control Block
DSCB

Objectives

1. Use the data set list utility to perform the following functions:
   a. browse or edit a data set or member
   b. delete a data set or member
   c. rename a data set or member
   d. print a data set or member
   e. display data set information
   f. catalog or uncatalog a data set
   g. print a data set index
   h. compress a data set
   i. free a data set's unused space

2. Use the repeat command to repeat the previous line command.

3. Execute a TSO command or CLIST or REXX procedure as a line command from a data set list or member list.

4. Use the FIND, SORT, LOCATE, and SAVE commands.

5. Use the data set list utility to print a data set list.

6. Use the data set list utility to display or print VTOC information.

Topic 2   Other utilities to manage libraries and data sets

As you saw in the last topic, you can use the data set list utility to perform most of the utility functions you use frequently. So if you need to perform a variety of functions, it's convenient to use the data set list utility. But if you need to perform a single function, or if you need to perform a function that's not available from the data set list utility, you can use one of the other TSO utilities.

In this topic, I'll present five utilities. First, I'll show you how to maintain partitioned data sets using the library utility. Second, I'll show you how to allocate, rename, delete, catalog, or uncatalog sequential or partitioned data sets using the data set utility. Third, I'll show you how to copy and move data sets using the move/copy utility. Fourth, I'll show you how to create, update, and delete statistics for members of partitioned data sets using the reset utility. Fifth, I'll show you how to print data sets using the hardcopy utility.

OPTION 3.1: THE LIBRARY UTILITY

The library utility, option 1 on the utility selection menu, lets you perform a variety of operations on partitioned data sets and their members. Figure 5-29 presents the library utility entry panel. As you can see, you can enter one of nine function codes in the OPTION field. The valid codes and their meanings are:

    C   Compress the library
    X   Print an index listing
    L   Print the entire library
    I   Display library information
    S   Display a shortened version of the library information
    P   Print a specific member
    R   Rename a member

```
------------------------------ LIBRARY UTILITY ------------------------------
OPTION  ===>

    blank - Display member list      B - Browse member
    C - Compress data set            P - Print member
    X - Print index listing          R - Rename member
    L - Print entire data set        D - Delete member
    I - Data set information         S - Data set information (short)

ISPF LIBRARY:
    PROJECT ===> DLOWE
    GROUP   ===> TEST        ===>              ===>            ===>
    TYPE    ===> COBOL
    MEMBER  ===>                     (If "P", "R", "D", "B", or blank selected)
    NEWNAME ===>                     (If "R" selected)

OTHER PARTITIONED OR SEQUENTIAL DATA SET:
    DATA SET NAME  ===>
    VOLUME SERIAL  ===>              (If not cataloged)

DATA SET PASSWORD ===>               (If password protected)
```

Figure 5-29   The library utility entry panel

D   Delete a member
B   Browse a member

You can also leave the OPTION field blank. If you do, ISPF displays a member list.

Notice that all these functions are also available with the DSLIST utility. Because of that, I'll present the library utility briefly. Since you already know how the functions work, I'll just show you how to invoke them from the library utility.

You can also print or display information from a sequential data set or print an entire sequential data set with this utility. However, you'll rarely need to use it for these functions, so I won't show you how to process sequential data sets here.

The C, X, L, I, and S options operate on an entire library, so all you need to enter with the option code is the name of the library you want to process. The other four options, B, P, R, and D, operate on a specific member, so you have to specify a member name in addition to the library name. If you leave the OPTION field blank, you can code the member name as a pattern. Then, ISPF displays a member list that consists of members that fit that pattern. Finally, if you enter the R option to rename a member, you also have to enter the new name for the member.

To illustrate how to use the library utility, consider figure 5-30. In part 1, I entered the R option to rename a member. In addition, I entered the library name, DLOWE.TEST.COBOL, the old member name, MKTG4100, and the new member name, MKTG1400. When I pressed the Enter key, ISPF renamed the member, as you can see from the message at the top of the panel in part 2 of the figure.

OPTION 3.2: THE DATA SET UTILITY

The data set utility lets you perform a variety of functions for non-VSAM data sets. Figure 5-31 presents the data set utility entry panel, which you can display by selecting option 2 from the utility selection menu. As you can see, you can enter one of seven function codes. The valid codes and their meanings are:

A   Allocate a new data set
R   Rename an existing data set
D   Delete an existing data set
C   Catalog an existing data set
U   Uncatalog an existing data set
S   Display shortened version of data set information
M   Allocate a new data set using SMS classes

You can also leave the option field blank. If you do, ISPF displays information about the data set you specify. Since you can perform all these functions except the two allocate functions, A and M, using the DSLIST utility, I'll show you only how to allocate data sets here.

How to create a sequential data set

Before you can use a data set on an MVS system, you must create it. Under ISPF, this is called allocating a data set. When you allocate a data set, you tell the system the data set's name, its characteristics, such as its organization and the length of its records, and

Part 1:

Specify the rename
option and the library
and member informa-
tion

```
------------------------------- LIBRARY UTILITY -------------------------------
OPTION  ===> R

     blank - Display member list          B - Browse member
     C - Compress data set                P - Print member
     X - Print index listing              R - Rename member
     L - Print entire data set            D - Delete member
     I - Data set information             S - Data set information (short)

  ISPF LIBRARY:
     PROJECT ===> DLOWE
     GROUP   ===> TEST      ===>          ===>          ===>
     TYPE    ===> COBOL
     MEMBER  ===> MKTG4100     (If "P", "R", "D", "B", or blank selected)
     NEWNAME ===> MKTG1400     (If "R" selected)

  OTHER PARTITIONED OR SEQUENTIAL DATA SET:
     DATA SET NAME  ===>
     VOLUME SERIAL  ===>          (If not cataloged)

  DATA SET PASSWORD ===>          (If password protected)
```

Part 2:

The member is
renamed

```
------------------------------- LIBRARY UTILITY -------- MEMBER MKTG4100 RENAMED
OPTION  ===>

     blank - Display member list          B - Browse member
     C - Compress data set                P - Print member
     X - Print index listing              R - Rename member
     L - Print entire data set            D - Delete member
     I - Data set information             S - Data set information (short)

  ISPF LIBRARY:
     PROJECT ===> DLOWE
     GROUP   ===> TEST      ===>          ===>          ===>
     TYPE    ===> COBOL
     MEMBER  ===>              (If "P", "R", "D", "B", or blank selected)
     NEWNAME ===>              (If "R" selected)

  OTHER PARTITIONED OR SEQUENTIAL DATA SET:
     DATA SET NAME  ===>
     VOLUME SERIAL  ===>          (If not cataloged)

  DATA SET PASSWORD ===>          (If password protected)
```

Figure 5-30   Renaming a member of a partitioned data set

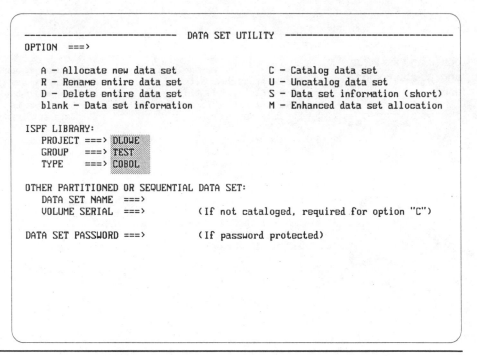

```
------------------------------ DATA SET UTILITY ------------------------------
OPTION ===>

    A - Allocate new data set              C - Catalog data set
    R - Rename entire data set             U - Uncatalog data set
    D - Delete entire data set             S - Data set information (short)
    blank - Data set information           M - Enhanced data set allocation

ISPF LIBRARY:
    PROJECT ===> DLOWE
    GROUP   ===> TEST
    TYPE    ===> COBOL

OTHER PARTITIONED OR SEQUENTIAL DATA SET:
    DATA SET NAME  ===>
    VOLUME SERIAL  ===>           (If not cataloged, required for option "C")

DATA SET PASSWORD ===>            (If password protected)
```

Figure 5-31   The data set utility entry panel

how much space it will require. Then, the system sets aside direct-access space for your file and adds your file's name to its catalog.

To allocate a data set under ISPF, you enter the data set name on the data set utility panel and select option A. If a data set already exists with that name, ISPF displays an error message. Otherwise, ISPF displays the allocate panel, shown in figure 5-32. Here, I'm allocating a sequential data set.

If you've worked with native TSO, you should understand that the word "allocate" under ISPF doesn't mean the same thing as it does under native TSO. As you already know, allocate under ISPF means to create. But under native TSO it may mean to create or to retrieve an existing data set to be processed by a program.

How to specify a volume   If you want to place a data set on a specific volume, you must enter that volume's serial number in the VOLUME SERIAL field. If you leave this field blank, MVS selects a default volume for the data set, unless you specify a generic unit. In the GENERIC UNIT field, you specify the type of DASD you want to use, such as 3380. Then, MVS selects an appro-

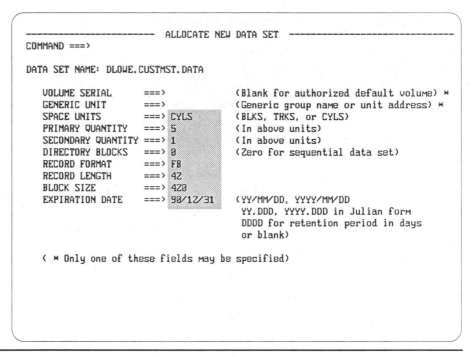

```
---------------------------  ALLOCATE NEW DATA SET  -----------------------------
COMMAND ===>

DATA SET NAME: DLOWE.CUSTMST.DATA

        VOLUME SERIAL      ===>            (Blank for authorized default volume) *
        GENERIC UNIT       ===>            (Generic group name or unit address) *
        SPACE UNITS        ===> CYLS       (BLKS, TRKS, or CYLS)
        PRIMARY QUANTITY   ===> 5          (In above units)
        SECONDARY QUANTITY ===> 1          (In above units)
        DIRECTORY BLOCKS   ===> 0          (Zero for sequential data set)
        RECORD FORMAT      ===> FB
        RECORD LENGTH      ===> 42
        BLOCK SIZE         ===> 420
        EXPIRATION DATE    ===> 90/12/31   (YY/MM/DD, YYYY/MM/DD
                                            YY.DDD, YYYY.DDD in Julian form
                                            DDDD for retention period in days
                                            or blank)

        ( * Only one of these fields may be specified)
```

Figure 5-32   Allocating a sequential data set

priate volume. Normally, you don't specify the volume serial
number or a generic unit.

How to specify space requirements   SPACE UNITS, PRIMARY
QUANTITY, and SECONDARY QUANTITY work together to specify
how much space is allocated to the data set. The SPACE UNITS
field determines the unit of measure for the other two fields. You
may allocate space in blocks, tracks, or cylinders of data by specifying BLKS, TRKS, or CYLS.

As a general rule, the primary quantity field, PRIMARY QUAN-
TITY, is the amount of space you think the data set will require. In
figure 5-32, for example, I think the data set will require 5 cylinders of disk space.

To allow for errors in estimation or changes in requirements,
the secondary quantity field, SECONDARY QUANTITY, allows for
extensions to the primary allocation. Then, if the primary allocation of space isn't large enough for the data set, the secondary allocation is made. If this still isn't enough space, the secondary allocation is repeated until 15 secondary allocations are made. After that,

the only way to allocate more space to the file is to copy or move it to a data set with a larger allocation.

In figure 5-32, I specified 5 cylinders of primary space and 1 cylinder of secondary space. As a result, the largest this file can become is 20 cylinders: 5 for the primary allocation, and 1 for each of the 15 secondary allocations. Incidentally, each allocation, both primary and secondary, is called an *extent*. A data set can have up to 16 extents: one primary and 15 secondary.

How to specify data set characteristics   The RECORD FORMAT, RECORD LENGTH, and BLOCK SIZE fields let you specify data set characteristics. RECORD FORMAT is normally FB, indicating that the file contains fixed-length, blocked records. It can also be F for fixed-length, unblocked records, or VB or V for variable-length, blocked or unblocked records. There are other options for record format, but you'll rarely use them. The RECORD LENGTH field, simply enough, specifies the length of each record. And the value you enter in the BLOCK SIZE field should be a multiple of RECORD LENGTH.

How to choose an efficient block size   One of the problems of allocating data sets is deciding what value to use for the block size. For reasons too complicated to explain here, it generally isn't possible to utilize 100% of the storage space available in each track of direct-access storage. Exactly what percentage of direct-access space you can utilize depends on the characteristics of the individual device and the block size of the file. As a result, the block size you choose for your file determines how efficiently that file utilizes direct-access space. Usually, a 95% utilization is considered excellent.

Because each type of direct-access device has different characteristics, a block size that is efficient for one type of device may waste a great deal of space on a different device type. For example, suppose you want to allocate a source library that will contain 10,000 80-byte records. You choose a block size of 3120; that's 39 80-byte records in each block. If the disk device is a 3350, you'll use about 97% of the available space on each track. That's an efficient utilization of disk space. However, the same file on a 3380 device will use only 84% of the available disk space. That's not an efficient utilization of disk space.

Determining the best block size for a file of any given record length on any given device type is a complex task. Fortunately,

Block size	Blocks/ track	Records/ track	Percent usage
47440	1	593	98.90
23440	2	586	97.73
15440	3	579	96.56
11440	4	572	95.40
9040	5	565	94.23
7440	6	558	93.06
6320	7	553	92.23
5440	8	544	90.73
4800	9	540	90.06

Figure 5-33   Optimum block sizes for 80-byte records on a 3380 device

most data sets you allocate under ISPF will contain 80-byte records. And although IBM manufactures many different types of disk devices, the 3380 is the most commonly used device in MVS installations. Selecting the best block size for a file containing 80-byte records on a 3380 is a manageable task. Figure 5-33 lists the block sizes that use disk space most efficiently for files of this type. If you select one of these values, you'll know you're not wasting disk space.

Figure 5-33 also shows the number of records per track for each block size listed. So, if you select a block size of 9040, 565 records are stored in each track. To determine the number of tracks to allocate for a data set, just divide the number of records per track for the block size you select into the number of records in the file and round the result up. For example, a 10,000-record data set with a block size of 9040 requires 18 tracks (10,000 / 565 = 17.7).

How to specify an expiration date   A file's *expiration date* is the date the file is no longer needed and can be deleted. You enter this date in the EXPIRATION DATE field in one of three formats: YY/MM/DD or YY.DDD for a specific date, or DDDD for a retention period. For example, in figure 5-32 I entered the expiration date 90/12/31, which means the file will expire on December 31, 1990. I could have accomplished the same thing by entering 90.365. Or, if the current date was 1/1/90, I could have entered 365 to get the same expiration date.

How to use default allocation values   Quite frankly, it's difficult at times to remember the correct coding for all the allocation values for a data set. Fortunately, ISPF allows you to model a new data set after an existing one. To do this, first, display the data set information for the existing file you want to use as a model by leaving the option field on the data set utility entry panel blank. Then, return to the entry panel and allocate a new data set. When you do, ISPF remembers the information it displayed for the existing file and supplies it as default values for the new data set.

How to create a partitioned data set

Figure 5-34 shows an example of allocating a partitioned data set. The only difference between allocating a sequential and a partitioned data set is the DIRECTORY BLOCKS field. This field indicates how many 255-byte directory blocks are allocated for the library. If you specify zero for this field, the data set is assumed to be sequential. If you enter a non-zero value, the data set will be partitioned.

The value you enter in the DIRECTORY BLOCKS field depends on the number of members you expect in the library and whether the library contains standard or non-standard members. If the library contains standard ISPF source members (members that have ISPF statistics), each directory block can accommodate six member entries. So if you expect 40 members, you should allocate at least seven directory blocks.

If the library contains non-standard ISPF source members (members that don't have ISPF statistics), each directory block can hold up to 21 member entries. Thus, only two directory blocks are required for a 40-member library. (You use the edit profile as described in topic 2 of chapter 4 to control the generation of ISPF statistics in source members.)

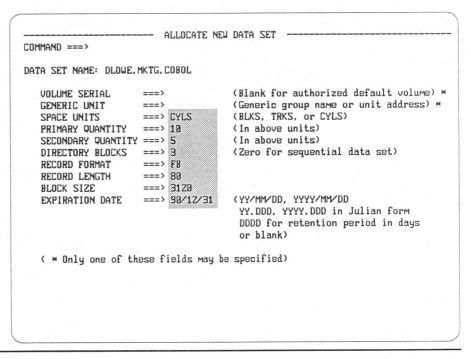

```
------------------------ ALLOCATE NEW DATA SET ------------------------------
COMMAND ===>

DATA SET NAME:  DLOWE.MKTG.COBOL

     VOLUME SERIAL      ===>           (Blank for authorized default volume) *
     GENERIC UNIT       ===>           (Generic group name or unit address) *
     SPACE UNITS        ===> CYLS      (BLKS, TRKS, or CYLS)
     PRIMARY QUANTITY   ===> 10        (In above units)
     SECONDARY QUANTITY ===> 5         (In above units)
     DIRECTORY BLOCKS   ===> 3         (Zero for sequential data set)
     RECORD FORMAT      ===> FB
     RECORD LENGTH      ===> 80
     BLOCK SIZE         ===> 3120
     EXPIRATION DATE    ===> 90/12/31  (YY/MM/DD, YYYY/MM/DD
                                        YY.DDD, YYYY.DDD in Julian form
                                        DDDD for retention period in days
                                        or blank)

     ( * Only one of these fields may be specified)
```

Figure 5-34   Allocating a partitioned data set

If you are allocating a *load library* (a load library contains executable programs), allow four members per directory block. Thus, ten directory blocks are required for a 40-member load library. Depending on the attributes of each load module, more than four entries might fit into each block. But four entries per block is the safest way to compute directory size for a load library.

How to create a data set managed by SMS

If you specify option M on the entry panel, you can use the Storage Management Subsystem to allocate a new data set. The panel ISPF displays when you specify this option is illustrated in figure 5-35. It's similar to the allocate panel I presented earlier, so I'll describe only the differences between the two.

The main difference is that this panel allows you to enter the management class, storage class, and data class of the data set

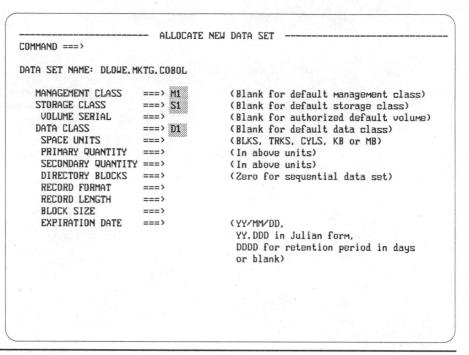

```
----------------------- ALLOCATE NEW DATA SET -----------------------------
COMMAND ===>

DATA SET NAME: DLOWE.MKTG.COBOL

     MANAGEMENT CLASS    ===> M1      (Blank for default management class)
     STORAGE CLASS       ===> S1      (Blank for default storage class)
      VOLUME SERIAL      ===>         (Blank for authorized default volume)
     DATA CLASS          ===> D1      (Blank for default data class)
     SPACE UNITS         ===>         (BLKS, TRKS, CYLS, KB or MB)
     PRIMARY QUANTITY    ===>         (In above units)
     SECONDARY QUANTITY  ===>         (In above units)
     DIRECTORY BLOCKS    ===>         (Zero for sequential data set)
     RECORD FORMAT       ===>
     RECORD LENGTH       ===>
     BLOCK SIZE          ===>
     EXPIRATION DATE     ===>         (YY/MM/DD,
                                       YY.DDD in Julian form,
                                       DDDD for retention period in days
                                       or blank)
```

Figure 5-35   Allocating a data set managed by SMS

you're allocating. When you enter values in these fields, SMS uses the characteristics of the classes you specify to allocate the data set. So you don't need to specify the volume serial, space units, and so on. But if you do specify values in these fields, they override the values specified in the class definition. Since this can cause inconsistencies, you usually enter values in only the MANAGEMENT CLASS, STORAGE CLASS, and DATA CLASS fields when you allocate a managed data set. Or, you can leave the entire screen blank and SMS will use its default classes to allocate the data set, if any are defined.

There are two other differences you should notice on this panel. First, GENERIC UNIT field isn't available. Second, if you enter a value in the SPACE UNITS field, you can enter KB or MB in addition to BLKS, TRKS, and CYLS. If you specify KB, the space is allocated in kilobytes. If you specify MB, the space is allocated in megabytes.

OPTION 3.3: THE MOVE/COPY UTILITY

The move/copy utility lets you move or copy sequential or partitioned data sets. It also lets you promote a data set or member into a library that's controlled by the Library Management Facility, or promote a member within a controlled library. I'll show you how to promote a data set or member in chapter 8 when I present the Library Management Facility. So I won't present the promote function here.

Before I describe how you use the move/copy utility, I want to explain the difference between a move and a copy operation. To copy a data set means to reproduce it in another location. After you copy a file, you have two versions of it: the original version and the copied version. To move a data set, however, means to copy the file and scratch the original, so only one version of the file remains.

How to move or copy a sequential data set

Before you can move or copy a sequential data set, you must first invoke the move/copy utility by selecting option 3 from the utility menu. Then, ISPF displays the entry panel in figure 5-36. On this panel, you enter an option code to specify the operation you want to perform. The eight valid option codes and their meanings are:

C   Copy a data set
M   Move a data set
L   Copy and lock a member
P   Promote a data set or member
CP Copy and print a data set
MP Move and print a data set
LP Copy, lock, and print a member
PP Promote and print a data set or member

In part 1 of figure 5-37, I entered C in the OPTION field. As a result, the data set will be copied. For the CP and MP options, the data set is printed as it's copied or moved. And for the LP option, the data set is printed and locked. The printed output is written to the ISPF list data set. You can route it to a printer when you terminate ISPF or print it without terminating ISPF using the LIST command.

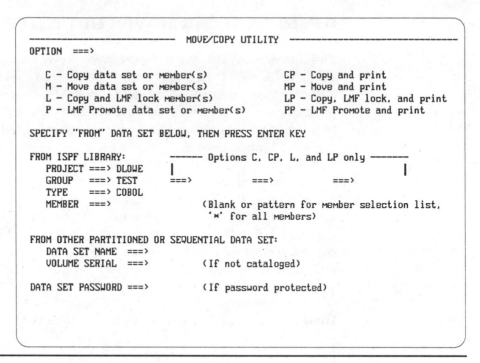

```
--------------------------- MOVE/COPY UTILITY ---------------------------
OPTION  ===>

     C - Copy data set or Member(s)              CP - Copy and print
     M - Move data set or Member(s)              MP - Move and print
     L - Copy and LMF lock member(s)             LP - Copy, LMF lock, and print
     P - LMF Promote data set or Member(s)       PP - LMF Promote and print

SPECIFY "FROM" DATA SET BELOW, THEN PRESS ENTER KEY

FROM ISPF LIBRARY:           ------ Options C, CP, L, and LP only -------
     PROJECT ===> DLOWE       |                                          |
     GROUP   ===> TEST       ===>          ===>           ===>
     TYPE    ===> COBOL
     MEMBER  ===>                 (Blank or pattern for member selection list,
                                  '*' for all members)

FROM OTHER PARTITIONED OR SEQUENTIAL DATA SET:
     DATA SET NAME  ===>
     VOLUME SERIAL  ===>          (If not cataloged)

DATA SET PASSWORD ===>          (If password protected)
```

Figure 5-36   The move/copy utility entry panel

Besides the option code, you also enter the data set name information for the input file, called the *from data set*, on the first entry panel. In figure 5-37, the *from* data set is DLOWE.TEST.DATA. For sequential data sets, you leave the member name blank.

Notice that you can enter up to four library names for the C, CP, L, and LP options. If you enter more than one name here, the libraries are concatenated. Then, ISPF searches for the data set in each of the libraries until it finds it.

After you enter the option code and the *from* data set name, ISPF displays the second entry panel, shown in part 2 of figure 5-37. On this panel, you enter the data set name information for the output file, called the *to data set*. In this example, the *to* data set is DLOWE.TEST1.DATA.

In addition to the *to* data set name, part 2 of figure 5-37 shows three questions you must answer:

```
IF PARTITIONED, REPLACE LIKED-NAMED MEMBERS ===>
IF SEQUENTIAL, "TO" DATA SET DISPOSITION    ===>
SPECIFY PACK OPTION FOR "TO" DATA SET       ===>
```

Part 1:

Specify the copy
option and the *from*
data set information

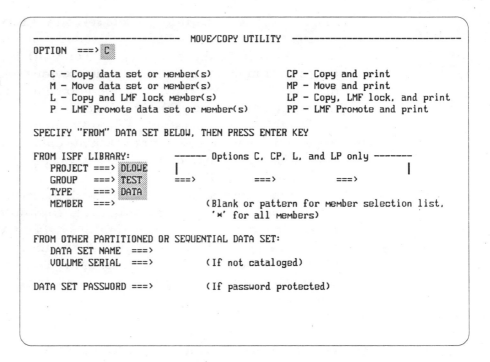

```
------------------------------- MOVE/COPY UTILITY -------------------------------
OPTION  ===> C

    C - Copy data set or member(s)        CP - Copy and print
    M - Move data set or member(s)        MP - Move and print
    L - Copy and LMF lock member(s)       LP - Copy, LMF lock, and print
    P - LMF Promote data set or member(s) PP - LMF Promote and print

SPECIFY "FROM" DATA SET BELOW, THEN PRESS ENTER KEY

FROM ISPF LIBRARY:            ------ Options C, CP, L, and LP only -------
    PROJECT ===> DLOWE        |                                          |
    GROUP   ===> TEST    ===>         ===>          ===>
    TYPE    ===> DATA
    MEMBER  ===>              (Blank or pattern for member selection list,
                              '*' for all members)


FROM OTHER PARTITIONED OR SEQUENTIAL DATA SET:
    DATA SET NAME  ===>
    VOLUME SERIAL  ===>           (If not cataloged)

DATA SET PASSWORD ===>           (If password protected)
```

Part 2:

Specify the *to* data
set information

```
COPY --- FROM DLOWE.TEST.COBOL ------------------------------------------------
COMMAND ===>

SPECIFY "TO" DATA SET BELOW.

TO ISPF LIBRARY:
    PROJECT ===> DLOWE
    GROUP   ===> TEST1
    TYPE    ===> DATA

TO OTHER PARTITIONED OR SEQUENTIAL DATA SET:
    DATA SET NAME  ===>
    VOLUME SERIAL  ===>           (If not cataloged)

DATA SET PASSWORD ===>           (If password protected)

"TO" DATA SET OPTIONS:
    IF PARTITIONED, REPLACE LIKE-NAMED MEMBERS ===> YES    (YES or NO)
    IF SEQUENTIAL, "TO" DATA SET DISPOSITION   ===>        (OLD or MOD)
    SPECIFY PACK OPTION FOR "TO" DATA SET      ===>        (YES, NO or blank)
```

Figure 5-37   Copying a sequential data set

The first applies to partitioned data sets only. I'll explain it in a moment. The second applies only to sequential files. It indicates the disposition for the *to* data set: OLD or MOD. If you specify OLD, the copy or move operation erases the previous contents of the *to* data set. If you specify MOD, the operation adds the copied or moved data to the end of the *to* data set.

The third question asks if you want to store the output data set in packed format. If you want to pack the data set, specify YES. Otherwise, specify NO, or leave the entry blank to use the same format as the *from* data set.

For any move or copy operation, both the *from* and *to* data sets must already exist. In other words, move/copy doesn't allocate a new *to* data set. To create a new copy of a data set, you must first allocate the new data set using the data set utility. Remember, you can easily allocate a new data set using the characteristics of an existing data set by first displaying the existing data set's information.

How to move or copy a partitioned data set

For partitioned data sets, you can move or copy a single member, all members, or selected members of the *from* library.

How to move or copy a single member   Figure 5-38 shows how to use move/copy to move a single member from one library to another. In part 1 of figure 5-38, I specified the option code and the *from* data set and member. Here, I'm going to move (M) a member named MKTG1200 from a library named DLOWE.TEST.COBOL.

In part 2, the *to* data set is DLOWE.TESTMKTG.COBOL and the member name is the same: MKTG1200. (If I wanted to, I could change the member name.) As a result, the member MKTG1200 is moved from DLOWE.TEST.COBOL to DLOWE.TESTMKTG.COBOL and deleted from DLOWE.TEST.COBOL.

For any move or copy operation involving libraries, your response to the question

```
IF PARTITIONED, REPLACE LIKE-NAMED MEMBERS ===>
```

is important. Whether you specify YES or NO here depends on how you want to handle members that exist in both the *from* and *to* libraries. YES means that duplicate members should be deleted

Part 1:

Specify the move
option and the *from*
data set information

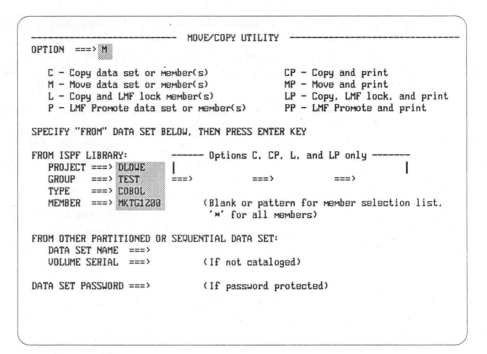

```
------------------------ MOVE/COPY UTILITY ------------------------------
OPTION  ===> M

   C - Copy data set or member(s)           CP - Copy and print
   M - Move data set or member(s)           MP - Move and print
   L - Copy and LMF lock member(s)          LP - Copy, LMF lock, and print
   P - LMF Promote data set or member(s)    PP - LMF Promote and print

SPECIFY "FROM" DATA SET BELOW, THEN PRESS ENTER KEY

FROM ISPF LIBRARY:            ------ Options C, CP, L, and LP only -------
   PROJECT ===> DLOWE      |                                           |
   GROUP   ===> TEST    ===>          ===>          ===>
   TYPE    ===> COBOL
   MEMBER  ===> MKTG1200      (Blank or pattern for member selection list,
                               '*' for all members)


FROM OTHER PARTITIONED OR SEQUENTIAL DATA SET:
   DATA SET NAME  ===>
   VOLUME SERIAL  ===>        (If not cataloged)

DATA SET PASSWORD ===>        (If password protected)
```

Part 2:

Specify the *to* data
set information

```
MOVE --- FROM DLOWE.TEST.COBOL(MKTG1200) ---------------------------------
COMMAND ===>

SPECIFY "TO" DATA SET BELOW.

TO ISPF LIBRARY:
   PROJECT ===> DLOWE
   GROUP   ===> TESTMKTG
   TYPE    ===> COBOL
   MEMBER  ===>              (Blank unless member is to be renamed)

TO OTHER PARTITIONED OR SEQUENTIAL DATA SET:
   DATA SET NAME  ===>
   VOLUME SERIAL  ===>            (If not cataloged)

DATA SET PASSWORD ===>            (If password protected)

"TO" DATA SET OPTIONS:
   IF PARTITIONED, REPLACE LIKE-NAMED MEMBERS ===> YES   (YES or NO)
   IF SEQUENTIAL, "TO" DATA SET DISPOSITION   ===>       (OLD or MOD)
   SPECIFY PACK OPTION FOR "TO" DATA SET      ===>       (YES, NO or blank)
```

Figure 5-38   Moving a library member

from the *to* library before they are copied or moved. NO means that duplicate members should not be copied or moved. So in figure 5-38, MKTG1200 is moved to DLOWE.TESTMKTG.COBOL even if that library already has a member with the same name.

How to move or copy an entire library   Figure 5-39 shows how to move or copy all members of a partitioned data set. In part 1, I entered an asterisk (*) as the member name for the *from* library. That means all members are included in the move or copy operation.

In part 2 of figure 5-39, I specified NO for REPLACE LIKE-NAMED MEMBERS. So each member of the *from* library is copied to the *to* library unless the *to* library already contains a member with the same name.

How to move or copy selected members   Figure 5-40 shows how to copy or move selected members of a partitioned data set. In part 1, I specified the *from* library but left the member name blank. Then, in part 2, I specified the *to* library.

Since I left the member name blank for the *from* library, ISPF displayed the member selection list shown in part 3 of figure 5-40. Here, you type an S next to each member you want copied. In this example, I copied two members: MKTG1200, and MKTG4100.

The RENAME column of the member list allows you to change the name of a member as it is copied or moved. For example, in part 3 of figure 5-40, I specified that MKTG4100 should be renamed to MKTG1400. Remember that the member name is changed only in the *to* library. The member name in the *from* library is not changed.

Part 4 of figure 5-40 shows the member list after the copy operation has completed. Here, ISPF indicates whether or not each member was replaced or added to the *to* library.

By the way, you can also browse a data set from the move/copy utility's member selection list. Just enter B next to the data set you want to browse and ISPF invokes the browse facility. When you exit from browse, ISPF returns you to the member selection list. Then, you can browse another member or select the member you want to move or copy.

Part 1:

Specify the copy option and the *from* data set information

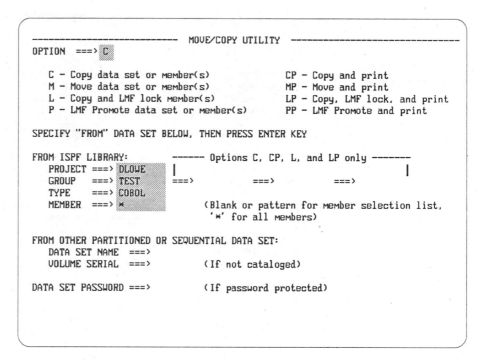

```
--------------------------------- MOVE/COPY UTILITY ---------------------------------
OPTION  ===> C

   C - Copy data set or member(s)             CP - Copy and print
   M - Move data set or member(s)             MP - Move and print
   L - Copy and LMF lock member(s)            LP - Copy, LMF lock, and print
   P - LMF Promote data set or member(s)      PP - LMF Promote and print

SPECIFY "FROM" DATA SET BELOW, THEN PRESS ENTER KEY

FROM ISPF LIBRARY:             ------ Options C, CP, L, and LP only -------
   PROJECT ===> DLOWE       |                                        |
   GROUP   ===> TEST     ===>          ===>           ===>
   TYPE    ===> COBOL
   MEMBER  ===> *           (Blank or pattern for member selection list,
                             '*' for all members)

FROM OTHER PARTITIONED OR SEQUENTIAL DATA SET:
   DATA SET NAME  ===>
   VOLUME SERIAL  ===>           (If not cataloged)

DATA SET PASSWORD ===>          (If password protected)
```

Part 2:

Specify the *to* data set information

```
COPY --- FROM DLOWE.TEST.COBOL(*) ---------------------------------------------
COMMAND ===>

SPECIFY "TO" DATA SET BELOW.

TO ISPF LIBRARY:
   PROJECT ===> DLOWE
   GROUP   ===> TESTMKTG
   TYPE    ===> COBOL

TO OTHER PARTITIONED OR SEQUENTIAL DATA SET:
   DATA SET NAME  ===>
   VOLUME SERIAL  ===>              (If not cataloged)

DATA SET PASSWORD ===>             (If password protected)

"TO" DATA SET OPTIONS:
   IF PARTITIONED, REPLACE LIKE-NAMED MEMBERS ===> NO    (YES or NO)
   IF SEQUENTIAL, "TO" DATA SET DISPOSITION   ===>       (OLD or MOD)
   SPECIFY PACK OPTION FOR "TO" DATA SET      ===>       (YES, NO or blank)
```

Figure 5-39   Copying an entire library

Part 1:

Specify the copy
option and the *from*
data set information

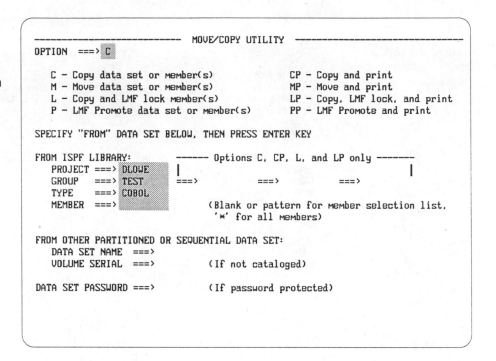

```
------------------------- MOVE/COPY UTILITY -------------------------------
OPTION ===> C

    C - Copy data set or member(s)              CP - Copy and print
    M - Move data set or member(s)              MP - Move and print
    L - Copy and LMF lock member(s)             LP - Copy, LMF lock, and print
    P - LMF Promote data set or member(s)       PP - LMF Promote and print

SPECIFY "FROM" DATA SET BELOW, THEN PRESS ENTER KEY

FROM ISPF LIBRARY:          ------ Options C, CP, L, and LP only -------
    PROJECT ===> DLOWE       |                                          |
    GROUP   ===> TEST        ===>         ===>            ===>
    TYPE    ===> COBOL
    MEMBER  ===>             (Blank or pattern for member selection list,
                             '*' for all members)

FROM OTHER PARTITIONED OR SEQUENTIAL DATA SET:
    DATA SET NAME  ===>
    VOLUME SERIAL  ===>          (If not cataloged)

DATA SET PASSWORD ===>           (If password protected)
```

Part 2:

Specify the *to* data
set information

```
COPY --- FROM DLOWE.TEST.COBOL ----------------------------------------------
COMMAND ===>

SPECIFY "TO" DATA SET BELOW.

TO ISPF LIBRARY:
    PROJECT ===> DLOWE
    GROUP   ===> TESTMKTG
    TYPE    ===> COBOL

TO OTHER PARTITIONED OR SEQUENTIAL DATA SET:
    DATA SET NAME  ===>
    VOLUME SERIAL  ===>          (If not cataloged)

DATA SET PASSWORD ===>           (If password protected)

"TO" DATA SET OPTIONS:
    IF PARTITIONED, REPLACE LIKE-NAMED MEMBERS ===> YES   (YES or NO)
    IF SEQUENTIAL, "TO" DATA SET DISPOSITION   ===>       (OLD or MOD)
    SPECIFY PACK OPTION FOR "TO" DATA SET       ===>      (YES, NO or blank)
```

Figure 5-40 Copying selected members

Part 3:

Specify the members
to be copied

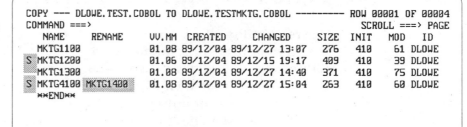

```
COPY --- DLOWE.TEST.COBOL TO DLOWE.TESTMKTG.COBOL ---------- ROW 00001 OF 00004
COMMAND ===>                                             SCROLL ===> PAGE
   NAME     RENAME     VV.MM CREATED   CHANGED      SIZE INIT  MOD   ID
   MKTG1100            01.08 89/12/04 89/12/27 13:07  276  410    61 DLOWE
 S MKTG1200            01.06 89/12/04 89/12/15 19:17  409  410    39 DLOWE
   MKTG1300            01.08 89/12/04 89/12/27 14:40  371  410    75 DLOWE
 S MKTG4100 MKTG1400   01.08 89/12/04 89/12/27 15:04  263  410    60 DLOWE
   **END**
```

Part 4:

The result of the
copy

```
COPY --- DLOWE.TEST.COBOL TO DLOWE.TESTMKTG.COBOL ---------- ROW 00001 OF 00004
COMMAND ===>                                             SCROLL ===> PAGE
   NAME     RENAME     VV.MM CREATED   CHANGED      SIZE INIT  MOD   ID
   MKTG1100            01.08 89/12/04 89/12/27 13:07  276  410    61 DLOWE
   MKTG1200 *REPL      01.06 89/12/04 89/12/15 19:17  409  410    39 DLOWE
   MKTG1300            01.08 89/12/04 89/12/27 14:40  371  410    75 DLOWE
   MKTG4100 *COPIED    01.08 89/12/04 89/12/27 15:04  263  410    60 DLOWE
   **END**
```

Figure 5-40   Copying selected members (continued)

OPTION 3.5: THE RESET UTILITY

The reset utility allows you to create, update, and delete ISPF statistics for members of partitioned data sets. If STATS mode is on, ISPF creates or updates statistics each time you edit a member of a partitioned data set. So if STATS mode is on, you won't usually need to use the reset utility. However, there are times when you'll want to create statistics for a member or an entire data set, modify existing statistics, or delete statistics.

When you select reset, option 5 on the utility menu, ISPF displays the entry panel presented in figure 5-41. Here, you can enter the following options:

R   Create or update ISPF statistics
D   Delete ISPF statistics

How to create or update ISPF statistics

To create or update statistics, enter R (for Reset) in the OPTION field on the entry panel. Next, if you want to change the user-id for existing statistics or if you want to create statistics under a user-id other than your own, enter a value in the NEW USERID field. If you don't enter a value in the NEW USERID field when creating statistics, ISPF records the statistics under your user-id. If you're modifying statistics and don't enter a user-id, the user-id remains unchanged.

If you want to change the version number of a member, enter the new number in the NEW VERSION NUMBER field. When you change the version number, ISPF changes some other statistics as well. It sets the creation date and change date to the current date. It changes the current number of lines and initial number of lines to the current number of data records. If you specify YES for the RESET MOD LEVEL field, ISPF sets the modification level to zero. And if you specify YES for the RESET SEQ NUMBERS field, ISPF changes the number of modified lines to zero.

After you enter the values you want to change, you need to identify the data set and members you want ISPF to change. To do that, enter the appropriate values for the ISPF LIBRARY or OTHER PARTITIONED DATA SET fields. If you leave the MEMBER field

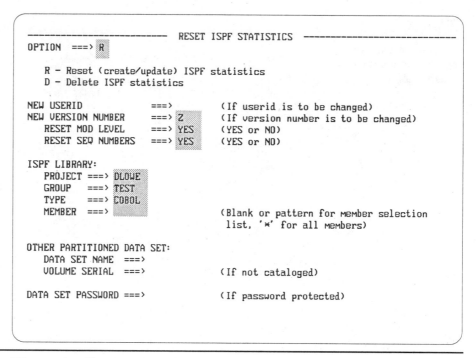

```
------------------------------- RESET ISPF STATISTICS -------------------------------
OPTION  ===> R

    R - Reset (create/update) ISPF statistics
    D - Delete ISPF statistics

NEW USERID              ===>              (If userid is to be changed)
NEW VERSION NUMBER      ===> Z            (If version number is to be changed)
    RESET MOD LEVEL     ===> YES          (YES or NO)
    RESET SEQ NUMBERS   ===> YES          (YES or NO)

ISPF LIBRARY:
    PROJECT ===> DLOWE
    GROUP   ===> TEST
    TYPE    ===> COBOL
    MEMBER  ===>                (Blank or pattern for member selection
                                 list, '*' for all members)

OTHER PARTITIONED DATA SET:
    DATA SET NAME  ===>
    VOLUME SERIAL  ===>         (If not cataloged)

DATA SET PASSWORD ===>          (If password protected)
```

Figure 5-41   The reset utility entry panel

blank or specify a pattern, ISPF displays a member list. You can
select any number of entries from this list by placing an S to the
left of each entry. If you want to update all the members in the
data set, enter an asterisk (*) for the member name on the entry
panel.

Figure 5-42 shows what happened when I processed the reset
function I entered in figure 5-41. In part 1 of figure 5-42, ISPF
displayed a member list, since I didn't specify a member name on
the entry panel. From this list, I selected the member MKTG1200.
Notice the value of the statistics for this member before I processed
the reset function. Part 2 shows the statistics for this member after
I reset the statistics. As you can see, ISPF changed the version
number to 2 and the modification level to zero. In addition, ISPF
changed the creation date and last changed date to the current
date. Finally, ISPF changed the initial and current sizes to the
current number of records, and the number of modified lines to
zero.

Part 1:

Select the members
you want to change
statistics for

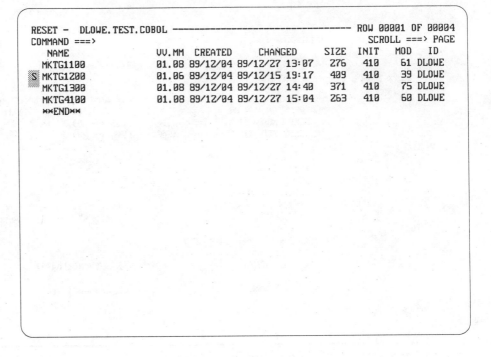

Part 2:

The statistics are
reset according to
the values you
entered on the entry
panel

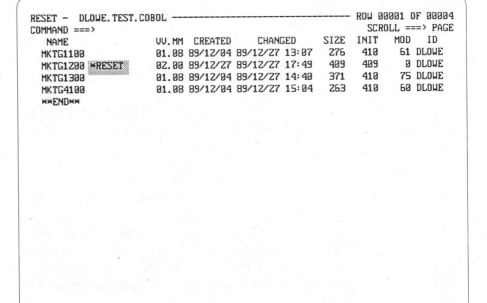

Figure 5-42   Changing ISPF statistics

How to delete ISPF statistics

To delete the statistics for a member or a group of members, enter the option D on the entry panel. Then, specify the members you want to process just like you do to create or update statistics. If you enter anything in any other fields on the panel, they're ignored.

Figure 5-43 illustrates the result of deleting the statistics for the member I updated in figure 5-42. In part 1, I entered D in the OPTION field, and the name of the library and member in the ISPF LIBRARY fields. In part 2, you can see that ISPF deleted the statistics.

OPTION 3.6: THE HARDCOPY UTILITY

You use the hardcopy utility to obtain a printed copy of a data set or library member immediately. Printed output from other sources, such as edit or move/copy, is recorded in ISPF's list file, which isn't actually printed until you exit ISPF or execute a LIST command.

The hardcopy utility can produce printed output at a local printer in foreground mode. Alternatively, you can specify job information for hardcopy to submit a background job to print the data set or member. Or, if the TSO/E Information Center Facility is installed, you can use it to print a data set.

You invoke the hardcopy utility by specifying option 6 from the utility menu. When you do, ISPF displays an entry panel that allows you to specify the requirements for the type of printing you want to do. The entry panel ISPF displays depends on whether you use the Information Center Facility to perform the print function.

How to print a data set at a local printer

Figure 5-44 presents the hardcopy entry panel ISPF displays if you don't use the Information Center Facility for printing. Here, you can select two options. PK keeps the data set or member you specify after it's printed. PD deletes it after it's printed.

The example in figure 5-44 shows how to print a data set at a local printer. Because I specified PK as the hardcopy option, the data set will be kept after it's printed. By the way, if you specify a

Part 1:

Specify the delete
option and the data
set and member
information

```
---------------------------- RESET ISPF STATISTICS ----------------------------
OPTION  ===> D

  R - Reset (create/update) ISPF statistics
  D - Delete ISPF statistics

NEW USERID            ===>           (If userid is to be changed)
NEW VERSION NUMBER    ===> Z         (If version number is to be changed)
  RESET MOD LEVEL     ===> YES       (YES or NO)
  RESET SEQ NUMBERS   ===> NO        (YES or NO)

ISPF LIBRARY:
  PROJECT ===> DLOWE
  GROUP   ===> TEST
  TYPE    ===> COBOL
  MEMBER  ===> MKTG1200            (Blank or pattern for member selection
                                    list, '*' for all members)


OTHER PARTITIONED DATA SET:
  DATA SET NAME  ===>
  VOLUME SERIAL  ===>               (If not cataloged)

DATA SET PASSWORD ===>              (If password protected)
```

Part 2:

The statistics are
deleted

```
RESET -  DLOWE.TEST.COBOL ----------------------------------- ROW 00001 OF 00004
COMMAND ===>                                                   SCROLL ===> PAGE
  NAME                VV.MM  CREATED      CHANGED        SIZE  INIT  MOD  ID
  MKTG1100            01.08 89/12/04 89/12/27 13:07      276   410   61  DLOWE
  MKTG1200 *RESET
  MKTG1300            01.08 89/12/04 89/12/27 14:40      371   410   75  DLOWE
  MKTG4100            01.08 89/12/04 89/12/27 15:04      263   410   60  DLOWE
  **END**
```

Figure 5-43   Deleting ISPF statistics

```
------------------------------ HARDCOPY UTILITY ------------------------------
OPTION  ===> PK

   PK - Print and keep data set
   PD - Print and delete data set




DATA SET NAME ===> TEST.COBOL(MKTG1200)
   VOLUME SERIAL      ===>                    (If not cataloged)
   DATA SET PASSWORD ===>                     (If password protected PDS)

PRINT MODE            ===> LOCAL             (BATCH or LOCAL)

SYSOUT CLASS          ===>
LOCAL PRINTER ID      ===> IBMT2IP1

JOB STATEMENT INFORMATION: (If not to local printer, verify before proceeding)
   ===> //DLOWEA   JOB (9999),'DOUG LOWE'
   ===> //*
   ===> //*
   ===> //*
```

Figure 5-44   Printing a data set at a local printer

member of a partitioned data set to be printed, it's always kept
regardless of the option you specify.

In the PRINT MODE field, enter LOCAL to print the data set at
a local printer. Then enter the printer-id in the LOCAL PRINTER ID
field. ISPF uses the value in this field to route the output to the
correct printer. In this example, the output is routed to a printer
named IBMT2IP1. Printer-ids vary from one installation to the
next, so you'll have to ask your supervisor what printer-id to use.

Unlike most other ISPF entry panels, the hardcopy panel
doesn't provide project, library, type, and member fields to specify
a data set. Instead, you enter the data set name in the usual TSO
format. In figure 5-44, I entered TEST.COBOL(MKTG1200) as the
data set name. Since ISPF adds the user-id (project) to the beginning of the data set name, the actual MVS data set name for the file
to be printed is DLOWE.TEST.COBOL(MKTG1200).

If you don't want ISPF to add your user-id to a data set name,
simply enclose the name in apostrophes. For example,

```
DATASET NAME ===> 'SYS2.COMMAND.CLIST($VER)'
```

If you use apostrophes, you must specify the fully qualified data set name.

If the data set isn't cataloged, you must enter a volume serial number in the VOLUME SERIAL field. And if the data set is protected by standard MVS security (not RACF), you must supply a password in the PASSWORD field. Otherwise, you leave these fields blank.

How to print a data set using a background job

To print a data set via a background job, you specify BATCH in the PRINT MODE field. Then, hardcopy generates the JCL necessary to print the data set using the JOB statement provided in the JOB STATEMENT INFORMATION field and the output class indicated in the SYSOUT CLASS field. If you're not familiar with JCL, find out from your supervisor what values to code in these fields.

Each time you complete the hardcopy entry panel, hardcopy generates a job step that invokes a system utility named IEBGENER to print the specified data set. As a result, you can print three data sets with a single job simply by completing the entry panel three times. The job isn't actually submitted for JES background processing until you return to the utilities menu by pressing PF3/15.

To illustrate, consider figure 5-45. In part 1, I specify the hardcopy option (PK), the data set and member name, the SYSOUT class (X), and the JOB statement information. Part 2 shows the next panel ISPF displays. It indicates that JCL has been generated. Here, you have three options: (1) enter PK or PD and another data set name to generate more JCL; (2) enter CANCEL to return to the utilities menu without submitting the job; or (3) press the End key, PF3/15, to submit the job. Part 3 shows the panel ISPF displays when you submit the job for background processing. Here, you can see that the job named DLOWEA has been submitted. The MVS job number for this job is JOB01777. When you press the Enter key, ISPF returns to the utility menu.

How to print a data set using the Information Center Facility

If you use the Information Center Facility to print a data set, ISPF displays the entry panel in figure 5-46 when you select the

Part 1:

Specify the option,
data set, and job
information

```
------------------------------ HARDCOPY UTILITY ----------------------------------
OPTION  ===> PK

   PK - Print and keep data set
   PD - Print and delete data set




DATA SET NAME ===> TEST.COBOL(MKTG1200)
   VOLUME SERIAL      ===>                    (If not cataloged)
   DATA SET PASSWORD ===>                     (If password protected PDS)

PRINT MODE            ===> BATCH         (BATCH or LOCAL)

SYSOUT CLASS          ===> X
LOCAL PRINTER ID      ===>

JOB STATEMENT INFORMATION: (If not to local printer, verify before proceeding)
   ===> //DLOWEA   JOB (9999),'DOUG LOWE'
   ===> //*
   ===> //*
   ===> //*
```

Part 2:

The JCL has been
generated; press the
End key to submit the
job

```
------------------------------ HARDCOPY UTILITY ------------------- JCL GENERATED
OPTION  ===> PK

   PK - Print and keep data set
   PD - Print and delete data set
   CANCEL - Exit without submitting job

Enter END command to submit job.

DATA SET NAME ===> TEST.COBOL(MKTG1200)
   VOLUME SERIAL      ===>                    (If not cataloged)
   DATA SET PASSWORD ===>                     (If password protected PDS)

PRINT MODE            ===> BATCH         (BATCH or LOCAL)

SYSOUT CLASS          ===> X
LOCAL PRINTER ID      ===>

JOB STATEMENT INFORMATION:
        //DLOWEA   JOB (9999),'DOUG LOWE'
        //*
        //*
        //*
```

Figure 5-45   Printing a data set via a background job

Part 3:

The job has been submitted for background processing

```
-------------------------------- HARDCOPY UTILITY -------------------- JCL GENERATED
OPTION  ===> PK

   PK - Print and keep data set
   PD - Print and delete data set
   CANCEL - Exit without submitting job

Enter END command to submit job.

DATA SET NAME ===> TEST.COBOL(MKTG1200)
   VOLUME SERIAL     ===>                  (If not cataloged)
   DATA SET PASSWORD ===>                  (If password protected PDS)

PRINT MODE         ===> BATCH       (BATCH or LOCAL)

SYSOUT CLASS       ===> X
LOCAL PRINTER ID   ===>

JOB STATEMENT INFORMATION:
       //DLOWEA  JOB (9999),'DOUG LOWE'
IKJ56250I JOB DLOWEA(JOB01777) SUBMITTED
***
```

Figure 5-45   Printing a data set via a background job (continued)

hardcopy utility. The options available from this panel are the same as for local or batch printing: PK and PD. You also enter the data set name, volume serial number, and password just as you do for the other printing methods. However, the last three fields on the screen are new.

In the PRINTER LOCATION field, you enter the location-id of the printer you want to use. In the PRINTER FORMAT field, enter the format you want to use. Both of these fields vary from one shop to the next, so check with your system administrator to find out what values to use. In figure 5-46, I entered MMA/PRT1 for the location id, and I entered STANDARD for the printer format.

You can also leave the PRINTER LOCATION and PRINTER FORMAT fields blank or enter partial names followed by an asterisk (*). If the names you specify don't identify a specific printer, ICF displays a list of the available printers. You can then select the printer you want from this list.

The last field you specify is the number of copies. After you enter all these fields, press the Enter key. Then, the information is sent to ICF for processing.

```
------------------------------ HARDCOPY UTILITY ------------------------------
OPTION  ===> PK


   PK - Print and keep data set
   PD - Print and delete data set




DATA SET NAME ===> TEST.COBOL(MKTG1200)
   VOLUME SERIAL    ===>                    (If not cataloged
   DATA SET PASSWORD ===>                   (If password protected PDS)

PRINTER LOCATION   ===> MMA/PRT1

PRINTER FORMAT     ===> STANDARD

NUMBER OF COPIES   ===> 1
```

Figure 5-46   Printing a data set using the Information Center Facility

DISCUSSION

When compared with MVS utility programs or TSO commands, ISPF's utilities make managing libraries and data sets easy. When you submit a background job to perform one of these functions, you typically have to code complicated JCL statements. And in native TSO, you have to code equally complicated parameters on the TSO commands.

Still, you can't use these utilities to perform all the functions you'll ever need. For example, you won't always be able to use the allocate function of the dataset utility to allocate your data sets. That's because both the JCL DD statement and the native TSO ALLOCATE command provide options that aren't available under ISPF. So if your data set requires one of these options (most don't), you won't be able to use ISPF. But, in most cases, ISPF provides all the functions you'll need to manage your libraries and data sets.

Terms

extent
expiration date
load library
from data set
to data set

Objectives

1. Use the library utility to perform any of its functions.

2. Use the data set utility to allocate, rename, delete, catalog, or uncatalog a data set.

3. Distinguish between a copy and a move operation.

4. Use the copy/move utility to reproduce a data set, either with or without printing it.

5. Use the reset utility to perform the following functions:

    a. Create or update the ISPF statistics for selected members of a partitioned data set

    b. Delete the ISPF statistics for selected members of a partitioned data set

6. Use the hardcopy utility to print a data set.

Topic 3   The compare and search utilities

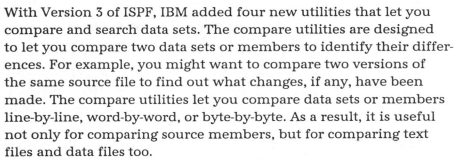

With Version 3 of ISPF, IBM added four new utilities that let you compare and search data sets. The compare utilities are designed to let you compare two data sets or members to identify their differences. For example, you might want to compare two versions of the same source file to find out what changes, if any, have been made. The compare utilities let you compare data sets or members line-by-line, word-by-word, or byte-by-byte. As a result, it is useful not only for comparing source members, but for comparing text files and data files too.

The search utilities are useful because they let you search a member, a group of members, or a group of libraries to locate all occurrences of a particular character string. For example, you could use the search utilities to locate all source members that refer to a particular data file, copy member, or subprogram.

The four compare and search utilities are implemented by a single IBM program called *SuperC*. SuperC is a versatile utility program that provides a variety of search and comparison functions. The four ISPF compare and search utilities are simply interfaces to the SuperC program that invoke different functions.

Unfortunately, the way IBM designed these interfaces can seem a little confusing at first. Although there are four search and compare utilities, only three of them are available from the utilities menu. Option 3.12, called SuperC, is the standard compare utility. You'll use SuperC to do a straightforward comparison of two data sets or members. Option 3.13, called SuperCE, is the extended compare utility. It lets you specify additional options to do more complicated comparisons. Option 3.14, called search-for, is the standard search utility. It lets you do a basic search operation.

The fourth search-and-compare utility, the extended search-for utility, doesn't appear on the utilities menu. Instead, you invoke it by specifying option S from the extended compare utility, option 3.13. To use the extended search-for utility directly from any ISPF panel, just type =3.13.S in the command area.

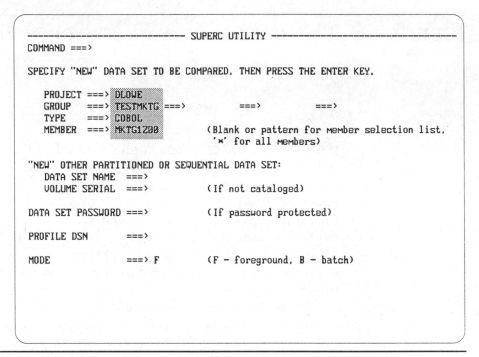

```
------------------------------- SUPERC UTILITY -------------------------------
COMMAND ===>

SPECIFY "NEW" DATA SET TO BE COMPARED, THEN PRESS THE ENTER KEY.

     PROJECT ===> DLOWE
     GROUP   ===> TESTMKTG ===>        ===>         ===>
     TYPE    ===> COBOL
     MEMBER  ===> MKTG1Z00      (Blank or pattern for member selection list,
                                 '*' for all members)


"NEW" OTHER PARTITIONED OR SEQUENTIAL DATA SET:
     DATA SET NAME  ===>
     VOLUME SERIAL  ===>        (If not cataloged)

DATA SET PASSWORD ===>          (If password protected)

PROFILE DSN       ===>

MODE              ===> F        (F - foreground, B - batch)
```

Figure 5-47   The first SuperC utility entry panel

OPTION 3.12: THE SUPERC UTILITY

The SuperC utility, option 3.12, lets you compare two data sets or
members. SuperC compares files on a line-by-line basis and creates
a listing of the differences.

How to specify the data sets to compare

You use two panels to specify the names of the data sets you want
to compare. On the first panel, illustrated in figure 5-47, you
specify the new data set, that is, the more current version of the
data set. On the second panel, illustrated in figure 5-48, you specify
the older version of the data set. If one of the data sets you're
comparing isn't an updated version of the other, it doesn't matter
which ones you specify as the new and old data sets.

   The data sets you compare using the SuperC utility can be
sequential data sets, partitioned data sets, members of partitioned
data sets, or concatenated data sets. The only restriction is that the

```
COMPARE -- DLOWE.TESTMKTG.COBOL(MKTG1200) ---------------------------------------
COMMAND ===>

SPECIFY "OLD" DATA SET TO BE COMPARED, THEN PRESS THE ENTER KEY.

    PROJECT ===> DLOWE
    GROUP   ===> TEST     ===>          ===>          ===>
    TYPE    ===> COBOL
    MEMBER  ===> MKTG1200

"OLD" OTHER PARTITIONED OR SEQUENTIAL DATA SET:
    DATA SET NAME  ===>
    VOLUME SERIAL  ===>                          (If not cataloged)

DATA SET PASSWORD ===>                           (If password protected)

LISTING TYPE       ===> DELTA                    (DELTA/CHNG/LONG/OVSUM/NOLIST)
LISTING DS NAME    ===> SUPERC.LIST
SEQUENCE NUMBERS   ===> COBOL                     (blank/SEQ/NOSEQ/COBOL)
```

Figure 5-48   The second SuperC utility entry panel

new and the old data sets must be the same type. So, for example, you can't compare a sequential data set with a member of a partitioned data set. In figures 5-47 and 5-48, I entered the names of members in two partitioned data sets.

If you want to compare all the members in the new partitioned data set with liked-named members in the old partitioned data set, enter an asterisk (*) in the MEMBER field on the first entry panel. If you want to select members in the new partitioned data set to compare with members in the old partitioned data set, leave the MEMBER field blank or enter a pattern. Then, ISPF displays a member list like the one in figure 5-49. From this list, you select the members you want to compare by entering an S to the left of the member names.

Notice that the member names in the list are from the new data set. If the members you want to compare them with in the old data set have the same names, you don't need to enter the old member names. However, if any of the old members have different names, you need to enter the names in the column labeled OLD-MEM.

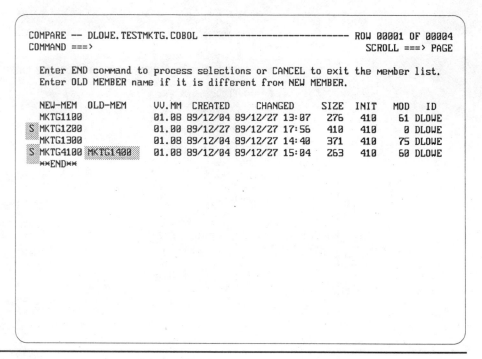

```
COMPARE -- DLOWE.TESTMKTG.COBOL ----------------------------- ROW 00001 OF 00004
COMMAND ===>                                                  SCROLL ===> PAGE

    Enter END command to process selections or CANCEL to exit the member list.
    Enter OLD MEMBER name if it is different from NEW MEMBER.

    NEW-MEM  OLD-MEM      VV.MM CREATED   CHANGED       SIZE  INIT   MOD  ID
    MKTG1100              01.08 89/12/04 89/12/27 13:07  276  410    61 DLOWE
  S MKTG1200              01.00 89/12/27 89/12/27 17:56  410  410     0 DLOWE
    MKTG1300              01.08 89/12/04 89/12/27 14:40  371  410    75 DLOWE
  S MKTG4100  MKTG1400    01.08 89/12/04 89/12/27 15:04  263  410    60 DLOWE
    **END**
```

Figure 5-49   A SuperC member selection list

In figure 5-49, for example, I selected two members to compare. The first one has the same name in both the new and old data sets, so I didn't need to specify the old member name. The second member, however, has a different name in the old data set, so I had to enter that name in the OLD-MEM column.

To process the members you select, press the End key, PF3/15. If you press the End key without selecting any members, ISPF returns to the previous panel. You can also exit from the member list without processing selections by entering the CANCEL command in the command area.

How to compare data sets in batch mode

Usually, you'll use the SuperC utility in foreground mode. However, if you're comparing two large members or two entire libraries, you may want to invoke SuperC in batch mode so you can continue your work while the comparison is done. To do that, enter B in the MODE field on the SuperC utility entry panel.

```
----------------------- SUPERC UTILITY - SUBMIT BATCH JOBS -----------------------
OPTION  ===>

blank  - Generate output listing to SYSOUT CLASS below.
  1    - Generate output listing to DATA SET NAME below.
  2    - Generate output listing using completed  //OUTDD DD  below.

SYSOUT CLASS  ===> A

DATA SET NAME ===> SUPERC.LIST

//OUTDD  DD   ===>
//            ===>
                                    LRECL for the Listing Output will be 133

JOB STATEMENT INFORMATION: (Required - Enter/Verify JOB control statements)
 ===> //DLOWEB   JOB (9999),'DOUG LOWE'
 ===> //*
 ===> //*
 ===>
```

Figure 5-50   A batch submit panel for a job that includes an output listing

If you select batch mode, ISPF displays a submit entry panel like the one in figure 5-50. Here, you can opt to send the output listing to a SYSOUT class or data set you specify, or you can enter the actual DD statement you want to include in the job. You can also enter the job statement information from this panel. When you make the appropriate entries and press the Enter key, ISPF submits a batch job to invoke the SuperC program.

How to request a listing

In the LISTING TYPE field of the second entry panel, you specify the type of output listing you want SuperC to prepare. As you can see, SuperC can prepare four types of listings: DELTA, CHNG, LONG, and OVSUM. If you specify NOLIST in this field, SuperC won't prepare any listing. Instead, SuperC just displays a message indicating the results of the comparison.

If you request a DELTA listing, the list output shows the differences between the two data sets, followed by a summary.

Figure 5-51, for example, is a DELTA list from a comparison of two partitioned data set members.

Notice in figure 5-51 that each difference included in the listing is prefixed by a code. This code indicates the type of difference SuperC found. For example, the letter I means that a line was inserted and the letter D means that a line was deleted. Two other codes you'll see frequently in a DELTA list output from a line compare are RN and RO, which stand for reformat new and reformat old. These codes indicate that the lines in the old and new data sets contain the same data, but with different spacing.

After the changed lines in a line compare listing are four columns that provide additional information about the changes. The first column, labeled TYPE, tells more about the differences that were found. Figure 5-52 lists all the codes you may find in this column. As you can see in figure 5-51, these codes usually appear after the lines they apply to. But one code, MAT=, appears between the changed lines, because this code doesn't indicate anything about the changed lines. Instead, it indicates there are lines between the changed lines that are the same in both of the data sets or members being compared.

The next column, labeled LEN, indicates the number of consecutive lines the type code refers to. For example, in figure 5-51, you can see that SuperC found 131 matching lines between the first two differences. And the last two columns, labeled N-LN# and O-LN#, indicate the line numbers in the new and old data sets where the changes were found.

On the last page of a DELTA listing is a summary of the differences that were found. For example, in figure 5-51, 407 lines were the same in both data sets, 3 lines were added to the new data set, 2 lines were deleted from the old data set, and 3 lines were changed. This summary is useful because it shows the extent of the differences between the two data sets.

If you specify CHNG for the listing type, the output is similar to the DELTA listing. The difference is that the CHNG listing includes up to ten unchanged lines before and after each changed line. This sometimes helps to determine the context of the change.

If you specify LONG for the listing type, the output listing contains every line in the new data set, whether it's changed or not, and any data from the old data set that's not in the new data set. This type of listing can be extensive, so unless you need all the information it contains, you should use the DELTA or CHNG listings.

```
   SUPERC - FILE/LINE/WORD/BYTE COMPARE PGM - V2.7(87/03/27)   90/01/26   17.54        PAGE   1
NEW: DLOWE.TESTMKTG.COBOL(MKTG1200)        OLD: DLOWE.TEST.COBOL(MKTG1200)

                   LISTING OUTPUT SECTION (LINE COMPARE)

ID     SOURCE LINES                                                       TYPE LEN N-LN# O-LN#
       ----+----1----+----2----+----3----+----4----+----5----+----6----+----7----+----8
I  -  018400 000-PRODUCE-SALES-REPORT.                                    RPL=   1 00184 00184
D  -  018400 000-PRODUCT-SALES-REPORT.

                                                                          MAT= 131
I  -  031600*                                                             INS=   1 00316 00316
                                                                          MAT=  87
I  -  040400                        / TOTAL-SALES-LAST-YTD                RPL=   1 00404 00403
D  -  040300                        / BRANCH-TOTAL-LAST-YTD
                                                                          MAT=   6


   SUPERC - FILE/LINE/WORD/BYTE COMPARE PGM - V2.7(87/03/27)   90/01/26   17.54        PAGE   2
NEW: DLOWE.TESTMKTG.COBOL(MKTG1200)        OLD: DLOWE.TEST.COBOL(MKTG1200)

              LINE COMPARE SUMMARY AND STATISTICS

407 NUMBER OF LINE MATCHES               3  TOTAL CHANGES (PAIRED+NONPAIRED CHNG)
  0 REFORMATTED LINES                    2  PAIRED CHANGES (REFM+PAIRED INS/DEL)
  3 NEW FILE LINE INSERTIONS             1  NON-PAIRED INSERTS
  2 OLD FILE LINE DELETIONS              0  NON-PAIRED DELETES
410 NEW FILE LINES PROCESSED
409 OLD FILE LINES PROCESSED

LISTING-TYPE = DELTA       COMPARE-COLUMNS =    7:80        LONGEST-LINE = 80
PROCESS OPTIONS USED: COBOL
```

Figure 5-51 A delta output listing for a comparison operation

Code	Description
MAT=	The lines in the two data sets being compared match.
RFM=	The lines have been reformatted in the new data set.
RPL=	The lines have been replaced in the new data set.
INS=	New lines were inserted in the new data set.
DEL=	Lines were deleted from the new data set.
IMV=	Lines were moved in the new data set.
DMV=	Lines were moved in the old data set.
IMR=	Lines were moved and reformatted in the new data set.
DMR=	Lines were moved and reformatted in the old data set.

Figure 5-52   Type codes that can appear on a comparison listing

The last listing type you can specify is OVSUM. This type of listing contains only a summary of the differences just like the summary page in figure 5-51. Since the individual differences aren't included in the listing, this type of listing is useful if you're interested in the extent of the differences between the two files, but don't need to know the specific differences.

After you specify the type of list output you want, you need to specify the name of the data set that will contain the output. You enter that name in the LISTING DS NAME field on the second entry panel. If you leave this field blank, SuperC uses a default of SUPERC.LIST, prefixed by your user-id.

After the comparison operation is complete, you can print the list output or you can view it at your terminal using browse. If you execute SuperC in foreground mode, the SuperC utility invokes browse automatically when the comparison operation finishes. When you finish browsing the output listing, press the End key, PF3/15, to return to the first entry panel.

How to handle sequence numbers

The last option you can specify for the SuperC utility determines how sequence numbers are handled. You enter this option in the SEQUENCE NUMBERS field on the second entry panel. The valid options are SEQ, NOSEQ and COBOL.

If you specify SEQ or leave the SEQUENCE NUMBERS field blank, sequence numbers are excluded from the comparison. Then, SuperC assumes the values in columns 73-80 of fixed-length 80-byte blocked data sets and the values in columns 1-8 of variable-length 255-byte blocked data sets are sequence numbers. If you specify NOSEQ, sequence numbers are treated as data. And if you specify COBOL, the data in columns 1-6 is assumed to be a sequence number and is ignored.

How to use a profile data set

If you specify only the names of the new and old data sets as in figures 5-47 and 5-48, the SuperC program uses defaults for its processing options. One way to change these defaults is to specify the name of a profile data set in the PROFILE DSN field on the first panel. A profile data set can specify the listing type and sequence numbers setting, and other options that are available with the SuperCE utility. To create a profile data set, you have to use the SuperCE utility, which I'll explain next.

OPTION 3.13: THE SUPERCE UTILITY

The SuperCE utility, option 3.13, is an extended version of the SuperC utility. Figure 5-53 shows the SuperCE entry panel. Like the SuperC utility, SuperCE lets you compare data sets or members. Unlike SuperC, however, SuperCE lets you specify a variety of options that affect the way the data is compared. For example, you can select one of four types of comparisons. You can also select from over 20 processing options, and supply control statements that provide precise control over the comparison.

The SuperCE utility also provides access to the extended search-for utility. I won't discuss that function here, though. Instead, I'll discuss the extended search-for utility separately later in this topic.

```
------------------------------ SUPERCE UTILITY ------------------------------
OPTION  ===> P

blank - Compare Data Sets                    P - Select Process Options
  B   - Submit Batch Data Set Compare        E - Edit Statements Data Set
  S   - Extended Search-For Compare Utility  A - Activate/Create Profiles

New DS Name     ===> TESTMKTG.COBOL(MKTG1200)
Old DS Name     ===> TEST.COBOL(MKTG1200)
PDS Member List ===>            (blank/pattern - member list, * - compare all)
   (Leave New/Old Dsn "blank" for concatenated-uncataloged-password panel)
                          Optional Section
Compare Type    ===> LINE                 (FILE/ LINE /WORD/BYTE)
Listing Type    ===> DELTA                (OVSUM/ DELTA /CHNG/LONG/NOLIST)
Listing Dsn     ===> SUPERC.LIST
Process Options ===>
                ===>
Statements Dsn  ===>
Update  Dsn     ===>
BROWSE  Output  ===> YES                   ( YES /NO/COND/UPD)
```

Figure 5-53   The SuperCE entry panel

How to specify the data sets to compare

To compare two data sets using SuperCE, enter the names of the
new and old data sets in the NEW DS NAME and OLD DS NAME
fields. Notice that you must enter the names using TSO naming
conventions. The PROJECT, GROUP, and TYPE fields aren't available like they are for most other ISPF functions.

If the data sets you're comparing are partitioned, you can
compare all their members by entering an asterisk (*) in the PDS
MEMBER LIST field. To display a member list, leave this field
blank or enter a pattern. The member list that's displayed is the
same as the one that's displayed for the SuperC utility.

If you want to compare concatenated, uncataloged, or password-
protected data sets, leave the NEW DS NAME and OLD DS NAME
fields blank. When you do, SuperCE displays the panel in figure
5-54. Here, you can enter up to four data sets to be concatenated, a
volume serial number for an uncataloged data set, and a password
for a password-protected data set. Note that if you submit a job in

```
 ------------------- SUPERCE - CONCATENATION INTERACTIVE ENTRY -------------------
COMMAND ===>

   "NEW"      DS1 ===>
CONCATENATION DS2 ===>
              DS3 ===>
              DS4 ===>
OTHER "NEW" PARTITIONED OR SEQUENTIAL DATA SET
    DATA SET NAME ===>
    VOLUME SERIAL ===>                        (If not cataloged)
    PASSWORD      ===>                        (If password protected)

   "OLD"      DS1 ===>
CONCATENATION DS2 ===>
              DS3 ===>
              DS4 ===>
OTHER "OLD" PARTITIONED OR SEQUENTIAL DATA SET
    DATA SET NAME ===>
    VOLUME SERIAL ===>                        (If not cataloged)
    PASSWORD      ===>                        (If password protected)
```

Figure 5-54   The SuperCE concatenation entry panel

batch mode by entering B in the OPTION field on the entry panel,
the PASSWORD fields aren't displayed on this panel.

How to specify types of comparisons

The SuperCE utility can perform four different types of comparisons: file, line, word, and byte. To specify one of these types, enter the appropriate value in the COMPARE TYPE field on the SuperCE entry panel. If you don't enter a value here, the default is LINE.

A *file comparison* quickly compares two data sets by calculating a *hash value* for each. A file comparison always produces a summary listing like the one shown in figure 5-55, so it doesn't matter what listing type you request. As you can see in figure 5-55, the hash value for the new data set is DF832F75, and the hash value for the old data set is 1DF2506F. That means the files are different. If the hash values were the same, you could assume the data sets were identical. Although file comparison is the fastest comparison method available, it provides the least amount of

```
    SUPERC - FILE/LINE/WORD/BYTE COMPARE PGM - V2.7(87/03/27)   90/01/11   12.47          PAGE    1
NEW: DLOWE.TESTMKTG.COBOL(MKTG1200)                         OLD: DLOWE.TEST.COBOL(MKTG1200)

DIFF SAME   N-BYTES   O-BYTES   N-LINES   O-LINES   N-HASH-SUM   O-HASH-SUM

**          32720     32800     409       410       DF832F75     1DF2506F
```

Figure 5-55 Sample output from a file comparison

useful information. So you should use it only if you're interested in finding out whether two files are identical.

If you specify a *line compare*, SuperC compares the two data sets line by line. This is the type of comparison you'll probably use most often. It's particularly useful for source programs because it's record-oriented and identifies inserted and deleted lines of code. I presented sample output from a line compare earlier in figure 5-51.

The *word compare* compares two data sets word by word. In this case, a word is a group of characters delimited by blanks or any other delimiter. A word compare is particularly useful for comparing text files.

The last compare type is BYTE. If you specify this option, the SuperC program compares the two data sets byte by byte. The output listing for a *byte compare* includes both hexadecimal and character representations of the data set contents. This type of compare is most useful for data sets that contain unreadable characters.

How to select process options

There are a variety of options you can specify that affect the execution of the SuperC program. Since you'll never use many of these options, I won't discuss all of them here. However, you can see most of them, along with a brief explanation, in the panels in parts 2, 3, and 4 of figure 5-56.

In part 1 of figure 5-56, I entered P in the OPTION field on the SuperCE entry panel to select process options. When I pressed the Enter key, ISPF displayed the screen in part 2 of figure 5-56. As you can see, the options are grouped into categories. The first category contains Input Process Control Options. The second contains Don't Process Control Options. In this example, I selected the COBOL input process control option so the sequence numbers in columns 1-6 of the data sets are ignored. I also selected the DPCBCMT option so that the lines that contain an asterisk in column 7 aren't processed. That way, COBOL comment statements won't be included in the comparison.

At the bottom of the panel in part 2, you can see a message that indicates the options are continued on the next page. So, after you select the options you want on the first option panel, press the Enter key. Then, ISPF displays a second option panel, illustrated in part 3 of figure 5-56. This panel contains Output Process Control

Part 1:

Enter the option to
select process
options

```
------------------------------ SUPERCE UTILITY ------------------------------
OPTION ===> P

blank - Compare Data Sets                      P - Select Process Options
  B   - Submit Batch Data Set Compare          E - Edit Statements Data Set
  S   - Extended Search-For Compare Utility     A - Activate/Create Profiles

New DS Name      ===> TESTMKTG.COBOL(MKTG1200)
Old DS Name      ===> TEST.COBOL(MKTG1200)
PDS Member List  ===>            (blank/pattern - member list, * - compare all)
    (Leave New/Old Dsn "blank" for concatenated-uncataloged-password panel)
                           Optional Section
Compare Type    ===> LINE              (FILE/ LINE /WORD/BYTE)
Listing Type    ===> DELTA             (OVSUM/ DELTA /CHNG/LONG/NOLIST)
Listing Dsn     ===> SUPERC.LIST
Process Options ===>
                ===>
Statements Dsn  ===>
Update  Dsn     ===>
BROWSE  Output  ===> YES               ( YES /NO/COND/UPD)
```

Part 2:

Select the options you
want from the first
option panel

```
-------------------- SUPERCE - LINE COMPARE PROCESS OPTIONS ----------- (1 of 3)
COMMAND ===>

Select Process Option(s) or "blank" to remove.  Press  ENTER to continue.

                        Input Process Control Options
        SEQ      - Ignore FB 80/VB 255 standard sequence number columns, or
        NOSEQ    - Process FB 80/VB 255 standard sequence number columns as data, or
     S  COBOL    - Ignore sequence number columns 1-6 in FB 80 records.
        ANYC     - Process Lower case as Upper case input characters.

                        Don't Process Control Options
        DPPLCMT  - Don't process /* ... */ comments and blank compare lines.
        DPPSCMT  - Don't process (* ... *) comments and blank compare lines.
        DPADCMT  - Don't process "--" comments and blank compare lines.
        DPACMT   - Don't process "assembler" lines with "*" in column 1.
        DPFTCMT  - Don't process lines with "C" in column 1.
     S  DPCBCMT  - Don't process lines with "*" in column 7.
        DPBLKCL  - Don't process blank compare lines.
                        (continued on next page)
```

Figure 5-56   Selecting process options for a compare operation

Part 3:

Select the options you
want from the second
option panel

```
-------------------- SUPERCE - LINE COMPARE PROCESS OPTIONS ------------ (2 of 3)
COMMAND ===>

Select Process Option(s) or "blank" to remove.   Press  ENTER to continue.

                          Output Process Control Options
     REFMOVR  - Reformat override.  Don't flag reformatted lines in listing.
     DLREFM   - Don't list reformatted old DS lines. Only new DS reformats.
     DLMDUP   - Don't list matched old DS lines in side-by-side listing.
     FMVLNS   - Flag Insert/Delete moved lines.
     LOCS     - List only changed and non-paired members in PDS summary list.
     CNPML    - Count all lines including non-paired members in PDS summary.

                           Listing Control Options
     WIDE     - Up to 80 columns side-by-side. Line length = 202/203, or
  S  NARROW   - Up to 55 columns side-by-side. Line length = 132/133, or
     LONGLN   - Lists up to 176 columns. Line length = 202/203.
     NOPRTCC  - No print control column and page separators.
     APNDLST  - Append listing report to listing data set.
                         (continued on next page)
```

Part 4:

Select the options you
want from the third
option panel

```
'-------------------- SUPERCE - LINE COMPARE PROCESS OPTIONS ------------ (3 of 3)
COMMAND ===>

Select Process Option(s) or "blank" to remove.   Press  ENTER to continue.

                           Update Data Set Options
     APNDUPD  - Append update report to update data set.

     UPDSUMO  - Overall summary statistics listed in a single line format, or
     UPDCMS8  - Cntl and new DS source using cols 73-80 (for CMS UPDATE), or
     UPDMVS8  - Cntl and new DS source using cols 73-80 (for MVS IEBUPDTE), or
     UPDSEQ0  - Cntl and new DS source using relative line numbers, or
     UPDCNTL  - Ins, del and mat control records using relative line numbers, or
     UPDPDEL  - Prefixed delta lines (maximum 32K columns in output line).
```

Figure 5-56   Selecting process options for a compare operation (continued)

Part 5:

The options you
selected are displayed
in the PROCESS
OPTIONS field on the
entry panel

```
---------------------------------- SUPERCE UTILITY ----------------------------------
OPTION  ===>

blank - Compare Data Sets                          P - Select Process Options
  B   - Submit Batch Data Set Compare              E - Edit Statements Data Set
  S   - Extended Search-For Compare Utility        A - Activate/Create Profiles

New DS Name      ===> TESTMKTG.COBOL(MKTG1200)
Old DS Name      ===> TEST.COBOL(MKTG1200)
PDS Member List ===>           (blank/pattern - member list, * - compare all)
    (Leave New/Old Dsn "blank" for concatenated-uncataloged-password panel)
                        Optional Section
Compare Type     ===> LINE                    (FILE/ LINE /WORD/BYTE)
Listing Type     ===> DELTA                   (OVSUM/ DELTA /CHNG/LONG/NOLIST)
Listing Dsn      ===> SUPERC.LIST
Process Options  ===> COBOL DPCBCMT NARROW
                 ===>
Statements Dsn   ===>
Update  Dsn      ===>
BROWSE  Output   ===> YES                      ( YES /NO/COND/UPD)
```

Figure 5-56   Selecting process options for a compare operation (continued)

options and Listing Control Options. The only option I selected
here is NARROW, which causes SuperC to list the two data sets
being compared side by side.

If you press the Enter key again, ISPF displays the third, and
last, option panel. This panel, illustrated in part 4 of figure 5-56,
contains Update Data Set Options. You can use these options to
create an *update data set* that contains information about the file
differences in one of several formats. The most interesting update
data set is UPDMVS8, which creates control cards that can be
processed by the standard MVS utility IEBUPDTE. You can use
IEBUPDTE with these control cards to update the old data set so it
will be identical to the new data set. (SuperCE stores the output in
the data set you specify in the UPDATE DSN field on the SuperCE
entry panel. If you don't specify an update data set name, SuperCE
uses the default SUPERC.UPDATE prefixed by your user-id.)

When you finish selecting all the options you want to use, press
the Enter key again and ISPF returns to the SuperCE entry panel.
Notice in part 5 of figure 5-56 that all the process options I selected
are listed in the PROCESS OPTIONS field. If you want to, you can

enter any of the process options directly into this field rather than selecting them from the option panels.

How to specify process statements

The SuperCE program also provides a set of process statements that control its execution. The statements you select are stored in a statements data set. Since you won't use these statements often, I won't discuss them in detail here. But you can find the details for coding these statements in the IBM manual *ISPF/PDF Services*.

If you want to use an existing statements data set, enter its name in the STATEMENTS DSN field on the SuperCE entry panel. To create a statements data set, or to display or modify the statements in an existing statements data set, enter the name of a new or an existing data set in the STATEMENTS DSN field and enter E in the OPTION field. That's what I did in part 1 of figure 5-57. If you select E without specifying the name of a statements data set, SuperCE uses the default SUPERC.STMTS, prefixed with your user-id.

If you enter the E option and press the Enter key, ISPF displays the panel in part 2 of figure 5-57. In the edit window at the top of this panel, you can enter any of the process statements listed at the bottom of the panel. The only statement I entered is

```
CMPLINE NTOP 'PROCEDURE DIVISION'
```

This statement tells SuperCE to start the comparison with the first line that contains the characters PROCEDURE DIVISION. After you enter all the statements you want to use, return to the SuperCE entry panel by pressing the End key, PF3/15.

How to browse SuperCE output

You learned earlier that the SuperC utility automatically invokes browse when the comparison is complete. Although the default for SuperCE is also to browse the output listing, you have other options as well. You can request that the output listing not be browsed, that it be browsed only if SuperCE finds differences in the data sets it compares, or that the update data set be browsed instead of the output listing. To select one of these options, enter the appropriate value in the BROWSE OUTPUT field on the

Part 1:

Select the option to
edit the statements
data set and enter the
name of the data set

```
---------------------------------- SUPERCE UTILITY ----------------------------------
OPTION  ===> E

blank - Compare Data Sets                    P - Select Process Options
  B   - Submit Batch Data Set Compare        E - Edit Statements Data Set
  S   - Extended Search-For Compare Utility  A - Activate/Create Profiles

New DS Name     ===> TESTMKTG.COBOL(MKTG1200)
Old DS Name     ===> TEST.COBOL(MKTG1200)
PDS Member List ===>          (blank/pattern - member list, * - compare all)
   (Leave New/Old Dsn "blank" for concatenated-uncataloged-password panel)
                           Optional Section
Compare Type    ===> LINE                    (FILE/ LINE /WORD/BYTE)
Listing Type    ===> DELTA                   (OVSUM/ DELTA /CHNG/LONG/NOLIST)
Listing Dsn     ===> SUPERC.LIST
Process Options ===> COBOL DPCBCMT NARROW
                ===>
Statements Dsn  ===> COBOL.STMTS
Update  Dsn     ===>
BROWSE  Output  ===> YES                     ( YES /NO/COND/UPD)
```

Part 2:

Enter the statements
you want to include in
the data set

```
EDIT ----- DLOWE.COBOL.STMTS ------------------------------- COLUMNS 001 072
COMMAND ===>                                               SCROLL ===> DATA

     Enter or change Process Statements in the EDIT window below:
****** ************************** TOP OF DATA *********************************
''''''  CMPLINE NTOP 'PROCEDURE DIVISION'
''''''
''''''
''''''
''''''
****** ************************** BOTTOM OF DATA ******************************
    Examples                         Explanation
 CMPCOLM 5:60  75:90        Compare using two column compare ranges
 LSTCOLM 25:90              List columns 25:90 from input
 DPLINE  'PAGE '            Exclude line if "PAGE " found anywhere on line
 DPLINE  'PAGE ',87:95      Exclude if "PAGE " found within columns 87:99
 SELECT  MEM1,NMEM2:OMEM2   Compare MEM1 with MEM1 and NMEM2 with OMEM2
 CMPLINE NTOP 'MACRO'       Start comparing after string found in new DSN
 LNCT    66                 Set lines per page to 66
 Others: DPLINEC  CMPBOFS  CMPCOLMN  CMPCOLMO  NTITLE  OTITLE  SLIST
         NCHGT    OCHGT     comment-lines ("*" and ".*")
```

Figure 5-57   Editing the statements data set for a compare operation

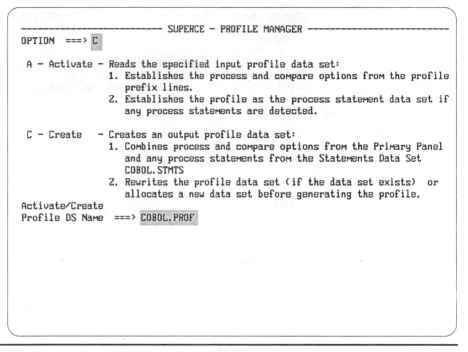

```
---------------------------- SUPERCE - PROFILE MANAGER ----------------------------
OPTION  ===> C

   A - Activate - Reads the specified input profile data set:
                  1. Establishes the process and compare options from the profile
                     prefix lines.
                  2. Establishes the profile as the process statement data set if
                     any process statements are detected.

   C - Create   - Creates an output profile data set:
                  1. Combines process and compare options from the Primary Panel
                     and any process statements from the Statements Data Set
                     COBOL.STMTS
                  2. Rewrites the profile data set (if the data set exists)  or
                     allocates a new data set before generating the profile.
Activate/Create
Profile DS Name  ===> COBOL.PROF
```

Figure 5-58   Creating a profile data set

SuperCE entry panel. The options are YES to display the output listing, NO to not display the listing, COND to display the listing if differences are found, and UPD to display the update data set.

How to use a profile

When I presented the SuperC utility, I mentioned that you can use a profile to define a compare operation. In other words, the profile contains the information you would otherwise enter into the fields on the SuperC or SuperCE entry panel.

To create a profile, you must first set all of the SuperCE options the way you want them in the profile. Then, enter A in the OPTION field on the SuperCE entry panel. When you do, SuperCE displays the profile manager panel shown in figure 5-58. On this panel, enter C in the OPTION field and the name of the profile you want to create in the PROFILE DS NAME field.

Once you've created a profile, you can use it for any compare operation. If you want to use it with the SuperC utility, all you

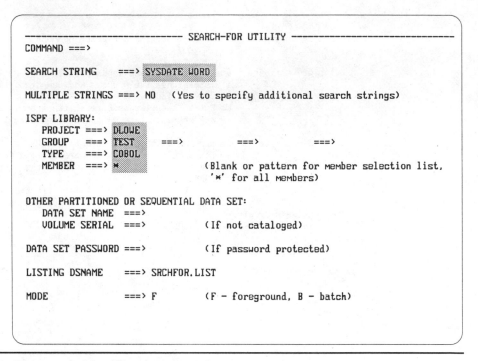

```
-------------------------------- SEARCH-FOR UTILITY --------------------------------
COMMAND ===>

SEARCH STRING      ===> SYSDATE WORD

MULTIPLE STRINGS ===> NO   (Yes to specify additional search strings)

ISPF LIBRARY:
   PROJECT ===> DLOWE
   GROUP   ===> TEST      ===>          ===>          ===>
   TYPE    ===> COBOL
   MEMBER  ===> *                      (Blank or pattern for member selection list,
                                        '*' for all members)

OTHER PARTITIONED OR SEQUENTIAL DATA SET:
   DATA SET NAME   ===>
   VOLUME SERIAL   ===>                 (If not cataloged)

DATA SET PASSWORD ===>                 (If password protected)

LISTING DSNAME    ===> SRCHFOR.LIST

MODE              ===> F               (F - foreground, B - batch)
```

Figure 5-59   The search-for utility entry panel

have to do is enter the name of the profile data set on the first
SuperC entry panel. But to use a profile with the SuperCE utility,
you have to activate it. To do that, enter A in the OPTION field on
the profile manager panel and enter the name of the profile you
want to activate in the PROFILE DS NAME field.

OPTION 3.14: THE SEARCH-FOR UTILITY

The search-for utility, option 3.14, allows you to search for one or
more character strings in a data set. You specify the character
strings and data set on the search-for entry panel, illustrated in
figure 5-59. If you leave the MEMBER field blank or enter a
pattern, search-for will display a member list. To select a member
for the search, enter S next to the member name. In figure 5-59, I
specified an asterisk, so all members of the library would be
searched.

You can process the search operation in either foreground or batch mode. Just enter your selection in the MODE field like you do for the SuperC utility. If you select batch, ISPF displays a panel that allows you to specify a destination for the output listing.

You can also specify the name of the data set where you want the output listing saved. Just enter the data set name in the LISTING DSNAME field. If you don't specify a name, SuperC uses the default SRCHFOR.LIST prefixed with your user-id. I'll show you an example of an output listing in a minute. But first, I'll show you how to specify a search string.

How to specify a search string

To specify a search string, enter the characters in the SEARCH STRING field on the search-for entry panel. If the string contains blanks, enclose it in single quotation marks. Also enclose the string in single quotation marks if it contains apostrophes, and enter two consecutive apostrophes for each apostrophe within the search string.

When you search for a string using the search-for utility, the SuperC program searches for the characters regardless of their case. So, for example, if you enter the string

```
'procedure division'
```

it is located whether the string occurs in the data set in lowercase letters, uppercase letters, or a combination of upper and lowercase letters. If you want to control the case of the characters SuperC searches for, you must use the extended search-for utility. I'll present that utility in a moment.

Although you can't specify the case of a character string, you do have some control over what character strings SuperC considers a match. To do that, you use the keywords PREFIX, SUFFIX, and WORD after the search string. If you specify PREFIX, SuperC locates the string only if it occurs at the beginning of a word. If you specify SUFFIX, SuperC locates the string only if it occurs at the end of a word. If you specify WORD, SuperC locates the string only if it is a separate word. The SuperC program considers any group of characters that begins and ends with a blank or another delimiter to be a word.

For example, in figure 5-59, I entered the search string

```
SYSDATE WORD
```

```
SEARCH --- DLOWE.TEST.COBOL --------------------------------------------------
COMMAND ===>


Specify 1 or more SEARCH STRINGS below:

   ===> SYSDATE WORD
   ===>
   ===>
   ===>
   ===>
   ===>
   ===>
   ===>
   ===>
   ===>

Press ENTER to start search or END command to exit.
```

Figure 5-60   The search-for panel for entering multiple search strings

Here, SuperC locates the string SYSDATE only if it appears as a
separate word. Note that the keyword is entered after the character
string.

You can specify only one keyword on each search string. So, for
example, you can't search for a string that's either a prefix or a
suffix. To do that, you'd have to perform two separate searches or
specify multiple search strings. If you don't use a keyword on the
search string, search-for will locate the string anywhere in the file,
whether it's an entire word itself or part of another word.

How to specify multiple search strings

If you want to specify more than one search string, enter YES in
the MULTIPLE STRINGS field on the search-for entry panel. When
you do, ISPF displays the panel in figure 5-60. As you can see, this
panel allows you to specify up to ten search strings. If you enter a
search string on the first entry panel, ISPF displays it in the first

field on the multiple search string panel, as you can see in figure 5-60.

Each search string you specify on this panel can contain one of the search keywords: PREFIX, SUFFIX, or WORD. If you specify multiple search strings, you can also use another keyword: C. The C keyword means that a search string you specify is located on the same line as the previous search string. In other words, it continues the search string you entered on the previous line.

For example, if I enter the search strings

```
MOVE WORD
```

and

```
TO WORD C
```

search-for will locate all lines that contain both the words MOVE and TO.

The search-for listing

Figure 5-61 presents the output from a search-for operation. The search-for utility created this listing as it processed the search in figure 5-59. As you can see, it lists the lines in each data set where the specified string was found. The last page presents a summary of the search operation, including the total number of lines that contain the search string, the number of members that contain the search string, and the number of members processed. Just like the compare utilities, the search-for utility invokes browse automatically after it completes the search operation.

OPTION 3.13.S:
THE EXTENDED SEARCH-FOR UTILITY

The extended search-for utility provides more flexibility than the search-for utility. With extended search-for, you can specify the case of the characters in a search string, and you can specify process options and statements. You invoke the extended search-for utility by selecting option S from the SuperCE utility entry panel or by selecting option 13.S from the utilities menu. Figure 5-62 presents the panel ISPF displays when you do that.

```
   SUPERC - FILE/LINE/WORD/BYTE COMPARE PGM - V2.7(87/03/27)  90/01/11   12.51        PAGE   1
LINE-#   SOURCE SECTION                      SRCH DSN: DLOWE.TEST.COBOL

MKTG1100            ----------  STRING(S) FOUND ------------
   162  020000       CALL 'SYSDATE' USING TODAYS-DATE.                           02000000
MKTG1200            ----------  STRING(S) FOUND ------------
   200  020000       CALL 'SYSDATE' USING TODAYS-DATE.                           02000000
MKTG1300            ----------  STRING(S) FOUND ------------
   182  020000       CALL 'SYSDATE' USING TODAYS-DATE.                           02000000
MKTG1400            ----------  STRING(S) FOUND ------------
   149  020000       CALL 'SYSDATE' USING TODAYS-DATE.                           02000000


   SUPERC - FILE/LINE/WORD/BYTE COMPARE PGM - V2.7(87/03/27)  90/01/11   12.51        PAGE   2
         SUMMARY SECTION                     SRCH DSN: DLOWE.TEST.COBOL

LINES-FOUND  MEMBERS-W/LNS  MEMBERS-PROC  LINES-PROC  COMPARE-COLS  LONGEST-LINE
    4             4              4           1320         1: 80          80

PROCESS OPTIONS USED: ANYC

THE FOLLOWING PROCESS STATEMENT(S) WERE PROCESSED:
   SRCHFOR 'SYSDATE',W
```

Figure 5-61 Sample output from a search operation

```
---------------------------- EXTENDED SEARCH-FOR UTILITY ----------------------------
OPTION  ===>

   blank - Search-For Strings               P - Select Process Options
     B   - Submit Batch Search-For          E - Edit Statements Data Set

Search DS Name  ===> TEST.COBOL
PDS Member List ===>                 (blank/pattern - member list, * - search all)
   (Leave Search Dsn "blank" for concatenated-uncataloged-password panel)

      Enter Search Strings and Optional operands (WORD/PREFIX/SUFFIX,C)

CAPS    ===> SYSDATE WORD
CAPS    ===>
CAPS    ===>
ASIS    ===>
ASIS    ===>

Listing DS Name ===> SRCHFOR.LIST
Process Options ===>
Statements Dsn  ===>
```

Figure 5-62   The extended search-for utility entry panel

There are four options you can choose from the entry panel in figure 5-62. If you leave the OPTION field blank, extended search-for searches for the strings you specify. If you enter B in the OPTION field, a job is submitted in batch mode. ISPF uses the same batch submit panel it uses for the SuperC, SuperCE, and search-for utilities. Option P lets you select process options. And option E lets you edit the statements data set. I'll show you how to use the P and E options in a minute. But first, I'll show you how to specify the search strings and how to specify the data set to search.

How to specify search strings

The format of the search strings you use with the extended search-for utility is the same as their format with the search-for utility. In other words, you use quotes and keywords in the same manner. However, when you enter a search string, you specify whether you want to search for uppercase characters or for upper or lowercase characters. To search for uppercase characters, enter the search

string in one of the CAPS fields. Then, the search string will be
found only if it occurs in all uppercase characters in the file. If you
enter the string in one of the ASIS fields, it will be found only if it
occurs in the file exactly as you enter it.

   If you specify the ANYC option, extended search-for ignores
case when it searches the file. In that case, it doesn't matter
whether you enter a search string in a CAPS or ASIS field. I'll show
you how to select the ANYC option in a moment.

How to specify the data set to search

You specify the data set you want to search by entering it in standard TSO format. If the data set is partitioned, you can display a
member list by leaving the PDS MEMBER LIST field blank or
entering a pattern. To search all the members in a partitioned data
set, enter an asterisk (*) in the PDS MEMBER LIST field. If you
want to concatenate data sets or if the data set is uncataloged or
password protected, leave the data set name field blank.

   Figure 5-63 presents the panel that's displayed if you don't
specify a data set name on the entry panel. You can enter up to
four data sets on this panel. If you want to search a data set that's
not cataloged, enter the data set name in the DATA SET NAME
field and enter the volume serial number in the VOLUME SERIAL
field. For a password-protected data set, enter the password in the
PASSWORD field.

How to select process options

A moment ago, I mentioned that you can use the ANYC option to
tell extended search-for to ignore case when it searches for the
search string. To specify the ANYC option, and other search
options, enter P in the OPTION field of the search-for entry panel.
Then, ISPF displays a panel shown in figure 5-64. Many of these
options are also available with the compare utilities. To select an
option, enter a non-blank character next to it. After you select the
options you want and press the Enter key, ISPF returns to the
search-for entry panel where the selected options are displayed in
the PROCESS OPTIONS field.

   Although the Don't Process Control Options, such as
DPPLCMT, DPPSCMT, etc., are available with the extended

```
----------- EXTENDED SEARCH-FOR - CONCATENATION DATA SET ENTRY ---------------
COMMAND ===>


  "SEARCH"    DS1 ===>
CONCATENATION DS2 ===>
              DS3 ===>
              DS4 ===>

OTHER "SEARCH" PARTITIONED OR SEQUENTIAL DATA SET
    DATA SET NAME ===>
    VOLUME SERIAL ===>                    (If not cataloged)
    PASSWORD      ===>                    (If password protected)
```

Figure 5-63   The extended search-for utility concatenation entry panel

```
--------------------- EXTENDED SEARCH-FOR - PROCESS OPTIONS ----------- (1 of 1)
COMMAND ===>

Select Process Option(s) or "blank" to remove.   Press  ENTER to continue.

                     Sequence Number Columns Processing
      SEQ      - Ignore FB 80/VB 255 standard sequence number columns, or
      NOSEQ    - Process FB 80/VB 255 standard sequence number columns as text or
  S   COBOL    - Ignore COBOL FB 80 sequence number columns 1-6.

      ANYC     - Text string matches on "any" (upper or lower) case.
      IDPFX    - List member name id as prefix to each search line found.
  S   LPSF     - List search and up to six preceding and following lines, or
      LMTO     - List member totals only, or
      LTO      - List total summary only.

      LONGLN   - Lists up to 176 columns. Line length = 202/203.
      NOPRTCC  - No print control column and page separators.
      APNDLST  - Append listing report to listing data set.
          Others: DPPLCMT, DPPSCMT, DPADCMT, DPACMT, DPFTCMT, DPCBCMT, DPBLKCL
          (Enter these keywords directly on Search-For panel options line)
```

Figure 5-64   Selecting process options for an extended search operation

---

The SRCHFOR/SRCHFORC statement

```
SRCHFOR
SRCHFORC     'string'[,search-type]
```

Explanation

string   The string you want to search for. It must be enclosed in single quotes.

search-type   A code that specifies what strings are considered a match. The valid codes
                  are P for prefix, S for suffix, and W for word.

Figure 5-65   The SuperC SRCHFOR and SRCHFORC process statements

search-for utility, you can't select them from the option panel. As the message at the bottom of the option panel indicates, you have to enter these options directly in the PROCESS OPTIONS field on the first entry panel. You can enter any of the available options in this field rather than selecting them from the option panel.

How to use process statements

In addition to the process options, you can also specify process statements for a search operation. All these statements except one are also available for the compare utilities. The only new statement is SRCHFOR/SRCHFORC.

You can use the SRCHFOR and SRCHFORC statements to specify the strings you want to search for. So if you search for the same string frequently, you can save it in a process statement data set. Then, you don't have to enter it each time you do the search.

Figure 5-65 presents the format of the SRCHFOR and SRCHFORC statements. As you can see, you must enclose the string you want to search for in single quotes. The string can optionally be followed by a search type. The search types, P, S, and W, correspond to the search keywords PREFIX, SUFFIX, and WORD. If you code one of these search types, you must separate it from the character string with a comma. Notice that there is no equivalent for the C keyword. To continue a search string within a line, use SRCHFORC.

```
EDIT ----- DLOWE.SEARCH.STMTS ------------------------------ COLUMNS 001 072
COMMAND ===>                                                 SCROLL ===> DATA

      Enter or change Process Statements in the EDIT window below:
******  ************************** TOP OF DATA *****************************
''''''  SRCHFOR 'SYSDATE',W
''''''
''''''
''''''
''''''
******  ************************** BOTTOM OF DATA **************************
      Examples                          Explanation
   SRCHFOR  'ABCD',W          Search for the word "ABCD"
   SRCHFORC 'DEFG'            "DEFG" must be on same line as word "ABCD"
   CMPCOLM  1:60  75:90       Search columns 1:60 and 75:90 for string(s)
   DPLINE   'PAGE ',87:95     Exclude line if "PAGE " found in columns 87:99
   DPLINE   'PAGE '           Exclude if "PAGE " found anywhere on line
   SELECT   MEM1,MEM2         Search only members MEM1 and MEM2 of PDS
 Others: DPLINEC LSTCOLM CMPLINE NTITLE NCHGT LNCT SLIST
         comment-lines ("*" and ".*")
```

Figure 5-66   Editing the process statements data set for an extended search operation

To create a statements data set, or to modify an existing data set, enter E in the OPTION field of the extended search-for entry panel and the name of the statements data set in the STATEMENTS DSN field. If the data set doesn't exist, ISPF allocates it, then displays the panel in figure 5-66. You can enter any of the process statements listed at the bottom of the panel in the edit window at the top of the panel.

To exit from the statements panel and save the statements data set, press the End key, PF3/15. If you want to exit without saving the data set, enter the CANCEL command. Either way, you're returned to the extended search-for entry panel. Then, if all the fields contain the values you want, press the Enter key to process the search operation.

DISCUSSION

As you've seen, the SuperC utilities are very powerful. For most uses, the basic SuperC and search-for options are sufficient. Use the extended SuperC options only when you need the additional features they provide.

Terms

SuperC program
file compare
line compare
word compare
byte compare
update data set

Objectives

1. Use the SuperC or SuperCE utility to compare the contents of two data sets. The data sets may be sequential data sets, partitioned data sets, members of partitioned data sets, or concatenated data sets. The operation may require process options or statements.

2. Create a profile data set for use with the SuperC or SuperCE utility.

3. Use the search-for or extended search-for utility to search a data set for a string. The data set may be a sequential data set, a partitioned data set, members of a partitioned data set, or a concatenated data set. The operation may require process options or statements.

Chapter 6

How to compile, link-edit, and debug a program in foreground mode

As a programmer, you'll probably use ISPF most for program development. You've already learned how to perform many basic program development tasks under ISPF: browsing, editing, allocating data sets, and so on. This chapter, though, explains the critical program development tasks of compiling, link-editing, and debugging programs.

This chapter is divided into three topics. In the first topic, I'll show you how to compile and link-edit programs in foreground mode using ISPF. In the second topic, I'll show you how to use the OS COBOL interactive debugger to debug your OS/VS COBOL programs. And in the third topic, I'll show you how to use the VS COBOL II interactive debugger to debug your VS COBOL II programs.

If your installation uses ISPF Version 3 and the Software Configuration and Library Manager (SCLM), you won't use the standard ISPF facilities for compiling and link-editing your programs. Instead, you'll use SCLM's build function. You'll learn how to use this, and other SCLM functions, in chapter 8.

Topic 1　How to compile and link-edit a program

There are several methods you can use to compile and link-edit programs under ISPF. This topic explains the method ISPF is designed for: compiling and link-editing programs in foreground mode using familiar ISPF selection and entry panels.

When you select option 4 from the primary option menu, ISPF displays a foreground selection panel similar to figure 6-1. Here, you have the option of compiling or assembling a program using one of the system compilers or the assembler, link-editing a program using the standard linkage editor, using the SCRIPT/VS text formatting program, interactively debugging a COBOL or FORTRAN program, or displaying a member parts list. Because most of these features require licensed program products, your shop may not have all of them. Or, your shop may have added additional compilers, such as VS BASIC or the CICS command level translator. Your shop may or may not have modified the foreground selection menu to reflect the products it has installed.

In addition to entering an option on the foreground selection panel, you also need to specify whether the source file you're processing contains packed data. If it does, enter YES in the SOURCE DATA PACKED field. If it doesn't, enter NO.

If the Session Manager is installed at your shop, another field may appear at the bottom of the foreground selection panel: ENTER SESSION MANAGER MODE. If you enter YES in this field, you can enter the Session Manager from any of the foreground processors. Since there usually isn't any reason to use the Session Manager when you're using the foreground processors, you'll usually enter NO in this field.

In this topic, I'll describe how you use two of the main types of options, assembling/compiling and link-editing, in a VS COBOL II environment. I'll also show you how to create a *member parts list*, which lets you see what modules are copied into or called from your program. Then, in the next two topics, I'll show you how to debug a COBOL program using the OS COBOL interactive

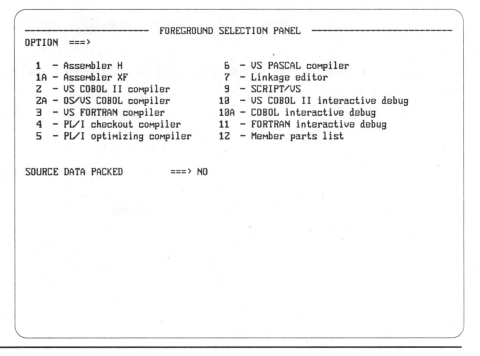

```
------------------------ FOREGROUND SELECTION PANEL ------------------------
OPTION ===>

    1 - Assembler H                 6 - VS PASCAL compiler
    1A - Assembler XF               7 - Linkage editor
    2 - VS COBOL II compiler        9 - SCRIPT/VS
    2A - OS/VS COBOL compiler       10 - VS COBOL II interactive debug
    3 - VS FORTRAN compiler         10A - COBOL interactive debug
    4 - PL/I checkout compiler      11 - FORTRAN interactive debug
    5 - PL/I optimizing compiler    12 - Member parts list


SOURCE DATA PACKED        ===> NO
```

Figure 6-1   The foreground selection panel

debugger and the VS COBOL II interactive debugger. With few exceptions, program development for other programming languages, like PL/I or assembler, is the same.

Libraries and output listings

Before I go on, I want to point out that foreground program development uses a variety of libraries and data sets. Figure 6-2 lists the data set names I created for this book. Although the naming conventions at your shop may be different and although you may not be working in COBOL, these names should serve as examples of the types of data sets you need.

Usually, you'll have at least two COBOL libraries: a test library that contains versions of programs under development and a COPY library that contains members included via COPY statements. (You maintain the members in these libraries using the editor as described in chapter 4.) Normally, you'll concatenate

Data set name	Function
DLOWE.TEST.COBOL	COBOL source library for programs under development
DLOWE.COPY.COBOL	COBOL COPY library
DLOWE.TEST.OBJ	Object library for the compiled versions of programs in DLOWE.TEST.COBOL
DLOWE.SUBPROG.OBJ	Subprogram object library
DLOWE.TEST.LOAD	Load library for the link-edited versions of programs in DLOWE.TEST.OBJ
DLOWE.member.LIST	COBOL compiler listing
DLOWE.member.LINKLIST	Linkage-editor listing

Figure 6-2   Data sets used for program development (VS COBOL II)

these libraries on the compile entry panel so they're searched in this order: first the test library, then the COPY library.

For a one-programmer project, a single test library is sufficient. For a multi-programmer project, however, you'll probably have one test library for each programmer. And for a large project, you may have an additional COBOL library: a master source library that contains only final versions of programs. If these libraries are controlled by LMF or SCLM as described in chapter 8, they will be organized into a hierarchy that may have other intermediate levels for testing purposes.

All the foreground compilers place the compiled version of a program, called an *object module*, in an OBJ library with the same name as the source library. Thus, if the source library is DLOWE.TEST.COBOL, the *object library* is DLOWE.TEST.OBJ. The member name for the source and object program is the same. In addition, any called subprograms must be kept in an object library. Generally, the subprogram library follows ISPF naming conventions, so DLOWE.SUBPROG.OBJ is a valid name.

The linkage editor places its output, called a *load module*, in a load library, again with the same name. So, in the above example, the *load library* is DLOWE.TEST.LOAD.

Output listings generated by the foreground compilers are placed in a sequential data set whose type is LIST. For example,

```
------------------------ FOREGROUND VS COBOL II COMPILE ------------------------
COMMAND ===>

ISPF LIBRARY:
   PROJECT ===> DLOWE
   GROUP   ===> TEST      ===> COPY      ===>          ===>
   TYPE    ===> COBOL
   MEMBER  ===> MKTG1200           (Blank or pattern for member selection list)

OTHER PARTITIONED OR SEQUENTIAL DATA SET:
   DATA SET NAME  ===>

LIST ID ===>                              PASSWORD ===>

COMPILER OPTIONS:    (Options LIB and OBJECT generated automatically)
   TEST  ===> TEST    (TEST or NOTEST)
   OTHER ===>

ADDITIONAL INPUT LIBRARIES:
        ===>
        ===>
```

Figure 6-3   The foreground VS COBOL II compile entry panel

DLOWE.MKTG1200.LIST is a valid name for a compiler listing. For
a linkage editor listing, the type qualifier is LINKLIST. Thus,
DLOWE.MKTG1200.LINKLIST is a valid name for a link listing.

Now, I'll show you how to use these files as you develop a
program in foreground mode.

How to compile a program

To compile a program, you select one of the compilers: options 1
through 6 in figure 6-1. To compile a VS COBOL II program, you
select option 2: the VS COBOL II compiler. Figure 6-3 shows the
panel ISPF displays when you select this compiler. On it, you
provide the name of the source program you want to compile. You
can do that by entering the appropriate values in the PROJECT,
GROUP, TYPE, and MEMBER fields, or by entering a name in the
DATA SET NAME field. In this example, I'm compiling MKTG1200
in DLOWE.TEST.COBOL. As usual, if you omit the member name
from this panel, ISPF displays a member list.

You can specify up to four libraries in the GROUP field of the compile entry panel. For example, if the program you're compiling contains COPY statements, you'll need to specify the COPY library. In figure 6-3, I specified COPY in the second LIBRARY field. As a result, DLOWE.COPY.COBOL is used as a COPY library for this compile.

Actually, all the libraries listed on the entry panel are searched when you use a COPY statement. So, DLOWE.TEST.COBOL is used as a COPY library too. For example, suppose MKTG1200 contains this COPY statement:

```
COPY CUSTMAST.
```

Since DLOWE.TEST.COBOL is the first library specified on the entry panel, it's the first library ISPF searches for the CUSTMAST member. If the COPY member isn't found there, ISPF searches the next library, DLOWE.COPY.COBOL.

If you want to change the search order for COPY libraries, you can specify the COPY library first, followed by your source library. But that changes the search order for the source member as well. In other words, the COPY library is searched before the TEST library to find MKTG1200.

You can also specify COPY libraries in the ADDITIONAL INPUT LIBRARIES fields. You use these fields to specify an input library if the library's project or type qualifier is different from that of the source file. If you enter a library name in one of these fields, it must be fully qualified and enclosed in single quotes. In figure 6-3, for example, I could enter a name like this:

```
'DLOWE.COPY.COBOL'
```

Any additional input libraries you specify are added to the end of the library search chain, so they're always searched last.

The LIST ID field in figure 6-3 requests a name for the data set that will contain the compiler listing. The full data set name follows this pattern:

```
project-id.list-id.LIST
```

The default list-id is the name of the source member. So since I left the LIST ID field blank in figure 6-3, the list data set is named DLOWE.MKTG1200.LIST.

Compiler options The *compiler options* control optional features of the VS COBOL II compiler. The VS COBOL II entry panel provides two lines for compiler options. The first indicates whether you intend to use the VS COBOL II debugger. If you do, you must specify TEST. Then, the compiler generates symbolic debugging information, which is stored in the object module. If you aren't going to use the debugger, specify NOTEST.

The OTHER option line lets you specify other compiler options. In some installations, you must specify a few specific compiler options for the compiler to work properly. Figure 6-4 lists some of the COBOL compiler options you're likely to use. Most of them control optional compiler output generated in the compiler listing, such as a Data Division map and a cross-reference listing. The underlined values are IBM standard defaults, though the defaults at your installation may be different. At any rate, you'll have to find out from your supervisor what options you must code.

Figure 6-4 also explains two compiler options automatically generated by ISPF: LIB and OBJECT. Since ISPF generates these options, you should *not* include them on the entry panel.

Compiler output Once you complete the entry panel and press the Enter key, your terminal temporarily enters native TSO mode. When the compiler begins execution, TSO displays the message

    VS COBOL II STARTED

on the top line of the screen. When the compilation is complete, TSO displays *** on the second line of the screen. Then, when you press the Enter key, ISPF enters browse mode automatically so you can look at the compiler output. The output contains a complete source listing, diagnostics, and other output depending on the compiler options you specify. When you're done looking at the compiler output, press the End key, PF3/15, to exit from browse.

When you exit from the browse display, ISPF displays the print options panel presented in figure 6-5. This panel lets you determine the disposition of the list output. Here, you can enter one of three options: D, K, PD, or PK.

If the program doesn't contain many compiler errors, you can just make a note of the errors as you browse the listing. Then, when you get to this panel, you can delete the listing by entering D in the OPTION field. On the other hand, if the compiler errors are extensive, you can print the compiler output by entering the PK or the PD option and specifying the destination for the listing. If you enter PK, ISPF prints the data set and keeps it. If you enter PD, ISPF prints the data set and deletes it. You can also keep the data

Option	Meaning
RESIDENT NORESIDENT	Determines whether subroutines in the COBOL library can be shared by other programs that are executing at the same time.
SOURCE NOSOURCE	Print the source listing.
MAP NOMAP	Print a Data Division map.
LIST NOLIST	Print a Procedure Division map.
OFFSET NOOFFSET	Print a condensed Procedure Division map—can't be used with PMAP.
XREF NOXREF	Print a cross-reference listing.
APOST QUOTE	Indicates whether apostrophes (') or quotes (") are used to mark non-numeric literals.
BUFSIZE(*n*)	Specifies how much buffer space to allow. You can specify *n* as an integer or use K to represent units of 1024 bytes. Thus, BUFSIZE(2048) and BUFSIZE(2K) have the same meaning.

Options supplied by ISPF

LIB	Allows the use of COPY statements.
OBJECT	Causes a permanent object module to be created.

Figure 6-4   VS COBOL II compiler options

set without printing it by entering the K option. If you use either the K or the PK option to keep the data set, you can use browse to display it at a later time.

If the TSO/E Information Center Facility is installed at your shop, the print options panel presented in figure 6-5 may look a bit different. That's because the print destination is specified differently for ICF. However, the options that are available are the same: D, PK, PD, and D.

```
------------------------- FOREGROUND PRINT OPTIONS -------------------------
OPTION  ===> PD

  PK - Print data set and keep        K - Keep data set (without printing)
  PD - Print data set and delete      D - Delete data set (without printing)

  If END command is entered, data set is kept without printing.

DATA SET NAME: DLOWE.MKTG1200.LIST

PRINT MODE   ===> BATCH          (BATCH or LOCAL)

SYSOUT CLASS ===>
PRINTER ID   ===>                (For 328x printer)

JOB STATEMENT INFORMATION:       (Required for system printer)
  ===> //DLOWEB  JOB (9999),'DOUG LOWE'
  ===> //*
  ===> //*
  ===> //*
```

Figure 6-5   The foreground print options panel

How to link-edit a program

Before you can execute a compiled program, you must *link-edit* it.
When you link-edit a program, the program is combined with any
subprograms you invoke with CALL statements along with any
compiler subroutines to form a load module that's ready to be
executed by MVS.

To invoke the *linkage editor*, select option 7 from the foreground menu. Then, ISPF displays the panel shown in figure 6-6.
On this panel, you enter the library and member name of the
object module created by the compiler. In this example, I'm link-
editing MKTG1200 in DLOWE.TEST.OBJ. The link-edited load
module is placed in DLOWE.TEST.LOAD using the same member
name.

If you need to include a subprogram library for the linkage
editor, specify it as one of the libraries in the GROUP fields on the
entry panel. The linkage editor searches up to four libraries you
specify in these fields to resolve subprogram calls. ISPF searches

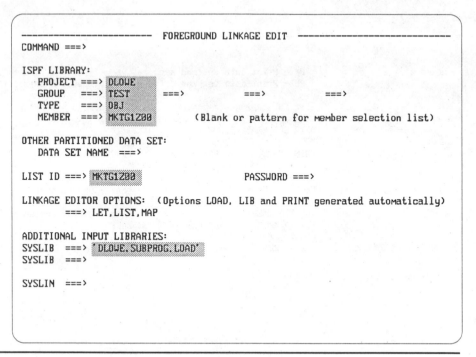

```
------------------------ FOREGROUND LINKAGE EDIT ---------------------------
COMMAND ===>

ISPF LIBRARY:
    PROJECT ===> DLOWE
    GROUP   ===> TEST      ===>          ===>           ===>
    TYPE    ===> OBJ
    MEMBER  ===> MKTG1200         (Blank or pattern for member selection list)

OTHER PARTITIONED DATA SET:
    DATA SET NAME ===>

LIST ID ===> MKTG1200                    PASSWORD ===>

LINKAGE EDITOR OPTIONS:  (Options LOAD, LIB and PRINT generated automatically)
        ===> LET,LIST,MAP

ADDITIONAL INPUT LIBRARIES:
SYSLIB  ===> 'DLOWE.SUBPROG.LOAD'
SYSLIB  ===>

SYSLIN  ===>
```

Figure 6-6   The foreground linkage-edit entry panel

the libraries in the order you list them, so if the same subprogram name occurs in more than one library, be sure to list the correct library first.

You can also enter a subprogram library in one of the SYSLIB fields near the bottom of the panel. You enter a library here if its project or type qualifier is different from that of the object library that contains the main program. Any library name you specify in one of these fields must be fully qualified and enclosed in single quotes. In figure 6-6, for example, I entered this library name:

```
'DLOWE.SUBPROG.LOAD'
```

Then, ISPF added this library to the end of the library search chain.

The LIST ID field works much like it does for a compiler. The full data set name for the list file follows this pattern:

```
project-id.list-id.LINKLIST
```

So, in figure 6-6, the list file is DLOWE.MKTG1200.LINKLIST.

The LINKAGE EDITOR OPTIONS field lets you specify linkage editor options. As you can see, ISPF generates three options automatically: LOAD, LIB, and PRINT. In addition, I specified the LET, LIST, and MAP options. The LET option tells the linkage editor to ignore minor linkage errors that routinely occur when linking a VS COBOL II program. And the LIST and MAP options provide useful information in the link-edit listing.

You use the last field on the link-edit entry panel, SYSLIN, only when you link a VS PASCAL program. So, for a VS COBOL II program, you leave this field blank.

When you complete the entry panel, press the Enter key to start the linkage editor. When you do, your terminal enters native TSO mode temporarily, just like it does when you compile a program. As the linkage editor executes, TSO displays any errors that are encountered. When the link-edit operation is complete, TSO displays three asterisks. Then, when you press the Enter key, ISPF enters browse mode so you can look at the output from the linkage editor.

After you've looked at the output and exited from browse mode, ISPF displays the print options panel I presented in figure 6-5. On this panel, you enter the disposition of the link-edit listing, then press the Enter key. When you do, ISPF returns to the link-edit entry panel.

How to display a member parts list

If the program you're compiling or link-editing contains COPY or CALL statements, it might be helpful to see a list of the copied and called modules before you compile or link-edit the program. That way, you can be sure you specify all the libraries you need for the compile or link-edit operation. You can view this information by selecting option 12 from the foreground menu. Figure 6-7 shows how it works.

Part 1 of figure 6-7 shows the member parts list entry panel. On it, you enter the name of the library and the member you want to display a parts list for. In figure 6-7, I specified DLOWE.TEST.COBOL for the library and MKTG1200 for the member. If you leave the MEMBER field blank, a member list is displayed. From the member list, you can select only one member at time. If you want to create a member parts list for more than one member, enter a pattern in the MEMBER field on the entry

Part 1:

Enter the name of the
library and member
you want to produce a
parts list for

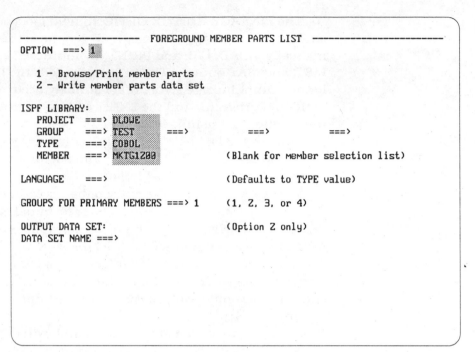

```
------------------------ FOREGROUND MEMBER PARTS LIST ------------------------
OPTION  ===> 1

    1 - Browse/Print member parts
    2 - Write member parts data set

ISPF LIBRARY:
    PROJECT  ===> DLOWE
    GROUP    ===> TEST      ===>            ===>            ===>
    TYPE     ===> COBOL
    MEMBER   ===> MKTG1200         (Blank for member selection list)

LANGUAGE   ===>                    (Defaults to TYPE value)

GROUPS FOR PRIMARY MEMBERS ===> 1   (1, 2, 3, or 4)

OUTPUT DATA SET:                   (Option 2 only)
DATA SET NAME ===>
```

Part 2:

ISPF displays the
member parts list in
browse mode

```
BROWSE - PARTS LIST FOR DLOWE.TEST.COBOL(MKTG1200) ----------------------------
COMMAND ===>                                             SCROLL ===> PAGE

FROM    VIA      FROM    VIA    MEMBER      TO    VIA       TO    VIA
-------  ---     -------  ---   --------   --------  ---   --------  ---
***************************************** TOP OF DATA *****************************************
                                (MKTG1200)  CUSTMAST  I*    MKTG120A  C*
                                (        )  RPTHDG14  I*    SALESMAN  I*
***************************************** BOTTOM OF DATA *****************************************
```

Figure 6-7   Creating a member parts list for a single member panel or enter an asterisk (*) to include all the members in the specified library.

You can also specify up to three additional libraries by entering their names in the GROUP fields. When ISPF creates the member parts list, it searches all the libraries you specify to locate the copied or called modules. In figure 6-7, I didn't enter any additional libraries.

In the LANGUAGE field, you enter the language of the member you're creating a parts list for. This field defaults to the value in the TYPE field, so in most cases, you can leave this field blank. In figure 6-7, for example, the language defaults to COBOL.

The GROUPS FOR PRIMARY MEMBERS field can be confusing. It tells ISPF how many of the libraries you listed in the GROUP field should be searched for *primary members*. A primary member is a member whose COPY and CALL references are tracked. If you specify a member name in the MEMBER field, there is only one primary member: the member you specify. If you specify a pattern in the MEMBER field, however, each member that matches the pattern is considered a primary member. ISPF creates a member parts list for each primary member. (If you specify an asterisk in the MEMBER field, every member is considered a primary member.)

The GROUPS FOR PRIMARY MEMBERS field lets you include a library in the GROUP field without searching it for primary members. For example, if you specify 1, only the first library listed is searched for primary members; other libraries are used to locate called subprograms or members included via a COPY statement. If you specify 2, 3, or 4, the first two, three, or four libraries are used to locate primary members. In most cases, you'll specify 1 for this field.

If you look at the top of the member parts list panel, you'll see that there are two options you can select. The first option lets you browse and, optionally, print the member parts list. The second option lets you create a data set that contains the member parts list information. Unless you're required to create a member parts list data set for documentation, you probably won't ever use the second option. But if you do, enter the name of the output data set in the DATA SET NAME field at the bottom of the panel.

In figure 6-7, I entered option 1 to browse the member parts list for MKTG1200. Then, when I pressed the Enter key, TSO cleared the screen and displayed the message

```
===> EXECUTING <===
```

on the first line. This indicates that the member parts list is being created. When it's done, TSO displays three asterisks on the second line of the screen. To display the member parts list, press the Enter key.

Part 2 of figure 6-7 presents the member parts list for MKTG1200. The column in the middle of the panel shows the member whose parts are displayed on this panel. In the TO columns on the right side of the panel, ISPF displays the names of the modules that are copied or called by the specified member. The VIA columns indicate whether a module is included (I) in the member with a COPY statement, or called (C) by the member with a CALL statement. In figure 6-7, you can see that the member MKTG1200 contains three COPY statements for the modules CUSTMAST, SALESMAN, and RPTHDG14 and a call statement for the module MKTG120A.

When you're done browsing a member parts list, exit from browse by pressing the End key, PF3/15. When you do, ISPF displays a print option panel like the one I presented in figure 6-5. This panel gives you the option of printing and keeping the member parts list, printing and deleting the list, keeping the list without printing it, or deleting the list. If you want to print the list, you can specify its destination on this panel.

The asterisks next to each of the copied and called modules in part 2 of figure 6-7 indicate that the modules weren't found in the library I specified on the entry panel. If you include the libraries that contain referenced members on the entry panel, the asterisks won't appear. However, including these libraries also causes the referenced members to be tracked in the member parts list. For example, figure 6-8 shows how the member list would appear if I had specified the COPY and SUBPROG libraries, which contain the copy members and the MKTG120A subprogram, on the entry panel in figure 6-7. As you can see, the member list includes entries for CUSTMAST, RPTHDG14, and SALESMAN because those members were referenced by MKTG1200. And, it includes an entry for MKTG120A, which also references the CUSTMAST and SALESMAN copy members. Note that the tracking of referenced members does *not* depend on the value you code in the GROUPS FOR PRIMARY

```
BROWSE - PARTS LIST FOR DLOWE.TEST.COBOL(MKTG1200) ----------------------------
COMMAND ===>                                                   SCROLL ===> PAGE

 FROM    VIA       FROM    VIA    MEMBER      TO      VIA       TO      VIA
 ------- ---       ------- ---    -------     ------- ---       ------- ---
********************************** TOP OF DATA **********************************
MKTG120A  I        MKTG1200  I    (CUSTMAST)
                   MKTG1200  C    (MKTG120A)  CUSTMAST  I       SALESMAN  I
                                  (MKTG1200)  CUSTMAST  I       MKTG120A  C
                                  (        )  RPTHDG14  I       SALESMAN  I
                   MKTG1200  I    (RPTHDG14)
MKTG120A  I        MKTG1200  I    (SALESMAN)
********************************* BOTTOM OF DATA ********************************
```

Figure 6-8   A member parts list for a single member that includes tracking of referenced members

MEMBERS field. Referenced members are tracked automatically if they're found in one of the libraries you specify.

Figure 6-9 presents a more comprehensive member parts list. To create this list, I included the TEST, COPY, and SUBPROG libraries on the entry panel, an asterisk for the MEMBER field, and 1 for the GROUPS FOR PRIMARY MEMBERS field. As a result, ISPF tracked the CALL and COPY references for all the members in DLOWE.TEST.COBOL, using DLOWE.COPY.COBOL and DLOWE.SUBPROG.COBOL to locate subprograms and copy members.

Discussion

In this chapter, I presented the techniques used to compile and link-edit programs in foreground mode using ISPF. There are, however, other program development techniques commonly used under TSO. Besides using the foreground option, you can invoke

FROM	VIA	FROM	VIA	MEMBER	TO	VIA	TO	VIA
MKTG1000	I	MKTG1100	I	(CUSTMAST)				
MKTG120A	I	MKTG1200	I	( )				
MKTG1300	I	MKTG1400	I	( )				
MKTG4100	I			( )				
				(MKTG1000)	CUSTMAST	I	RPTHDG14	I
				( )	SALESMAN	I	SYSDATE	C
				( )	SYSTIME	C		
				(MKTG1100)	CUSTMAST	I	RPTHDG14	I
				( )	SALESMAN	I	SYSDATE	C
				( )	SYSTIME	C		
				(MKTG120A)	CUSTMAST	I	SALESMAN	I
				(MKTG1200)	CUSTMAST	I	MKTG120A	C
				( )	RPTHDG14	I	SALESMAN	I
				(MKTG1300)	CUSTMAST	I	RPTHDG14	I
				( )	SALESMAN	I	SYSDATE	C
				( )	SYSTIME	C		
				(MKTG1400)	CUSTMAST	I	RPTHDG14	I
				( )	SYSDATE	C	SYSTIME	C
				(MKTG4100)	CUSTMAST	I	RPTHDG14	I
				( )	SYSDATE	C	SYSTIME	C
MKTG1000	I	MKTG1100	I	(RPTHDG14)				
MKTG120A	I	MKTG1200	I	( )				
MKTG1300	I	MKTG1400	I	( )				
MKTG4100	I			( )				
MKTG1000	I	MKTG1100	I	(SALESMAN)				
MKTG120A	I	MKTG1200	I	( )				
MKTG1300	I			( )				
MKTG1000	C	MKTG1100	C	(SYSDATE)				
MKTG1300	C	MKTG1400	C	( )				
		MKTG4100	C	( )				
MKTG1000	C	MKTG1100	C	(SYSTIME)				
MKTG1300	C	MKTG1400	C	( )				
		MKTG4100	C	( )				

Figure 6-9   A member parts list for an entire library

the foreground compilers directly using TSO commands. Furthermore, you can place the commands in a CLIST to make them easier to use. Under ISPF, you can invoke these commands or CLISTs using option 6 from the primary option menu, or you can invoke them from a member list displayed by the data set list utility (option 3.4) as described in chapter 5.

Another alternative for program development is background processing. I'll explain how you can use ISPF features for background program development in chapter 7.

Terms

member parts list
object module
object library
load module
load library
compiler option
link-edit
linkage editor

Objective

Use the ISPF foreground option to compile and link-edit a program and display a member parts list.

Topic 2   How to debug programs using OS COBOL Interactive Debug

In a traditional batch-oriented system, the most common way to test and debug a program is to submit the program for processing in a background region. Then, when the program completes, you inspect its output to determine if it executed properly. If the output is in error, or if the program ends abnormally and produces a storage dump, you review the program listing in an attempt to locate the bug. For the most part, there are few effective tools to help you locate a bug in this manner.

Under TSO, however, you can use one of two interactive debuggers to help you test and debug programs interactively. If you coded and compiled your program in OS/VS COBOL, you can use *OS COBOL Interactive Debug*, also called *TESTCOB*. If you coded and compiled your program in VS COBOL II, you can use *VS COBOL II Interactive Debug*, also called *COBTEST*. In this topic, I'll present the OS COBOL interactive debugger. I'll present the VS COBOL II interactive debugger in the next topic.

Basically, the COBOL interactive debugger lets you monitor the execution of your program at your terminal. You can control how statements in your program are executed. You can examine the contents of data fields and change them if you want. You can trace the flow of paragraphs or sections in your program. And unlike storage-dump debugging, the COBOL interactive debugger is symbolic. That means you use actual COBOL data names and statement numbers rather than hexadecimal addresses.

I'll begin this topic by describing how to invoke the COBOL interactive debugger. Then, I'll describe how to use the basic tools of the debugger: how to monitor your program's execution, how to manage its data, and how to list segments of the source program. Finally, I'll show you how to use some of the advanced features of TESTCOB, such as command lists and techniques for debugging subprograms.

Before I go on, I want to point out that I am *not* trying to teach you how to debug COBOL programs in this topic. So I'm not going to explain the likely causes of various abend codes. Instead, I want to teach you how to use the COBOL interactive debugger so you'll be able to debug your programs more easily.

HOW TO INVOKE THE DEBUGGER

Before you invoke TESTCOB, you must be sure the program you're debugging was compiled with the TEST option. The TEST option produces the symbolic data necessary for you to use a program with TESTCOB. The OS/VS COBOL compiler stores this symbolic data in a file that's separate from the object file. So, before you compile a program with the TEST option, you must allocate the partitioned data set that will contain the symbolic file. The data set should have the same name as the data set that contains the source file, except the type qualifier should be SYM. For example, if the source file is stored in a library named DLOWE.TEST.COBOL, you store the symbolic debugging file in a library named DLOWE.TEST.SYM. Then, when you compile the program, ISPF stores the symbolic debugging file with the same name as the source file.

If you want to create print output from the debugging session, you must also allocate a print data set. To do that, use the data set utility as described in chapter 5, specifying a record length of at least 121. You should use standard ISPF naming conventions, specifying TESTLIST as the type qualifier. For example, DLOWE.MKTG1200.TESTLIST is an appropriate name.

Option 10A from the foreground menu provides access to the COBOL interactive debugger. When you select this option, ISPF displays the debug entry panel presented in figure 6-10. Here, you specify the project and group qualifiers and the member name for the load module you want to debug. TESTCOB assumes a type qualifier of LOAD. Then, in the PROG ID fields, you specify up to four program names for the programs and subprograms you want to debug. Each must have a corresponding member in the SYM library. Normally, the first PROG ID field and the MEMBER field are the same. They don't have to be, though.

It's easy to become confused about the PROG ID and MEMBER fields, so let me explain them more carefully. The PROG ID fields identify up to four program modules to debug. These names correspond to the names you specify in the PROGRAM-ID paragraphs of

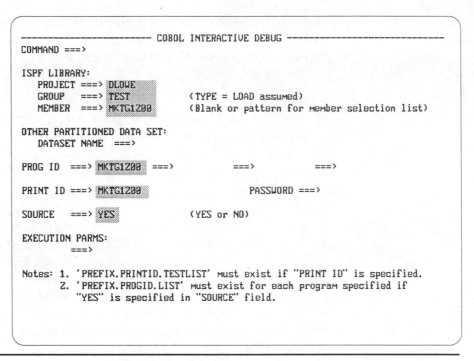

```
------------------------ COBOL INTERACTIVE DEBUG ------------------------
COMMAND ===>

ISPF LIBRARY:
    PROJECT ===> DLOWE
    GROUP   ===> TEST                    (TYPE = LOAD assumed)
    MEMBER  ===> MKTG1200                (Blank or pattern for member selection list)

OTHER PARTITIONED DATA SET:
    DATASET NAME ===>

PROG ID  ===> MKTG1200  ===>              ===>              ===>

PRINT ID ===> MKTG1200                          PASSWORD ===>

SOURCE   ===> YES                 (YES or NO)

EXECUTION PARMS:
        ===>

Notes: 1. 'PREFIX.PRINTID.TESTLIST' must exist if "PRINT ID" is specified.
       2. 'PREFIX.PROGID.LIST' must exist for each program specified if
          "YES" is specified in "SOURCE" field.
```

Figure 6-10   The foreground debug entry panel

the COBOL source programs. As a result, if you're debugging a
program named PROG1 that calls a COBOL subprogram named
SUBPROG1 and you want to debug both the main program and the
subprogram, you specify both PROG IDs. But remember that for
each PROG ID, there must be a corresponding member in the SYM
library. Thus, in this example, there must be members named
PROG1 and SUBPROG1 in the SYM library.

Most of the time, the subprograms your main program uses are
already tested and debugged. If that's the case, specify just the
main program name in the PROG ID field. In other words, you
don't have to name all the subprograms your main program uses,
just the ones you actually want to debug. Likewise, if you're
writing a new subprogram and you want to test and debug it, you
can specify just the subprogram name in the PROG ID field; you
don't have to specify the name of the main program.

As for the MEMBER field, it specifies the member name of a
load module in the load library. That member is the one that's
loaded and executed first during a debugging session. Again, in
our example, suppose that PROG1 and SUBPROG1 were link-
edited together to form a load module named LOAD1. Then, you

would specify LOAD1 in the MEMBER field. Typically, however, the member name for the load module is the same as the program name for the main program it contains. So the MEMBER field is usually the same as one of the PROG ID fields.

If you want to route debugging output to a print file, you must specify a print-id. The print-id identifies the print file you allocated before you invoked the debugger. For example, if you allocated a data set named DLOWE.MKTG1200.TESTLIST, you'd enter MKTG1200 in the PRINT ID field.

If you want to examine the source listing during the debugging session, enter YES in the SOURCE field. If you do, the compiler list file (.LIST) must exist for each PROG ID you specify.

Finally, enter any parameters you want to pass to the program you're debugging in the EXECUTION PARMS field. Since most programs don't require execution time parameters, you usually leave this field blank.

HOW TO MONITOR YOUR PROGRAM'S EXECUTION

TESTCOB lets you monitor your program's execution in two ways. First, you can establish *breakpoints* at one or more statements in your program. Then, whenever those statements are about to execute, TESTCOB interrupts your program and displays a message telling what statement is about to execute. At that point, you can resume your program's execution or enter a command to display the contents of a field, set another breakpoint, or do some other TESTCOB processing.

The second way to monitor program execution is to use a *trace*. A trace displays information about your program's execution without actually interrupting the program.

To monitor your program's execution, you have to understand how TESTCOB refers to individual statements in your program. TESTCOB follows this format when it refers to a particular Procedure Division statement:

```
program-id.statement-number.verb-number
```

Program-id identifies the program that contains the statement. Normally, this is the name of the program you're executing.

However, if your program calls subprograms, program-id names the subprogram if that's where the interrupt occurs.

Statement-number identifies the number of the Procedure Division statement that was about to execute when the interrupt occurred. This number corresponds to the number you code in columns 1-6 of the source program; it's *not* the compiler-generated line number that appears in the source listing.

Verb-number is significant only when you code more than one COBOL verb on a single line. It indicates what verb was about to execute when the interrupt occurred: if it's one, the first verb on the line was about to execute; if it's two, the second verb was about to execute; and so on. It's a good practice to limit yourself to one COBOL verb on each line of your Procedure Division. If you do that, the verb number is always one.

To illustrate TESTCOB's statement-referral notation, consider this message:

```
MKTG1200.018800.1
```

This refers to the first verb on line 18800 in the program named MKTG1200.

Now that you know how TESTCOB refers to Procedure Division statements, I'll show you how to use TESTCOB commands to start or resume a program's execution, to use breakpoints, and to establish a program trace.

How to start or resume your program's execution

Although you can invoke TESTCOB from ISPF, it executes in native TSO mode. So, after you select option 10A from the foreground menu, your terminal enters native TSO mode and displays the message TESTCOB. This message tells you that TESTCOB is executing and is waiting for you to enter a TESTCOB command. When this message appears, you can set a breakpoint, establish a trace, or just start your program executing.

TESTCOB provides two commands for starting your program's execution. The one you'll use most often is GO. If you enter the GO command, your program begins executing and continues until a breakpoint occurs, an abend occurs, or your program executes a STOP RUN statement. Then, TSO displays the TESTCOB message again and you can enter another command.

The RUN command is like the GO command except it ignores any breakpoints you've established. So the RUN command causes your program to execute to its completion: either an abend or a STOP RUN.

As I've already mentioned, you use the RUN or GO command to start your program executing when you first enter TESTCOB. In addition, you use the RUN or GO command to resume your program's execution after it's been interrupted by a breakpoint or an abend. But once your program ends by executing a STOP RUN, you can't resume it with a RUN or GO command.

If you specify a statement number on a RUN or GO command, program execution starts at the specified statement. For example, if you enter the command

```
GO MKTG1200.021100.1
```

execution begins at the first verb in line 21100 in MKTG1200. You can achieve the same result like this:

```
GO 021100
```

Here, TESTCOB assumes the first verb in line 21100 because you omitted the verb number. And, assuming that MKTG1200 is the program that's executing, you can omit the program-id.

Coding a statement number on a RUN or GO command is the same as issuing a GO TO statement in a COBOL program. You'll use this feature most when you're testing a single section of code repeatedly, perhaps changing the value of a data field between each execution.

How to use breakpoints

One of the most powerful features of the interactive debugger is the ability to use breakpoints. Basically, a breakpoint is a specific point in your program where you want to temporarily interrupt program execution. During a program interruption, you can use other TESTCOB commands to inspect data fields, display the status of files, or perform other debugging functions.

TESTCOB provides three types of breakpoints. A *NEXT break-point* lets you execute your program one statement at a time by setting a breakpoint at the next statement that's executed. An *unconditional breakpoint* sets a breakpoint at a specific statement number you supply; TESTCOB interrupts your program whenever that statement is about to execute. And a *conditional breakpoint* interrupts your program whenever a condition you specify occurs, for example, whenever a particular field's value changes.

How to use a NEXT breakpoint   A NEXT command establishes a breakpoint at the next statement that's executed. To set a NEXT breakpoint, enter the NEXT command with no operands, like this:

```
NEXT
```

Then, when you enter a GO command, TESTCOB executes only one statement of your program before it takes another breakpoint.

There are two situations where a NEXT breakpoint is particularly useful. The first is when your program reaches a decision point, such as an IF statement, and you want to see what statement of your program executes next. By setting a NEXT breakpoint, you cause TESTCOB to interrupt your program after the current statement executes, but before the following statement executes, even though you don't know in advance what the next statement is.

The second situation where a NEXT breakpoint is helpful is when you first enter TESTCOB. Before you start your program with a GO command, you *cannot* use certain TESTCOB commands, including the ones you use to examine and change your program's data. That's because TESTCOB doesn't actually load your program into storage until you issue a GO or RUN command. But if you enter a NEXT command followed by a GO command, TESTCOB loads your program and interrupts it *before* the first statement executes. Then, you can enter any TESTCOB command you want.

How to use an unconditional breakpoint   An unconditional breakpoint causes TESTCOB to interrupt your program whenever a particular statement is about to execute. To use unconditional breakpoints, you need to know about two TESTCOB commands: AT and OFF. Figure 6-11 gives the format of these commands.

You use the AT command to establish one or more breakpoints in your program. Basically, you provide one or more statement numbers in the AT command. Then, whenever one of those statements is about to execute, TESTCOB interrupts your program's execution and lets you enter one or more commands. When you enter a GO or RUN command, your program continues until the next breakpoint.

The AT command

```
AT statement-list [(command-list)]
```

The OFF command

```
OFF [statement-list]
```

Explanation

statement-list   One or more statement numbers specified as: (1) a single number; (2) several numbers separated by commas and enclosed in parentheses; or (3) a range of numbers separated by a colon. If no statements are specified in an OFF command, all unconditional breakpoints are deleted.

command-list   A series of TESTCOB commands, separated by semicolons, that is automatically executed when the specified breakpoint occurs.

Figure 6-11   TESTCOB commands used for unconditional breakpoints

To set one breakpoint, enter AT followed by the statement number where you want the breakpoint to occur. For example, if you enter the command

```
AT 21200
```

TESTCOB establishes a breakpoint at statement 21200.

To specify more than one statement number in an AT command, separate them with commas and enclose the entire list in parentheses. For example, the command

```
AT (21200,21900,22300)
```

sets three breakpoints, at lines 21200, 21900, and 22300.

You can also specify a range of statement numbers in an AT command, like this:

```
AT 21200:23700
```

Here, TESTCOB establishes a breakpoint at every statement between, and including, lines 21200 and 23700. This form of the AT command is useful when you want to "single-step" a segment of your program to locate an elusive program bug.

As you can see in figure 6-11, you can also specify a command list on an AT command. A *command list* is a list of commands that is executed when the AT breakpoint occurs. Each TESTCOB command in the list is separated by semicolons, and the entire list is enclosed in parentheses. TESTCOB executes the commands in the list before control returns to your terminal. If the list contains a GO command, control doesn't return to your terminal at all; instead, your program automatically resumes execution.

To illustrate, suppose you want to list the contents of a field named CM-CUSTOMER-KEY each time statement 21200 is executed, but you don't want to type LIST and GO commands repeatedly. To do that, you can enter this command:

```
AT 21200 (LIST CM-CUSTOMER-KEY;GO)
```

This command establishes a breakpoint at statement 21200. Then, whenever the breakpoint is taken, the LIST and GO commands are automatically executed. (I'll present the LIST command later in this topic.) The effect of this breakpoint is that the value of CM-CUSTOMER-KEY is listed each time statement 21200 is executed.

You use the OFF command to remove one or more breakpoints you've previously set using the AT command. On an OFF command, you specify statement numbers just as you do on an AT command. You can specify a single statement number like this:

```
OFF 21200
```

Here, TESTCOB removes the breakpoint at line 21200. To specify more than one statement number, separate them by commas and enclose the entire list in parentheses, like this:

```
OFF (21200,21900,22300)
```

Here, TESTCOB removes the three breakpoints at lines 21200, 21900, and 22300. You can specify a range of statements, like this:

```
OFF (21200:23700)
```

Here, TESTCOB removes all the breakpoints between, and including, lines 21200 and 23700. Finally, you can specify an OFF command with no operands. In that case, TESTCOB removes all your unconditional breakpoints.

How to use a conditional breakpoint   A conditional breakpoint interrupts your program based on the contents of a particular data field. As a result, conditional breakpoints let you monitor the

---

The WHEN command

```
WHEN identifier {data-name
                 (expression)}
```

The OFFWN command

```
OFFWN [identifier]
```

Explanation

identifier   A one- to four-character string that uniquely identifies a conditional breakpoint. For an OFFWN command, you can specify more than one identifier by separating them with commas and enclosing the list in parentheses. If no identifiers are specified in an OFFWN command, all conditional breakpoints are deleted.

data-name   If you specify a data name rather than an expression, the breakpoint is taken whenever the contents of that data name change.

expression   A relational condition in this form:

```
data-name operator value
```

where operator is a relational operator selected from the list in figure 6-13 and value is another data name or a literal value.

Figure 6-12   TESTCOB commands used for conditional breakpoints

contents of specific data fields to see when they change or when they attain a particular value.

You use two TESTCOB commands for conditional breakpoints. The WHEN command establishes a conditional breakpoint. And the OFFWN command removes one or more conditional breakpoints. These commands are shown in figure 6-12.

For the WHEN command, you specify a one- to four-character identifier. You use this identifier later to remove the breakpoint, and TESTCOB displays this identifier whenever it interrupts your program as a result of the breakpoint. The identifier must be unique during a TESTCOB session.

After the identifier, you specify either a single data name or an expression. If you specify a data name, that field is evaluated each time TESTCOB executes a program statement. Whenever the

Operator	Meaning
EQ =	Equal to
GT >	Greater than
LT <	Less than
NE ¬ =	Not equal to
GE >=	Greater than or equal to
LE <=	Less than or equal to

Figure 6-13   Relational operators for conditions

field's value changes, TESTCOB interrupts your program. For
example, suppose you enter this command:

    WHEN CUST CM-CUSTOMER-KEY

Then, TESTCOB interrupts your program whenever the value of
CM-CUSTOMER-KEY changes. CUST is the identifier associated
with this conditional breakpoint.

You can test a field for a specific value by coding an expression
that compares the field with another field or a literal. To do this,
you use one of the six relational operators shown in figure 6-13.
For example, suppose you code this command:

    WHEN HIT (CM-SALES-THIS-YTD LT CM-SALES-LAST-YTD)

Then, TESTCOB interrupts your program whenever the value of
CM-SALES-THIS-YTD is less than the value of CM-SALES-LAST-YTD.
Notice that the entire expression must be enclosed in parentheses.
Even so, complex or compound conditions aren't allowed.

To remove one or more conditional breakpoints, specify one or
more identifiers from WHEN commands in an OFFWN command.
For example, if you enter the command

    OFFWN CUST

TESTCOB removes the CUST conditional breakpoint. To specify more than one conditional breakpoint, enclose the list in parentheses, like this:

```
OFFWN (CUST,HIT)
```

Here, TESTCOB removes two conditional breakpoints. Finally, if you enter the OFFWN command without any identifiers, TESTCOB removes all the conditional breakpoints you've set.

The LISTBRKS command   The LISTBRKS command displays all your active breakpoints, including NEXT breakpoints, unconditional breakpoints, and conditional breakpoints. In addition, the LISTBRKS command tells you if a program trace is in effect. I'll describe the program trace feature next. LISTBRKS has no operands.

How to trace program flow

Figure 6-14 gives the format of the TRACE command. You use the TRACE command to initiate or terminate a program trace. A program trace helps you track your program's execution by displaying information about the program as it executes. The output generated by a TRACE command is similar to the output generated by COBOL's TRACE statement. If you specify PRINT, TESTCOB routes the output to the print file specified on the TESTCOB entry panel.

The ENTRY operand starts a trace of programs and subprograms. Each time a program transfers control to another program via a CALL statement, TESTCOB displays the new program's name (taken from the PROGRAM-ID paragraph). When control returns to the calling program, TESTCOB displays the calling program's name. This type of trace helps you check that your subprograms are invoked in the correct sequence.

The PARA and NAME operands both start a trace of the execution of your program's paragraphs and sections. If you say PARA, TESTCOB displays the statement number of each paragraph or section whenever that paragraph or section is about to execute. If you say NAME, TESTCOB displays the actual paragraph or section name rather than the statement number. Since the output created by NAME is much easier to follow than that created by PARA, I recommend you use NAME.

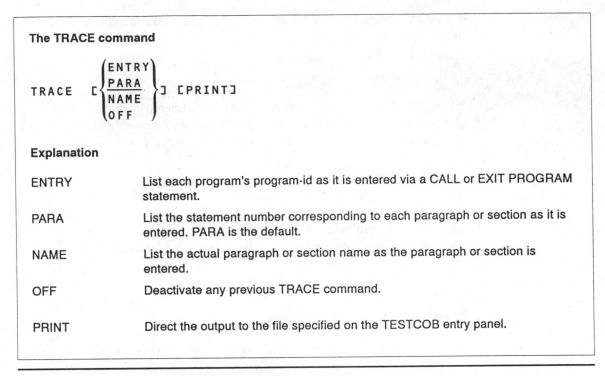

The TRACE command

```
TRACE   [ { ENTRY
            PARA
            NAME
            OFF  } ] [PRINT]
```

Explanation

ENTRY   List each program's program-id as it is entered via a CALL or EXIT PROGRAM
             statement.

PARA   List the statement number corresponding to each paragraph or section as it is
             entered. PARA is the default.

NAME   List the actual paragraph or section name as the paragraph or section is
             entered.

OFF   Deactivate any previous TRACE command.

PRINT   Direct the output to the file specified on the TESTCOB entry panel.

Figure 6-14   The TRACE command

If you enter a TRACE command with no operands, PARA is assumed. So you'll normally enter the TRACE command like this:

    TRACE NAME

Then, TESTCOB displays actual paragraph and section names rather than statement numbers.

To stop a program trace, enter the TRACE command with the OFF operand, like this:

    TRACE OFF

Then, the trace ends.

Figure 6-15 shows output typical of that generated by the TRACE command. As you can see, a list of paragraph and section names makes it easy to follow the execution of a program.

```
TRACE NAME
 TESTCOB
GO
 TRACING MKTG1200
 000242 100-FORMAT-REPORT-HEADING
 000251 200-PRODUCESALES-REPORT-LINES
 000281 210-READ-CUSTOMER-RECORD
 000287 220-PRINT-CUSTOMER-LINE
 000346 230-READ-SALESMAN-RECORD
 000352 240-PRINT-REPORT-LINE
 000359 250-PRINT-HEADING-LINES
 000378 260-WRITE-PAGE-TOP-LINE
 000384 270-WRITE-REPORT-LINE
 000384 270-WRITE-REPORT-LINE
 000390 280-ACCUMULATE-SALES-TOTALS
 000281 210-READ-CUSTOMER-RECORD
 000287 220-PRINT-CUSTOMER-LINE
 000352 240-PRINT-REPORT-LINE
 000384 270-WRITE-REPORT-LINE
 000390 280-ACCUMULATE-SALES-TOTALS
 .
 .
 .
```

Figure 6-15   Typical TRACE command output

HOW TO MANAGE YOUR PROGRAM'S DATA

Besides monitoring your program's statements as they execute,
TESTCOB lets you manage your program's data. You use the LIST
command to display the contents of one or more data fields. You
use the SET command to change the contents of data fields. And
because COBOL data names can be cumbersome to type repeatedly, the EQUATE and DROP commands let you substitute a
shorter name for a longer one. Finally, the LISTFILE command lets
you display the status of a file.

How to list data fields

Figure 6-16 shows the format of the LIST command, used to
display the contents of one or more data fields. On a LIST
command, you specify one or more *identifiers*. Each identifier can
be a data name, an index name, or one of the COBOL special

The LIST command

```
LIST    {identifier-list}  [PRINT]
        {ALL            }
```

Explanation

identifier-list   One or more identifiers specified as: (1) a single data name; (2) several data names separated by commas and enclosed in parentheses; or (3) a range of data names separated by a colon. An identifier can be a COBOL data name, an index name, or a COBOL special register.

ALL   List all of the program's data names, index names, special registers, and the TGT table.

PRINT   Direct the output to the file specified on the TESTCOB entry panel.

Figure 6-16   The LIST command

registers like DATE or TALLY. If you specify PRINT on the LIST command, TESTCOB routes output to the print file specified on the TESTCOB entry panel.

You specify the identifiers much like you specify statement numbers on an AT command. You can specify just one identifier, like this:

```
LIST CM-CUSTOMER-KEY
```

This command causes TESTCOB to display the value of the field named CM-CUSTOMER-KEY. Or, you can specify several identifiers separated by commas and enclosed in parentheses, like this:

```
LIST (CM-CUSTOMER-KEY,CM-CUSTOMER-NAME,CM-SALES-THIS-YTD)
```

This command causes TESTCOB to display the contents of three fields. Finally, you can specify a range of identifiers, like this:

```
LIST CM-CUSTOMER-NAME:CM-SALES-LAST-YTD
```

This command causes TESTCOB to display the value of each data field between, and including, CM-CUSTOMER-NAME and CM-SALES-LAST-YTD.

Type code	Meaning
A	Alphabetic
AN	Alphanumeric
ANE	Alphanumeric edited
NE	Numeric edited
ND	Numeric display (external decimal)
ND-OT	Numeric display, overpunch sign trailing
ND-OL	Numeric display, overpunch sign leading
ND-ST	Numeric display, separate sign trailing
ND-SL	Numeric display, separate sign leading
NP	Numeric packed decimal (COMP-3)
NP-S	Numeric packed decimal, signed
NB	Numeric binary (COMP)
NB-S	Numeric binary, signed
F	Floating point (COMP-1 or COMP-2)
FD	Floating point display
*	Subscripted item

Figure 6-17   LIST type codes

TESTCOB formats LIST output according to how you define the field in the COBOL program. TESTCOB displays alphanumeric items in standard character format if possible; if they contain unprintable characters, TESTCOB displays them in hexadecimal. TESTCOB displays numeric items, whether they're zoned decimal or packed decimal, as decimal values. If you specify a group item, TESTCOB displays the elementary items that make up the group on separate lines. If the field is subscripted, TESTCOB displays each occurrence on a separate line, preceded by its subscript value. And if you specify an index name, TESTCOB displays the occurrence number corresponding to the index name's value.

Each item TESTCOB displays as a result of a LIST command is labeled by the field's location in storage, its statement number, level number, name, and type code. The type code says how the field is defined in the COBOL program: whether it's alphanumeric, packed decimal, or some other data type. Figure 6-17 shows the type codes along with their meanings.

```
LIST CUSTOMER-MASTER-RECORD
                002700    01  CUSTOMER-MASTER-RECORD
                002900    02  CM-CUSTOMER-KEY
                003000    03  CM-SALESMAN-KEY
11B818          003100    04  CM-BRANCH-NUMBER          AN        01
11B81A          003200    04  CM-SALESMAN-NUMBER        AN        01
11B81C          003300    03  CM-CUSTOMER-NUMBER        AN                 1
11B81D          003400    02  CM-CUSTOMER-NAME          AN        GEORGE DONALDSON
11B840          003500    02  CM-SALES-THIS-YTD         NP-S      +00456.38
11B844          003600    02  CM-SALES-LAST-YTD         NP-S      +00235.49
```

Figure 6-18   Typical LIST command output

LIST displays each item's level number as a *normalized level number*. That means that level numbers are numbered sequentially from one, even though you might number by two's or five's in your source program. For example, if you code three levels numbered 01, 05, and 10, the corresponding normalized level numbers are 01, 02, and 03.

If you specify ALL on a LIST command, TESTCOB displays all your program's data. That includes all index names, data names, and special registers. It also includes the contents of a special table called the *task global table*, or *TGT*. The TGT contains many fields used to control the proper execution of your program. Most of these fields are of little concern to you. You probably won't use the ALL operand often. That's because it can result in a large quantity of output. It's usually better to specify the field or fields you want to display.

Figure 6-18 shows output typical of the LIST command. Here, I enter this command:

```
LIST CUSTOMER-MASTER-RECORD
```

Since CUSTOMER-MASTER-RECORD is a group item, TESTCOB lists its subordinate fields individually. The level numbers are normalized (my program contains 05, 10, and 15 levels, not 02, 03, and 04 levels), and the content of each field is formatted according to the field's PICTURE.

The SET command

$$\text{SET} \quad \text{identifier-1} = \begin{Bmatrix} \text{identifier-2} \\ \text{literal} \end{Bmatrix}$$

Explanation

identifier-1   The data name or index name whose value is to be changed.

identifier-2   The data name or index name whose value is moved to identifier-1.

literal   A literal value that's moved to identifier-1.

Note: The move operation follows the standard COBOL MOVE rules.

Figure 6-19   The SET command

How to change a data field

Figure 6-19 shows the format of the SET command, used to change the contents of a data field. The operation of the SET command is simple: the contents of identifier-1 are replaced by the contents of identifier-2 or the literal. For example, consider this SET command:

```
SET SALESMAN-TOTAL-THIS-YTD = 0
```

This command causes TESTCOB to change the value of SALESMAN-TOTAL-THIS-YTD to zero.

If the lengths or types of the sending and receiving fields differ, the SET command follows the rules for a standard COBOL MOVE statement. Thus, TESTCOB truncates values or pads them with spaces as necessary, and converts data from one form to another, just as when you code a MOVE statement in your COBOL program. And, of course, certain combinations of sending and receiving fields aren't valid. For example, you can't move an alphanumeric value to a numeric packed-decimal field.

Because the rules for certain types of moves are obscure, it's a good idea to check the results of your SET command by following it with a LIST command. That way, you'll know if your SET command worked as you intended.

How to shorten data names

In your COBOL programs, I strongly recommend that you use data names that are meaningful. A data name like TOTAL-SALES-THIS-YTD is much more meaningful than X or TSLS. Since one of the primary goals of program development is to create programs that are easy to read and maintain, I can't stress this point too much.

Still, longer data names can be an irritation during a TESTCOB session. Fortunately, TESTCOB provides two commands that let you substitute a shorter name for a longer one. Figure 6-20 presents these two commands: EQUATE and DROP.

The EQUATE command lets you assign a *symbol* to a data name or index name. For example, consider this EQUATE command:

```
EQUATE CUSTKEY CM-CUSTOMER-KEY
```

Once you've entered this command, you can use the symbol CUSTKEY instead of the data name CM-CUSTOMER-KEY throughout your TESTCOB session.

The DROP command lets you remove a previously defined symbol. So if you enter:

```
DROP CUSTKEY
```

you can no longer use CUSTKEY to refer to CM-CUSTOMER-KEY. You can specify several symbols in a single DROP command, like this:

```
DROP (CUSTKEY,NAME,YTDSALES)
```

Here, TESTCOB deletes three symbols. If you enter DROP with no symbols, TESTCOB deletes all your symbols.

How to display the status of a file

The LISTFILE command, whose format is given in figure 6-21, displays the status of a data set at your terminal. On the LISTFILE command, you specify a file name that's defined in your program by an FD statement. If you include the PRINT operand, TESTCOB routes the output to the print data set you specified on the TESTCOB entry panel.

Figure 6-22 shows output that's typical of the LISTFILE command. Here, I entered a LISTFILE command like this:

```
LISTFILE CUSTMST
```

The EQUATE command

```
EQUATE symbol data-name
```

The DROP command

```
DROP [symbol]
```

Explanation

symbol	A character string that follows the rules for forming a COBOL data name. Usually shorter than the actual data name it will stand for. For a DROP command, you can specify more than one symbol by separating them with commas and enclosing the entire list in parentheses. (If no symbols are specified in a DROP command, all symbols are deleted.)
data-name	The data name that the specified symbol represents. Can also be an index name or a special register like TALLY.

Figure 6-20   The EQUATE and DROP commands

The LISTFILE command

```
LISTFILE  file-name [PRINT]
```

Explanation

file-name	The name of the file whose status is to be listed.
PRINT	Direct the output to the file specified on the TESTCOB entry panel.

Figure 6-21   The LISTFILE command

```
LISTFILE CUSTMST
 FD CUSTMST
 DSORG PS
 DSNAME DLOWE.CUSTMAST.DATA
 OPEN INPUT , LRECL 00042, BLKSIZE 00840, RECFM F
 TESTCOB
```

Figure 6-22   Typical LISTFILE command output

In response, TESTCOB displays significant information about the file, including the file's organization (PS means sequential), data set name (DLOWE.CUSTMAST.DATA), open mode (input), record length (42), block size (840), and recording mode (fixed). As you debug your program, this information can help you determine the cause of file-related problems.

HOW TO USE
THE IF COMMAND IN A COMMAND LIST

Although there are many possible uses for coding a command list on an AT command, the most common is to list the contents of one or more data fields and resume program execution. In some cases, however, you want to resume program execution only under certain conditions. For example, you may want to list the contents of a field and resume program execution if that field is less than another field. The IF command, whose format is shown in figure 6-23, lets you do just that. You can enter an IF command by itself, if you want, but you normally use it in a command list.

You specify an expression on an IF command just as you do on a WHEN command, so I won't restate the rules here. After the expression, you say either HALT or GO to tell TESTCOB what to do if the expression is true. If you say HALT, TESTCOB stops your program's execution and returns control to your terminal. If you say GO, TESTCOB resumes your program's execution. In either case, control returns to the next command in the list if the expression is false.

The IF command

$$\text{IF (expression)} \begin{Bmatrix} \text{GO} \\ \text{HALT} \end{Bmatrix}$$

Explanation

expression	A relational condition formed following the rules for an expression in a WHEN command.
GO	Says that program execution should be immediately resumed if the expression is true.
HALT	Says that control should return to the user immediately if the expression is true.

Figure 6-23 The IF command

To illustrate, consider this AT command:

```
AT 29300 (IF (LASTYTD LT THISYTD) HALT;GO)
```

Here, TESTCOB executes the IF command each time it takes the breakpoint at line 29300, and compares the symbol LASTYTD with THISYTD. If the expression is true, that is, if LASTYTD is less than THISYTD, TESTCOB halts the program and returns control to the terminal. Otherwise, TESTCOB executes the next command in the list. In this case, the next command is GO, so the program continues.

Suppose you entered this AT command:

```
AT 29300 (IF (LASTYTD GE THISYTD) GO)
```

Here, program execution continues if LASTYTD is greater than or equal to THISYTD. Otherwise, control returns to the terminal, since there are no more commands in the list to execute. If you compare this command list with the previous one, you'll see that they both have the same effect: the program continues executing until LASTYTD is less than THISYTD at line 29300.

The SOURCE command

SOURCE $\begin{Bmatrix} \text{line-1} \\ \text{line-1:line-2} \end{Bmatrix}$

Explanation

line-1   The starting line number. If line-2 isn't specified, only line-1 is listed.

line-2   The ending line number when a range of lines is to be listed.

Figure 6-24 The SOURCE command

HOW TO DISPLAY SOURCE STATEMENTS

Figure 6-24 gives the format of the SOURCE command, which you can use to display one or more lines of your source program at your terminal. To use the SOURCE command, you must have specified YES in the SOURCE field on the debug entry panel. In addition, you must have compiled the program with the SOURCE compiler option.

On the SOURCE command, you supply a single line number or a range of line numbers separated by a colon. For example, to display line 29300, code this command:

```
SOURCE 29300
```

And to display lines 29000 to 29500, code this command:

```
SOURCE 29000:29500
```

Quite frankly, the SOURCE command isn't very useful. In my opinion, it's far better to have a printed version of the compiler listing available as you debug your program. That way, you won't erase important debugging information (like LIST output) to display source lines. And you'll be able to mark corrections directly on the source listing. In short, you probably won't use the SOURCE command much unless your installation has a policy that restricts printouts of compiler listings or the turnaround time for hardcopy output is excessive.

HOW TO DEBUG A SUBPROGRAM

Up to now, I've assumed you're debugging a program that doesn't call subprograms. If your program does call one or more subprograms, you use some of the TESTCOB features differently.

As your program executes and interrupts occur, the statement numbers TESTCOB displays reflect the program or subprogram that is currently executing. For example, if TESTCOB displays the statement number

    SYSDATE.1500.1

you know that the subprogram named SYSDATE is executing.

To debug a program that's not currently executing, you have to specify the program name on the TESTCOB commands. For example, suppose you need to debug the SYSDATE subprogram and that line 20200 in MKTG1200 is the CALL statement that invokes SYSDATE. Assuming that MKTG1200 is currently executing, you first set a breakpoint at line 20200 like this:

    AT 20200

Then, TESTCOB interrupts your program just before line 20200 executes. Now, you want to set a range of breakpoints in SYSDATE so you can single-step through the subprogram from lines 1000 to 3000. If you enter the command

    AT 1000:3000

TESTCOB sets the breakpoints for lines 1000 through 3000 of MKTG1200, since that's the program currently executing. So you have to enter the AT command like this:

    AT SYSDATE.1000:SYSDATE.3000

Then, the breakpoints are established for lines 1000 through 3000 of SYSDATE.

You can also refer to data names in this fashion. For example, if you enter the command

    LIST TODAYS-DATE

TESTCOB lists the value of TODAYS-DATE in the current program. But if you enter

    LIST SYSDATE.TODAYS-DATE

TESTCOB lists the value of TODAYS-DATE in the subprogram named SYSDATE.

Finally, remember that you can use the ENTRY operand of the TRACE command to trace subprogram execution. As a result, you can make sure the correct subprograms are executing at the right times.

HOW TO TERMINATE TESTCOB

There are two ways to exit from TESTCOB. Normally, you issue an END command, like this:

```
END
```

Then, control returns to ISPF.

The other way to end TESTCOB is to enter a DUMP command, like this:

```
DUMP
```

Then, control returns to ISPF and a storage dump is generated. To use the DUMP command, you must issue an ALLOCATE command for ddname SYSUDUMP or SYSABEND *before* you start your TESTCOB session. Normally, you'll use SYSUDUMP, and allocate it to a SYSOUT class, like this:

```
ALLOCATE DDNAME(SYSUDUMP) SYSOUT(A)
```

If you use SYSABEND, the dump is much larger, containing a lot of information you don't need. In any event, you should use the DUMP command only as a last resort when you can't isolate a program bug using the interactive debugger.

DISCUSSION

As a testing and debugging tool, the COBOL interactive debugger is vastly superior to the storage-dump approach. So if you're still debugging your programs in batch mode using storage dumps, I suggest you start using the interactive debugger right now, if it's available. Having read the introduction this topic presents, you'll be able to learn how to use TESTCOB quickly.

Terms

OS COBOL Interactive Debug
TESTCOB
VS COBOL II Interactive Debug
COBTEST
breakpoint
trace
program-id
statement-number
verb-number
NEXT breakpoint
unconditional breakpoint
conditional breakpoint
command list
identifier
normalized level number
task global table
TGT
symbol

Objectives

1. Invoke TESTCOB to debug a COBOL program. The program
    may or may not use called subprograms.

2. Describe how to use the following TESTCOB features:

    a. NEXT breakpoint
    b. unconditional breakpoint
    c. conditional breakpoint
    d. program trace

3. Use TESTCOB commands to examine and change the contents
    of data fields as your program executes.

Topic 3 How to debug programs using VS COBOL II Interactive Debug

VS COBOL II provides a debugging tool similar to OS COBOL Interactive Debug called VS COBOL II Interactive Debug, or COBTEST. COBTEST is part of VS COBOL II and provides a number of functions that aren't provided by OS COBOL Interactive Debug. The most significant difference between OS COBOL Interactive Debug and VS COBOL II Interactive Debug is that VS COBOL II Interactive Debug can be used in either batch or interactive mode. And interactive mode provides for both line mode and full-screen mode. You must have ISPF Version 2 or later to use full-screen mode.

In this topic, I'll cover only the basic functions of full-screen interactive mode of VS COBOL II Interactive Debug. Specifically, you'll learn how to invoke COBTEST in full-screen mode, how to use the full-screen panel, how to use COBTEST to monitor your program's execution and manage its data, how to use the IF command, how to debug subprograms, and how to terminate COBTEST.

Before I go on, I want to point out that I will *not* try to teach you how to debug COBOL programs in this topic; that's beyond the scope of this book. Instead, I'll teach you how to use COBTEST in full-screen mode so you'll be able to debug your programs more easily.

HOW TO INVOKE COBTEST

Before you invoke COBTEST, you must be sure the program you're debugging was compiled with the TEST option. The TEST option produces the symbolic data necessary for you to debug a program with COBTEST. You also need to be sure you've allocated any data sets required by the program you're debugging before you invoke COBTEST.

```
-------------------------- VS COBOL II DEBUG INVOCATION --------------------------
COMMAND ===>

ISPF LIBRARY:
   PROJECT ===> DLOWE
   GROUP   ===> TEST
   TYPE    ===> LOAD
   MEMBER  ===> MKTG1200          (Blank for member selection list)

OTHER PARTITIONED DATA SET:
   DATASET NAME  ===>

PASSWORD ===>                      MIXED MODE ===> NO  (YES or NO)

VS COBOL II PROGRAM PARAMETERS:
   ===>
   ===>

LOG      ===> NO   (Yes or No)
LOG DSN ===>
RESTART ===> NO   (Yes or No)
RESTART DSN ===>
```

Figure 6-25   The foreground debug entry panel

To invoke VS COBOL II Debug, select option 10 from the Foreground Selection Panel. When you do, the full-screen debug invocation panel shown in figure 6-25 is displayed. On this panel, you specify the name of the program to be debugged and its run-time parameters.

If you're using ISPF naming conventions, enter the name of the program you want to execute under ISPF LIBRARY. Otherwise, enter the data set name under OTHER PARTITIONED DATA SET. If the program you're using is password protected, be sure to enter the password. And, if you'll be using characters from the Double Byte Character Set in the debugging session, specify YES in the MIXED MODE field.

You can enter run-time parameters in the area labeled VS COBOL II PROGRAM PARAMETERS. Since most COBOL programs don't use run-time options or parameters, I won't present the details for coding them.

The LOG, LOG DSN, RESTART, and RESTART DSN fields provide for two optional debugging files. The first one is created during your debugging session and contains any COBTEST commands you enter as well as any output that's sent to your terminal. If you want to log your debugging session, specify YES in the LOG field, and, in the LOG DSN field, enter the name of the data set you want created to contain the log. This data set will consist of fixed-length, 80-character records.

The second file allows you to restart a debugging session at a specific point. In most cases, you'll use it to restart a session at the point it was previously terminated. To do that, specify YES in the RESTART field and the name of the restart data set in the RESTART DSN field. The restart data set is an existing file that contains COBTEST commands. Usually, you'll use the log file created during the previous execution of a debugging session as the restart file. Then, all you have to do is specify the name of the log file under RESTART DSN, and the input commands in the log file are executed, returning you to the previous termination point. From there, you can continue by entering additional debugging commands.

HOW TO USE THE FULL-SCREEN PANEL

Once you invoke the full-screen debugger, ISPF displays the main debugging panel. From this panel, you can enter COBTEST commands and view the execution of the debugging session. This panel is illustrated in figure 6-26.

Areas of the full-screen panel

The top of the debugging panel contains heading information. In the upper left-hand corner is the name of the debug tool, COBTEST. Then, after the heading QUALIFY: is the *qualify field*, which contains the name of the current program. In figure 6-26, the current program is MKTG1200. After the heading WHERE: is the statement number of the next statement to be executed. When the debugging panel is first displayed, the statement number specified is always the first executable statement of the program, since COBTEST doesn't automatically begin executing your program when you invoke it in interactive mode. In figure 6-26, the first executable statement is number 228.

Heading area

Source area

Log area

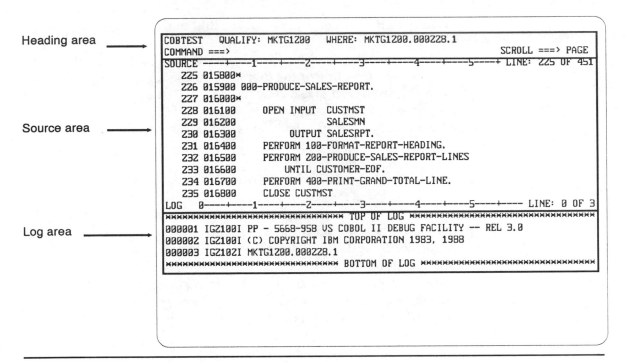

```
COBTEST    QUALIFY: MKTG1200   WHERE: MKTG1200.000228.1
COMMAND ===>                                        SCROLL ===> PAGE
SOURCE ----+----1----+----2----+----3----+----4----+----5----+ LINE: 225 OF 451
    225 015800*
    226 015900 000-PRODUCE-SALES-REPORT.
    227 016000*
    228 016100     OPEN INPUT  CUSTMST
    229 016200               SALESMN
    230 016300          OUTPUT SALESRPT.
    231 016400     PERFORM 100-FORMAT-REPORT-HEADING.
    232 016500     PERFORM 200-PRODUCE-SALES-REPORT-LINES
    233 016600          UNTIL CUSTOMER-EOF.
    234 016700     PERFORM 400-PRINT-GRAND-TOTAL-LINE.
    235 016800     CLOSE CUSTMST
LOG    0----+----1----+----2----+----3----+----4----+----5----+---- LINE: 0 OF 3
******************************* TOP OF LOG ***********************************
000001 IGZ100I PP - 5668-958 VS COBOL II DEBUG FACILITY -- REL 3.0
000002 IGZ100I (C) COPYRIGHT IBM CORPORATION 1983, 1988
000003 IGZ102I MKTG1200.000228.1
********************************* BOTTOM OF LOG ******************************
```

Figure 6-26   The full-screen debugging panel

The second line of the screen is the standard ISPF command line. The rest of the screen consists of the log area and the source area. The *log area* is where ISPF displays the COBTEST commands you issue during your debugging session as well as any output from COBTEST that's routed to your terminal. The log area always occupies the part of the screen not allocated to the source area. Lines similar to those in the log area in figure 6-26 always appear when you first invoke the debugger. Here, the first two lines identify the software and the third line indicates the next line of code to be executed, in this case, the first executable statement of the program.

The *source area* is where you can display your source programs. The default is for the source area to consist of 12 lines of 80 characters each, including a heading line. As you can see, that's what's displayed in figure 6-26. You can change the size of the source area using the SOURCE command, which I'll present later in this topic.

A header line appears at the beginning of the log and source areas. This line consists of the name of the area, a scale indicating the column numbers, and a line counter that indicates the line number of the first line of the display and the total number of lines in the area. In figure 6-26, you can see that all three lines of the log area are displayed. In the source area, the first line displayed is line 225 and there are 451 lines in the source listing.

How to scroll the full-screen panel

You can scroll within the source and log areas of the full-screen panel using the ISPF scrolling commands or the PF keys associated with the commands. ISPF determines what area you want to scroll by the location of the cursor at the time you issue the command. If the cursor is located anywhere in the source area, ISPF scrolls the source listing. If the cursor is located anywhere outside the source area, ISPF scrolls the log listing.

Entering commands on the full-screen panel

There are three areas where you can enter COBTEST commands on the full-screen panel: the qualify field, the command area, and the prefix area. These areas are shown in figure 6-27.

In the qualify field, you can enter the name of a source statement listing you want to display. Of course, the source listing must be available to COBTEST. Note that entering a program name here only changes the qualified program during the current program interruption. Once program execution is continued, the program that's actually executing is displayed in the source area at the next program interrupt.

You'll enter most of your COBTEST commands in the command area. I'll present the most useful of these commands in this topic. You can also enter three COBTEST commands in the *prefix area*. When you enter a command in the prefix area, it operates only on the line where you enter it. I'll present all three prefix commands later in this topic.

You should enter commands in only one panel area at a time. If you enter commands in more than one area, the areas are recognized in the following order: (1) qualify field, (2) prefix area, (3) log area, and (4) command line. Only the first command recognized is

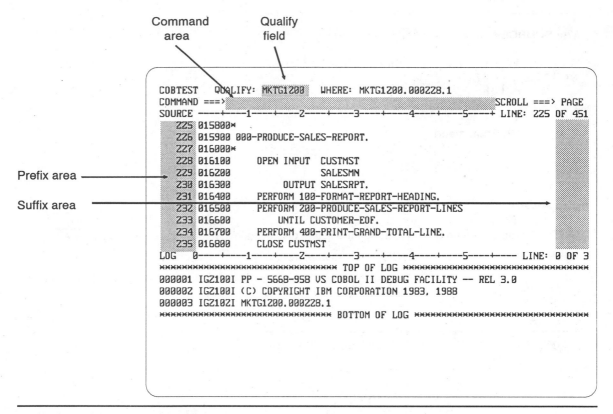

Figure 6-27   COBTEST command entry areas

executed; all others are ignored. If you enter more than one
command in the same area, only the first one is executed, except
on the command line. On the command line, you can enter
multiple commands by separating them with semicolons, and
they're all executed.

How to display source listings

Although the source area is optional, you'll almost always use it.
When you do, you need to know how to use the two commands
presented in figure 6-28: SOURCE and RESTORE.

The SOURCE command   You use the SOURCE command to
change the size of the source area. Just type the SOURCE command

---

The SOURCE command

```
              (LISTING program-name)
SOURCE  [{OFF                       }  ]
              (ON                     )
```

The RESTORE command

```
RESTORE
```

Explanation

LISTING program-name	Change the listing displayed in the source area to *program-name*.
OFF	Close the source area.
ON	Open the source area using the default size settings on the profile panel.

Figure 6-28 The SOURCE and RESTORE commands

without any operands in the command line, place the cursor where you want the bottom left corner of the source area to be, and press the Enter key. The new source area will extend from the top right corner of the old source area to the cursor position.

Figure 6-29 illustrates this use of the SOURCE command. In part 1, I placed the cursor so the source area would consist of 10 lines of 40 columns. Then, I issued the SOURCE command. The results are illustrated in part 2 of figure 6-29. If you change the size of the source area frequently, you'll probably want to assign the SOURCE command to a PF key.

If you want to close the source area completely, issue the command

```
SOURCE OFF
```

To reopen the source area, position the cursor and reissue the SOURCE command or issue the command

```
SOURCE ON
```

If you use the ON operand, COBTEST uses its default to determine the size of the source area. As I mentioned earlier in this topic, the

Part 1:

To change the size of the source area, position the cursor where you want the bottom left corner to be, and enter the SOURCE command

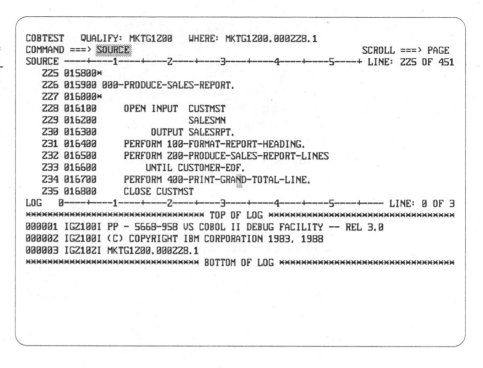

Part 2:

When you press the Enter key, the source area is changed to the indicated size

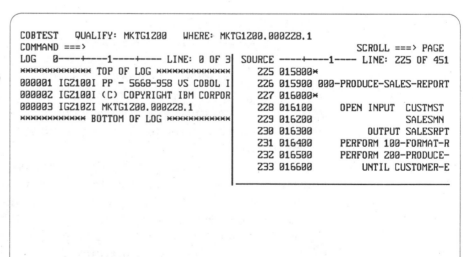

Figure 6-29   The SOURCE command as it's used to define the size of the source area

330   Chapter 6

default size of the source area is 12 lines. However, when you use the SOURCE command to change the size of the source area, the default is also changed. In other words, the default is always the size of the last source area that was displayed.

You can also use the SOURCE command to select a different listing to be displayed. You do that using the LISTING *program-name* operand. For example, if a subprogram named DATEDIT is called by the currently executing program, I can display its source listing by issuing the command

```
SOURCE LISTING DATEDIT
```

The effect is the same as entering DATEDIT in the qualify field.

The RESTORE command   Sometimes during a debugging session, you'll need to scroll the source listing of the currently executing program or display the source listing for a program other than the one that's executing. When you do one of those things, you lose the display of the line that's currently executing. To restore the display to the currently executing line, issue the RESTORE command. The RESTORE command has no operands.

HOW TO MONITOR
YOUR PROGRAM'S EXECUTION

Now that you know how to invoke COBTEST and how to use the full-screen panel, you're ready to learn the commands you'll use to debug your programs. Here, I'll show you how to monitor your program's execution. Next, I'll show you how to manage your program's data.

COBTEST lets you monitor your program's execution in two ways. First, you can establish *breakpoints* at one or more statements in your program. Whenever your program comes to a breakpoint, it stops executing temporarily. As a result, using breakpoints allows you to look at your program at specific times during its execution. The second way to monitor program execution is to use a *trace*. A trace displays information about your program's execution without actually interrupting the program.

Before I go on, I want you to understand how COBTEST refers to individual statements in your program. COBTEST follows this format when it refers to a particular Procedure Division statement:

```
program-id.line-number.verb-number
```

Program-id identifies the program that contains the statement. Normally, this is the name of the program you're executing. However, if your program calls subprograms, program-id is the name of the subprogram if that's where the interrupt occurs.

Line-number identifies the line number of the line containing the Procedure Division statement that was *about* to execute when the interrupt occurred. This number corresponds to the compiler-generated line number that appears in the source listing.

Verb-number is significant only when you code more than one COBOL verb on a single line. It indicates what verb was about to execute when the interrupt occurred: if it's one, the first verb on the line was about to execute; if it's two, the second verb was about to execute; and so on. Of course, it's a good practice to limit yourself to one COBOL verb on each line of your Procedure Division. If you do that, the verb number is always one.

To illustrate COBTEST's statement-referral notation, consider this message:

```
MKTG1200.000228.1
```

This refers to the first verb on line 228 in the program named MKTG1200.

Now that you know how COBTEST refers to Procedure Division statements, I'll show you how to use its commands to start or resume a program's execution, to use breakpoints, and to establish a program trace.

How to start or resume your program's execution

When you invoke COBTEST in interactive mode, your program doesn't automatically begin execution. Instead, it waits for you to enter a command to tell it what to do. Here, you can set a breakpoint, establish a trace, or just start your program executing.

There are three commands for starting your program's execution. They are presented in figure 6-30. The command you'll use most often to start program execution is GO. If you enter GO, your

The GO command

```
GO [statement-number]
```

The RUN command

```
RUN [statement-number]
```

The RESTART command

```
RESTART
```

Explanation

statement-number   A statement number in the COBOL source program. Must be in the form [program-id.] line-number [.verb-number].

Figure 6-30   COBTEST commands used to start or resume program execution

program begins executing and continues until a breakpoint occurs, an abend occurs, or your program executes a STOP RUN statement.

The RUN command is like the GO command except that it ignores any breakpoints you established. So the RUN command causes your program to execute to its completion: either an abend or a STOP RUN.

You can also use the RUN or GO command to resume your program's execution after it's interrupted by a breakpoint. Usually, when an interrupt occurs, you'll issue other COBTEST commands to find out what's happening in your program or to set additional breakpoints. Then you'll issue a RUN or GO command to continue execution. Once your program ends by executing a STOP RUN, however, you can't resume it with a RUN or GO command.

If you specify a statement number on a RUN or GO command, program execution starts at the specified statement. For example, if you enter this command:

```
GO MKTG1200.000251.1
```

execution begins at the first verb in line 251 of MKTG1200. You can achieve the same result like this (assuming MKTG1200 is the program that's been executing):

```
GO 251
```

Here, the first verb in line 251 is assumed because you omitted the verb number. And MKTG1200 is the program that's executed since you omitted the program-id.

Coding a statement number on a RUN or GO command is the same as issuing a GO TO statement in a COBOL program. You'll use this feature most when you're testing a single section of code repeatedly, perhaps changing the value of a data field between each execution.

You can also use the RESTART command to start program execution. When you issue the RESTART command, the previous version of the program invoked by the debugger is deleted and the program is reloaded. In the process, all program variables are initialized. However, all debug tool settings, such as breakpoints, remain unchanged. The RESTART command makes it easy to test a program several times without having to get out of COBTEST. For example, you might want to restart a program after an abend occurs.

How to use breakpoints

One of the most powerful features of COBTEST is its ability to use breakpoints. Basically, a breakpoint is a specific point in your program where you want to temporarily interrupt program execution. Once the program stops, you can use other COBTEST commands to inspect data fields, display the status of files, or perform other debugging functions.

COBTEST provides four types of breakpoints. A *NEXT breakpoint* lets you execute your program one statement at a time by setting a breakpoint at the next statement that's executed. A *STEP breakpoint* lets you step through your program, executing a specified number of verbs at a time. An *unconditional breakpoint* sets a breakpoint at a specific statement number you supply, so your program is interrupted whenever that statement is about to execute. And a *conditional breakpoint* interrupts your program whenever a condition you specify occurs, for example, whenever a particular field's value changes.

The NEXT command

```
NEXT [(command-list)]
```

Explanation

command-list   A series of COBTEST commands, separated by semicolons, that are automatically executed when the specified breakpoint occurs. The entire list is enclosed in parentheses.

Figure 6-31   The NEXT command

How to use a NEXT breakpoint   The NEXT command establishes a breakpoint at the next statement that's executed. Figure 6-31 present its format. To set a NEXT breakpoint, issue the NEXT command with no operands, like this:

```
NEXT
```

Then, when program execution continues, COBTEST executes only one statement of your program before it takes the next breakpoint.

As you can see in figure 6-31, you can also specify a command list on a NEXT command. A *command list* is a list of COBTEST commands that is executed when a specified condition occurs. In the case of the NEXT command, the command list is executed before the statement that follows the current statement is executed.

When you code a command list, each command is separated by semicolons and the entire list is enclosed in parentheses. The commands in the list are executed before control returns to your terminal. For example, consider this command:

```
NEXT (LIST CM-CUSTOMER-KEY)
```

When COBTEST executes this command, three things happen. First, COBTEST executes the current statement. Second, COBTEST executes the single LIST command in the command list. (I'll present the LIST command later in this topic.) Third, COBTEST takes the breakpoint before it executes the next statement. Of course, you can accomplish the same thing by entering the NEXT command without a command list, then entering the LIST command when COBTEST takes the next breakpoint. However, if

---

The STEP command

```
STEP [number]
```

Explanation

number   The number of verbs to be executed before the next breakpoint is taken. One
                is the default.

Figure 6-32   The STEP command

you want to issue the same command repeatedly, it's more efficient to enter it once in a command list. Then, you can use the ISPF RETRIEVE command to redisplay the NEXT command in the command area and execute it again.

There are two situations where a NEXT breakpoint is particularly useful. The first is when your program reaches a decision point, such as an IF statement, and you want to see what statement of your program is executed next. By setting a NEXT breakpoint, you cause COBTEST to interrupt your program after the current statement executes, but before the next statement executes, even though you don't know in advance what the next statement is.

The second situation where a NEXT breakpoint is helpful is when you first enter COBTEST in interactive mode. Before you begin the execution of your program, you can't use certain COBTEST commands, including the ones you use to examine and change your program's data. That's because COBTEST doesn't actually load your program into storage until you issue a GO or RUN command. But if you enter a NEXT command followed by a GO command, COBTEST loads your program and interrupts it *before* the first statement executes. Then, you can enter any COBTEST command you want.

How to use a STEP breakpoint   Figure 6-32 presents the format of the STEP command. This command causes COBTEST to execute a specified number of verbs before it takes the next breakpoint. For example, if you specify

```
STEP 5
```

COBTEST executes five verbs.

The STEP command is probably most useful for executing one verb at a time. Then, you can assign the STEP function to a PF key so that each time you press the PF key, COBTEST executes one verb. To execute one verb at a time, you can code the STEP command

    STEP 1

or just

    STEP

since one is the default. Notice that this is the same as issuing a NEXT command followed by a GO command.

How to use an unconditional breakpoint   An unconditional breakpoint causes COBTEST to interrupt your program whenever it's about to execute a particular statement. To use unconditional breakpoints, you need to know about three debugging commands: AT, OFF, and PEEK. Figure 6-33 presents the formats of these commands.

You use the AT command to establish one or more breakpoints in your program. As you can see, there are two different formats. In the first format, AT ENTRY, you specify the name of one or more programs or ALL. ALL includes all programs in the load module. Then, COBTEST stops before it executes the first verb in each program you specify.

This form of the AT command is particularly useful for debugging subprograms. For example, suppose you want to stop program execution when a subprogram called SYSDATE is first entered. Then, all you do is enter this command:

    AT ENTRY SYSDATE

If you do, COBTEST stops program execution before it executes the first verb in the subprogram.

In the second format of the AT command, you specify one or more statement numbers where you want COBTEST to interrupt program execution. To set one breakpoint, code AT followed by the statement number for the breakpoint you want to set. For example, if you enter the command

    AT 252

COBTEST sets a breakpoint at statement 252.

The AT command

```
AT ENTRY {program-name}
         {ALL         }
```

```
AT statement-list [(command-list)]
```

The OFF command

```
OFF [statement-list]
```

The PEEK command

```
PEEK
```

Explanation

program-name   The name of the COBOL program for which the breakpoint applies. Multiple programs can be specified by separating them with commas and enclosing them in parentheses.

ALL   Apply the breakpoint to all programs in the run unit.

statement-list One or more statements in the form [program-id.]line-number[.verb-number] where statement-number is specified as: (1) a single number; (2) several numbers separated by commas and enclosed in parentheses; or (3) a range of numbers separated by a colon. If no statements are specified on an OFF command, all unconditional breakpoints are deleted.

command-list   A series of COBTEST commands, separated by semicolons, that are automatically executed when the specified breakpoint occurs. The entire list is enclosed in parentheses.

Figure 6-33 COBTEST commands used for unconditional breakpoints

To specify more than one statement number in an AT command, separate the numbers with commas and enclose the entire list in parentheses. For example, the command

```
AT (252,259,263)
```

sets three breakpoints at lines 252, 259, and 263. You can also specify a range of statement numbers in an AT command, like this:

```
AT 252:263
```

Here, COBTEST establishes a breakpoint at every statement between, and including, lines 252 and 263. This form of the AT command is useful when you want to "single-step" a segment of your program to locate an elusive program bug.

In the statement-list form of the AT command, you can also specify a list of commands that are executed automatically when the breakpoint occurs just as you can for the NEXT command. For example, the command

```
AT 252 (LIST CUSTOMER-EOF-SW)
```

sets a breakpoint at line 252. Before line 252 is executed, however, COBTEST displays the contents of CUSTOMER-EOF-SW. Then, you can enter GO to continue processing, or you can enter additional COBTEST commands.

You use the OFF command to remove one or more breakpoints you've previously set using the AT command. On an OFF command, you specify statement numbers just as on an AT command. For instance, you can specify a single statement number like this:

```
OFF 252
```

Here, the breakpoint at line 252 is removed. Or, you can specify more than one statement number by separating them with commas and enclosing the entire list in parentheses, like this:

```
OFF (252,259,263)
```

Here, the three breakpoints at lines 252, 259, and 263 are removed. Or, you can specify a range of statements, like this:

```
OFF 252:263
```

Here, all the breakpoints between, and including, lines 252 and 263 are removed. Finally, you can specify an OFF command with no operands. In that case, all the unconditional breakpoints are deleted.

You can also use AT and OFF commands in the prefix area to set or clear breakpoints at particular lines. For example, to set a breakpoint at line 252, you can type AT in the prefix area of that line. To remove the breakpoint, enter OFF in the prefix area. If

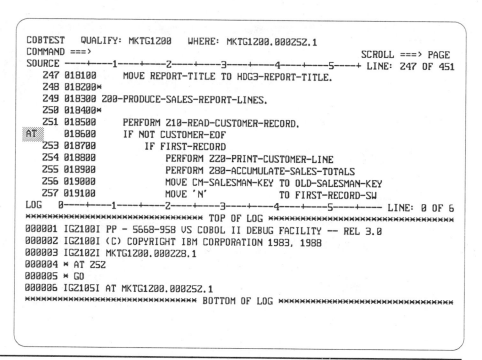

```
COBTEST   QUALIFY: MKTG1200   WHERE: MKTG1200.000252.1
COMMAND ===>                                              SCROLL ===> PAGE
SOURCE ----+----1----+----2----+----3----+----4----+----5----+ LINE: 247 OF 451
    247 018100      MOVE REPORT-TITLE TO HDG3-REPORT-TITLE.
    248 018200*
    249 018300 200-PRODUCE-SALES-REPORT-LINES.
    250 018400*
    251 018500      PERFORM 210-READ-CUSTOMER-RECORD.
 AT     018600      IF NOT CUSTOMER-EOF
    253 018700          IF FIRST-RECORD
    254 018800              PERFORM 220-PRINT-CUSTOMER-LINE
    255 018900              PERFORM 280-ACCUMULATE-SALES-TOTALS
    256 019000              MOVE CM-SALESMAN-KEY TO OLD-SALESMAN-KEY
    257 019100              MOVE 'N'              TO FIRST-RECORD-SW
LOG    0----+----1----+----2----+----3----+----4----+----5----+---- LINE: 0 OF 6
************************************** TOP OF LOG ******************************
000001 IGZ100I PP - 5668-958 VS COBOL II DEBUG FACILITY -- REL 3.0
000002 IGZ100I (C) COPYRIGHT IBM CORPORATION 1983, 1988
000003 IGZ102I MKTG1200.000228.1
000004 * AT 252
000005 * GO
000006 IGZ105I AT MKTG1200.000252.1
************************************** BOTTOM OF LOG ***************************
```

Figure 6-34   Feedback in the source area from an AT command

there's more than one statement on the line, you can enter a number following AT or OFF. So AT 2 sets a breakpoint at the second statement on the line and OFF 2 clears it.

The only other command you can enter in the prefix area is the PEEK command. You use this command to display a line number that's obscured by the feedback of a previous AT command, as in figure 6-34. From here, when you type PEEK right over AT and press the Enter key, line number 252 reappears in the prefix area.

How to use a conditional breakpoint   A conditional breakpoint interrupts your program based on the contents of a particular data field. As a result, conditional breakpoints let you monitor the contents of specific data fields to see when they change or when they attain a particular value.

You use two commands for conditional breakpoints. The WHEN command establishes a conditional breakpoint. And the OFFWN command removes one or more conditional breakpoints. These commands are presented in figure 6-35.

The WHEN command

```
WHEN identifier {data-name    } [(command-list)]
                {(expression)}
```

The OFFWN command

```
OFFWN [identifier]
```

Explanation

identifier   A one- to four-character string that uniquely identifies a conditional breakpoint. For an OFFWN command, you can specify more than one identifier by separating them with commas and enclosing the list in parentheses. If no identifiers are specified on an OFFWN command, all conditional breakpoints are deleted.

data-name   If you specify a data name, the breakpoint is taken whenever the contents of that data name change.

expression   A relational condition in this form:

```
data-name operator value
```

where *operator* is a relational operator selected from the list in figure 6-36 and *value* is another data name or literal value. A breakpoint is taken when the expression is true.

command-list A series of COBTEST commands, separated by semicolons, that are automatically executed when the specified breakpoint occurs. The entire list is enclosed in parentheses.

Figure 6-35   COBTEST commands used for conditional breakpoints

On the WHEN command, you must specify a one- to four-character identifier. You use this identifier later to remove the breakpoint. As a result, the identifier must be unique during a debugging session.

After the identifier, you specify either a single data name or an expression. If you specify a data name, COBTEST evaluates that field each time it executes a program statement. Whenever the field's value changes, COBTEST interrupts your program. For example, suppose you enter this WHEN command:

```
WHEN CUST CM-CUSTOMER-KEY
```

Operator	Meaning
EQ =	Equal to
GT >	Greater than
LT <	Less than
NE ¬ =	Not equal to
GE >=	Greater than or equal to
LE <=	Less than or equal to

Figure 6-36 Relational operators for conditions

Then, COBTEST interrupts your program whenever the value of CM-CUSTOMER-KEY changes. CUST is the identifier associated with this conditional breakpoint.

You can test a field for a specific value by coding an expression that compares the field with another field or a literal. To do this, you use one of the relational operators shown in figure 6-36. For example, suppose you code this WHEN command:

```
WHEN HIT (CM-SALES-THIS-YTD = CM-SALES-LAST-YTD)
```

Then, COBTEST interrupts your program whenever the value of CM-SALES-THIS-YTD equals the value of CM-SALES-LAST-YTD. Notice that you must enclose the entire expression in parentheses. Even so, complex or compound conditions are not allowed. You can also specify a command list on the WHEN command just as you can on the NEXT and AT commands.

To remove one or more conditional breakpoints, you specify one or more identifiers from WHEN commands in an OFFWN command. For example, if you enter the command

```
OFFWN CUST
```

The LISTBRKS command

```
LISTBRKS [PRINT]
```

Explanation

PRINT   Direct the output to a print file instead of to the terminal.

Figure 6-37   The LISTBRKS command

COBTEST removes the CUST conditional breakpoint. To specify
more than one conditional breakpoint, you enclose the list in
parentheses, like this:

```
OFFWN (CUST,HIT)
```

Here, COBTEST removes two conditional breakpoints. And, if you
enter the OFFWN command without any identifiers, COBTEST
removes all the conditional breakpoints you've set.

How to display active breakpoints   The LISTBRKS command
displays all your active breakpoints set with AT, NEXT, and WHEN
commands. In addition, the LISTBRKS command tells you if a
program trace or frequency tallying is in effect. I'll show you how
to trace a program later in this topic, but I won't present frequency
tallying.

As you can see in figure 6-37, the only operand of the
LISTBRKS command is PRINT. If you specify PRINT during a
debugging session, COBTEST writes the list of active breakpoints
to a print file (SYSDBOUT) instead of to the terminal.

How to trace program flow

Figure 6-38 presents the format of the TRACE command. You use
the TRACE command to initiate or terminate a program trace. A
program trace helps you track your program's execution by
displaying information about the program as it executes. If you
specify PRINT on the TRACE command, COBTEST routes the

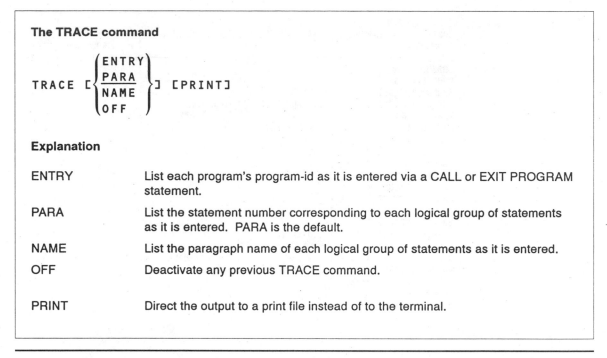

The TRACE command

```
TRACE [ { ENTRY
          PARA
          NAME
          OFF  } ] [PRINT]
```

Explanation

ENTRY   List each program's program-id as it is entered via a CALL or EXIT PROGRAM statement.

PARA   List the statement number corresponding to each logical group of statements as it is entered. PARA is the default.

NAME   List the paragraph name of each logical group of statements as it is entered.

OFF   Deactivate any previous TRACE command.

PRINT   Direct the output to a print file instead of to the terminal.

Figure 6-38   The TRACE command

output to the print file associated with SYSDBOUT instead of displaying it on your terminal.

The ENTRY operand starts a trace of programs and subprograms. Each time a program transfers control to another program via a CALL statement, COBTEST lists the new program's name (taken from the PROGRAM-ID paragraph). When control returns to the calling program, COBTEST lists the calling program's name. This type of trace helps you check that your subprograms are being invoked in the correct sequence.

The PARA and NAME operands both trace the execution of the logical groups of statements in your program. By a logical group of statements, I mean a paragraph or any sequence of statements that can cause a change in the program logic. For example, an IF-THEN-ELSE statement and an EVALUATE statement are both considered logical groups.

If you say PARA, COBTEST lists the statement number of the first statement in a logical group of statements whenever that group is about to be executed. If you say NAME, COBTEST lists the name of the paragraph containing the logical group in addition to

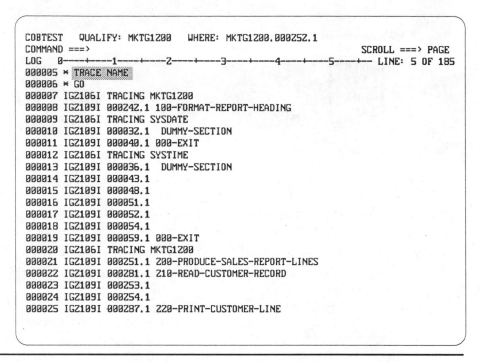

Figure 6-39   Sample TRACE output

the statement number. Since the output created by NAME is much easier to follow than that created by PARA, I recommend you use NAME. Since PARA is the default, you'll normally enter the TRACE command like this:

TRACE NAME

To stop a program trace, enter the TRACE command with the OFF operand, like this:

TRACE OFF

Figure 6-39 shows output typical of that generated by the TRACE command. (In this figure, I closed the source area so you can see more of the trace output.) As you can see, the list of paragraph names makes it easy to follow the execution of the program. Notice in this example that the statements in the subprograms SYSDATE and SYSTIME are traced as well as the statements in the main program.

HOW TO MANAGE YOUR PROGRAM'S DATA

Besides monitoring your program's statements as they execute, COBTEST lets you manage your program's data. You use the LIST command to display the contents of one or more data fields. You use the SET command to change the contents of data fields. And because COBOL data names can be cumbersome to type repeatedly, you use the EQUATE and DROP commands to substitute a short name for a longer one.

How to list data fields

Figure 6-40 shows the format of the LIST command, which you use to list the contents of one or more data fields. To do that, you specify one or more identifiers on the LIST command. Each identifier can be an FD name, a data name, an index name, or one of several COBOL special registers.

You specify the identifiers much as you specify statement numbers in an AT command. You can specify a single identifier, like this:

```
LIST CM-CUSTOMER-KEY
```

Here, COBTEST lists the value of the field named CM-CUSTOMER-KEY. Or, you can specify several identifiers separated by commas and enclosed in parentheses, like this:

```
LIST (CM-CUSTOMER-KEY,CM-SALES-THIS-YTD,CM-SALES-LAST-YTD)
```

Here, COBTEST lists the contents of three fields. Finally, you can specify a range of identifiers, like this:

```
LIST CM-CUSTOMER-KEY:CM-SALES-LAST-YTD
```

Here, COBTEST lists the value of each data field coded in the record description between and including CM-CUSTOMER-KEY and CM-SALES-LAST-YTD.

If you specify ALL on a LIST command, COBTEST lists all your program's data. That includes all FD names, index names, data names, and pointer data items, but COBOL special registers are not included. You probably won't use the ALL operand often because it can result in a large quantity of output. It's usually better to specify the field or fields you want to list.

The LIST command

$$\text{LIST} \begin{Bmatrix} \text{identifier-list} \\ \text{literal} \\ \text{ALL} \end{Bmatrix} \text{[GROUP] [} \begin{Bmatrix} \underline{\text{DISPLAY}} \\ \text{HEX} \\ \text{BOTH} \end{Bmatrix} \text{] [PRINT]}$$

Explanation

identifier-list	One or more identifiers specified as: (1) a single data name; (2) several data names separated by commas and enclosed in parentheses; or (3) a range of data names separated by a colon. An identifier can be a COBOL FD name, a data name, an index name, or one of several special registers.
literal	Any literal value enclosed in quotes.
ALL	List all of the program's FD names, data names, index names, and pointer data items.
GROUP	List each identifier at the highest level possible.
DISPLAY	List the data in EBCDIC format.
HEX	List the data in hexadecimal format.
BOTH	List the data in both EBCDIC and hexadecimal format.
PRINT	Direct the output to a print file instead of to the terminal.

Figure 6-40   The LIST command

The remaining operands determine how COBTEST displays the fields specified in the LIST command. If you code GROUP, COBTEST displays the fields as elementary items whether they are part of a group item or not. If you omit GROUP, COBTEST displays the fields with their *normalized level numbers* (numbered sequentially from 01 so that if you used 01 and 05 levels in your program, they'd become 01 and 02 levels in the display). The DISPLAY, HEX, and BOTH operands determine whether COBTEST displays the data in EBCDIC format, hex format, or both formats. DISPLAY is the default. If you code the PRINT operand, COBTEST writes the data to a print file instead of displaying it on the terminal.

You can also code the LIST command without any operands. But if you do, you must place the cursor under a variable name in

Type code	Meaning
CMP3	Numeric packed decimal
COMP	Numeric binary
DISP	Alphabetic, alphanumeric, alphanumeric-edited, unsigned numeric, numeric-edited
DSL	Numeric (overpunch sign leading)
DSLS	Numeric (separate sign leading)
DSP1	Double-byte character
DSPF	External floating point
DSTS	Numeric (separate sign trailing)

Figure 6-41 LIST type codes

the source display before you press the Enter key. Then, COBTEST displays the contents of that variable. You can simplify this function even further by assigning a PF key to the LIST function.

Each item COBTEST displays as a result of a LIST command is labeled by its statement number, normalized level number, name, and type code. The type code says how the field is defined in the COBOL program: whether it's alphanumeric, packed decimal, or some other data type. Figure 6-41 shows the type codes along with their meanings.

COBTEST formats the LIST output according to how you define the field in the COBOL program. It displays alphabetic and alphanumeric items in standard character format. It displays numeric items, whether they're zoned decimal or packed decimal, as decimal values. If you specify a group item, COBTEST displays the elementary items that make up the group on separate lines. If a field is subscripted, COBTEST displays each occurrence on a separate line, preceded by its subscript value. If you specify an index name, COBTEST displays the type code and occurrence number corresponding to the index name's value. And if you specify an FD or SD name, COBTEST displays the statement number, type code, information obtained from the file's control blocks, and a list of the records associated with the FD or SD.

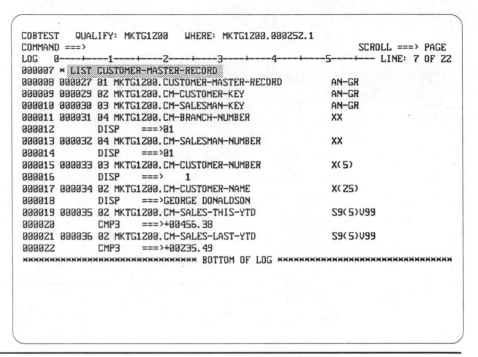

```
COBTEST   QUALIFY: MKTG1200   WHERE: MKTG1200.000252.1
COMMAND ===>                                                          SCROLL ===> PAGE
LOG  0----+----1----+----2----+----3----+----4----+----5----+---- LINE: 7 OF 22
000007 × LIST CUSTOMER-MASTER-RECORD
000008 000027 01 MKTG1200.CUSTOMER-MASTER-RECORD         AN-GR
000009 000029 02 MKTG1200.CM-CUSTOMER-KEY                AN-GR
000010 000030 03 MKTG1200.CM-SALESMAN-KEY                AN-GR
000011 000031 04 MKTG1200.CM-BRANCH-NUMBER               XX
000012        DISP   ===>01
000013 000032 04 MKTG1200.CM-SALESMAN-NUMBER             XX
000014        DISP   ===>01
000015 000033 03 MKTG1200.CM-CUSTOMER-NUMBER             X(5)
000016        DISP   ===>    1
000017 000034 02 MKTG1200.CM-CUSTOMER-NAME               X(25)
000018        DISP   ===>GEORGE DONALDSON
000019 000035 02 MKTG1200.CM-SALES-THIS-YTD              S9(5)V99
000020        CMP3   ===>+00456.38
000021 000036 02 MKTG1200.CM-SALES-LAST-YTD              S9(5)V99
000022        CMP3   ===>+00235.49
×××××××××××××××××××××××××××××× BOTTOM OF LOG ×××××××××××××××××××××××××××××××××
```

Figure 6-42   Sample LIST output

Figure 6-42 shows output typical of the LIST command. (I closed the source area in this example so you can see all the LIST output.) Here, I entered this command:

    LIST CUSTOMER-MASTER-RECORD

Since CUSTOMER-MASTER-RECORD is a group item, COBTEST displays its subordinate fields individually. The level numbers are normalized (my program contains 05, 10, and 15 levels, not 02, 03, and 04 levels), and the content of each field is formatted according to the field's picture.

How to change a data field

Figure 6-43 shows the format of the SET command, which you use to change the contents of a data field. The operation of the SET command is simple: the contents of identifier-1 are replaced by

---

The SET command

$$SET\ identifier-1\ =\ \begin{Bmatrix} identifier-2 \\ literal \end{Bmatrix}$$

Explanation

identifier-1   The data name, index name, or special register whose value is to be changed.

identifier-2   The data name, index name, or special register whose value is moved to identi-fier-1.

literal   A literal value that's moved to identifier-1.

Figure 6-43   The SET command

the contents of identifier-2 or the literal. For example, consider this SET command:

```
SET SALESMAN-TOTAL-THIS-YTD = 0
```

This command causes COBTEST to change the value of SALESMAN-TOTAL-THIS-YTD to zero.

If the lengths or types of the sending and receiving fields differ, the SET command follows the rules for a standard COBOL MOVE statement. Thus, COBTEST truncates or pads with spaces as necessary, and converts data from one form to another, just as when you code a MOVE statement in a COBOL program. And, of course, certain combinations of sending and receiving fields aren't valid. For example, you can't move an alphanumeric value to a numeric packed-decimal field.

Because the rules for certain types of moves are obscure, it's a good idea to check the results of your SET command by following it with a LIST command. That way, you'll know if your SET command worked as you intended.

How to shorten data names

I strongly recommend that you use data names that are mean-ingful in your COBOL programs. For example, a data name like

---

The EQUATE command

```
EQUATE symbol [program-name.]identifier
```

The DROP command

```
DROP [symbol]
```

The LISTEQ command

```
LISTEQ [PRINT]
```

Explanation

symbol	A character string that follows the rules for forming a COBOL data name. Usually shorter than the actual data name it will stand for. For a DROP command, you can specify more than one symbol by separating them with commas and enclosing the entire list in parentheses. If no symbols are specified in a DROP command, all symbols are deleted.
program-name	The name of a COBOL program currently resident in storage. The default is the program currently executing or referenced by a QUALIFY command.
identifier	The data name, file name, index name, or special register that the specified symbol represents.
PRINT	Direct the output to a print file instead of to the terminal.

Figure 6-44   The EQUATE, DROP, and LISTEQ commands

TOTAL-SALES-THIS-YTD is much more meaningful than X or TSLS. Since one of the primary goals of program development is to create programs that are easy to read and maintain, I can't stress this point too much.

Still, longer data names can be an irritation during a debugging session. That's why COBTEST provides three commands that make it easy for you to substitute a shorter name for a longer one. These three commands, EQUATE, DROP, and LISTEQ, are shown in figure 6-44.

The EQUATE command assigns a *symbol* to a data name, file name, index name, or special register. For example, consider this EQUATE command:

```
EQUATE CUSTKEY CM-CUSTOMER-KEY
```

Once you've entered this command, you can use the symbol CUSTKEY instead of the data name CM-CUSTOMER-KEY throughout your debugging session.

The DROP command removes a previously defined symbol. So if you enter:

```
DROP CUSTKEY
```

you can no longer use CUSTKEY to refer to CM-CUSTOMER-KEY. You can specify several symbols in a single DROP command, like this:

```
DROP (CUSTKEY,NAME,YTDSALES)
```

Here, COBTEST deletes three symbols. If you enter DROP with no symbols, COBTEST deletes all your symbols.

The LISTEQ command lists all symbols you've assigned using the EQUATE command during the current debugging session. To write this list to an output file instead of to the terminal, specify the PRINT operand. Then, COBTEST writes the output to the file associated with SYSDBOUT.

HOW TO USE THE IF COMMAND IN A COMMAND LIST

Although there are many possible uses for coding a command list in an AT or NEXT breakpoint, the most common is to list the contents of one or more data fields and then resume program execution. I showed you how to do that when I presented the NEXT and AT commands. In some cases, however, you'll want to resume program execution only under certain circumstances. The IF command, whose format is shown in figure 6-45, lets you do just that. Although you can enter an IF command by itself, it's normally used in a command list.

On an IF command, you specify an expression that COBTEST tests when it executes the command. The format of the expression is the same as for a WHEN command, so you can review that

The IF command

$$\text{IF (expression)} \begin{Bmatrix} \text{(command-list)} \\ \text{HALT} \\ \text{GO} \end{Bmatrix}$$

Explanation

expression   A relational condition in the form

                   `data-item operator value`

                   where *operator* is a relational operator selected from the list in figure 6-36 and
                   value is another data item or literal value.

command-list   A series of COBTEST commands separated by semicolons that are automati-
                   cally executed when the specified condition occurs.

HALT   Return control to the terminal.

GO   Resume program execution.

Figure 6-45   The IF command

command if you need to. After the expression, you specify either
HALT, GO, or a command list to tell COBTEST what to do if the
expression is true. If you say GO, COBTEST resumes program
execution. If you say HALT, COBTEST returns control to your
terminal. If you code a command list, COBTEST executes the
commands in the list. If the expression specified by the IF
command is false, COBTEST executes the command in the list that
follows the IF command. If there are no more commands in the
list, COBTEST returns control to the terminal.

To illustrate, consider this AT command:

`AT 252 (IF (LASTYTD LT THISYTD) HALT;GO)`

Here, COBTEST executes the IF command each time the breakpoint at line 252 is taken, and compares the symbol LASTYTD with
THISYTD. If the expression is true, that is, if LASTYTD is less than
THISYTD, COBTEST halts program execution and returns control
to the terminal. Otherwise, COBTEST executes the next command
in the list. In this case, the next command is GO, so program execution continues.

Suppose you enter this AT command:

```
AT 252 (IF (LASTYTD GE THISYTD) GO)
```

Here, COBTEST continues program execution if LASTYTD is greater than or equal to THISYTD. Otherwise, COBTEST returns control to the terminal, since there are no more commands in the list for it to execute. If you compare this command list with the previous one, you'll see that they both have the same effect: the program continues executing until LASTYTD is less than THISYTD.

As you can imagine, you can use IF commands within command lists to code quite complicated commands. You can even nest IF commands by coding them within the command list of another IF command. However, there shouldn't be too many occasions when you need to code anything much more complicated than what I've presented here.

HOW TO DEBUG
A SUBPROGRAM AND ITS CALLING PROGRAM

Throughout most of this topic, I've assumed you're debugging a main program. But COBTEST provides features that make it easy to debug subprograms and their calling programs as well. You already know how to use the ENTRY operand of the TRACE command to trace subprogram execution. In addition, you need to know how to qualify the operands of your COBTEST commands so they refer to your subprogram.

How to qualify operands of COBTEST commands

As your program executes and interrupts occur, the statement numbers COBTEST displays reflect the program or subprogram that is currently executing. For example, if COBTEST displays the statement number

```
SYSDATE.000032.1
```

you know that the subprogram named SYSDATE is executing.

To debug a program that's not currently executing, you have to specify the program name on the COBTEST commands. For example, suppose you need to debug the SYSDATE subprogram and that line 242 in MKTG1200 is the CALL statement that invokes SYSDATE. Assuming that MKTG1200 is currently executing, you first set a breakpoint at line 242 like this:

```
AT 242
```

Then, COBTEST interrupts your program just before line 242 executes. Now, you want to set a range of breakpoints in SYSDATE so you can single-step through the subprogram from lines 32 to 36. If you enter the command

```
AT 32:36
```

COBTEST sets the breakpoints for lines 32 through 36 of MKTG1200, since that's the program currently executing. So you have to enter the AT command like this:

```
AT SYSDATE.32:SYSDATE:36
```

Then, the breakpoints are established for lines 32 through 36 of SYSDATE.

You can also refer to data names in this fashion. For example, if you enter the command

```
LIST TODAYS-DATE
```

COBTEST lists the value of TODAYS-DATE in the current program. But if you enter

```
LIST SYSDATE.TODAYS-DATE
```

COBTEST lists the value of TODAYS-DATE in the subprogram named SYSDATE.

HOW TO TERMINATE COBTEST

To terminate COBTEST, issue a QUIT command like this:

```
QUIT
```

Then, control returns to ISPF.

You can also use the DUMP command to terminate COBTEST. Besides terminating COBTEST, it produces a dump of your program's storage areas (not including register information). The output goes to the data set associated with SYSABOUT.

DISCUSSION

In this topic, I've presented the COBTEST commands you'll use most often in your interactive debugging sessions. However, there are many more functions provided by COBTEST that you may want to know about. If you want to learn more about VS COBOL II debug, I recommend our book *VS COBOL II: A Guide for Programmers and Managers*.

Terms

qualify field
command area
log area
source area
prefix area
suffix area
program-name
breakpoint
trace
program-id
line-number
verb-number
NEXT breakpoint
STEP breakpoint
unconditional breakpoint
conditional breakpoint
command list
normalized level number
symbol

Objectives

1. Invoke COBTEST to debug a COBOL program on your system using interactive full-screen mode.

2. Identify each of the COBTEST command entry areas and explain how you use them.

3. Use COBTEST full-screen commands to set screen parameters and display source listings.

4. Use the following COBTEST features in your debugging sessions:

    a. NEXT breakpoint
    b. STEP breakpoint
    c. unconditional breakpoint
    d. conditional breakpoint
    e. program trace

5. Use COBTEST commands to examine and change the contents of data fields during your debugging sessions.

Chapter 7

How to process background jobs

As you know, MVS provides two basic types of processing: foreground and background. Foreground processing lets you interact directly with the computer via a terminal. In contrast, background processing does not interact with a terminal. So you can't control background processing using the ISPF commands this book teaches. Instead, you control background processing using Job Control Language statements, or JCL.

Foreground processing under TSO provides many advantages over background processing, but background processing is often more appropriate for many common tasks. For example, although you can compile and link-edit programs using foreground processing, it ties up your terminal so you can't do other work until the compile and link-edit finishes. Using background processing, you can use your terminal to perform other foreground tasks while the compile and link-edit executes in background mode.

The two topics in this chapter present ISPF facilities for managing background jobs. In topic 1, you'll learn how to use standard ISPF facilities to submit background jobs, monitor their status, and display their output. In topic 2, you'll learn how to use an optional program called the *System Display and Search Facility*, or *SDSF*. SDSF provides more advanced features to control your background jobs, so you'll want to use it if it's available at your installation.

Topic 1   How to use standard ISPF facilities to process background jobs

This topic describes the standard facilities that are available with ISPF for processing background jobs. I'll begin by describing the life cycle of a typical background job under MVS. Then, I'll show you the different ways you can submit a background job. Finally, I'll show you how to use the outlist utility to monitor your jobs and display their output.

THE LIFE CYCLE OF A JOB

Figure 7-1 describes the life cycle of a typical background job under MVS. First, a system operator or a TSO user submits the job for execution. Once a job is submitted, the job entry subsystem (JES2 or JES3) places it in a job queue, where it waits until an MVS component called an *initiator* is available to execute it. How long it waits in the job queue depends on a number of factors, including its storage and I/O device requirements and the job class assigned to it when it's submitted.

Every job you submit for execution under MVS must have a *job name*. You specify this name, which is one to eight characters in length, in the JCL for the job. When you refer to a job you've submitted, you usually use its job name. However, MVS doesn't require you to use unique job names. As a result, it's perfectly acceptable to submit two jobs with the same job name. MVS assigns a unique *job-id* to each job as it's submitted. So if you submit more than one job with the same job name, you must use the job-id rather than the job name to identify each job.

When an initiator becomes available for your job, JES2/JES3 assigns the job for execution. As your job executes, MVS generates informational messages that are collected in the job output and stored in a SYSOUT queue. In addition, programs executed by the job's steps can generate output that's written to a SYSOUT queue.

1. The job is submitted for execution by a system operator or a TSO user.

2. The job waits in a job queue.

3. The job is selected for execution by JES.

4. The job executes.

5. The job output is collected and held in a SYSOUT queue.

6. The job output is routed to its final destination and removed from the SYSOUT queue.

Figure 7-1   The life cycle of a background job

Data in a SYSOUT queue is held there until it's printed at a local or remote printer, copied to a data set, or deleted.

Each data set written to a SYSOUT queue is assigned a one–character *SYSOUT class* that determines how MVS prints the output. Each SYSOUT class is normally associated with a printer or a group of printers. Typically, SYSOUT class A is used for the installation's main printer or printers. Other SYSOUT classes may be assigned to specific printers or other devices.

If a SYSOUT class isn't associated with a printer or other device, it's called a *reserved class.* MVS holds any output written to a reserved class in the SYSOUT queue until an operator (1) directs it to a specific printer, (2) directs it to another SYSOUT class, or (3) deletes it. At my installation, class X is defined as a reserved class.

When you submit a background job from TSO, you usually want to direct the output to a reserved class. Then, you can examine the output at your terminal and determine if you should print it or delete it.

As a TSO user, you need to know how to do three things before you can effectively manage background jobs. First, you need to know how to submit a job for background processing. Second, you need to know how to monitor the status of a job you've submitted to see if it's waiting for execution, executing, or waiting for its output to print. Third, you need to know how to retrieve the output for a job that's completed.

```
------------------------- BATCH SELECTION PANEL -------------------------
OPTION  ===>

    1 - Assembler H               5 - PL/I optimizing compiler
    1A - Assembler XF             6 - VS PASCAL compiler
    2 - VS COBOL II compiler      7 - Linkage editor
    2A - OS/VS COBOL compiler     10 - VS COBOL II interactive debug
    3 - VS FORTRAN compiler       12 - Member parts list
    4 - PL/I checkout compiler


SOURCE DATA ONLINE ===> YES     (YES or NO)
SOURCE DATA PACKED ===> NO       (YES or NO)


JOB STATEMENT INFORMATION:   (Verify before proceeding)

   ===> //DLOWEA    JOB (9999),'DOUG LOWE',CLASS=R,MSGCLASS=R
   ===> //*
   ===> //*
   ===> //*
```

Figure 7-2   The batch selection panel

HOW TO SUBMIT A BACKGROUND JOB

ISPF provides three basic methods for submitting jobs for background processing. The first is the batch option, option 5 on the
primary option menu. This option is designed specifically for
submitting jobs for language processing. The batch option automatically generates the JCL necessary to process your job, so you don't
have to create any JCL yourself. The second method is issuing a
SUBMIT command from the ISPF editor. And the third method is
issuing a SUBMIT command from the data set list utility, option
3.4. When you use the SUBMIT command in either of these cases,
you must create the job's JCL statements yourself.

How to use the batch option to submit a job

When you select the batch option from the primary option menu,
ISPF displays a selection panel like the one shown in figure 7-2.

This panel is similar to the foreground processing panel I described in chapter 6. The main difference is that the batch option generates JCL statements that are submitted for background processing, while the foreground option invokes the language processors for immediate processing in foreground mode. In addition, you must supply job statement information on the batch selection panel. I'll explain how you code this information in a moment.

On the batch selection panel, you can select one of eight compilers (FORTRAN, PASCAL, and two versions each of assembler, COBOL, and PL/I), the linkage editor, and the VS COBOL II interactive debugger. These options all work the same in background mode as they do in foreground mode, so I won't present them here.

You can also select the member parts list function on this panel. The only difference between this option in foreground and background mode is that you can't browse a parts list created in background mode.

When you select one of the batch options, ISPF displays a second panel. On it, you enter data set information, compiler options, and so on. Once you've completed this panel, ISPF generates the JCL necessary to process the function you selected. Then, it returns to the batch menu, where you can select another batch option. ISPF adds the JCL for the second and subsequent batch options you select to the end of the JCL already generated. As a result, you can create a job with more than one step by selecting more than one batch option. The job isn't submitted for processing until you return to the primary option menu by pressing the End key, PF3/15.

How to supply job information   To submit a job for background processing using the batch option, you must supply information ISPF uses to create a JOB statement. On the batch selection panel, ISPF provides four lines for this purpose. You can change the information in these lines to reflect your own JOB statement requirements.

ISPF generates a default job name for the JOB statement. This name consists of your user-id followed by a single character. Initially, this character is the letter A. Thus, for my user-id, the initial job name is DLOWEA. Each time you submit a job, ISPF increments this character. So, the second job I submit has DLOWEB for its job name, followed by DLOWEC, and so on. Once the job name reaches DLOWEX, it cycles back to DLOWEA. If you want to, you can change the job name to any name within the limits of your installation.

Figure 7-3 shows four examples of JOB statement information. In example 1, I coded the minimum JOB statement information: an account number (9999) and a programmer name.

Example 2 is more complex. Here, I supplied some additional JOB statement parameters. I coded the CLASS parameter so my job executes in class R. And I coded the MSGCLASS parameter to tell MVS where to route job output.

Example 3 shows how to specify a JOBLIB for your JOB. Here, I coded a JOBLIB DD statement that identifies DLOWE.PROGLIB as the JOBLIB following the JOB statement. For background jobs created by the batch option, you won't normally specify a JOBLIB. That's because the assembler, compilers, and linkage editor are usually stored in the system program library (SYS1.LINKLIB).

Example 4 shows how you can specify JES2 or JES3 control statements along with the JOB statement. Here, I coded the /*PRIORITY statement to assign job dispatching priority 4 to my job. And I coded the /*ROUTE statement to route all the printed output generated by the job to a remote printer named RMT193.

My purpose here is not to teach you JCL. Instead, I just want to show how you can use the JOB statement field to supply various JCL parameters. If you don't understand any of the parameters or control statements, don't worry about it. Just remember that you can code more than a simple JOB statement in the JOB statement field.

A sample compile-and-link job   To illustrate how you submit a background job with the batch option, consider figure 7-4. Here, I generate a job to compile and link-edit a VS COBOL II program. In part 1, I select option 2, the VS COBOL II compiler. Then, ISPF displays the batch VS COBOL II compile panel, shown in part 2. (Note that the panel is similar to the entry panel for a foreground VS COBOL II compile as described in chapter 6.) Here, I supply the library and member names for the program I want to compile. In this case, the library is DLOWE.TEST.COBOL and the member is MKTG1200. In addition, I specify a list output id (MKTG1200) and appropriate compiler options.

All the batch options require that you enter either a LIST ID or a SYSOUT CLASS to determine how MVS handles printed output. If you specify a SYSOUT CLASS, the output is routed to a JES2/JES3

```
Example 1

JOB STATEMENT INFORMATION:  (Verify before proceeding)
  ===> //DLOWEA   JOB (9999),'DOUG LOWE'
  ===> //*
  ===> //*
  ===> //*


Example 2

JOB STATEMENT INFORMATION:  (Verify before proceeding)
  ===> //DLOWEA   JOB (9999),'DOUG LOWE',
  ===> //            CLASS=R,
  ===> //            MSGCLASS=R
  ===> //*


Example 3

JOB STATEMENT INFORMATION:  (Verify before proceeding)
  ===> //DLOWEE   JOB (9999),'DOUG LOWE'
  ===> //JOBLIB   DD   DSN=DLOWE.PROGLIB,DISP=SHR
  ===> //*
  ===> //*


Example 4

JOB STATEMENT INFORMATION:  (Verify before proceeding)
  ===> /*PRIORITY 4
  ===> //DLOWEE   JOB (9999),'DOUG LOWE'
  ===> /*ROUTE PRINT RMT193
  ===> //*
```

Figure 7-3   Examples of JOB statement information

output queue. If you specify a LIST ID, MVS adds the output to a list data set whose name follows this format:

```
project-id.list-id.LIST
```

Thus, if I specify MKTG1200 as the LIST ID, MVS stores the compiler output in a data set named DLOWE.MKTG1200.LIST. In this case, the output is not routed to a JES2/JES3 output queue.

Whether you use a LIST ID or a SYSOUT CLASS depends on factors unique to your installation. In either case, you can examine the output at your terminal or route it to a local or remote printer. If you specify a LIST ID, you use the browse option to examine the output and you use the hardcopy utility to print it. If you specify a SYSOUT CLASS, you use the outlist utility or the System Display and Search Facility to perform these functions. (I'll describe the outlist utility later in this chapter, and I'll describe the System Display and Search Facility in the next topic.)

Once you complete the VS COBOL II entry panel and press the Enter key, ISPF returns to the batch selection panel, as shown in part 3 of figure 7-4. There are a couple points to note here. First, notice the message at the upper right-hand corner of the screen: JOB STEP GENERATED. That means ISPF generated the JCL necessary to process the COBOL compiler. ISPF adds any batch options selected now to the end of the JCL stream, creating additional job steps.

Second, notice the three options explained in the center of the screen. Here, you can enter another option to generate more JCL, enter the CANCEL command to return to the primary option menu without submitting the JCL generated, or press the End key, PF3/15, to submit the JCL generated. In part 3 of figure 7-4, I select option 7 to generate the JCL to link-edit the program.

Part 4 of figure 7-4 shows the batch linkage edit panel. Like the compile panel, it's very similar to the entry panel for a foreground link-edit job. Here, I supply the data set information (MKTG1200 is the member name, DLOWE.TEST.OBJ is the library name), a LIST ID (MKTG1200), appropriate link-edit options, and the name of the library that contains the subprogram load modules I want to link-edit with the main program (DLOWE.SUBPROG.LOAD). After I complete this panel and press the Enter key, the display is just like part 3 of figure 7-4.

To submit the job for background processing, press the End key, PF3/15. Then, ISPF issues a TSO SUBMIT command to submit the job for processing in a background region. The SUBMIT command generates a message, shown in part 5 of figure 7-4, to verify that the job was submitted. Then, when you press the Enter key, ISPF returns to the primary option menu.

JCL generated by the batch option   Figure 7-5 shows the actual job stream that was generated by the batch options selected in

Part 1:

Specify the processor
option for the compile

```
------------------------- BATCH SELECTION PANEL -------------------------
OPTION  ===> Z

    1  - Assembler H              5 - PL/I optimizing compiler
    1A - Assembler XF             6 - VS PASCAL compiler
    Z  - VS COBOL II compiler     7 - Linkage editor
    ZA - OS/VS COBOL compiler    10 - VS COBOL II interactive debug
    3  - VS FORTRAN compiler     12 - Member parts list
    4  - PL/I checkout compiler


SOURCE DATA ONLINE ===> YES     (YES or NO)
SOURCE DATA PACKED ===> NO      (YES or NO)



JOB STATEMENT INFORMATION:  (Verify before proceeding)

    ===> //DLOWEA    JOB (9999),'DOUG LOWE',CLASS=R,MSGCLASS=R
    ===> //*
    ===> //*
    ===> //*
```

Part 2:

Enter the information
needed for the compile

```
------------------------- BATCH VS COBOL II COMPILE -------------------------
COMMAND ===>

ISPF LIBRARY:
    PROJECT ===> DLOWE
    GROUP   ===> TEST      ===> COPY      ===>           ===>
    TYPE    ===> COBOL
    MEMBER  ===> MKTG1Z00              (Blank or pattern for member selection list)

OTHER PARTITIONED OR SEQUENTIAL DATA SET:
    DATA SET NAME  ===>

LIST ID      ===> MKTG1Z00            (Blank for hardcopy listing)
SYSOUT CLASS ===>                     (If hardcopy requested)

COMPILER OPTIONS:
   TERM  ===> NOTERM                  (TERM or NOTERM)
   OTHER ===> SOURCE,XREF,OFFSET,MAP

ADDITIONAL INPUT LIBRARIES:
        ===>
        ===>
```

Figure 7-4   Generating a background compile-and-link job

Part 3:

Specify the processor option for the link

```
-------------------------- BATCH SELECTION PANEL ---------- JOB STEP GENERATED
OPTION  ===> ?

   1 - Assembler H               5 - PL/I optimizing compiler
   1A - Assembler XF             6 - VS PASCAL compiler
   2 - VS COBOL II compiler      7 - Linkage editor
   2A - OS/VS COBOL compiler     10 - VS COBOL II interactive debug
   3 - VS FORTRAN compiler       12 - Member parts list
   4 - PL/I checkout compiler

INSTRUCTIONS:
    Enter option to continue generating JCL.
    Enter CANCEL command to exit without submitting job.
    Enter END command to submit job.

SOURCE DATA ONLINE ===> YES      (YES or NO)
SOURCE DATA PACKED ===> NO       (YES or NO)

JOB STATEMENT INFORMATION:
    //DLOWEA   JOB (9999),'DOUG LOWE',CLASS=R,MSGCLASS=R
    //*
    //*
    //*
```

Part 4:

Enter the information needed for the link

```
-------------------------- BATCH LINKAGE EDIT --------------------------------
COMMAND ===>

ISPF LIBRARY:
    PROJECT ===> DLOWE
    GROUP   ===> TEST     ===>          ===>          ===>
    TYPE    ===> OBJ
    MEMBER  ===> MKTG1200             (Blank or pattern for member selection list)

OTHER PARTITIONED DATA SET:
    DATA SET NAME  ===>

LIST ID       ===> MKTG1200          (Blank for hardcopy listing)
SYSOUT CLASS ===>                    (If hardcopy requested)

LINKAGE EDITOR OPTIONS:
    TERM  ===>                        (TERM or Blank)
    OTHER ===> LET.LIST.MAP

ADDITIONAL INPUT LIBRARIES:          (LOAD libraries only)
SYSLIB  ===> 'DLOWE.SUBPROG.LOAD'
SYSLIB  ===>

SYSLIN  ===>
```

Figure 7-4 Generating a background compile-and-link job (continued)

Part 5:

The job has been
submitted

```
---------------------------- BATCH SELECTION PANEL ---------- JOB STEP GENERATED
OPTION  ===>

     1  - Assembler H               5 - PL/I optimizing compiler
    1A  - Assembler XF              6 - VS PASCAL compiler
     2  - VS COBOL II compiler      7 - Linkage editor
    2A  - OS/VS COBOL compiler     10 - VS COBOL II interactive debug
     3  - VS FORTRAN compiler      12 - Member parts list
     4  - PL/I checkout compiler

INSTRUCTIONS:
    Enter option to continue generating JCL.
    Enter CANCEL command to exit without submitting job.
    Enter END command to submit job.

SOURCE DATA ONLINE ===> YES      (YES or NO)
SOURCE DATA PACKED ===> NO       (YES or NO)

JOB STATEMENT INFORMATION:
    //DLOWEA  JOB (9999),'DOUG LOWE',CLASS=R,MSGCLASS=R
IKJ56250I JOB DLOWEA(JOB06798) SUBMITTED
***
```

Figure 7-4   Generating a background compile-and-link job (continued)

figure 7-4. If you're not familiar with JCL, you can skip this section;
it's not crucial to your understanding of background processing.

Notice that ISPF generated two job steps for each batch option I
selected. The first step for the compile option (line 3) invokes a
program named ISRLEMX. This program searches the libraries
supplied in the batch selection panel for the specified member. If
it finds the member, ISRLEMX copies it to a temporary data set
named &&TEMP1. It also expands any included members and
unpacks any packed members. Then, the second step for the
compile (line 8) invokes the COBOL compiler using the &&TEMP1
data set as input. Notice the &&TEMP1 data set is deleted when
this step completes.

The first step for the link-edit option (line 23) invokes a
program named ISRSCAN. This program also copies the specified
member to a temporary data set named &&TEMP1. Then, the
second step for the link-edit (line 26) invokes the linkage editor,
which processes &&TEMP1 as input, then deletes it.

```
1 //DLOWEE    JOB (9999),'DOUG LOWE',CLASS=R,MSGCLASS=R
  *** $ACFJ219 ACF2 ACTIVE MVSDDC
3 //SCAN     EXEC PGM=ISRLEMX,COND=(12,LE),
  //    PARM=(COB,MKTG1200,B,N, ,4, ,OO,ENU,4,7',
  //       '1,/,SYSDA')
  ***
  *** INSERT A STEPLIB DD HERE IF ISRLEMX IS NOT IN YOUR SYSTEM LIBRARY
  ***
4 //ISRLCODE DD   DSN=DLOWE.TEST.COBOL,DISP=SHR
5 //         DD   DSN=DLOWE.COPY.COBOL,DISP=SHR
6 //ISRLEXPD DD   UNIT=SYSDA,DISP=(NEW,PASS),SPACE=(CYL,(2,2)),
  //              DSN=&&TEMP1
7 //ISRLMSG  DD   SYSOUT=(*)
8 //COBOL EXEC    PGM=IGYCRCTL,REGION=640K,COND=(12,LE),
  // PARM=NOTERM,
  // 'SOURCE,XREF,OFFSET,MAP')
9 //SYSPRINT DD   DSN=DLOWE.MKTG1200.LIST,UNIT=SYSDA,
  //              SPACE=(CYL,(2,2)),DISP=(MOD,CATLG),
  //              DCB=(RECFM=FBA,LRECL=133,BLKSIZE=3059)
10 //SYSIN    DD   DSN=&&TEMP1,DISP=(OLD,DELETE)
11 //SYSPUNCH DD   DUMMY
12 //SYSUT1   DD   UNIT=SYSDA,SPACE=(CYL,(2,2))
13 //SYSUT2   DD   UNIT=SYSDA,SPACE=(CYL,(2,2))
14 //SYSUT3   DD   UNIT=SYSDA,SPACE=(CYL,(2,2))
15 //SYSUT4   DD   UNIT=SYSDA,SPACE=(CYL,(2,2))
16 //SYSUT5   DD   UNIT=SYSDA,SPACE=(CYL,(2,2))
17 //SYSUT6   DD   UNIT=SYSDA,SPACE=(CYL,(2,2))
18 //SYSUT7   DD   UNIT=SYSDA,SPACE=(CYL,(2,2))
19 //SYSLIB   DD   DSN=SYS1.MACLIB,DISP=SHR
20 //         DD   DSN=DLOWE.TEST.COBOL,DISP=SHR
21 //         DD   DSN=DLOWE.COPY.COBOL,DISP=SHR
22 //SYSLIN   DD   DSN=DLOWE.TEST.OBJ(MKTG1200),DISP=OLD
23 //SCAN     EXEC PGM=ISRSCAN,PARM='MKTG1200',COND=(12,LE)
  ***
  *** INSERT A STEPLIB DD HERE IF ISRSCAN IS NOT IN YOUR SYSTEM LIBRARY
  ***
24 //IN       DD   DSN=DLOWE.TEST.OBJ,DISP=SHR
25 //OUT      DD   UNIT=SYSDA,DISP=(NEW,PASS),SPACE=(CYL,(2,2)),
  //              DSN=&&TEMP1
26 //LINK     EXEC PGM=IEWL,REGION=512K,COND=(12,LE),
  // PARM=(,
  //       'LET,LIST,MAP')
27 //SYSPRINT DD   DSN=DLOWE.MKTG1200.LIST,UNIT=SYSDA,
  //              SPACE=(CYL,(2,2)),DISP=(MOD,CATLG),
  //              DCB=(RECFM=VBA,LRECL=121,BLKSIZE=3146)
28 //SYSLIN   DD   DSN=&&TEMP1,DISP=(OLD,DELETE)
29 //OBJECT   DD   DSN=DLOWE.TEST.OBJ,DISP=SHR
30 //SYSLIB   DD   DSN=DLOWE.TEST.LOAD,DISP=SHR
31 //         DD   DSN=DLOWE.SUBPROG.LOAD,DISP=SHR
32 //SYSLMOD  DD   DSN=DLOWE.TEST.LOAD(MKTG1200),
  //              DISP=SHR,DCB=(BLKSIZE=3072)
33 //SYSUT1   DD   UNIT=SYSDA,SPACE=(CYL,(2,2)),DISP=NEW
34 //SYSGO    DD   DSN=DLOWE.TEST.OBJ(MKTG1200),DISP=OLD
```

Figure 7-5   JCL generated for the compile-and-link job

How to submit a job using the SUBMIT command of edit

The batch option I just described is useful, but it has one major drawback: it lets you generate JCL only for the specific processing options it allows. If you want to invoke any other processing program, such as the CICS command-level translator, you can't do it using the batch option. Instead, you must create the JCL yourself.

The SUBMIT command of edit (option 2 from the primary option menu) makes it easy to create JCL streams and submit them for processing. First, you use the editing features you already know to create the JCL statements you need. Normally, you save this JCL as a member of a JCL library. (JCL libraries have CNTL as their type qualifier.) Then you enter SUBMIT as a primary command, and ISPF submits the JCL in the member you're editing for processing as a background job.

To illustrate, consider figure 7-6. Here, I'm editing a member named COB2UCG in a library named DLOWE.TEST.CNTL. This member contains the JCL statements necessary to compile and execute MKTG1200 in DLOWE.TEST.COBOL. In part 1 of figure 7-6, you can see that I entered a SUBMIT primary command. Part 2 shows how TSO responded with a one-line message saying it submitted the job. You must press the Enter key here to return to edit mode.

Frankly, I prefer the SUBMIT command of edit over the batch option. That's because once I've created the JCL to compile and link-edit a program, all I have to do is submit it. In contrast, if you use the batch option, you have to go through the COBOL and link-edit panels each time you want to submit the job.

How to submit a job from the data set list utility, option 3.4

In chapter 5, you learned that you can enter a variety of TSO commands to process individual members in a member selection list generated by the data set list utility, option 3.4. One of the most useful commands you can use here is SUBMIT, which submits a job for background processing. You can submit a background job simply by typing the word SUBMIT next to the name of the member that contains the JCL for the job you want to submit.

Part 1:

Enter the SUBMIT
command during the
edit of a JCL file

```
EDIT ---- DLOWE.TEST.CNTL(COB2UCG) - 01.00 ------------------- COLUMNS 001 072
COMMAND ===> SUBMIT                                          SCROLL ===> 0020
****** ****************************** TOP OF DATA ********************************
000100 //DLOWEA    JOB  (9999),'DOUG LOWE',CLASS=R,TIME=(1),MSGCLASS=R
000200 //          EXEC COB2UCG,PARM.COB2='APOST,OBJECT'
000210 //COB2.SYSPRINT DD SYSOUT=*
000220 //COB2.SYSIN   DD DSNAME=DLOWE.TEST.COBOL(MKTG1200),DISP=SHR
000230 //COB2.SYSLIB  DD DSNAME=DLOWE.COPY.COBOL,DISP=SHR
000240 //GO.SYSLMOD   DD DSNAME=DLOWE.TEST.LOAD(MKTG1200),DISP=SHR
000250 //GO.SYSPRINT  DD SYSOUT=*
000260 //GO.SYSOUT    DD SYSOUT=*
000270 //GO.CUSTMST   DD DSNAME=MMAV.T6825.CUSTOMER.MASTER,DISP=SHR
000280 //GO.SALESMN   DD DSNAME=MMAV.T6825.SALESMAN.MASTER,DISP=SHR
000290 //GO.SALESRPT  DD SYSOUT=*
****** *************************** BOTTOM OF DATA *******************************
```

Part 2:

The JCL you're editing
is submitted as a job

```
EDIT ---- DLOWE.TEST.CNTL(COB2UCG) - 01.00 ------------------- COLUMNS 001 072
COMMAND ===> SUBMIT                                          SCROLL ===> 0020
****** ****************************** TOP OF DATA ********************************
000100 //DLOWEA    JOB  (9999),'DOUG LOWE',CLASS=R,TIME=(1),MSGCLASS=R
000200 //          EXEC COB2UCG,PARM.COB2='APOST,OBJECT'
000210 //COB2.SYSPRINT DD SYSOUT=*
000220 //COB2.SYSIN   DD DSNAME=DLOWE.TEST.COBOL(MKTG1200),DISP=SHR
000230 //COB2.SYSLIB  DD DSNAME=DLOWE.COPY.COBOL,DISP=SHR
000240 //GO.SYSLMOD   DD DSNAME=DLOWE.TEST.LOAD(MKTG1200),DISP=SHR
000250 //GO.SYSPRINT  DD SYSOUT=*
000260 //GO.SYSOUT    DD SYSOUT=*
000270 //GO.CUSTMST   DD DSNAME=MMAV.T6825.CUSTOMER.MASTER,DISP=SHR
000280 //GO.SALESMN   DD DSNAME=MMAV.T6825.SALESMAN.MASTER,DISP=SHR
000290 //GO.SALESRPT  DD SYSOUT=*
****** *************************** BOTTOM OF DATA *******************************
IKJ56250J JOB DLOWEA(JOB06814) SUBMITTED
***
```

Figure 7-6   Using the SUBMIT command of edit

Figure 7-7 shows an example of submitting a job using this method. In part 1, I used the data set list utility to display a list of the members in the library DLOWE.TEST.CNTL. Then, I typed the word SUBMIT next to the member named COB2UCG. Part 2 shows the resulting one-line message TSO displayed to confirm that the job was submitted.

Other methods of submitting background jobs

Besides the batch option and the SUBMIT command issued from edit or the data set list utility, ISPF provides several additional methods of submitting background jobs. Throughout ISPF, you'll find options for routing printed output to a local printer or for submitting a job to print the output. These options generate their own JCL, though you must supply the job statement information. You've seen several examples so far in this book. For instance, in chapter 5, you saw how to use the hardcopy utility to submit background print jobs. And in chapter 2, you saw how to print the log and list files using a background job.

OPTION 3.8: THE OUTLIST UTILITY

Once you've submitted a job for background processing, you can use the outlist utility to monitor its progress or display its output. You invoke the outlist utility by selecting option 8 from the utilities menu. Then, ISPF displays the outlist utility panel, shown in figure 7-8.

OUTLIST provides five options. You invoke four of them using a one-letter option code, as follows:

L   List the names of active background jobs
D   Delete job output
P   Print job output
R   Requeue job output to a different output class

The fifth option is to display job output at your terminal. You select this option by leaving the OPTION field blank.

Part 1:

Enter the SUBMIT
command next to the
name of a member
that contains JCL

```
DSLIST -- DLOWE.TEST.CNTL ------------------------------- ROW 00001 OF 00011
COMMAND ===>                                                SCROLL ===> PAGE
             NAME    RENAME      UU.MM     CHANGED     SIZE  INIT  MOD   ID
             COBUC               01.06 90/03/08 12:36    6     5     2 MMA001
             COBUCG              01.02 90/02/20 18:59   10    11     4 MMA001
             COBUCL              01.03 90/04/10 20:24    8     7     3 MMA001
             COBUCLG             01.03 90/02/21 18:20   11    11     1 MMA001
   SUBMIT    COBZUCG             01.00 90/02/21 18:54   11    11     0 MMA001
             COMPLINK            01.05 90/04/10 18:12   37    37     4 MMA001
             IEFBR14             01.02 90/05/22 19:20    5     4     3 MMA001
             LDCSTMST            01.02 90/02/08 19:06    9     9     2 MMA001
             LDSLSMAN            01.02 90/02/08 18:10    9     9     2 MMA001
             MKTG1200            01.15 90/02/08 19:43   11    11    11 MMA001
             SUBPROG             01.00 90/02/07 14:06    5     5     0 MMA001
             **END**
```

Part 2:

The JCL in the
member is submitted
as a job

```
DSLIST -- DLOWE.TEST.CNTL ------------------------------- ROW 00001 OF 00011
COMMAND ===>                                                SCROLL ===> PAGE
             NAME    RENAME      UU.MM     CHANGED     SIZE  INIT  MOD   ID
             COBUC               01.06 90/03/08 12:36    6     5     2 MMA001
             COBUCG              01.02 90/02/20 18:59   10    11     4 MMA001
             COBUCL              01.03 90/04/10 20:24    8     7     3 MMA001
             COBUCLG             01.03 90/02/21 18:20   11    11     1 MMA001
   SUBMIT    COBZUCG             01.00 90/02/21 18:54   11    11     0 MMA001
             COMPLINK            01.05 90/04/10 18:12   37    37     4 MMA001
             IEFBR14             01.02 90/05/22 19:20    5     4     3 MMA001
             LDCSTMST            01.02 90/02/08 19:06    9     9     2 MMA001
             LDSLSMAN            01.02 90/02/08 18:10    9     9     2 MMA001
             MKTG1200            01.15 90/02/08 19:43   11    11    11 MMA001
             SUBPROG             01.00 90/02/07 14:06    5     5     0 MMA001
             **END**

IKJ56250J JOB DLOWEA(JOB06197) SUBMITTED
***
```

Figure 7-7   Using the SUBMIT command from the data set list utility

```
---------------------------- OUTLIST UTILITY ----------------------------
OPTION ===>

    L - List job names/id's via the TSO STATUS command
    D - Delete job output from SYSOUT hold queue
    P - Print job output and delete from SYSOUT hold queue
    R - Requeue job output to a new output class
    blank - Display job output

FOR JOB TO BE SELECTED:
   JOBNAME ===>
   CLASS   ===>
   JOBID   ===>

FOR JOB TO BE REQUEUED:
   NEW OUTPUT CLASS ===>

FOR JOB TO BE PRINTED:                    (A for ANSI    )
   PRINTER CARRIAGE CONTROL ===>          (M for machine )
                                          (Blank for none)
```

Figure 7-8   The OUTLIST utility panel

How to list job names

Option L issues a TSO STATUS command to display the status of
jobs you've submitted for background processing. Figure 7-9 shows
an example of listing job names. Here, I specify L in the option
field. When I press the Enter key, ISPF issues a STATUS command.
The STATUS command displays a line near the bottom of the
screen indicating that I submitted one job for background
processing, DLOWEA, and that the job finished processing and is
waiting in an output queue. If I had submitted more than one job,
additional lines would be displayed.

How to display or print job output

Once a background job has completed processing and is waiting in
an output queue, you can use the outlist utility to display or print
its output. On the outlist utility panel, specify the job name and, if

```
---------------------------  OUTLIST UTILITY  ---------------------------
OPTION  ===> L

   L - List job names/id's via the TSO STATUS command
   D - Delete job output from SYSOUT hold queue
   P - Print job output and delete from SYSOUT hold queue
   R - Requeue job output to a new output class
   blank - Display job output

FOR JOB TO BE SELECTED:
   JOBNAME ===>
   CLASS   ===>
   JOBID   ===>

FOR JOB TO BE REQUEUED:
   NEW OUTPUT CLASS ===>

FOR JOB TO BE PRINTED:                      (A for ANSI    )
   PRINTER CARRIAGE CONTROL ===>            (M for machine )
                                            (Blank for none)
IKJ56192J JOB DLOWEA(JOB06798) ON OUTPUT QUEUE
***
```

Figure 7-9   Listing job names

you've submitted more than one job with the same name, the job-id. (You can find the job-id by listing the job name. In figure 7-9, the job-id for the job named DLOWEA is JOB06798.) If you want, you can also specify a job class to further identify the job. I usually leave the CLASS field blank, though.

If you leave the OPTION field blank, ISPF retrieves the job output and displays it at your terminal. Figure 7-10 shows the first panel of a typical job display. Here, you can see the system messages indicating the completion status of each step in the job. You use standard browse commands to display the entire job output.

If you specify P as the option, ISPF displays the panel in figure 7-11. Here, you specify what to do with the job output. The four options are to print the data set and keep it (PK), print the data set and delete it (PD), keep the data set without printing it (K), and delete the data set without printing (D). If you select the print data set option, you can print output at a local printer (specify LOCAL in the PRINT MODE field and a local printer-id) or submit it as a

```
SDSF OUTPUT DISPLAY DLOWEA    JOB  4107 DSID     2 LINE        0 COLUMNS 02- 81
COMMAND INPUT ===>                                             SCROLL ===> DATA
********************************** TOP OF DATA ********************************
                     J E S 2   J O B   L O G  --  S Y S T E M   M V S B  --  N O D
--------- JOB 4107  IEF097I DLOWEA  - USER DLOWE   ASSIGNED
19.05.02 JOB 4107  $HASP373 DLOWEA   STARTED - INIT 64 - CLASS R - SYS MVSB
19.05.02 JOB 4107  IEF403I DLOWEA - STARTED - TIME=19.05.02
19.05.04 JOB 4107  -                                          --TIMINGS (MINS.)--
19.05.04 JOB 4107  -JOBNAME  STEPNAME PROCSTEP    RC   EXCP    CPU    SRB  CLOCK
19.05.04 JOB 4107  -DLOWEA   SCAN                 00     24    .00    .00    .0
19.05.11 JOB 4107  -DLOWEA   COBOL                12    166    .00    .00    .1
19.05.12 JOB 4107  -DLOWEA   SCAN              FLUSH      0    .00    .00    .0
19.05.12 JOB 4107  -DLOWEA   LINK              FLUSH      0    .00    .00    .0
19.05.12 JOB 4107  IEF404I DLOWEA - ENDED - TIME=19.05.12
19.05.12 JOB 4107  -DLOWEA   ENDED.   NAME-DOUG LOWE            TOTAL CPU TIME=
19.05.12 JOB 4107  $HASP395 DLOWEA   ENDED
------ JES2 JOB STATISTICS ------
   22 FEB 90 JOB EXECUTION DATE
         56 CARDS READ
        167 SYSOUT PRINT RECORDS
          0 SYSOUT PUNCH RECORDS
          9 SYSOUT SPOOL KBYTES
       0.16 MINUTES EXECUTION TIME
          1 //DLOWEA  JOB (9999),'DOUG LOWE',CLASS=R,MSGCLASS=R
```

Figure 7-10   Displaying job output

background job (specify BATCH in the PRINT MODE field, a
SYSOUT class, and the JOB statement information). In figure 7-11, I
printed the output at a local printer named IBMT2IP1, then
deleted it.

Another way to print held job output is to change its SYSOUT
class from a reserved class to a class assigned to an appropriate
printer. For example, suppose class X is defined as a reserved print
class in your installation, while class M is assigned to a printer in
your group or department. To direct output held in class X to your
printer, all you need to do is change its output class from X to M.

That's where the requeue option on the outlist utility panel
comes in. If you specify option R, a job name, and a new output
class, MVS assigns the held output for the specified job to the
output class you specify.

The exact procedures for printing job output vary from one
installation to the next. So you'll have to find out from your supervisor what the correct procedures are and when you should use
each one.

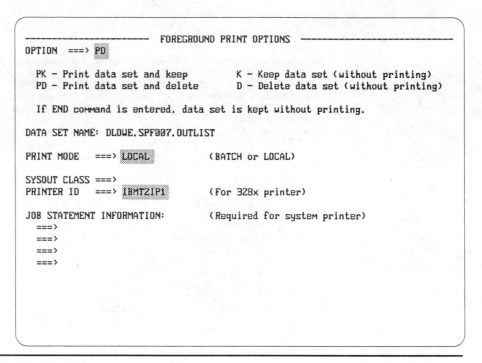

```
---------------------- FOREGROUND PRINT OPTIONS ---------------------------
OPTION  ===> PD

  PK - Print data set and keep        K - Keep data set (without printing)
  PD - Print data set and delete      D - Delete data set (without printing)

  If END command is entered, data set is kept without printing.

DATA SET NAME: DLOWE.SPF007.OUTLIST

PRINT MODE   ===> LOCAL            (BATCH or LOCAL)

SYSOUT CLASS ===>
PRINTER ID   ===> IBMTZIP1         (For 328x printer)

JOB STATEMENT INFORMATION:         (Required for system printer)
  ===>
  ===>
  ===>
  ===>
```

Figure 7-11   Printing job output

How to delete job output

Besides displaying job names or displaying, printing, or requeuing
job output, the outlist utility lets you delete job output. You've
already seen how you can do that from the foreground print
options menu. You can also delete job output by selecting option D
from the outlist utility panel and entering the name of the job
whose output you want to delete. Note that if you requeue job
output using option R, MVS automatically deletes the output after
it prints it. But if you display the output rather than print it, MVS
keeps it in the queue. So remember to delete your jobs after you
display them.

DISCUSSION

Whether you use the foreground or the batch facility to compile
and link-edit programs depends mostly on your personal prefer-

ence and your shop's standards. Response time is generally better when you use the foreground option. But when you use a background job, you can code your own JCL to invoke programs other than the standard language processors and linkage editor. And as an added bonus, you can use your terminal for other functions while your job is executing in a background region.

Although the features I've presented in this topic are enough to manage simple background job processing, they are crude. In particular, most of the outlist features are limited because they use line-oriented TSO commands to implement their functions. In contrast, SDSF provides much better control over background processing. If your installation has it, you should learn how to use it by reading the next topic.

Terms

initiator
job name
job-id
SYSOUT class
reserved class

Objectives

1. Use the ISPF background option to create and submit a background job that compiles and link-edits a program.

2. Use the SUBMIT command of edit to submit a background job.

3. Use the SUBMIT command from the data set list utility to submit a background job.

4. Use the outlist utility to (1) monitor job status and (2) display or print job output.

Topic 2

How to manage background jobs with SDSF

The *System Display and Search Facility*, commonly referred to as *SDSF*, is a utility program that allows you to monitor and, to some extent, control the operation of an MVS JES2 system. (It isn't available under JES3.) As an application programmer, you'll use it most often to monitor the background jobs you submit to JES2. So that's what you'll learn to do in this topic.

You should know that SDSF is a separately-licensed program. In other words, it's not a standard part of TSO or ISPF, so it may not be available at your installation. Although the outlist utility, which is a part of ISPF, provides some of the same functions as SDSF, SDSF is more convenient to use. So, if SDSF's available, you'll want to learn how to use it.

I'll begin this topic by introducing you to the basic SDSF operations. Then, I'll show you how to use the SDSF display panels that let you monitor your jobs. Finally, I'll present some advanced operations you can use within SDSF. When you finish this chapter, you'll know everything you need to know as a programmer to use SDSF efficiently.

BASIC SDSF OPERATIONS

SDSF is similar to most of the ISPF facilities you already know. As a result, you shouldn't have any trouble learning how to use it.

How to invoke SDSF

You can invoke SDSF from either TSO or ISPF. Starting SDSF from TSO is easy: just enter the command SDSF from the READY prompt. To use SDSF from ISPF, it must be included on one of the ISPF menus. Typically, it's included on the primary option menu.

On the primary option menu in figure 7-12, for example, it's option S. When you invoke SDSF by entering the appropriate option, it displays the SDSF primary option menu, as shown in figure 7-13.

The SDSF primary option menu

As you can see, the SDSF primary option menu is different than the ISPF primary option menu. Instead of entering a single number or letter to select an option, you must enter the command for that option. For example, to display the system log, you enter the LOG command.

The system programmer who installs SDSF can restrict access to some or all of the SDSF options that are available. So, the SDSF primary option menu at your installation may not contain all the options shown in figure 7-13. In any event, only a few of the options are useful for most purposes.

Incidentally, the SDSF command area also accepts MVS or JES2 operator commands. But in most installations, those commands are restricted to certain users. So I won't describe them in this book.

SDSF display panels

The SDSF primary option menu in figure 7-13 lets you select one of four display panels. Figure 7-14 shows an example of each of these displays. If you select option I, SDSF displays the contents of the JES2 *input queue*. This display lists jobs that are waiting for execution as well as jobs that are currently executing. From it, you can determine how many jobs in the queue are ahead of yours. And, if you wish, you can change the job class or cancel the job altogether.

Options O and H display the contents of the JES2 *output queue* and *held output queue*. These displays show jobs that have completed execution and are awaiting final disposition. Jobs that are waiting to be printed are in the output queue, while jobs that are held or assigned to a reserved class are in the held output queue. From these displays, you can display job output at your terminal, change the disposition of the job output, or delete the job output.

```
------------------------ ISPF/PDF PRIMARY OPTION MENU ------------------------
OPTION  ===>
                                                           USERID  - DLOWE
        0  ISPF PARMS  - Specify terminal and user parameters  TIME    - 13:19
        1  BROWSE      - Display source data or output listings TERMINAL - 3278
        2  EDIT        - Create or change source data           PF KEYS - 24
        3  UTILITIES   - Perform utility functions
        4  FOREGROUND  - Invoke language processors in foreground
        5  BATCH       - Submit job for language processing
        6  COMMAND     - Enter TSO command or CLIST
        7  DIALOG TEST - Perform dialog testing
        8  LM UTILITIES- Perform library administrator utility functions
        9  IBM PRODUCTS- Additional IBM program development products
       10  SCLM        - Software Configuration and Library Manager
        C  CHANGES     - Display summary of changes for this release
        S  SDSF        - Spool Display and Search Facility
        T  TUTORIAL    - Display information about ISPF/PDF
        X  EXIT        - Terminate ISPF using log and list defaults

Enter END command to terminate ISPF.
```

Figure 7-12   An ISPF primary option menu that includes SDSF

```
------------------------- SDSF PRIMARY OPTION MENU -------------------------
COMMAND INPUT ===>                                      SCROLL ===> DATA

    Type an option or command and press Enter.

        I         - Display jobs in the JES2 input queue
        O         - Display jobs in the JES2 output queue
        H         - Display jobs in the JES2 held output queue
        ST        - Display status of jobs in the JES2 queues

        TUTOR     - Short course on SDSF (ISPF only)
        END       - Exit SDSF

    Use Help key for more information.
```

Figure 7-13   The SDSF primary option menu

Option ST displays the *status panel*, which combines information from all of the JES2 queues into one display. On it, you can follow the progress of a job as it waits on the input queue, executes, and prints.

Before I describe the individual operation of these displays, I'd like you to notice several elements they all have in common. To begin, the first two columns of each display's queue listing are labeled NP and JOBNAME. The JOBNAME column, obviously, displays the name of the job. The NP column lets you enter line commands to control specific jobs. SDSF calls these line commands *action characters*.

The other element these screens have in common is the LINE field on the right side of the top line. This field tells you how many lines are in the queue and which lines are currently being displayed. For example, the input queue panel in figure 7-14 is currently displaying lines 1-3, and there are 3 lines in the queue.

Finally, I want you to be aware that you can change the values of certain SDSF fields simply by overtyping them. For example, you can change the output class of a job in an output queue by typing the new class value in the column labeled C. I'll be sure to point out what fields can be overtyped as I explain how each queue display works.

How to terminate SDSF

You terminate an SDSF session just like you do any of the ISPF functions. You can either press the Return key, PF4/16, from any SDSF panel, or you can press the End key, PF3/15, from the SDSF primary option menu. Then, you're returned to the ISPF menu where you invoked SDSF.

If you're not on the SDSF primary option menu and you press PF3/15, you're returned to the previous panel. For example, pressing PF3/15 from the held output panel in figure 7-14 returns you to the SDSF primary option menu in figure 7-13. So to end a session from a panel other than the primary option menu, you may have to press PF3/15 more than once.

The input queue panel

```
SDSF INPUT QUEUE DISPLAY ALL CLASSES                      LINE 1-3 (3)
COMMAND INPUT ===>                                          SCROLL ===> DATA
:NP JOBNAME TYPE JNUM  PRTY C  POS DEST     RMT NODE SAFF ASYS STAT
    DLOWEX  JOB   803   12 R      LOCAL          1            HOLD
    DLOWEB  JOB  1025    7 R      LOCAL          1       MVSB
    DLOWEA  JOB  1232    7 R    1 LOCAL          1
```

The output queue panel

```
SDSF OUTPUT ALL CLASSES    ALL FORMS LINES    1,159  LINE 1-1 (1)
COMMAND INPUT ===>                                      SCROLL ===> DATA
:NP JOBNAME TYPE JNUM  PRTY C FORM FCB  DEST        TOT-REC  PRT-REC DEVICE   ST
    DLOWEB  JOB  1025    4 R STD  **** LOCAL          1,159
```

The held output queue panel

```
SDSF HELD OUTPUT DISPLAY ALL CLASSES          1863 LINES LINE 1-4 (4)
COMMAND INPUT ===>                                      SCROLL ===> DATA
:NP JOBNAME TYPE JNUM  DN  CRDATE  C FORM FCB  DEST     RMT NODE  TOT-REC RNUM
    DLOWEX  JOB   813   3  2/05/90 R STD  **** LOCAL          1        54
    DLOWEB  JOB  1025   5  2/06/90 R STD  **** LOCAL          1     1,159
    DLOWEA  JOB  1232   4  2/06/90 R STD  **** LOCAL          1       426
    DLOWEX  JOB  1672   3  2/06/90 R STD  **** LOCAL          1       215
```

The status panel

```
SDSF STATUS DISPLAY ALL CLASSES                        LINE 1-4 (4)
COMMAND INPUT ===>                                      SCROLL ===> DATA
:NP JOBNAME TYPE JNUM  PRTY QUEUE        C  POS HDN DEST    SAFF ASYS STAT
    DLOWEX  JOB   803   12 EXECUTION     R          LOCAL             HOLD
    DLOWEB  JOB  1025    7 EXECUTION     R          LOCAL        MVSB
    DLOWEA  JOB  1232    7 EXECUTION     R    1     LOCAL
    DLOWE   TSU  3574   15 EXECUTION                LOCAL   MVSB MVSB
```

Figure 7-14   SDSF queue panels

All panels

S   Displays output data sets.
?   Displays a list of the output data sets.

Input queue

A   Releases a held job.
C   Cancels a job.

Output queue

H   Holds a job's output.
O   Releases a held job.

Held output queue

P   Purges a job's output.

Note: All of these commands can be used from the status panel.

Figure 7-15   SDSF action characters

HOW TO MONITOR BACKGROUND JOBS

Now that you're familiar with the general operation of the SDSF display panels, I want to show you how to use it to monitor your background jobs. First, I'll show you how to monitor jobs using the status panel, which is the most flexible SDSF panel. Then, I'll show you how to use three other SDSF panels that provide functions that aren't available with the status panel: input, output, and held output.

Figure 7-15 lists most of the action characters you can use with these panels. You use these characters to change the status of a job displayed on the status, input queue, output, or held output panels.

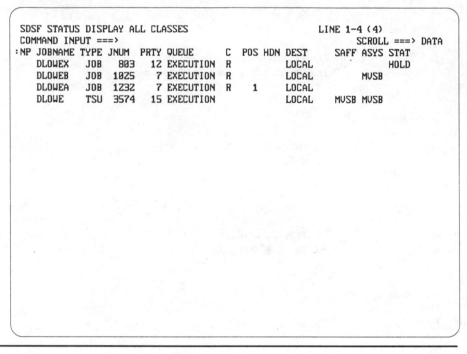

```
SDSF STATUS DISPLAY ALL CLASSES                      LINE 1-4 (4)
COMMAND INPUT ===>                                      SCROLL ===> DATA
:NP JOBNAME TYPE JNUM  PRTY QUEUE      C  POS HDN DEST     SAFF ASYS STAT
    DLOWEX  JOB   803   12 EXECUTION   R            LOCAL            HOLD
    DLOWEB  JOB  1025    7 EXECUTION   R            LOCAL       MVSB
    DLOWEA  JOB  1232    7 EXECUTION   R   1        LOCAL
    DLOWE   TSU  3574   15 EXECUTION               LOCAL  MVSB MVSB
```

Figure 7-16   A status panel with four entries in the execution queue

How to monitor jobs using the status panel

As you know, background jobs go through three distinct phases as they are processed. First, the job waits in an input queue until it can be executed. Second, the job is executed. And third, the job's output is gathered and held in an output queue until it can be printed. The easiest way to monitor a job as it progresses through these phases is to use the status panel. To do that, enter the ST command from any SDSF panel. Then, SDSF displays the status panel, shown in figure 7-16.

In figure 7-16, three jobs have been submitted for execution. (The fourth entry in the status queue indicates that you are logged on the system as a TSO user.) If you look at the QUEUE column, you can see that all three of these jobs are in the JES2 execution queue; that means they are waiting to be executed or are currently executing. The first job is on hold, as you can see in the STAT column for the job. The second job is currently executing. You can tell a job is executing if there's a value in the ASYS column. This column contains the system-id of the system that's executing the job. The third job is waiting to be executed.

If there's more than one job waiting to be executed, you can tell what job will execute next by looking in the POS column. This column contains the position of a job in the JES2 queue within its job class. The job class is listed in the C column.

If a job isn't currently executing, you can change its status using the A and H action characters. If you enter A in the NP column for a job and the job is currently held, the job is released. If you enter H for a non-held job, the job is put on hold.

You can also change a job's priority or destination by over-typing the appropriate fields on the status panel. For example, if you want to change the priority of a job so it will be executed sooner, you can type the new priority right over the current priority. Note that you can change a job's priority and destination only if the job isn't currently executing.

As a job executes, it creates SYSOUT data sets that are held in a JES2 output queue. You can display a list of the SYSOUT data sets that are allocated to a job by entering the ? action character in the NP column beside the job. When you do, SDSF displays a job data set panel like the one in figure 7-17. Here, you can see that the job named DLOWEB has created five SYSOUT data sets so far.

When a job finishes executing, its output is moved to a JES2 output queue. In the status panel in figure 7-18, the PRINT entry in the QUEUE column indicates that the output for job DLOWEB is in the JES2 print queue. The number in the HDN column indicates how many held SYSOUT data sets there are for the job. As you can see, there are five SYSOUT data sets being held in the print queue for DLOWEB.

If you want to release held job output for printing, you can enter the O action character on the status panel. You can also enter the C and P action characters from the status panel to manage the SYSOUT data for a job. If you enter C, all the output for the job is purged from the JES2 print queue. If you enter P, the SYSOUT data is purged from the system.

How to monitor jobs using the input queue, output, and held output panels

Three SDSF panels let you monitor jobs in specific JES2 queues: the input queue panel lets you monitor jobs in the JES2 input

```
 SDSF JOB DATA SET DISPLAY - JOB DLOWEB  (J1025   )      LINE 1-5 (5)
 COMMAND INPUT ===>                                    SCROLL ===> DATA
:NP DDNAME    STEP-NAME PROC-STEP DSID C REC-CNT PAGE-CNT CC RMT NODE 0-GRP-N  PR
    $JESZLOG  JESZ                  2 R      20             1        1        LI
    $JCLIMG   JESZ                  3 R      38             1        1        LI
    $SYSMSGS  JESZ                  4 R      81             1        1        LI
    SYSPRINT  COBZ               101 R     928             1        1        LI
    SALESRPT  GO                 108 R      11             1        1        LI
```

Figure 7-17   A job data set panel for a job that's currently executing

```
 SDSF STATUS DISPLAY ALL CLASSES                       LINE 1-4 (4)
 COMMAND INPUT ===>                                    SCROLL ===> DATA
:NP JOBNAME TYPE JNUM  PRTY QUEUE     C  POS HDN DEST     SAFF ASYS STAT
    DLOWEX   JOB  803   12 EXECUTION  R          LOCAL              HOLD
    DLOWEB   JOB  1025   7 PRINT      R    5 LOCAL
    DLOWEA   JOB  1232   7 EXECUTION  R          LOCAL         MVSB
    DLOWE    TSU  3574  15 EXECUTION             LOCAL    MVSB MVSB
```

Figure 7-18   A status panel that contains held output for a job queue, the output panel lets you monitor jobs in the JES2 output queue, and the held output panel lets you monitor jobs in the JES2 held output queue. Although the status panel is usually more useful, the input queue, output, and held output panels provide a few features that aren't available with the status panel. You can display these panels by entering the appropriate command from any SDSF panel.

To display an input queue panel, enter the I command from any SDSF panel. You can perform the same functions from this panel that you can from the status panel. In addition, you can change the job class by overtyping it. As with the other fields you can overtype, you can change the class only if the job isn't currently executing.

To display a non-held output panel, enter the O command from any SDSF panel. On this panel, you can enter the ? action character to display the JES2 data sets for a job just like you can from the status panel. You can also enter C to purge the output from the output queue, P to purge the output from the system, or H to hold the output. And you can overtype most of the fields to change the job output print characteristics.

To display a held output panel, enter the H command from any SDSF panel. This panel contains information about held SYSOUT data sets for all jobs. Like the status and output panels, you can display JES2 data sets for a single job by entering the ? action character in the NP column for that job. You can also enter the C, O, and P action characters on the held output panel, just like you can on the status panel. And you can overtype the C or DEST field to change the job's output class or destination.

How to display SYSOUT data

There's one more action character you should know: S. It lets you display the contents of the SYSOUT data sets produced by a job. You can use it from any of the SDSF panels I've presented here. If you use it from an input, output, held-output, or status display, SDSF will display all of the SYSOUT data sets for a job. If you use it from the job-data-set panel (displayed with the ? action character), SDSF displays just the SYSOUT data set you select.

```
SDSF OUTPUT DISPLAY DLOWEB    JOB  1025 DSID    Z LINE      0 COLUMNS 02- 81
COMMAND INPUT ===>                                          SCROLL ===> DATA
********************************** TOP OF DATA ********************************
                    J E S 2   J O B   L O G  --  S Y S T E M   M V S B  --  N O D
-------- JOB 1025  IEF097I DLOWEB - USER DLOWE    ASSIGNED
17.00.18 JOB 1025  $HASP373 DLOWEB  STARTED - INIT 64 - CLASS R - SYS MVSB
17.00.18 JOB 1025  IEF403I DLOWEB - STARTED - TIME=17.00.18
17.00.31 JOB 1025  -                                        --TIMINGS (MINS.)--
17.00.31 JOB 1025  -JOBNAME  STEPNAME PROCSTEP   RC   EXCP    CPU   SRB  CLOCK
17.00.31 JOB 1025  -DLOWEB   COB2                00    300    .00   .00    .2
17.00.36 JOB 1025  -DLOWEB   GO                  00    360    .00   .00    .0
17.00.36 JOB 1025  IEF404I DLOWEB - ENDED - TIME=17.00.36
17.00.36 JOB 1025  -DLOWEB   ENDED.   NAME-DOUG LOWE            TOTAL CPU TIME=
17.00.36 JOB 1025  $HASP395 DLOWEB   ENDED
------ JES2 JOB STATISTICS ------
    08 FEB 90 JOB EXECUTION DATE
           12 CARDS READ
        1,159 SYSOUT PRINT RECORDS
            0 SYSOUT PUNCH RECORDS
           87 SYSOUT SPOOL KBYTES
         0.30 MINUTES EXECUTION TIME
         1//DLOWEB    JOB (9999),'DOUG LOWE',CLASS=R,TIME=(1),MSGCLASS=R
         *** $ACFJZ19 ACF2 ACTIVE MVSDC
         2//          EXEC COB2UCG,PARM.COB2='APOST,OBJECT'
```

Figure 7-19   An output data set panel

Figure 7-19 shows a typical SDSF output display. Here, the first SYSOUT data set for a job is displayed. You can use the normal ISPF scrolling commands to browse this output, and you can use the FIND and LOCATE commands to find a particular line.

To move from one SYSOUT data set to another, you use the NEXT and PREV commands, shown in figure 7-20. The NEXT command moves forward a specified number of data sets. For example, the command

    NEXT 2

moves forward two data sets. If you don't enter a number on the NEXT command, the display moves forward one data set. And if you specify NEXT 0, the display is scrolled to the top of the current data set.

The PREV command works just the opposite of the NEXT command: it moves the display back one or more data sets.

The NEXT/PREV commands

```
NEXT
PREV    [n]
```

Explanation

NEXT   Moves the display forward one or more data sets.

PREV   Moves the display backwards one or more data sets.

n   The number of data sets to move in the specified direction. If omitted, 1 is
              assumed. If 0, the display is repositioned to the top of the current data set.

Figure 7-20   The NEXT and PREV commands

ADVANCED SDSF OPERATIONS

There are some additional operations you can perform within SDSF to control the information that's displayed on its panels. Here, I'll show you how to limit the jobs SDSF displays on a panel and how to refresh a panel automatically.

How to limit the jobs SDSF displays

If the JES2 queues contain many jobs, you might want to limit the jobs SDSF displays. You can do that in two ways: by their names or by their destinations. The formats of the two commands you use to limit the jobs SDSF displays are illustrated in figure 7-21.

How to limit the jobs by name   To limit the jobs SDSF displays on its panels by their names, you use the PREFIX command. The format of this command is shown in figure 7-21. On the PREFIX command, you specify a character string. Then, SDSF displays only jobs with names that match the character string. For example, if I enter the command

```
PREFIX DLOWEX
```

SDSF displays only jobs with the job name DLOWEX.

The PREFIX command

```
PREFIX [character-string]
```

The DEST command

```
DEST [destination-name]
```

Explanation

character-string   The name of the jobs you want to display. You can also use * to represent any string of characters and % to represent any one character. If you omit the character string, SDSF displays all the jobs.

destination-name   Up to four destinations of the jobs you want to display. If you do not enter a destination name, SDSF displays all the jobs.

Figure 7-21   The format of the PREFIX and DEST commands

You can also code a generic name on the PREFIX command by including the symbols * and %. An asterisk (*) represents any string of characters. For example, the command

```
PREFIX DLO*
```

displays all jobs that begin with the characters DLO. It doesn't matter how many additional characters follow these characters. So both the jobs DLOWEX and DLOWEA2 would be displayed.

The percent sign (%) represents a single character. So, the command

```
PREFIX DLO%%
```

displays all the jobs that begin with DLO and that are five characters long.

Note that when you use the PREFIX command, it remains in effect from one SDSF session to the next. The only way you can change it is by entering another PREFIX command. If you want to display all the jobs in the queues regardless of their names, enter the PREFIX command without a parameter.

How to limit the jobs by destination   You can also limit the jobs SDSF displays on the input, output, and held output panels by their destination. To do that, you use the DEST command. The format of this command is shown in figure 7-21. On the DEST command, you can specify up to four destination names. For example, you enter this command:

```
DEST LOCAL
```

to display only those jobs whose destination is LOCAL. If you don't enter any destination names on the DEST command, SDSF displays all the jobs regardless of their destination.

Like PREFIX, DEST remains in effect from one SDSF session to the next. To change it, enter another DEST command.

How to refresh a panel display

If you're monitoring the progress of a job or an output data set, you may want to update, or refresh, the display periodically. There are two ways you can do that. First, you can do it manually by entering the command again to display the queue you're monitoring. For example, if you're displaying the input queue and you enter the I command, SDSF refreshes the input queue display.

The second way to refresh a display is to use the & command. When you use &, you specify a time interval in seconds. Then, SDSF refreshes the display each time the specified number of seconds elapse. For example, if I enter the command

```
&30
```

SDSF refreshes the display every 30 seconds.

DISCUSSION

There are panels you can display and operations you can perform with SDSF other than the ones presented in this topic. For example, SDSF can display SYSLOG data, information about the active users on the system, and information about JES2 printers and initiators. Along with these panels, there are additional action characters you can use. However, as an application programmer, you'll seldom need to use these features. Those presented here should be all you need to know to use SDSF effectively. And if you understand the material presented in this topic, you should have no problem learning to use the other panels and operations if you need to.

Terms

System Display and Search Facility
SDSF
input queue
output queue
held output queue
status panel
action character

Objectives

1. Explain how you invoke SDSF from ISPF.

2. Control the operation of a job or output data set by entering an action character or by overtyping a field on the panel.

3. Use the PREFIX and DEST commands to limit the information that's displayed on an SDSF panel.

4. Use the & command to automatically refresh the SDSF display.

Chapter 8

How to use libraries managed by LMF and SCLM

Most programming projects require several types of ISPF libraries: source libraries, object libraries, load libraries, copy libraries, and so on. It's a good idea to maintain several sets of these libraries, organized into a hierarchy, for all but the smallest programming projects. Then, the highest set of libraries in the hierarchy contains programs that have been fully tested and put into production. The lowest-level libraries contain programs that are under development or in maintenance. And libraries in the middle levels of the hierarchy contain programs in various phases of testing.

The difficulty of maintaining a hierarchy like this is coordinating the movement of library members within the hierarchy. For example, when a programmer finishes coding a program, he or she must move it up to the next level of the hierarchy. And when a program needs some maintenance work, a copy of it must be moved down the hierarchy. Then, when the maintenance work is done, it must be moved back up the hierarchy. In all cases, the project coordinator must keep track of the most current version of each member, and must make sure that two programmer's aren't working on the same member at the same time. If these controls aren't enforced, library hierarchies can quickly get out of hand.

A relatively recent trend in program development is to automate library management tasks using *change control software*. ISPF provides two distinct change control systems. Beginning with ISPF Version 2, IBM introduced the *Library Management Facility*, or *LMF*. With ISPF Version 3, IBM introduced another change control system, called the *Software Configuration and Library Manager*, or *SCLM*. Although both LMF and SCLM let you organize libraries into a hierarchy and control the movement of members within that hierarchy, SCLM provides more sophisticated change control tools. I'll show you how to use both features in this chapter.

For both LMF and SCLM, a project administrator is responsible for setting up the library hierarchy and establishing its controls. As a result, I won't show you how to perform those functions here. Instead, I'll show you how to use the LMF and SCLM functions a programmer needs to use to work on an LMF- or SCLM-managed project.

This chapter is divided into two topics. The first shows you how to use LMF; the second covers SCLM. If your installation uses ISPF Version 2, you can read just topic 1, since SCLM isn't supported under ISPF Version 2. If your installation is using ISPF Version 3, you can read either topic, depending on which change control system you need to use.

Topic 1   How to use LMF-managed libraries

The Library Management Facility is a relatively simple change control system that lets you create a hierarchy of libraries and control how members move up and down that hierarchy. By using LMF, an installation can insure that the location of the most current version of each library member is always known. LMF is available under ISPF Versions 2 and 3.

To use LMF properly, you must first understand how LMF lets you set up a hierarchy and control the movement of members within it. So this topic starts by explaining those concepts. Then, it shows you how to use the LMF functions needed most by application programmers.

Keep in mind that to use LMF successfully, a project administrator must set up the library hierarchy and controls. I won't show you how to do those tasks in this chapter. Instead, I'll concentrate on the functions an application programmer needs to know to work with LMF-controlled libraries.

LMF CONCEPTS

Although LMF is relatively simple, there are a few concepts you need to understand before you can use it properly. In particular, you need to understand the structure of LMF library hierarchies, and how LMF controls the movement of members within the hierarchy.

The structure of an LMF library hierarchy

LMF lets a project administrator organize libraries into a hierarchy, like the one shown in figure 8-1. As you can see, this hierarchy consists of four levels. LMF controls only the top three of these levels, which include four libraries. The libraries in a hierarchy that are within the control of LMF are called *controlled*

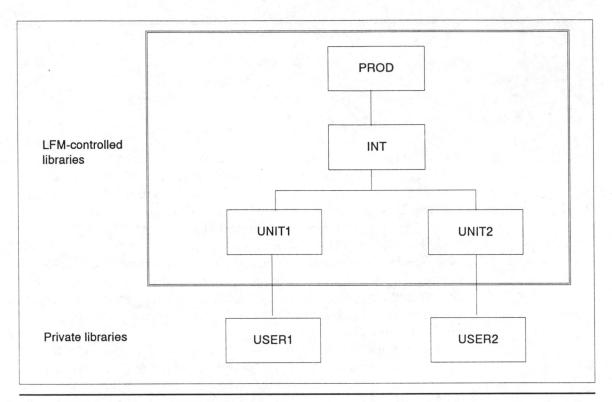

Figure 8-1   An LMF library hierarchy

libraries. The bottom level of the hierarchy, the one that's outside the control of LMF, consists of *private libraries.*

Each box in figure 8-1 actually represents a *group* of libraries. Each group consists of several *types* of libraries, such as COBOL, COPY, OBJ, LOAD, LIST, and so on. To identify each library's project, group, and type, LMF uses ISPF's standard naming conventions. Thus, if the name of the project is MKTG, the COBOL source library in the UNIT1 group would be MKTG.UNIT1.COBOL. And the object library in the INT group would be MKTG.INT.OBJ.

When a program in a private library is completed, its members are *promoted* into one of the libraries in the bottom level of the controlled hierarchy. These libraries are called *entry level libraries,* because this is where members enter into the controlled hierarchy. In figure 8-1, there are two entry level libraries: UNIT1 and UNIT2.

Once the various phases of program testing are complete, the programs are promoted to their *target libraries.* A member's target library is always the next highest level in the hierarchy. In figure 8-1, for example, the target library for all the members in UNIT1 and UNIT2 is INT, and the target library for all the members in INT is PROD. Because LMF automatically promotes members up the hierarchy, the hierarchy is sometimes called a *promotion hierarchy*.

How LMF controls the members of a library hierarchy

LMF imposes strict controls on how you can access, update, and move members within a hierarchy. To begin with, LMF won't let you edit a member of a controlled library directly. Instead, you have to copy the member to a private library and edit it there. When you copy a member in a controlled library to your private library, LMF *locks* the member in the controlled library so no one else can access it.

When you finish editing a member, you can either abandon the changes you made and delete the member from your private library, or you can promote the member back into an entry-level library. If you delete the member, LMF removes the lock on the member in the controlled library so others can access it. If you promote the member, LMF retains the lock on the higher-level copy of the member. In figure 8-1, for example, suppose you copy a member in the PROD group to your private library to edit it, and then you promote the member into the UNIT1 group. Now, a copy of the member exists in both the PROD and UNIT1 groups. When that happens, LMF locks all copies of the member except the one at the lowest level. That way, LMF insures that you can access only the most current version of the member.

If the project administrator wants to, he or she can restrict promotion into entry-level libraries to members that have been *predefined*. Then, you can promote a member into the entry-level library only if its name appears in the list of predefined members. Alternatively, the project administrator can allow *undefined* members in the entry level library. Then, you can promote any member you wish into the hierarchy.

Another way the project administrator can control members within libraries is by restricting certain LMF functions to specific users. For example, the administrator can specify what users can promote members into an entry-level library, what users can promote members through the hierarchy, and what users can access members for editing.

HOW TO USE LMF FUNCTIONS

As an application programmer, you need to know how to perform
three tasks for LMF-controlled libraries: (1) edit an LMF-controlled
member; (2) promote a member from a private library into the hierarchy or delete it to remove the lock; and (3) promote a member
that's already in the hierarchy to a higher group.

You may have noticed that there's an option on the primary
option menu for LMF functions. The functions provided by that
option let the project administrator set up the hierarchy and establish its controls. As an application programmer, you won't use this
option. Instead, you'll perform the LMF tasks I'll describe here
using the ISPF options you're already familiar with.

How to edit a member of a controlled library

To edit a member of a controlled library, you have to copy it into a
private library. The easiest way to do that is to use the Edit entry
panel to concatenate your private library with the controlled
library where the member resides, as illustrated in figure 8-2. As
you'll recall, when you concatenate libraries on the edit entry
panel, ISPF searches all the libraries to retrieve the member, but
always stores the saved member in the first library you specify. In
figure 8-2, I specified a private library, USER1, in the first GROUP
field. Then, I specified UNIT1, INT, and PROD in the remaining
GROUP fields. That way, ISPF will search the entire LMF library
hierarchy to locate the member. Then, it will save the edited
member in the USER1 library.

The LMF LOCK field determines whether or not the member
should be locked when it is retrieved from an LMF-controlled
library. You should almost always leave this field at its default,
YES. If the member is already locked by another user, you can
change this field to NO. Then, LMF will let you retrieve the
member, but you won't be able to promote it back into the library
hierarchy later on. So you should do this only if you don't need to
return the member to the controlled library.

If you want to copy more than one member to a private library,
you can use the move/copy utility, option 3.3. Figure 8-3 shows
how to do that. In part 1, I entered the three controlled library
groups in the GROUP fields, and entered the L command in the
OPTION field to copy and lock the member. (You can also use the

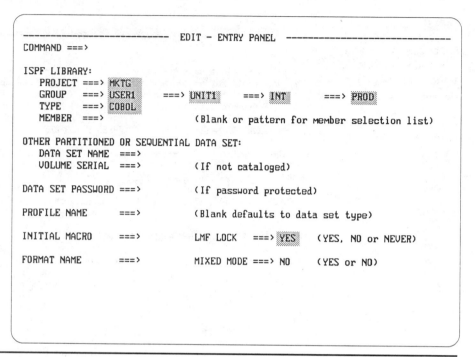

Figure 8-2   The edit entry panel as it's used to copy a controlled library member to a private library

LP command to copy, lock, and print the member.) In the member field, you can enter a member name to copy and lock one member, an asterisk to copy and lock all members in the library, or leave the field blank or enter a pattern to display a member list. In part 1 of figure 8-3, I entered MKTG1200 as the member name.

After you've selected the members you want to copy and lock, move/copy displays the panel shown in part 2 of figure 8-3. Here, you enter the private library you want to copy the member or members to. In this case, the library is MKTG.USER1.COBOL.

How to promote a member

LMF allows two basic types of promotions: (1) promoting a member from a private library into an entry-level library and (2) promoting a member from a controlled library to the next higher library in the promotion hierarchy. To perform either of these

Part 1:

Specify the copy and
lock option and the
name of the member
you want to copy

```
------------------------------ MOVE/COPY UTILITY ------------------------------
OPTION  ===> L

     C - Copy data set or member(s)              CP - Copy and print
     M - Move data set or member(s)              MP - Move and print
     L - Copy and LMF lock member(s)             LP - Copy, LMF lock, and print
     P - LMF Promote data set or member(s)       PP - LMF Promote and print

SPECIFY "FROM" DATA SET BELOW, THEN PRESS ENTER KEY

FROM ISPF LIBRARY:          ------ Options C, CP, L, and LP only -------
     PROJECT ===> MKTG           |                                      |
     GROUP   ===> UNIT1    ===> INT      ===> PROD      ===>
     TYPE    ===> COBOL
     MEMBER  ===> MKTG1200        (Blank or pattern for member selection list,
                                   '*' for all members)

FROM OTHER PARTITIONED OR SEQUENTIAL DATA SET:
     DATA SET NAME  ===>
     VOLUME SERIAL  ===>          (If not cataloged)

DATA SET PASSWORD ===>           (If password protected)
```

Part 2:

Enter the name of the
private library where
you want the member
copied

```
COPY --- FROM MKTG.UNIT1.COBOL(MKTG1200) --------------------------------------
COMMAND ===>

SPECIFY "TO" DATA SET BELOW.

TO ISPF LIBRARY:
     PROJECT ===> MKTG
     GROUP   ===> USER1
     TYPE    ===> COBOL
     MEMBER  ===>             (Blank unless member is to be renamed)

TO OTHER PARTITIONED OR SEQUENTIAL DATA SET:
     DATA SET NAME  ===>
     VOLUME SERIAL  ===>          (If not cataloged)

DATA SET PASSWORD ===>           (If password protected)

"TO" DATA SET OPTIONS:
     IF PARTITIONED, REPLACE LIKE-NAMED MEMBERS ===> NO    (YES or NO)
     IF SEQUENTIAL, "TO" DATA SET DISPOSITION   ===>       (OLD or MOD)
     SPECIFY PACK OPTION FOR "TO" DATA SET      ===>       (YES, NO or blank)
```

Figure 8-3   The move/copy utility as it's used to copy a member of a controlled library
to a private library

functions, you use the move/copy utility, option 3.3 from the primary option menu.

Figure 8-4 shows how to promote a member from a private library into an entry level library. First, enter the promote (P) or promote and print (PP) command along with the name of the member you want to promote and the private library where it resides. In part 1 of figure 8-4, I entered the P command and the member MKTG1200 in MKTG.USER1.COBOL. To promote all the members in the library, enter an asterisk (*) in the MEMBER field. To promote several members at once, either leave the MEMBER field blank or specify a pattern. Then, ISPF displays a member selection list, and you can select the members you want to promote from there.

After you select the members you want to promote, ISPF displays the panel in part 2 of figure 8-4. Here, you enter the name of the entry-level library you want the members promoted to. In this case, I promoted MKTG1200 to the library named MKTG.UNIT1.COBOL. Although you usually won't want to, you can also change the name of a member if you're copying a single member. To do that, just enter the new name in the MEMBER field.

In the ACTION field of this panel, you can enter MOVE or FREE. If you enter MOVE, ISPF moves the member into the controlled library and deletes it from the private library. If you enter FREE, ISPF deletes the member from the private library but does *not* move it to the controlled library. FREE lets you release the lock established for a member you previously copied for editing, but then decided you didn't want to change.

You can enter any information you want in the REASON CODE field, but it can't be longer than 26 characters. ISPF writes this information to an activity log that helps the project administrator keep track of promotions. If the project administrator uses this log, he or she will tell you what to enter in the REASON CODE field. Otherwise, you can ignore it.

To save space in the controlled libraries, specify YES in the PACK DATA field. Then, the member is stored in a compressed format that requires considerably less disk space. The disadvantage of packing a member is that it takes longer to retrieve and save it, since ISPF has to pack and unpack the data.

To promote a member from one level of a controlled library to the next level, you use the move/copy utility in the same way. The only difference is that since LMF tracks the promotion hierarchy, it automatically determines where to promote the member or

Part 1:

Specify the promote option and the member to be promoted

```
--------------------------------- MOVE/COPY UTILITY ---------------------------------
OPTION  ===> P

     C - Copy data set or member(s)           CP - Copy and print
     M - Move data set or member(s)           MP - Move and print
     L - Copy and LMF lock member(s)          LP - Copy, LMF lock, and print
     P - LMF Promote data set or member(s)    PP - LMF Promote and print

SPECIFY "FROM" DATA SET BELOW, THEN PRESS ENTER KEY

FROM ISPF LIBRARY:              ------ Options C, CP, L, and LP only ------
     PROJECT ===> MKTG         |                                          |
     GROUP   ===> USER1   ===>          ===>          ===>
     TYPE    ===> COBOL
     MEMBER  ===> MKTG1200     (Blank or pattern for member selection list,
                                '*' for all members)


FROM OTHER PARTITIONED OR SEQUENTIAL DATA SET:
     DATA SET NAME  ===>
     VOLUME SERIAL  ===>       (If not cataloged)

DATA SET PASSWORD ===>         (If password protected)
```

Part 2:

Specify the target library and the MOVE action

```
PROMOTE --- FROM MKTG.USER1.COBOL(MKTG1200) ------------------------------------
COMMAND ===>

SPECIFY "TARGET" CONTROLLED LIBRARY BELOW.

TO ISPF LIBRARY:
     PROJECT ===> MKTG
     GROUP   ===> UNIT1
     TYPE    ===> COBOL
     MEMBER  ===>              (Blank unless member is to be renamed)

ACTION       ===> MOVE        (MOVE to copy and delete source
                               FREE to only delete source)

REASON CODE  ===>

PACK DATA    ===>             (YES, NO, or blank to default to library controls)
```

Figure 8-4 The move/copy utility as it's used to promote a member from a private library into a controlled library members you select. So it doesn't ask you to enter the target library. Instead, once you've selected the member you want to promote, the member is automatically promoted to its target library.

DISCUSSION

From an application programer's point of view, working on an LMF-controlled project is not that much different than working on a project that doesn't use LMF. Unless you're responsible for setting up and maintaining the library hierarchy, all you have to do is learn how to access a member for editing and promote a member back into the hierarchy.

Unfortunately, even these simple tasks can become burdensome. For example, it's a simple matter to promote a member from a COBOL source library into an LMF-controlled source library. But most real programs involve members in many different types of libraries: source libraries, copy libraries, object libraries, load libraries, JCL libraries, and perhaps even documentation libraries. Promoting members from all these library types with LMF is both tedious and error-prone. That's why IBM introduced SCLM with ISPF Version 3. SCLM can track all the members that belong to a single program or application as a single unit. You'll learn how SCLM works in the next topic.

Terms

change control software
Library Management Facility
LMF
Software Configuration and Library Manager
SCLM
controlled library
private library
group
type
promote
entry-level library
target library

promotion hierarchy
lock
predefined member
undefined member

Objectives

1. Describe a promotion hierarchy and explain how it's controlled
    by LMF.

2. Copy a member from a controlled library into a private library
    for editing using either the edit function or the move/copy
    utility.

3. Use the move/copy utility to promote a member from a private
    library into an entry-level library or from one controlled library
    to another.

Topic 2　How to use SCLM-managed libraries

The Software Configuration and Library Manager is a sophisticated change management system that helps you manage large programming projects. Like LMF, SCLM lets you organize libraries into a hierarchy and control the movement of data up and down the hierarchy. But SCLM provides more sophisticated change management tools than LMF's simple controls. For example, SCLM includes a facility to define a software architecture, so you can specify what program components (like source modules, subprograms, copy members, and so on) make up individual programs, and what programs make up complete applications. It also includes a facility that automates the process of compiling and link-editing software architectures, so you can keep all components of a program current.

In this topic, you'll learn some basic SCLM concepts that you need to understand before you can begin to use SCLM effectively. Then, you'll learn how to use SCLM's basic program development features.

I want you to be aware at the outset that SCLM is complicated. In the long run, it can simplify program development for large projects. However, it requires a significant effort to learn how SCLM works, how to set it up properly, and how to create architecture definitions. Fortunately, most of that work must be done by the project administrator who is responsible for SCLM's use. As an application programmer working on an SCLM project, you need to understand only the basic SCLM concepts and functions I'll present here.

SCLM CONCEPTS

Before you can use SCLM, you must understand some of its basic concepts. I'll start by explaining how you define software architectures using SCLM. Then, I'll explain how SCLM manages the libraries in a hierarchy.

```
LOAD   MKTG1200 LOAD
INCLD  MKTG1200 COBOL
INCLD  MKTG1210 COBOL
INCLD  MKTG1220 COBOL
```

Figure 8-5   The SCLM architecture definition for the MKTG1200 program

An introduction to software architectures

In SCLM, an *architecture* is a coded specification of each component that makes up a complete application. At the most basic level,
each program that makes up an application has its own architecture. The architecture for a complete application consists of the
architectures for each of the application's programs.

A program architecture specifies all the software components
that make up a program. For example, figure 8-5 shows an architecture definition for a program named MKTG1200 that calls two
subprograms named MKTG1210 and MKTG1220. This architecture
definition lists four software components for the program: the load
module, named MKTG1200, and the three COBOL source
programs that are required to create the load module. By relating
these four components to one another, SCLM lets you treat them as
a single unit.

In addition to the four components listed in figure 8-5, SCLM
can automatically manage other software components. For
example, before the MKTG1200 load module can be created, the
MKTG1200, MKTG1210, and MKTG1220 source programs must be
compiled to create object modules that can be link-edited. So SCLM
also keeps track of the object modules, even though they aren't
listed in figure 8-5. Similarly, SCLM tracks the compiler listings
and link-edit maps created for the program, even though they
aren't listed in the architecture, either.

One of the major benefits of SCLM architectures is that they
enable SCLM to track the *dependencies* within an application. For
example, if a change is made to the MKTG1210 subprogram, SCLM
knows that MKTG1210 needs to be recompiled and MKTG1200
needs to be link-edited to include the new version of MKTG1210.
Likewise, SCLM knows that the MKTG1200 and MKTG1220
programs do *not* need to be recompiled, since those programs
haven't changed.

The function that checks a program's dependencies, compiles the source modules that have changed since they were last compiled, and link-edits them to create an up-to-date load module is called the *build* function. So, as a programmer working on a project managed by SCLM, you'll use SCLM's build function rather than ISPF's standard compilation functions to compile and link-edit your programs.

Besides dependencies created by subprograms, SCLM also tracks dependencies introduced by COPY statements. For example, suppose that the MKTG1220 subprogram included a COPY statement that referenced a source member named CUSTMAST. Then, if a change is made to CUSTMAST, SCLM knows that the MKTG1220 program is out of date and needs to be recompiled. Unlike subprogram dependencies, which have to be spelled out in an architecture definition, SCLM tracks COPY dependencies automatically. It does this by scanning the source program using a program called a *parser*. The parser simply locates and records any COPY statements that appear in the program.

The actual process of creating an SCLM architecture definition is complicated and, frankly, beyond the scope of this book. Suffice it to say that SCLM includes a simple programming language for specifying architectures, and architecture specifications are stored in source form as members of a library controlled by SCLM.

How SCLM manages library hierarchies

To manage the multiple versions of software components that are created as a program moves from various stages of testing into final production, SCLM lets a project administrator organize libraries into a hierarchy. Then, SCLM controls the movement of software components from one level of the hierarchy to the next.

Figure 8-6 illustrates a typical SCLM library hierarchy. Each level, or *layer*, of an SCLM hierarchy corresponds to a different stage of project development. The hierarchy in figure 8-6 contains four layers: the development layer, the unit test layer, the integration layer, and the production layer. More complicated projects might include additional layers, while less complicated projects might contain fewer layers.

Each layer of an SCLM library hierarchy contains one or more *groups* of libraries. For example, the unit test layer in figure 8-6 contains two groups, UNIT1 and UNIT2. Each of these groups, in

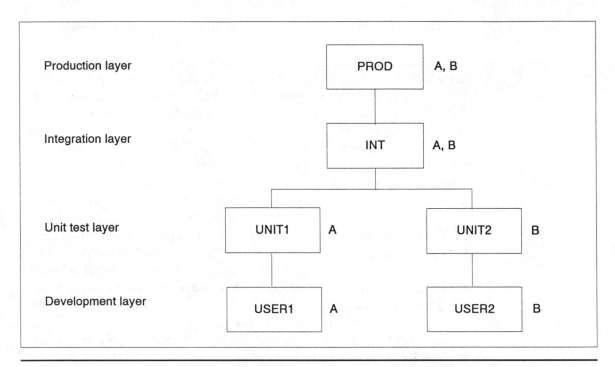

Production layer   PROD   A, B

Integration layer   INT   A, B

Unit test layer   UNIT1   A   UNIT2   B

Development layer   USER1   A   USER2   B

Figure 8-6   An SCLM library hierarchy

turn, consists of several types of libraries. For a typical COBOL
application, each group in the hierarchy would consist of COBOL,
OBJ, LOAD, LIST, and LINKLIST libraries. In addition, architecture
definitions are usually stored in libraries of type ARCHDEF. There
may be other library types as well, such as JCL libraries, documentation libraries, and so on.

The lowest level of an SCLM hierarchy is called the *development
layer*, and the libraries in the development layer are called *private
libraries*. SCLM allows you to edit members only in private
libraries; you can't directly edit members of higher-level libraries.
To edit a member in a higher-level library, you must *draw down*
the member, which means simply to copy it to a private library. As
you'll see later in this topic, if the member you're drawing down
exists in more than one level of the hierarchy, SCLM always draws
down the member at the lowest level, since it's always the most
current version.

When you draw down a member into a private library, SCLM
automatically locks the member in the higher-level library so that
no one else can work on it at the same time. When you've finished

working on a member in a private library, you can either *promote* it to a higher-level library or delete it. When you promote a member in a private library, the member is moved to the next layer of the hierarchy and the lock is removed. When you delete the member, it is removed from the private library and the lock is removed. As a result, the version that you originally drew down is restored as the current version of the member.

Notice the letters A and B next to each group in figure 8-6. These are *authorization codes*, which the project administrator can use to control how members move from one group to another. In this example, the USER1 and UNIT1 groups have authorization code A, while the USER2 and UNIT2 groups have authorization code B. The INT and PROD groups have both codes. When you create a member in a development library, SCLM assigns the development library's authorization code to it by default. From then on, SCLM won't allow you to move the member to a group that doesn't have the correct authorization code. The result of this arrangement is that members created in either group USER1 or USER2 can be promoted all the way up the hierarchy, but a member can be drawn down only to the development group where it was first created. In other words, a member created in group USER1 and promoted to group INT can *not* be drawn down to group USER2.

SCLM uses standard ISPF naming conventions to identify libraries in a hierarchy. The high-level qualifier of the data set name identifies the project the library belongs to. Thus, if the library hierarchy in figure 8-6 was for a project named MKTG, the COBOL source library for the UNIT1 group would be named MKTG.UNIT1.COBOL. And the load library in the USER2 group would be named MKTG.USER2.LOAD.

To specify the organization of an SCLM library hierarchy, a project administrator must create a *project definition*. The project definition consists of a series of macro instructions that must be assembled and link-edited before the library hierarchy can be used. The project definition is stored in a special group called PROJDEFS, which is not itself a part of the SCLM hierarchy for the project.

Figure 8-7 shows a portion of the project definition for the library hierarchy shown in figure 8-6. As you can see, the first set of macro instructions indicate what types of libraries are included in each group. Thus, each group consists of a COBOL, COPY, LOAD, OBJ, LIST, and ARCHDEF library. The EXTEND keyword on the macro that defines the COBOL type tells SCLM that COPY

```
*
*   TYPE DEFINITIONS
*
COBOL     FMLTYPE EXTEND=COPY
COPY      FMLTYPE
LOAD      FMLTYPE
OBJ       FMLTYPE
LIST      FMLTYPE
ARCHDEF   FMLTYPE
*
*   GROUP DEFINITIONS
*
USER1     FMLGROUP AC=(A),PROMOTE=UNIT1
USER2     FMLGROUP AC=(B),PROMOTE=UNIT2
UNIT1     FMLGROUP AC=(A),PROMOTE=INT
UNIT2     FMLGROUP AC=(B),PROMOTE=INT
INT       FMLGROUP AC=(A,B),PROMOTE=PROD
PROD      FMLGROUP AC=(A,B)
```

Figure 8-7   A portion of an SCLM project definition

members included in COBOL source programs can be found in the COPY library type.

The second set of macros in figure 8-7 specifies the groups included in the hierarchy. The PROMOTE keyword controls the structure of the hierarchy by specifying the library where members from each group will be promoted. The PROD group, whose macro doesn't have a PROMOTE keyword, is the highest-level library in the hierarchy. The AC keywords specify the authorization codes for each group.

SCLM FUNCTIONS

You can't use standard ISPF functions to manage SCLM libraries. Instead, you invoke SCLM functions from the SCLM primary option menu, shown in figure 8-8. To display this menu, select option 10 from the ISPF primary option menu. From it, you can invoke the standard browse and edit options to browse or edit an SCLM-controlled member, perform SCLM utility functions, build a member, or promote a member. Here, I'll cover just the functions you'll use most: the edit option to draw down and edit a member, the build option to compile and link-edit a member, the utilities

```
----------------------- SCLM PRIMARY OPTION MENU -----------------------
OPTION ===>

    1  BROWSE       - ISPF/PDF Browse
    2  EDIT         - Create or change source data in SCLM databases
    3  UTILITIES    - Perform SCLM database utility/reporting functions
    4  BUILD        - Construct SCLM-controlled components
    5  PROMOTE      - Move components up SCLM hierarchy
    X  EXIT         - Terminate SCLM

SPECIFY SCLM PROJECT CONTROL INFORMATION:
    PROJECT    ===> MKTG     (Project high-level qualifier)
    ALTERNATE  ===>          (Project definition: defaults to project)
    DEV GROUP  ===> USER1    (Development group: defaults to user ID)
```

Figure 8-8   The SCLM primary option menu

option to delete a member, and the promote option to move a
member up in the hierarchy.

Before you can invoke any SCLM function, you must enter the
SCLM project name in the PROJECT field on the SCLM primary
option menu. In figure 8-8, I entered MKTG in this field so I could
work on the MKTG project. Also, in the DEV GROUP field, you
specify the group name for your private development library. This
field defaults to your user-id, so you'll usually leave it unchanged.

One more thing you should know if you use SCLM is that while
you're in SCLM, the SCLM primary option menu temporarily
replaces the ISPF primary option menu. This affects you in two
ways. First, the Cancel key, PF4/16, doesn't work the same as it
does on the other ISPF panels. Pressing PF4/16 from an SCLM
panel returns you to the SCLM primary option menu instead of the
ISPF primary option menu. Second, prefixing the menu option
with an equals sign invokes the option from the SCLM primary
option menu, not the ISPF primary option menu. For example, if
you're editing an SCLM file and you enter

       COMMAND ===> =4

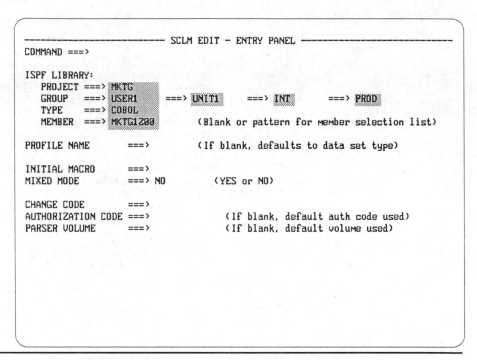

```
------------------------- SCLM EDIT - ENTRY PANEL -------------------------
COMMAND ===>

ISPF LIBRARY:
   PROJECT ===> MKTG
   GROUP   ===> USER1     ===> UNIT1    ===> INT      ===> PROD
   TYPE    ===> COBOL
   MEMBER  ===> MKTG1200         (Blank or pattern for member selection list)

PROFILE NAME       ===>         (If blank, defaults to data set type)

INITIAL MACRO      ===>
MIXED MODE         ===> NO       (YES or NO)

CHANGE CODE        ===>
AUTHORIZATION CODE ===>                 (If blank, default auth code used)
PARSER VOLUME      ===>                 (If blank, default volume used)
```

Figure 8-9   The SCLM edit entry panel

and then press the Enter key, ISPF executes option 4 from the
SCLM primary option menu.

If you want to go directly to an ISPF option from an SCLM
panel, you must chain two commands together. For example, to go
directly to the data set list utility from an SCLM panel, enter this
command:

    COMMAND ===> =X;3.4

Here, the =X command issues the X option from the SCLM primary
option menu, which terminates SCLM and returns you to the ISPF
primary option menu. Then, the 3.4 option takes you to the
DSLIST utility panel.

SCLM option 2: The Edit function

To edit a member in an SCLM library hierarchy, select option 2
from the SCLM primary option menu. Then, SCLM displays the
SCLM edit entry panel, shown in figure 8-9. On this panel, you

enter the name of the library and member you want to edit. If you leave the member name field blank or enter a pattern, SCLM displays a member list so you can select the member you want to edit.

Although the SCLM edit entry panel is similar to the standard ISPF edit entry panel, there are a few differences you need to be aware of. The most obvious is that the PROJECT field and the first GROUP field default to the PROJECT and DEV GROUP you specified on the SCLM primary option menu. SCLM won't let you change these fields. That way, any members you edit are saved in your development library even if they are retrieved from another level in the hierarchy. This is the process of drawing down I mentioned earlier.

The other three GROUP fields in the ISPF library specification default to the next three higher levels of the library hierarchy. As a result, SCLM searches for the member you specify starting with your development library and proceeding up in the hierarchy. This insures that you're editing the most current version of a program. Although you can change these three GROUP specifications, you normally don't need to. If you do change them, the groups you enter must be in order according to the library hierarchy defined by SCLM. Otherwise, SCLM won't let you edit the member.

Notice the CHANGE CODE field on the SCLM edit entry panel. In this field, you enter a code that indicates why you are changing the member. SCLM doesn't automatically do anything with the change code you enter. Instead, each installation must modify SCLM to handle the change code field in whatever manner is appropriate. As a result, your installation may or may not require you to enter a value in this field. If it does, you'll be supplied with a list of valid change codes.

You can usually omit the last two fields: AUTHORIZATION CODE and PARSER VOLUME. The AUTHORIZATION CODE field lets you enter an authorization code for the member. You should almost always let this field default to the default authorization code the project administrator set up for your development library. The PARSER VOLUME field lets you supply the name of the volume where you want the SCLM parser to store its output. If you omit this field (which you normally should), SCLM stores the parser output on a default volume.

When you save a member using the SCLM editor, the SCLM edit profile panel in figure 8-10 is displayed. Here, you enter the

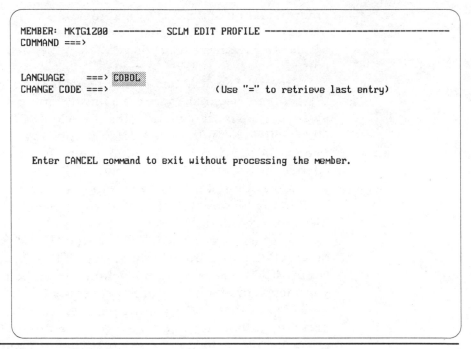

```
MEMBER: MKTG1200 --------- SCLM EDIT PROFILE -----------------------------------
COMMAND ===>


LANGUAGE    ===> COBOL
CHANGE CODE ===>                          (Use "=" to retrieve last entry)




   Enter CANCEL command to exit without processing the member.
```

Figure 8-10   The SCLM edit profile panel

language the member is written in and a change code. That way,
SCLM knows what compiler to use when you compile the program
using the build function.

The SCLM editor provides four primary commands that aren't
available under the standard ISPF editor. Figure 8-11 lists these
commands. The first three are SCLM variations of the CREATE,
REPLACE, and MOVE commands. SCREATE and SREPLACE create
a new member or replace an existing member with a range of lines
from the current member, and SMOVE moves data from another
member into the current member. The only difference between
these commands and their standard ISPF equivalents is that they
update the statistics that SCLM maintains for members in its
controlled libraries. So whenever you use SCLM, you should use
the SCREATE, SREPLACE, and SMOVE commands instead of
CREATE, REPLACE, and MOVE. There isn't a SCOPY command
because the standard COPY command doesn't affect SCLM statistics.

The SCREATE command   **Meaning**

```
SCREATE   member-name
          [range]
```
Create a new member with the range of lines marked by C or M commands.

The SREPLACE command

```
SREPLACE   member-name
           [range]
```
Create a new member or replace an existing member with the range of lines marked by C or M commands.

The SMOVE command

```
SMOVE   member-name

      [{BEFORE}  label ]
       {AFTER  }
```
Copy the named member to the position marked by an A or B line command, then delete the member from its original location.

The SPROF command

```
SPROF
```
Display the SCLM profile panel.

Figure 8-11   Primary commands for the SCLM editor

The fourth command is the SPROF command. This command simply displays the SCLM profile panel, illustrated in figure 8-10, so you can respecify the member's language and change code.

Other than these differences, the SCLM editor works the same as the ISPF editor. Thus, you can use all the editing features you learned about in chapter 4.

SCLM option 4: The build function

SCLM's build function lets you compile and link-edit the programs in a program architecture. To use the build function, select option 4 from the SCLM primary option menu. Then, SCLM displays the build entry panel shown in figure 8-12.

On the build panel, you enter the name of the architecture you want to build. Then, you enter EXECUTE or SUBMIT in the

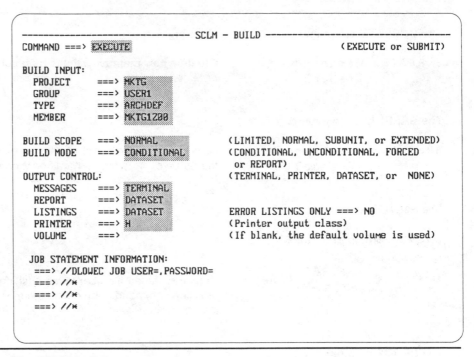

```
--------------------------------- SCLM - BUILD ----------------------------------
COMMAND ===> EXECUTE                                             (EXECUTE or SUBMIT)

BUILD INPUT:
   PROJECT    ===> MKTG
   GROUP      ===> USER1
   TYPE       ===> ARCHDEF
   MEMBER     ===> MKTG1200

BUILD SCOPE   ===> NORMAL          (LIMITED, NORMAL, SUBUNIT, or EXTENDED)
BUILD MODE    ===> CONDITIONAL     (CONDITIONAL, UNCONDITIONAL, FORCED
                                     or REPORT)
OUTPUT CONTROL:                    (TERMINAL, PRINTER, DATASET, or  NONE)
   MESSAGES   ===> TERMINAL
   REPORT     ===> DATASET
   LISTINGS   ===> DATASET         ERROR LISTINGS ONLY ===> NO
   PRINTER    ===> H               (Printer output class)
   VOLUME     ===>                 (If blank, the default volume is used)

JOB STATEMENT INFORMATION:
===> //DLOWEC JOB USER=,PASSWORD=
===> //*
===> //*
===> //*
```

Figure 8-12   The SCLM build entry panel

command line to execute the build operation in foreground mode
or submit it for execution as a batch job. In figure 8-12, I'm
building the architecture named MKTG1200 in foreground mode.
When you execute this function, SCLM analyzes the architecture,
determines all of the dependencies, compiles any source programs
that have been updated since the last time the architecture was
built, and invokes the linkage-editor to produce a load module.

The other fields on the build panel provide advanced
processing options you aren't likely to need. Usually, you'll leave
the BUILD SCOPE field at its default of NORMAL and the BUILD
MODE field at its default of CONDITIONAL. The OUTPUT
CONTROL fields specify how you want to handle the output from
the build function. Usually, you'll direct the messages to the
terminal and the report and listings to data sets.

As build executes, it displays messages like the ones in figure
8-13 at your terminal. These messages indicate build's progress, let
you know what source modules are being compiled, and inform
you of any errors that result. Build also displays a message telling
you the name of the data set that contains the report and listings it

```
FLM49000 - INVOKING BUILD PROCESSOR
FLM09002 - THE REPORT WILL APPEAR IN DLOWE.BUILD.REPORT31
FLM09006 - THE LISTING WILL APPEAR IN DLOWE.BUILD.LIST31
FLM42000 - BUILD PROCESSOR INITIATED - 13:36:48 ON 90/07/30
FLM44500 - >>>>> INVOKE TRANSLATOR(S) FOR TYPE: COBOL    MEMBER:  MKTG1200
FLM06501 - TRANSLATOR RETURN CODE FROM ===> COBOL                  ===> 0
FLM44500 - >>>>> INVOKE TRANSLATOR(S) FOR TYPE: COBOL    MEMBER:  MKTG1210
FLM06501 - TRANSLATOR RETURN CODE FROM ===> COBOL                  ===> 0
FLM44500 - >>>>> INVOKE TRANSLATOR(S) FOR TYPE: ARCHDEF  MEMBER:  MKTG1200
FLM06501 - TRANSLATOR RETURN CODE FROM ===> LKED/370               ===> 0
FLM46000 - BUILD PROCESSOR COMPLETED - 13:36:57 ON 90/07/30
FLM09008 - RETURN CODE = 0
***
```

Figure 8-13   Build messages

creates. In this case, the build report will be in the file DLOWE.BUILD.REPORT31, and the list output will be in DLOWE.BUILD.LIST31.

Figure 8-14 shows the *build report* for the MKTG1200 build. This report indicates what members were created during the build. In this case, MKTG1200 and MKTG1210 were both compiled to create new object modules, and a new MKTG1200 load module was created. Near the bottom of the report, you can see that build recompiled the MKTG1200 and MKTG1210 programs because they both depend on the CUSTMAST COPY member, which was modified since the last time MKTG1200 was built.

SCLM option 5: The promote function

When you finish working on an SCLM member, you can promote it from your private library to a higher-level SCLM library. To do that, you use the promote function, option 5 from the SCLM primary option menu. Figure 8-15 shows the promote entry panel.

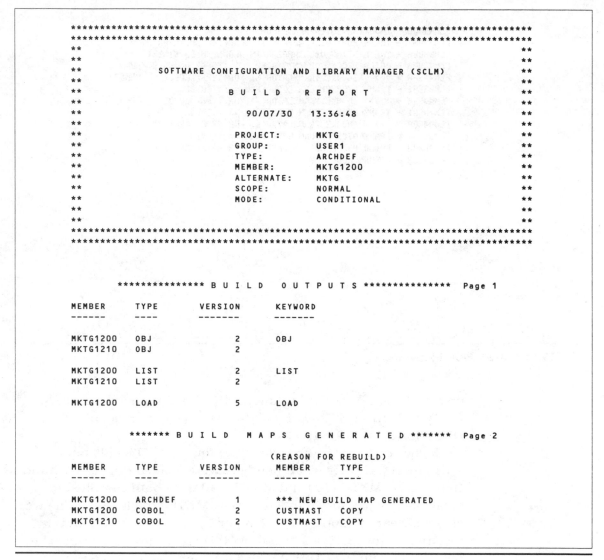

```
**********************************************************************
**********************************************************************
**                                                                  **
**                                                                  **
**          SOFTWARE CONFIGURATION AND LIBRARY MANAGER (SCLM)        **
**                                                                  **
**                    B U I L D   R E P O R T                       **
**                                                                  **
**                     90/07/30   13:36:48                          **
**                                                                  **
**                   PROJECT:      MKTG                             **
**                   GROUP:        USER1                            **
**                   TYPE:         ARCHDEF                          **
**                   MEMBER:       MKTG1200                         **
**                   ALTERNATE:    MKTG                             **
**                   SCOPE:        NORMAL                           **
**                   MODE:         CONDITIONAL                      **
**                                                                  **
**                                                                  **
**********************************************************************
**********************************************************************


           *************** B U I L D   O U T P U T S *************** Page 1

   MEMBER      TYPE       VERSION      KEYWORD
   ------      ----       -------      -------

   MKTG1200    OBJ           2         OBJ
   MKTG1210    OBJ           2

   MKTG1200    LIST          2         LIST
   MKTG1210    LIST          2

   MKTG1200    LOAD          5         LOAD


           ******* B U I L D   M A P S   G E N E R A T E D ******* Page 2

                                     (REASON FOR REBUILD)
   MEMBER      TYPE       VERSION      MEMBER      TYPE
   ------      ----       -------      ------      ----

   MKTG1200    ARCHDEF       1         *** NEW BUILD MAP GENERATED
   MKTG1200    COBOL         2         CUSTMAST    COPY
   MKTG1210    COBOL         2         CUSTMAST    COPY
```

Figure 8-14   A build report for the MKTG1200 build

In the PROMOTE INPUT fields, you enter the name of the architecture definition for the software component you want to promote. The PROMOTE SCOPE and PROMOTE MODE fields let you provide the same advanced processing options available with the build function. Usually, you'll use the defaults. The OUTPUT CONTROL fields specify how you want to handle the output from the promote function. Usually, you'll send the messages to your terminal and the report to a data set.

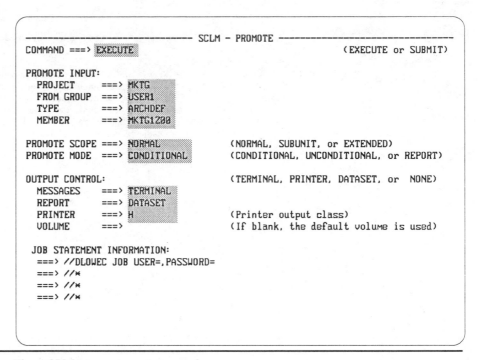

```
------------------------------ SCLM - PROMOTE ------------------------------
COMMAND ===> EXECUTE                                          (EXECUTE or SUBMIT)

PROMOTE INPUT:
    PROJECT     ===> MKTG
    FROM GROUP  ===> USER1
    TYPE        ===> ARCHDEF
    MEMBER      ===> MKTG1200

PROMOTE SCOPE ===> NORMAL            (NORMAL, SUBUNIT, or EXTENDED)
PROMOTE MODE  ===> CONDITIONAL       (CONDITIONAL, UNCONDITIONAL, or REPORT)

OUTPUT CONTROL:                      (TERMINAL, PRINTER, DATASET, or  NONE)
    MESSAGES    ===> TERMINAL
    REPORT      ===> DATASET
    PRINTER     ===> H               (Printer output class)
    VOLUME      ===>                 (If blank, the default volume is used)

JOB STATEMENT INFORMATION:
===> //DLOWEC JOB USER=,PASSWORD=
===> //*
===> //*
===> //*
```

Figure 8-15   The SCLM promote entry panel

To initiate the promote function, you must enter EXECUTE or
SUBMIT in the command area, just as you do for the build function. The promote function first analyzes the architecture to determine what members need to be promoted. Then, it copies those
members to the next highest level in the hierarchy and deletes
them from the private library. Notice that there is no place to enter
the name of the group where you want the members promoted.
Since the promotion hierarchy is specified by the project definition, SCLM determines where to promote the members. In this
case, the members from the USER1 groups will be promoted to the
UNIT1 group.

One of the most useful aspects of the promote function is that
it won't promote an architecture if any of its members have been
modified since the last time the member was built. As a result, you
can be assured that when you promote an architecture, all of its
components are up to date.

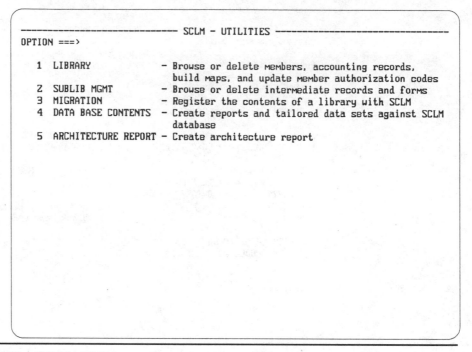

```
------------------------------ SCLM - UTILITIES ------------------------------
OPTION ===>

    1  LIBRARY            - Browse or delete Members, accounting records,
                            build Maps, and update Member authorization codes
    2  SUBLIB MGMT        - Browse or delete intermediate records and forms
    3  MIGRATION          - Register the contents of a library with SCLM
    4  DATA BASE CONTENTS - Create reports and tailored data sets against SCLM
                            database
    5  ARCHITECTURE REPORT - Create architecture report
```

Figure 8-16   The SCLM utilities menu

SCLM option 3.1: The library delete function

If you draw down a member, edit it, and then decide to abandon
your changes, you can use the SCLM utilities option to delete the
member. Then, SCLM releases the lock that was placed on the
member. When you select option 3 from the SCLM primary option
menu, SCLM displays the utility menu shown in figure 8-16. To
delete a member, you must use the library utility, option 3.1.
Figure 8-17 shows the library utility entry panel.

The SCLM library utility is similar to the standard ISPF library
utility, so I won't present the details of using it. On its entry panel,
you specify the name of the library you want to process. If you
leave the MEMBER field blank, SCLM displays a member list.
From there, you can delete a member by typing D next to the
member name.

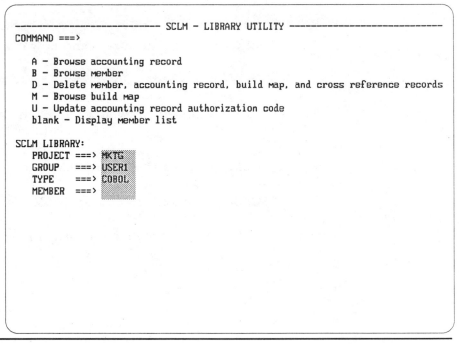

```
--------------------------- SCLM - LIBRARY UTILITY ---------------------------
COMMAND ===>

   A - Browse accounting record
   B - Browse member
   D - Delete member, accounting record, build map, and cross reference records
   M - Browse build map
   U - Update accounting record authorization code
   blank - Display member list

SCLM LIBRARY:
   PROJECT ===> MKTG
   GROUP   ===> USER1
   TYPE    ===> COBOL
   MEMBER  ===>
```

Figure 8-17   The SCLM library utility panel

DISCUSSION

As I said at the start of this topic, SCLM is a complicated software product. To use it effectively, the project administrator must maintain complete control of the library hierarchy. Thus, as an application programmer, the SCLM functions I've presented in this topic should be the only ones you'll need to use.

Terms

architecture   private library
dependency   draw down
build   promote
parser   authorization code
layer   project definition
group   build report
development layer

Objectives

1. Explain what an architecture is and how it's used in SCLM.

2. Explain the terms library hierarchy, draw down, and promote.

3. Use SCLM option 2 to draw down and edit an SCLM-controlled member.

4. Use SCLM option 4 to build an SCLM architecture.

5. Use SCLM option 5 to promote an SCLM architecture.

6. Use SCLM option 3.1 to delete an SCLM member.

Appendix A

ISPF reference summary

This appendix summarizes the ISPF options and the ISPF commands you'll use most often. For each option or command, you'll find a complete format or brief description. For the elements covered in this book, you'll also find chapter references where you will find more detailed information. You can use this summary as a quick refresher on how to use a particular ISPF feature.

ISPF OPTIONS

PROGRAM FUNCTION AND PROGRAM ACCESS KEYS

PA1	Interrupt a TSO command.	Chapter 1, Topic 3
PA2	Redisplay the current screen contents.	Chapter 1, Topic 3
PF1/13	Help (tutorial).	Chapter 2, Topic 1
PF2/14	Enter split screen mode.	Chapter 2, Topic 1
PF3/15	End the current operation.	Chapter 2, Topic 1
PF4/16	End the current operation and return to the primary option menu.	Chapter 2, Topic 1
PF5/17	Repeat the previous FIND command.	Chapter 3, Topic 1
PF6/18	Repeat the previous CHANGE command.	
PF7/19	Move the window up.	Chapter 3, Topic 1
PF8/20	Move the window down.	Chapter 3, Topic 1
PF9/21	Alternate between split screens.	Chapter 2, Topic 1
PF10/22	Move the window left.	Chapter 3, Topic 1
PF11/23	Move the window right.	Chapter 3, Topic 1
PF12/24	Move the cursor to the command area on line 2.	

SCROLL AMOUNTS   Chapter 3, Topic 1

HALF	Move the screen window half a page (11 lines or 40 columns).
PAGE	Move the screen window one page (22 lines or 80 columns).
n	Move the screen window n lines or columns.
MAX	Move the screen window to the top, bottom, left, or right margin.
CSR	Move the screen window so data at the cursor position ends up at the top, bottom, left, or right of the screen.
DATA	Move the screen window one line or one column less than a full page.

MEMBER SELECTION LIST COMMANDS

Line commands

S	Select the member (any option other than 3.1 and 3.4).	Chapter 3, Topic 1 Chapter 4, Topic 1 Chapter 5, Topic 2 Chapter 5, Topic 3
P	Print the member (options 3.1 and 3.4 only).	Chapter 5, Topic 1
R	Rename the member (options 3.1 and 3.4 only).	Chapter 5, Topic 1
D	Delete the member (options 3.1 and 3.4 only).	Chapter 5, Topic 1
B	Browse the member (options 3.1, 3.3, and 3.4 only).	Chapter 5, Topic 1 Chapter 5, Topic 2
E	Edit the member (option 3.4 only).	Chapter 5, Topic 1

Primary commands   Chapter 5, Topic 1

The LOCATE command

```
LOCATE sort-string
```

The SAVE command

```
SAVE [data-set-name]
```

The SELECT command

```
SELECT pattern [line-command]
```

The SORT command

```
SORT [field-1 [field-2]]
```

Special characters in primary commands

Jump directly to panel

```
=option
```
                                                          Chapter 2, Topic 1

Chain commands

```
command;command...
```
                                                          Chapter 2, Topic 1

Repeat a command

```
&command
```
                                                          Chapter 3, Topic 1

BROWSE COMMANDS

Establish a label   Chapter 3, Topic 1

```
.label
```

The BROWSE command   Chapter 3, Topic 2

```
BROWSE [member-name]
```

The COLUMNS command   Chapter 3, Topic 1

```
COLUMNS [ {ON
           OFF} ]
```

The DISPLAY command   Chapter 3, Topic 2

```
DISPLAY  {CC
          NOCC}   [character]
```

The FIND command   Chapter 3, Topics 1 and 2

```
FIND string [ {NEXT
               PREV
               FIRST}]  [{CHARS
               LAST        PREFIX}]  [column-1 [column-2]]
               ALL         SUFFIX
                           WORD
```

The HEX command   Chapter 3, Topic 2

```
HEX  [ {ON
        OFF} ]
```

The LOCATE command   Chapter 3, Topic 1

```
LOCATE  {line-number
         label}
```

EDIT COMMANDS

Line commands

Copying lines   Chapter 4, Topic 1

C	Copy this line.
Cn	Copy n lines starting with this line.
CC	Copy a block of lines.

A	Place the copied lines after this line.
An	Repeat the copied lines n times after this line.
B	Place the copied lines before this line.
Bn	Repeat the copied lines n times before this line.

Deleting lines   Chapter 4, Topic 1

D	Delete this line.
Dn	Delete n lines starting with this line.
DD	Delete the block of lines beginning with the first DD command and ending with the second DD command.

Excluding and redisplaying source lines   Chapter 4, Topic 3

X	Exclude this line.
Xn	Exclude n lines starting with this line.
XX	Exclude a block of lines.

S	Show one line of the excluded text.
Sn	Show n lines.

F	Show the first line of the excluded text.
Fn	Show the first n lines.

L	Show the last line of the excluded text.
Ln	Show the last n lines.

Inserting lines   Chapter 4, Topic 1

| I | Insert a single line following this line. |
| In | Insert *n* lines following this line. |

Moving lines   Chapter 4, Topic 1

M	Move this line.
Mn	Move *n* lines starting with this line.
MM	Move a block of lines.

A	Place the moved lines after this line.
An	Repeat the moved lines *n* times after this line.
B	Place the moved lines before this line.
Bn	Repeat the moved lines *n* times before this line.

Repeating lines   Chapter 4, Topic 1

R	Repeat this line.
Rn	Repeat this line *n* times.
RR	Repeat a block of lines.
RRn	Repeat a block of lines *n* times.

Shifting data   Chapter 4, Topic 3

Data shift command	Column shift command	Meaning
<	(	Shift this line left two positions.
<n	(n	Shift this line left *n* positions.
<<	((	Shift a block of lines left two positions.
<<n	((n	Shift a block of lines left *n* positions.
>	)	Shift this line right two positions.
>n	)n	Shift this line right *n* positions.
>>	))	Shift a block of lines right two positions.
>>n	))n	Shift a block of lines right *n* positions.

Other line commands   Chapter 4, Topic 2

TABS   Display a tab definition line.
COLS   Display a column line.
BOUNDS   Display a boundary line.
MASK   Display a mask line.

Primary commands

The AUTOLIST command   Chapter 4, Topic 2

AUTOLIST $\left[\begin{matrix} \underline{ON} \\ OFF \end{matrix} \right]$

The AUTONUM command   Chapter 4, Topic 2

AUTONUM $\left[\begin{matrix} \underline{ON} \\ OFF \end{matrix} \right]$

The AUTOSAVE command   Chapter 4, Topic 2

AUTOSAVE $\left[\begin{matrix} \underline{ON} \\ OFF\ \underline{PROMPT} \\ OFF\ NOPROMPT \end{matrix} \right]$

The BOUNDS command   Chapter 4, Topic 2

BOUNDS [left-column right-column]

The CANCEL command   Chapter 4, Topic 1

CANCEL

The CAPS command   Chapter 4, Topic 2

CAPS $\left[\begin{matrix} \underline{ON} \\ OFF \end{matrix} \right]$

The CHANGE command   Chapter 4, Topic 3

$$
\texttt{CHANGE string-1 [string-2] [range] }\left[\begin{array}{l}\underline{\texttt{NEXT}}\\ \texttt{PREV}\\ \texttt{FIRST}\\ \texttt{LAST}\\ \texttt{ALL}\end{array}\right]\ \left[\begin{array}{l}\underline{\texttt{CHARS}}\\ \texttt{PREFIX}\\ \texttt{SUFFIX}\\ \texttt{WORD}\end{array}\right]\ \left[\begin{array}{l}\texttt{X}\\ \texttt{NX}\end{array}\right]
$$

```
        [col-1  [col-2]]
```

The COPY command   Chapter 4, Topic 3

$$
\texttt{COPY [member] }\left[\begin{array}{l}\texttt{AFTER}\\ \texttt{BEFORE}\end{array}\right]\quad \texttt{label]}
$$

The CREATE command   Chapter 4, Topic 3

```
CREATE [member] [range]
```

The DELETE command   Chapter 4, Topic 3

$$
\texttt{DELETE [ALL] [range] }\left[\begin{array}{l}\texttt{X}\\ \texttt{NX}\end{array}\right]
$$

The EDIT command   Chapter 4, Topic 3

```
EDIT [member-name]
```

The EXCLUDE command   Chapter 4, Topic 3

$$
\texttt{EXCLUDE string [range] }\left[\begin{array}{l}\underline{\texttt{NEXT}}\\ \texttt{PREV}\\ \texttt{FIRST}\\ \texttt{LAST}\\ \texttt{ALL}\end{array}\right]\ \left[\begin{array}{l}\underline{\texttt{CHARS}}\\ \texttt{PREFIX}\\ \texttt{SUFFIX}\\ \texttt{WORD}\end{array}\right]\ \texttt{[col-1 [col-2]]}
$$

The FIND command   Chapter 4, Topic 3

$$
\texttt{FIND string [range] }\left[\begin{array}{l}\underline{\texttt{NEXT}}\\ \texttt{PREV}\\ \texttt{FIRST}\\ \texttt{LAST}\\ \texttt{ALL}\end{array}\right]\ \left[\begin{array}{l}\underline{\texttt{CHARS}}\\ \texttt{PREFIX}\\ \texttt{SUFFIX}\\ \texttt{WORD}\end{array}\right]\ \left[\begin{array}{l}\texttt{X}\\ \texttt{NX}\end{array}\right]
$$

```
        [col-1  [col-2]]
```

The HEX command   Chapter 4, Topic 2

```
HEX  [ {ON }]
       {OFF}
```

The IMACRO command   Chapter 4, Topic 2

```
IMACRO  {macro-name}
        {NONE      }
```

The LOCATE command   Chapter 4, Topic 3

```
LOCATE  {Line-number}
        {label      }
```

```
                {NEXT }   {CHANGE  }
                {PREV }   {LABEL   }
LOCATE  [{FIRST}]  {EXCLUDED}  [range]
                {LAST }   {ERROR   }
                          {COMMAND }
                          {SPECIAL }
```

The MOVE command   Chapter 4, Topic 3

```
MOVE [member] [{AFTER }  label]
               {BEFORE}
```

The NONUMBER command   Chapter 4, Topic 2

```
NONUMBER
```

The NOTES command   Chapter 4, Topic 2

```
NOTES  [{ON }]
        {OFF}
```

The NULLS command   Chapter 4, Topic 2

```
         {ON STD}
NULLS  [{ON ALL}]
         {OFF   }
```

The NUMBER command   Chapter 4, Topic 2

NUMBER [{<u>ON</u> / OFF}] [{<u>STD</u> / COBOL / STD COBOL}] [DISPLAY]

The PACK command   Chapter 4, Topic 2

PACK [{<u>ON</u> / OFF}]

The PROFILE command   Chapter 4, Topic 2

PROFILE [profile-name]

PROFILE {LOCK / UNLOCK}

The RECOVERY command   Chapter 4, Topic 2

RECOVERY [{<u>ON</u> / OFF}]

The RENUM command   Chapter 4, Topic 2

RENUM [{<u>ON</u> / OFF}] [{<u>STD</u> / COBOL / STD COBOL}] [DISPLAY]

The REPLACE command   Chapter 4, Topic 3

REPLACE [member] [range]

The RESET command   Chapter 4, Topic 1

RESET

The SAVE command   Chapter 4, Topic 1

SAVE

The STATS command   Chapter 4, Topic 2

STATS [{<u>ON</u> / OFF}]

The TABS command   Chapter 4, Topic 2

$$\text{TABS } [\{ \begin{matrix} \underline{\text{ON}} \\ \text{OFF} \end{matrix} \}] \ [\{ \begin{matrix} \underline{\text{STD}} \\ \text{ALL} \end{matrix} \}] \ [\text{tab-character}]$$

The UNDO command   Chapter 4, Topic 2

UNDO

The UNNUM command   Chapter 4, Topic 2

UNNUM

SCLM EDIT COMMANDS   Chapter 8, Topic 2

The SCREATE command

SCREATE member-name [range]

The SMOVE command

$$\text{SMOVE member-name } [\{ \begin{matrix} \text{BEFORE} \\ \text{AFTER} \end{matrix} \} \ \text{label}]$$

The SPROF command

SPROF

The SREPLACE command

SREPLACE member-name [range]

DATA SET LIST UTILITY COMMANDS

Line commands   Chapter 5, Topic 1

B	Browse the data set.
E	Edit the data set.
D	Delete the data set.
R	Rename the data set.
I	Display data set information.
S	Display shortened version of data set information.
C	Catalog the data set.
U	Uncatalog the data set.
P	Print the data set.
X	Print an index listing.
M	Display the member list.
Z	Compress the data set.
F	Free unused space.
=	Repeat the last command.

Primary commands   Chapter 5, Topic 1

The CONFIRM command

```
CONFIRM [{ ON
           OFF }]
```

The FIND command

$$
\text{FIND string } \left[\begin{cases} \underline{\text{NEXT}} \\ \text{ALL} \\ \text{FIRST} \\ \text{LAST} \\ \text{PREV} \end{cases} \right] \left[\begin{cases} \underline{\text{CHARS}} \\ \text{PREFIX} \\ \text{SUFFIX} \\ \text{WORD} \end{cases} \right] \text{ [column-1 [column-2]]}
$$

The LOCATE command

```
LOCATE sort-string
```

The SAVE command

```
SAVE [data-set-name]
```

The SELECT command

SELECT pattern [line-command]

The SHOWCMD command

SHOWCMD [{ON/OFF}]

The SORT command

SORT [field-1 [field-2]]

Appendix B

OS COBOL and VS COBOL II Interactive Debug reference summary

This appendix summarizes the commands you'll use most often when you use either OS COBOL Interactive Debug or full-screen mode of VS COBOL II Interactive Debug to debug your COBOL programs. I've included the commands for both these products in the same appendix because many of them have the same format. If there is a difference in a command for OS COBOL and VS COBOL II or if a command isn't valid for both products, I've noted it along with the command syntax.

The AT command (VS COBOL II only)

```
AT ENTRY { program-name }
         { ALL          }
```

```
AT statement-list [(command-list)]
```

The DROP command

```
DROP [symbol]
```

The DUMP command

```
DUMP
```

The END command (OS COBOL only)

```
END
```

The EQUATE command

```
EQUATE symbol [program-name.]identifier
```
Note: You cannot specify a file name as the identifier under OS COBOL.

The GO command

```
GO [statement-number]
```

The IF command

```
                     { (command-list) }
IF (expression)      { HALT            }
                     { GO              }
```

Note: You cannot specify a command list under OS COBOL.

The LIST command

```
     { identifier-list }            { DISPLAY }
LIST { literal         } [GROUP] [  { HEX     } ] [PRINT]
     { ALL             }            { BOTH    }
```

Note: The GROUP and DISPLAY/HEX/BOTH operands are not valid under OS COBOL.

The LSTBRKS command

```
LISTBRKS [PRINT]
```

The LISTEQ command (VS COBOL II only)

```
LISTEQ [PRINT]
```

The LISTFILE command (OS COBOL only)

```
LISTFILE file-name [PRINT]
```

The NEXT command

```
NEXT [(command-list)]
```

The OFF command

```
OFF [statement-list]
```

The OFFWN command

```
OFFWN [identifier]
```

The PEEK command (VS COBOL II only)

```
PEEK
```

The QUIT command (VS COBOL II only)

```
QUIT
```

The RESTART command (VS COBOL II only)

```
RESTART
```

The RESTORE command (VS COBOL II only)

```
RESTORE
```

The RUN command

```
RUN [statement-number]
```

The SET command

```
SET identifier-1 = { identifier-2 }
                   { literal      }
```

The SOURCE command (VS COBOL II only)

```
         { LISTING program-name }
SOURCE [ { OFF                  } ]
         { ON                   }
```

The SOURCE command (OS COBOL only)

```
         { line-1        }
SOURCE   { line-1:line-2 }
```

The STEP command (VS COBOL II only)

```
STEP [number]
```

The TRACE command

```
          { ENTRY }
          { PARA  }
TRACE   [ { NAME  } ] [PRINT]
          { OFF   }
```

The WHEN command

```
                    { data-name    }
WHEN identifier     { (expression) }  [(command-list)]
```

Note: You cannot specify a command list under OS COBOL.

Appendix C

SDSF reference summary

This appendix summarizes the commands you'll use most often when you use the System Display and Search Facility (SDSF) to manage background jobs.

PROGRAM FUNCTION AND PROGRAM ACCESS KEYS

PA1-3	Redisplay the screen.
PF1/13	Help.
PF2/14	Enter split screen mode.
PF3/15	Return to previous panel.
PF4/16	Return to ISPF.
PF5/17	Repeat the previous FIND command.
PF6/18	Find the next condition code when displaying job output.
PF7/19	Move the window up.
PF8/20	Move the window down.
PF9/21	Alternate between split screens.
PF10/22	Move the window left.
PF11/23	Move the window right.
PF12/24	Retrieve the previous command.

PRIMARY COMMANDS TO DISPLAY SDSF PANELS

LOG	Display the system log.
DA	Display active users on the system.
I	Display the JES2 input queue.
O	Display the JES2 output queue.
H	Display the JES2 held output queue.
ST	Display the JES2 status queue.
PR	Display JES2 printers.
INIT	Display JES2 initiators.

OTHER SDSF PRIMARY COMMANDS

Display alternate list of fields

?

Reissue a command

[command] &seconds

Display a column header

```
COLS
```

Limit panels by destination

```
DEST destination
```

Find a character string

```
FIND [{ *      }] [col-1 [col-2]] [{PREV }] [{CHARS }]
     { string }                    {NEXT }   {WORD  }
                                    {FIRST}   {PREFIX}
                                    {LAST }   {SUFFIX}
                                    {ALL  }
```

Include SYSIN data sets in display

```
INPUT { ON  }
      { OFF }
```

Locate a line

```
LOCATE { line-number           }
       { hh:mm:ss [mm/dd/yy]    }
```

Scroll forward through data sets

```
NEXT [number]
```

Limit panels by prefix

```
PREFIX [{ ?      }]
        { string }
```

Scroll backwards through data sets

```
PREV [number]
```

Print a portion of an output data set

```
PRINT [first-line last-line]
```

Close a print data set

PRINT CLOSE

Open a print data set

PRINT OPEN [class [copies [form]]]

Remove a column header

RESET

Set screen characteristics

SET SCREEN

Set hexadecimal display mode

SET HEX $\left\{ \begin{array}{l} ON \\ OFF \end{array} \right\}$

Display information about the current user

WHO

ACTION CHARACTERS

Character	Function	Panels
?	Display output data sets.	DA, I, O, H, ST
A	Release a held job.	DA, I, ST
Bnnn	Backspace a printer nnn pages.	PR
C	Cancel a job or purge output.	DA, I, O, H, ST, PR
CD	Cancel and dump a job.	DA, I, ST
D	Display jobs, printers, or initiators on SYSLOG.	DA, I, ST, PR, INIT
E	Restart a job or printer.	DA, I, ST, PR
Fnnn	Foreward space a printer nnn pages.	PR
H	Hold a job or output.	DA, I, O, ST
I	Interrupt a printer.	PR
L	List output status on SYSLOG.	DA, I, O, ST
N	Print selected output.	PR
O	Release held output.	H, ST
P	Purge output data sets.	DA, I, O, H, ST, PR, INIT
S	Select and display output data sets.	DA, I, O, H, ST, job data set
S	Start a printer or initiator.	PR, INIT
V	View graphics output.	Job data set
Z	Halt a printer or initiator.	PR, INIT

Appendix D

Installation dependent information

This appendix provides space for you to record information that's unique to your installation, such as your logon id and the procedures for accessing TSO. There are four copies of this information form, so you can record information about four systems.

MVS INSTALLATION DEPENDENT INFORMATION

Operating system

MVS/370, MVS/XA, or MVS/ESA?

JES2 or JES3?

TSO/E Version?

ISPF Version?

Information required to access the system

TSO user-id:

Network access procedure:

JOB statement accounting information:

DASD allocation information

Data set name high-level qualifier:

Valid generic or group names for JCL UNIT parameter:

Eligible DASD volumes (list type and vol-ser; e.g., 3380 TSO0001):

Processing classes

Job classes: SYSOUT classes:

Default: Default (MSGCLASS):

Other installation dependent information

MVS INSTALLATION DEPENDENT INFORMATION

Operating system

MVS/370, MVS/XA, or MVS/ESA?

JES2 or JES3?

TSO/E Version?

ISPF Version?

Information required to access the system

TSO user-id:

Network access procedure:

JOB statement accounting information:

DASD allocation information

Data set name high-level qualifier:

Valid generic or group names for JCL UNIT parameter:

Eligible DASD volumes (list type and vol-ser; e.g., 3380 TSO0001):

Processing classes

Job classes: SYSOUT classes:

Default: Default (MSGCLASS):

Other installation dependent information

MVS INSTALLATION DEPENDENT INFORMATION

Operating system

MVS/370, MVS/XA, or MVS/ESA?

JES2 or JES3?

TSO/E Version?

ISPF Version?

Information required to access the system

TSO user-id:

Network access procedure:

JOB statement accounting information:

DASD allocation information

Data set name high-level qualifier:

Valid generic or group names for JCL UNIT parameter:

Eligible DASD volumes (list type and vol-ser; e.g., 3380 TSO0001):

Processing classes

Job classes: SYSOUT classes:

Default: Default (MSGCLASS):

Other installation dependent information

MVS INSTALLATION DEPENDENT INFORMATION

Operating system

MVS/370, MVS/XA, or MVS/ESA?

JES2 or JES3?

TSO/E Version?

ISPF Version?

Information required to access the system

TSO user-id:

Network access procedure:

JOB statement accounting information:

DASD allocation information

Data set name high-level qualifier:

Valid generic or group names for JCL UNIT parameter:

Eligible DASD volumes (list type and vol-ser; e.g., 3380 TSO0001):

Processing classes

Job classes: SYSOUT classes:

Default: Default (MSGCLASS):

Other installation dependent information

Index

MVS TSO

Part 2: Commands and Procedures (CLIST and REXX)   **Doug Lowe**

Once you know how to use ISPF, you're ready to learn how to use the underlying TSO system directly, through TSO commands. And once you're skilled at using TSO commands, you're going to want to combine those commands into procedures for the jobs you do most often, so you don't have to enter all the commands individually each time.

That's why you need a copy of *MVS TSO, Part 2*. It starts by teaching you how to use TSO commands for programming tasks. Then, it shows you how to create procedures with those commands using either of TSO's procedure facilities—CLIST or REXX. To be specific, you'll learn:

- how to use TSO commands to compile and run programs in foreground mode, submit jobs for background processing, and manage data sets and libraries
- what key tasks have to be done using TSO commands (they can't be done with ISPF options)
- how to allocate files manged by the Storage Management Subsystem (SMS), an MVS/ESA option that controls DASD storage and data set allocation
- how to combine commands into CLIST or REXX procedures
- how to write and use edit macros (an edit macro is a CLIST or REXX procedure that you invoke from the ISPF editor as if it were an ISPF primary command; that means you can use edit macros to tailor the ISPF editor to your working style)

- how to use ISPF dialog manager to create CLIST or REXX procedures that interact with the terminal user via full-screen panels instead of line-by-line I/O
- how to use built-in variables, functions, and subprocedures in CLIST
- how to use arrays, the stack, and parsing commands in REXX
- and more!

Chock-full of practical examples

TSO commands and procedures are easier to master if you have plenty of practical examples to study. So *MVS TSO, Part 2* is loaded with illustrations...240 of them, to be exact. You'll find: command formats that clearly explain each operand...examples of TSO commands coded with different operands...sample CLIST and REXX procedures...and before-and-after screen images that show you how the commands and procedures work.

These illustrations not only help you understand TSO in the first place. They also serve as handy references when you're working at your terminal, so you don't have to spend your time digging through the IBM manuals.

So why wait to become a TSO expert?

Get your copy of *MVS TSO, Part 2* TODAY. I think you'll be delighted at how quickly you'll master TSO, CLIST, and REXX.

MVS TSO, Part 2, 10 chapters, 450 pages, **$36.50**
ISBN 0-911625-57-7

MVS JCL

MVS/ESA • MVS/XA • MVS/370   **Doug Lowe**

Anyone who's worked in an MVS shop knows that JCL is tough to master. You learn enough to get by...but then you stick to that. It's just too frustrating to try to put together a job using the IBM manuals. And too time-consuming to keep asking your co-workers for help...especially since they're often limping along with the JCL they know, too.

That's why you need a copy of *MVS JCL*. It zeroes in on the JCL you need for everyday jobs...so you can learn to code significant job streams in a hurry.

You'll learn how to compile, link-edit, load, and execute programs. Process all types of data sets. Code JES2/JES3 control statements to manage job and program execution, data set allocation, and SYSOUT processing. Create and use JCL procedures. Execute general-purpose utility programs. And much more.

But that's not all this book does. Beyond teaching you JCL, it explains how MVS works so you can apply that understanding as you code JCL. You'll learn about the unique interrelationship between virtual storage and multiprogramming under MVS. You'll learn about data management: what data sets are and how data sets, volumes, and units are allocated. You'll learn about job

management, including the crucial role played by JES2/JES3 as MVS processes jobs. And you'll learn about the components of a complete MVS system, including the role of system generation and initialization in tying the components together. That's the kind of perspective that's missing in other books and courses about MVS, even though it's background you must have if you want to bring MVS under your control.

Note to TSO users: For some TSO and ISPF functions, you have to provide JCL statements. Normally, you can get appropriate statements from your supervisor or co-workers. But the more you know about JCL, the more control you'll have over your TSO jobs, the more you'll understand about MVS, and the more independent you'll be.

So if you don't feel sure of yourself when it comes to coding job control language, get a copy of *MVS JCL* today.

MVS JCL, 17 chapters, 496 pages, **$42.50**
ISBN 0-911625-85-2

OS Utilities

                                                             Doug Lowe

OS Utilities is designed to free you from the IBM manuals and teach you how to use the OS utilities that will help you most in your day-to-day programming.

That means you'll learn how to: create, print, rename, reformat, and scratch various types of data sets...use the sort/merge utility...list important system information, such as catalog or VTOC entries...create large test files with just a few control statements...and more!

If you've ever written a program in a high-level language because you couldn't figure out how to use the utility for that function, this is the book for you.

Covers 13 utilites in all: IEBGENER, IEBPTPCH, IEBISAM, IEBCOPY, IEBUPDTE, IEBDG, IEBCOMPR, IEHLIST, IEHMOVE, IEHPROGM, IEFBR14, Sort/Merge, AMS

OS Utilities, 14 chapters, 185 pages, **$17.50**
ISBN 0-911625-11-9

VS COBOL II: A Guide for Programmers and Managers

Second Edition   **Anne Prince**

This book builds on your COBOL knowledge to quickly teach you everything you need to know about VS COBOL II, the IBM 1985 COBOL compiler for MVS shops: how to code the language elements that are new in the compiler (and what language elements you can't use any more)...CICS considerations...how to use the debugger...how the compiler's features can make your programs compile and run more efficiently...plus, guidelines for converting to VS COBOL II (that includes coverage of the conversion aids IBM supplies).

So if you're in a shop that's already converted to VS COBOL II, you'll learn how to benefit from the language elements and features the compiler has to offer. If you aren't yet working in VS COBOL II, you'll learn how to write programs now that will be easy to convert later on. And if you're a manager, you'll get some practical ideas on when to convert and how to do it as painlessly as possible.

VS COBOL II, 7 chapters, 271 pages, **$27.50**
ISBN 0-911625-54-2

Structured ANS COBOL

A 2-part course in 1974 and 1985 ANS COBOL   **Mike Murach and Paul Noll**

This 2-part course teaches you how to use standard COBOL the way the top professionals do.

Part 1: A Course for Novices teaches people with no programming experience how to design and code COBOL programs that prepare reports. Because report programs often call subprograms, use COPY members, handle one-level tables, and read indexed files, it covers these subjects too. But the real emphasis in this book is on the structure and logic of report programs, because most beginning programmers have more trouble with structure and logic than they do with COBOL itself.

Part 2: An Advanced Course also emphasizes program structure and logic, focusing on edit, update, and maintenance programs. But beyond that, it's a

complete guide to the language elements that all COBOL programmers should know how to use (though many don't). So it covers: sequential, indexed, and relative file handling...alternate indexing and dynamic processing... internal sorts and merges...the COPY library...subprograms...multi-level table handling using indexes as well as subscripts...character manipulation...and more! In fact, no matter how much COBOL experience you've had, you'll value *Part 2* as a handy reference to all the COBOL elements you'll ever want to use.

COBOL, Part 1, 13 chapters, 438 pages, **$32.50**
ISBN 0-911625-37-2

COBOL, Part 2, 12 chapters, 498 pages, **$32.50**
ISBN 0-911625-38-0

Structured COBOL Methods

Practical guidelines and model programs   **Paul Noll**

Unlike other books with "structured" in the title, this little book presents ideas on COBOL program development that are simple, cost-effective, time-tested, and yet revolutionary in many shops. It doesn't teach the COBOL language itself; instead, it teaches you how to design, code, and test your COBOL programs so they're easier to debug, document, and maintain.

Just open up to any page, take a look at the concepts or the sample design and code, and picture what a difference these methods can make in the program you're working on right now. Then, go to work and start experimenting. You'll be delighted at the results!

Structured COBOL Methods, 6 chapters + 5 model programs, 208 pages, **$25.00**
ISBN 0-911625-94-1

VSAM

Access Method Services and Application Programming   **Doug Lowe**

As its title suggests, *VSAM: Access Method Services and Application Programming* has two main purposes: (1) to teach you how to use the Access Method Services (AMS) utility to define and manipulate VSAM files; and (2) to teach you how to process VSAM files using various programming languages. To be specific, you'll learn:

- how VSAM data sets and catalogs are organized and used

- how to use AMS commands to define VSAM catalogs, space, clusters, alternate indexes, and paths

- how to set AMS performance options so you make the best possible use of your system's resources

- what recovery and security considerations are important when you use AMS

- how to code MVS and DOS/VSE JCL for VSAM files, and how to allocate VSAM files under TSO and VM/CMS

- how to process VSAM files in COBOL, CICS, and assembler language

You'll find the answers to questions like these

- How much primary and secondary space should I allocate to my VSAM files?

- What's an appropriate free space allocation for a KSDS?

- What's the best control interval size for VSAM files that are accessed both sequentially and directly?

- Do I always need to use VERIFY to check the integrity of my files?

- What's the difference between regular VSAM catalogs and the ICF catalog structure?

- When should I...and shouldn't I...use the IMBED and REPLICATE options to improve performance?

- It's easy to find out how many records are in a file's index component. But how do I find out how many of those records are in the sequence set?

- How do I determine the best buffer allocation for my files?

- What's the best way to back up my VSAM files— REPRO, EXPORT, or something else?

So why wait any longer to sharpen your VSAM skills? Get your copy of *VSAM: AMS and Application Programming* TODAY!

VSAM: AMS & Application Programming,
12 chapters, 260 pages, **$27.50**
ISBN 0-911625-33-X

VSAM for the COBOL Programmer

Second Edition   **Doug Lowe**

If you're looking for a no-frills approach to VSAM that teaches you only what you need to know to code COBOL programs, this is the book for you. You'll learn: the meanings of the critical terms and concepts that apply to VSAM files; the COBOL elements for handling VSAM files; how to handle alternate indexes and dynamic access; why error processing is a must; how to use the Access Method Services utility (AMS) to create,

print, copy, and rename VSAM files; how to code the MVS and VSE JCL to run programs that use VSAM files; and how your COBOL code is affected if you're working under VS COBOL II.

VSAM for COBOL, 6 chapters, 187 pages, **$22.50**
ISBN 0-911625-45-3

IMS for the COBOL Programmer

Part 1: DL/I Database Processing   **Steve Eckols**

This how-to book will have you writing batch DL/I programs in a minimum of time—whether you're working on a VSE or an MVS system. But it doesn't neglect the conceptual background you must have to create programs that work. So you'll learn:

- what a DL/I database is and how its data elements are organized into a hierarchical structure
- the COBOL elements for creating, accessing, and updating DL/I databases...including logical databases and databases with secondary indexing
- how to use DL/I recovery and restart features
- the basic DL/I considerations for coding interactive programs using IMS/DC or CICS

- how databases with the 4 common types of DL/I database organizations are stored (this material will help you program more logically and efficiently for the type of database you're using)
- and more!

7 complete COBOL programs show you how to process DL/I databases in various ways. Use them as models for production work in your shop, and you'll save hours of development time.

IMS, Part 1, 16 chapters, 333 pages, **$36.50**
ISBN 0-911625-29-1

IMS for the COBOL Programmer

Part 2: Data Communications and Message Format Service   **Steve Eckols**

The second part of *IMS for the COBOL Programmer* is for MVS programmers only. It teaches how to develop online programs that access IMS databases and run under the data communications (DC) component of IMS. So you'll learn:

- why you code message processing programs (MPPs) the way you do (DC programs are called MPPs because they process messages sent from and to user terminals)
- what COBOL elements you use for MPPs
- how to use Message Format Service (MFS), a facility for formatting complex terminal displays so you can enhance the look and operation of your DC programs
- how to develop applications that use more than one screen format or that use physical and logical paging

- how to develop batch message processing (BMP) programs to update IMS databases in batch even while they're being used by other programs
- how to use Batch Terminal Simulator (BTS) to test DC applications using IMS resources, but without disrupting the everyday IMS processing that's going on
- and more!

8 complete programs—including MFS format sets, program design, and COBOL code—show you how to handle various DC and MFS applications. Use them as models to save yourself hours of coding and debugging.

IMS, Part 2, 16 chapters, 398 pages, **$36.50**
ISBN 0-911625-30-5

CICS for the COBOL Programmer

Second Edition   **Doug Lowe**

This 2-part course is designed to help COBOL programmers become outstanding CICS programmers.

Part 1: An Introductory Course covers the basic CICS elements you'll use in just about every program you write. So you'll learn about basic mapping support (BMS), pseudo-conversational programming, basic CICS commands, sensible program design using event-driven design techniques, testing and debugging using IBM-supplied transactions (like CEMT, CECI, and CEDF) or a transaction dump, and efficiency considerations.

Part 2: An Advanced Course covers CICS features you'll use regularly, though you won't need all of them for every program. That means you'll learn about browse commands, temporary storage, transient data, data tables (including the shared data table feature of CICS 3.3), DB2 and DL/I processing considerations,

distributed processing features, interval control commands, BMS page building, and more! In addition, *Part 2* teaches you which features do similar things and when to use each one. So you won't just learn how to code new functions...you'll also learn how to choose the best CICS solution for each programming problem you face.

Both books cover all versions of CICS up through 3.3. Both cover OS/VS COBOL, VS COBOL II, and COBOL/370, so it doesn't matter which COBOL compiler you're using. And all the program examples in both books conform to CUA's Entry Model for screen design.

CICS, Part 1, 12 chapters, 409 pages, **$36.50**
ISBN 0-911625-60-7

CICS, Part 2, 12 chapters, 352 pages, **$36.50**
ISBN 0-911625-67-4

The CICS Programmer's Desk Reference

Second Edition   **Doug Lowe**

Ever feel buried by IBM manuals?

It seems like you need stacks of them, close at hand, if you want to be an effective CICS programmer. Because frankly, there's just too much you have to know to do your job well; you can't keep it all in your head.

That's why Doug Lowe decided to write *The CICS Programmer's Desk Reference*. In it, he's collected all the information you need to have at your fingertips, and organized it into 12 sections that make it easy for you to find what you're looking for. So there are sections on:

• BMS macro instructions—their formats (with an explanation of each parameter) and coding examples

• CICS commands—their syntax (with an explanation of each parameter), coding examples, and suggestions on how and when to use each one most effectively

• MVS and DOS/VSE JCL for CICS applications

• AMS commands for handling VSAM files

• details for MVS users on how to use ISPF

• complete model programs, including specs, design, and code

• a summary of CICS program design techniques that lead to simple, maintainable, and efficient programs

• guidelines for testing and debugging CICS applications

• and more!

So clear the IBM manuals off your terminal table. Let the *Desk Reference* be your everyday guide to CICS instead.

CICS Desk Reference, 12 sections, 507 pages, **$42.50**
ISBN 0-911625-68-2

Order Form

Our Unlimited Guarantee

To our customers who order directly from us: You must be satisfied. Our books must work for you, or you can send them back for a full refund...no questions asked.

Name & Title _____

Company (if company address) _____

Street Address _____

City, State, Zip _____

Phone number (including area code) _____

Fax number (if you fax your order to us) _____

Qty	Product code and title	*Price
MVS		
___ TSO1	MVS TSO, Part 1: Concepts and ISPF	$36.50
___ TSO2	MVS TSO, Part 2: Commands and Procedures (CLIST and REXX)	36.50
___ MJLR	MVS JCL (Second Edition)	42.50
___ MBAL	MVS Assembler Language	36.50
___ OSUT	OS Utilities	17.50
CICS		
___ CC1R	CICS for the COBOL Programmer Part 1 (Second Edition)	$36.50
___ CC2R	CICS for the COBOL Programmer Part 2 (Second Edition)	36.50
___ CRFR	The CICS Programmer's Desk Reference (Second Edition)	42.50
COBOL		
___ VC2R	VS COBOL II (Second Edition)	$27.50
___ SC1R	Structured ANS COBOL, Part 1	32.50
___ SC2R	Structured ANS COBOL, Part 2	32.50
___ SCMD	Structured COBOL Methods	25.00

Qty	Product code and title	*Price
Database		
___ DB1R	DB2 for the COBOL Programmer Part 1 (Second Edition)	$45.00
___ DB2R	DB2 for the COBOL Programmer Part 2 (Second Edition)	**Available June 1999**
___ DB22	DB2 for the COBOL Programmer Part 2 (First Edition—DB2 Version 2.2)	36.50
___ IMS1	IMS for the COBOL Programmer Part 1: DL/I Data Base Processing	36.50
___ IMS2	IMS for the COBOL Programmer Part 2: Data Communications and MFS	36.50
VSAM		
___ VSMX	VSAM: Access Method Services and Application Programming	$27.50
___ VSMR	VSAM for the COBOL Programmer (Second Edition)	22.50
PC programming		
___ VB60	Murach's Visual Basic 6	$45.00
___ VB50	Client/Server Programming: Visual Basic 5	40.00
___ AC97	Client/Server Programming: Access 97	40.00

☐ Charge the books plus UPS shipping and handling (and sales tax within California) to my
___Visa ___MasterCard ___American Express:

Card number _____

Valid thru (mo/yr) _____

Cardowner's signature _____

☐ Bill my company.
P.O.# _____

☐ I want to **SAVE** shipping and handling charges. Here's my check or money order for the books ($_____).
California residents, please add sales tax to your total.
(Offer valid in U.S.)

*Prices are subject to change. Please call for current prices.

To order now,

Call toll-free 1-800-221-5528
(Weekdays, 8 am to 5 pm Pacific Time)

Fax: 1-559-440-0963

Web: www.murach.com

Mike Murach & Associates, Inc.
2560 West Shaw Lane, Suite 101
Fresno, California 93711-2765
(559) 440-9071 • murachbooks@murach.com

Comment Form

Your opinions count

If you have any comments, criticisms, or suggestions for us, I'm eager to hear from you. Your opinions today will affect our products of tomorrow. And if you find any errors in this book, typographical or otherwise, please point them out so we can correct them in the next printing.

Thanks for your help.

Mike Murach

Book title: MVS TSO, Part 1: Concepts and ISPF

Dear Mike: _____

_____

_____

_____

_____

_____

_____

_____

_____

_____

_____

_____

_____

_____

_____

_____

_____

Name _____

Company (if company address) _____

Address _____

City, State, Zip _____

Fold where indicated and tape closed.

No postage needed if mailed in the U.S.

NO POSTAGE
NECESSARY
IF MAILED
IN THE
UNITED STATES

BUSINESS REPLY MAIL

FIRST-CLASS MAIL   PERMIT NO. 3063   FRESNO, CA

POSTAGE WILL BE PAID BY ADDRESSEE

Mike Murach & Associates, Inc.

2560 W SHAW LN STE 101
FRESNO CA 93711-9866